The dBASE Book

Developing Windows Applications
with dBASE PLUS

Ken Mayer

Third Edition

Volume 2

The dBASE Book
Developing Windows Applications with dBASE PLUS
Volume 2
by Ken Mayer

Copyright © 2005, 2007, 2013 by Kenneth *(Ken)* J. Mayer
ISBN: 978-0-9892875-1-7 (sc) print

First Printing, 2005; Second Printing, 2007; Third Printing, 2013
Printed in the United States of America

Trademark and Copyright acknowledgments:
- *Visual dBASE*, *dBASE*, *dBASE PLUS*, *dQuery* and variations of these product names and words are registered trademarks of dBase, LLC.
- *Borland Database Engine*, *BDE*, *Paradox*, *InterBase* and *Delphi* are registered trademarks of Borland International, Inc. and/or Embarcadero.
- *Firebird* is a registered trademark of Firebird Foundation Corporation.
- *Microsoft*, *Windows XP, Vista, Windows 7, Windows 8* (and all other forms of the names of the Windows operating system), *Word*, *Excel*, *FoxPro* are registered trademarks of Microsoft Corporation.
- *Quicken* is a registered trademark of Intuit, Inc.
- *Inno Setup* is copyrighted to Jordan Russel and Martijn Laan
- *Apache* is copyrighted to the Apache Software Foundation

No attempt has been made to designate as trademarks or service marks all personal computer words or terms in which proprietary rights might exist. The inclusion, exclusion or definition of a word or term is not intended to affect, or express any judgement on, the validity or legal status of any proprietary right which may be claimed in that word or term.

Disclaimer

The author and publisher have used their best efforts in preparing this book, and the programs contained herein. However, the author and publisher make no warranties of any kind, express or implied, with regard to the documentation or programs contained in this book, and specifically disclaim without any limitations, any implied warranties of merchantability and fitness for a particular purpose with respect to program listings in the book and/or the techniques described in the book. In no event shall the author or publisher be responsible or liable for any loss or profit or any other commercial damages, including but not limited to special, incidental, consequential or any other damages in connection with or arising out of furnishing, performance, or use of this book or the programs.

Table of Contents

X

About the Author

Ken Mayer has used dBASE both as a hobbyist and as a professional coder for many years, starting with dBASE III+ and working up to dBASE PLUS.

Ken worked for Borland, Intl. for two years as a Senior Quality Assurance Engineer on the Intrabuilder and dBASE products (Intrabuilder 1.0, Visual dBASE 7.0 and 7.01), and also worked for five years for dBASE Inc. as a Senior Quality Assurance Engineer, also working on dBASE (Visual dBASE 7.5, dB2K and dBASE PLUS, as well as dQuery). Ken was a contributing editor to dBASE Advisor magazine for the one and a half years or so it was in publication.

He served on Borland's TeamB (volunteer technical support) when Borland owned dBASE, and has helped many in the dBASE developer community. At this time he is a member of the dBVIPS for dataBased Intelligence, Inc., doing the same things he did with TeamB. He authored a good portion of the Knowledgebase articles that ship with dBASE PLUS, and authored the original dBASE PLUS tutorial. Some of the material in this book will look suspiciously familiar to any who have used the Knowledgebase.

Ken has also been the librarian of a freeware library of code made available to all dBASE developers called the dBASE Users' Function Library Project (dUFLP) for so long he's lost count. He has been a speaker at Borland and other conferences on dBASE, speaking about coding techniques.

Ken's current job is as a full-time instructor at Heald College (in Concord, CA) for over 5 years, teaching Microsoft Office courses, and other Business classes (e-Commerce, Entrepreneurship, Human Resources, etc.).

When not working, Ken is very active in the Society for Creative Anachronism, Inc. (http://www.sca.org), and enjoys cooking, movies, games, and reading.

Ken lives in Walnut Creek, CA with his wife Carolyn Eaton and their two cats Rebo and Zootie *(named after a pair of comedians from the science fiction TV show Babylon 5)*.

(Photograph of the author is by Sandra Linehan, December, 2012)

Introduction

Between dBASE II and Visual dBASE 5.x, a great number of books were written about dBASE. With the 32-bit versions of dBASE (Visual dBASE 7.x, dB2K and dBASE PLUS), even data became objects, ruled by object-oriented programming. In order to deal with these new data objects (data modules, queries, rowsets, and even field objects) a new language was created: OODML. This has created a steep learning curve for developers fluent in the 16-bit versions of dBASE, as well as those new to dBASE. When books were needed more than ever, only one book was published until now about the 32-bit versions of dBASE (Ted Blue's courseware book <u>The dBASE Developer – Book 1: Getting Started</u>).

<u>The dBASE Book: Developing Windows Applications With dBASE PLUS</u> is a bridge to those coders who are having a difficult time with the OOP model of dBL (the dBASE Language), and will help them develop solid Windows database applications. In addition, many dBASE coders are self-taught or have learned from those who were self-taught, and in the process have picked up a lot of bad coding techniques that can cause problems in their own code. This book will attempt to put dBASE developers on the "right path" to better coding techniques as well. Understanding object oriented development is essential to designing a proper Windows application, and this book will focus heavily on this aspect of dBASE.

Attempts have been made to make this book usable by developers using dBASE PLUS ranging from beginner to advanced.

The 3rd Edition of this book *(the one in your hands or on your screen)* is an update with fixes to the text and some of the code samples as suggested by a variety of folk from the first and second editions, and attempts have been made to include as many important updates to the software as possible at the time of printing. In addition, as the folk at dBase, LLC have been working on improving the software, I have attempted to update various parts of the book that deal with those improvements, enhancements and changes through release 2.8 of dBASE Plus *(released in the spring of 2012, with upgrades/bug fixes up until the time of this printing)*. The chapters that deal with deploying applications have been completely re-written/overhauled to deal with Windows Vista and Windows 7/8 and UAC issues, in order to make your applications work better with Windows itself. A new chapter (2) was added that explains the Windows UAC requirements for applications, and how dBASE has been modified to work with it *(rather than fighting with Windows and the UAC as dBASE developers have tended to do)*.

Why Did I Split the Book into Two Volumes?

Faithful readers will note that the first two editions of this book were a single volume. This is a HUGE book, as you know. There are two problems with it all being in one book – the first is just plain weight. The printed version is very large and a bit unwieldy. The publisher, AuthorHouse also has a page limit issue. You may recall – for the 2nd Edition I had to remove a chapter so that it could be printed. By splitting this into two volumes, the page count issue will go away for each of the two volumes, and the general weight of the book will be smaller for the individual books. While it does mean purchasing two books to obtain the set, I think the benefits outweigh the cost. I hope you agree.

Acknowledgments and Thanks

I would like to thank the people who have helped make this book possible. While I cannot thank by name every single person who may have contributed indirectly to the writing of this book, I would like to thank the following specifically.

The dBASE Community

Thanks to the dBASE community for the encouragement which helped me to decide that writing this book was a good idea. I cannot possibly name everyone who sent me "Please do this!" messages, either in private email or in the newsgroups, but my thanks to you all.

In addition, when I posted messages asking for ideas or specific information in the dBASE newsgroups many people came forward with their thoughts, advice, and assistance, sometimes providing code samples. Some of these folk are mentioned by name in the book, where I have referenced posts by them in the dBASE newsgroups, code I am using of theirs, etc. Again, thanks to you all.

Contributors

Others who have contributed to this book, and who have given me permission to use or reference materials of their own – in no specific order: Lane Coddington, Rich Muller and Peter Rorlick. A special thanks to Ivar B. Jessen for helping fine-tune the book title from what I had posted in the newsgroups, and to everyone who responded to requests for ideas for a title for the book. It was an interesting series of discussions, and I learned a lot from them.

Editors

I wish to thank **Jean-Pierre Martel** and **Professor Michael Nuwer**, who helped immensely from the beginning of this process right up to publication of the first two editions – their work permeates the book in many places, and I couldn't have done this without them.

These two gentlemen helped with the book proposal, table of contents *(which continues to evolve right up to publication)*, and much more. In addition to basic editing, they helped with the explanation of concepts, and to ensure that the sequence of the content made sense. They were great as sounding boards – being ready and willing to field questions and concerns I had, and were not shy about telling me when I was going in the wrong direction. The reason they did this is that they agreed with me that a good book on dBASE was needed.

In addition to the above, Jean-Pierre created the cover for this book *(he came out of retirement to do a new cover for me for the 3rd edition!)* – and what a great job he did, too! I cannot thank him enough for his generosity and the excellent job he has done!

Additionally several others stepped up to the plate for specific chapters that they had expertise in. Jim Sare kindly rewrote the Windows API (Chapter 22). Frank Polan helped with the chapter on Working in a Shared Environment (Chapter 9) having recently dealt with several of the issues covered by that chapter. These two did this with no thought of any reward or even mention in this book, but I have always believed in "credit where credit is due", and I owe them a debt of gratitude.

For the Second Edition of this book, I have to thank Frank Polan for stepping up and helping edit the chapters that were heavily modified, which meant walking through a bunch of exercises, and telling me what didn't make sense, etc.

For the Third Edition of this book:

James Peterson has over 10 years' experience in the analysis and development of enterprise computer systems. He joined The M Corporation in 2005 as an analyst / programmer and in 2008, was promoted to product manager - Subscribe systems with responsibility for the support and ongoing development of our subscription management systems. Prior to joining TMC, he developed his skills implementing and supporting ERP & CRM systems with UBA-Unicomp. James has a Bachelor of Science (Information Technology) and a Bachelor of Business from The University of Technology, Sydney. James has been invaluable in helping fix the grammar and sentence structure throughout the book.

Gerald Lightsey's career in management spanned 39 years in automobile Assembly Plant operations. He learned dBASE 3 in the early 80s, writing applications for his department. He has worked with dBASE through dBASE IV, dBASE 5 … When he retired in the mid-90s he got involved with Visual dBASE 5 and has continued working with the dBASE community testing the software, and helping users. He was extremely helpful with this book in the latter chapters (in Volume 2), where he made me re-think some of my approaches and explanations.

Michael Rozlog, CEO of dBase, LLC
Michael worked with me to produce and make available the 2nd Edition of the book as a PDF, which is being distributed with dBASE Plus 2.8. This process included my rebuilding the book completely in Word™ (2010), and avoiding using a third party tool to produce the book. I had to re-do all the screen shots for that version, as Word didn't like the ones I was using for earlier versions. This started me thinking that since the book was converted to Word, maybe I could just work on a 3rd Edition, which is where we are now.

With the plans for moving forward into the future that Michael has presented, I would expect a 4th Edition of this book at some point. Once I complete the third edition, I anticipate starting right in on changes for the 4th Edition. I cannot speak to most of these changes as they are under NDA *(non-disclosure agreement)*, and some of them are still being worked out as I write.

Also at dBASE, LLC
Marty Kay, head of R&D has always been pretty straightforward, although quite politic, when dealing with issues. I worked with Marty when the company was dBASE, Inc., and I was still there. The interesting thing is that I have never met him. Suffice it to say that when I bring an issue to his attention he is usually very fast to turn things around, even it if it means telling me I forgot something or made a stupid error in my own code.

Kathy Kolosky, a woman of many talents. Again I have never met Kathy, but she's always tried her best to be helpful, whether in a Tech Support position, QA (my old job), or working on the Project Explorer and trying to provide as much help as she can. She has tried hard to provide assistance as I stumbled through aspects of this edition of the book.

My Wife
Last, but far from the least, I need to thank my wife of nineteen years *(as of the time this version of the book becomes available)*, Carolyn Eaton, for being supportive of pretty much everything I do. When I wrote the 1st and 2nd Editions of the book, it was a tough time financially. However, she supported this effort despite the difficulties with nary a complaint. All the time I worked on the book I was also looking for work, and trying to pick up some paying contracts. Now she puts up with me muttering and mumbling while I work on the text, and sometimes cursing and swearing when a code example doesn't work. She has always been supportive – how can you ask for more? There are simply not enough words to thank her … except to say "I love you!"

Terminology

A minor note about terminology throughout the book …:

When I write I tend to sound things out in my head. When I discuss things like file extensions, I tend to pronounce the period as "dot". Hence you will see interesting syntax such as:

"A .INI file"

In this case, if you pronounce the period as "dot", using the letter "A" is correct. If you do not, and instead pronounce it without, then correct English would be to state:

"An .INI file"

I prefer the former option. My editors questioned this in various places throughout the book, and I chose to leave the text as is in these cases. I hope this does not offend anyone's sensibilities (*although if it does, well, it's my book …*)! And many thanks to my editors for putting up with my quirks and helping me correct my English, making this book easier to read.

Sample Code

It should be noted that throughout the book there are code samples. The sample code can be found on my website for this book, through my main dBASE webpage:

> http://www.goldenstag.net/dbase

If you go to this page, and find the information about my books, the page for the 3rd Edition of the books will have a link for the source code. This is contained in a .zip file with all of the code samples provided in folders, one folder per chapter, with a few folders as they are suggested in specific chapters of the book.

NOTES:

Chapter 19: Creating Menus, Popup Menus, Speedbars and Toolbars

This chapter is dedicated to helping you work with the other user-interface aspects of dBASE, when creating an application.

So far we have looked at creating forms, using custom components, custom forms, and more. However, most applications developed in dBASE are considered incomplete if they do not use menus, toolbars or speedbars and perhaps popup menus.

Does this mean that it is required that you use these features? No, it is not. Most applications at least use a menu – and of course much depends on the purpose of the application, the end-user's needs and all those considerations that any application developer must try to consider.

This chapter contains some "walk through" like instructions, but it is not necessary to actually do them – the steps are shown for your edification. While you may benefit by using them, nothing in later chapters of this book will require that you have done these steps.

Creating Menus

A menu is a set of options, normally at the top of the main application's form, or at the top of the form in use.

Menus can have sub-menus, separators, can be enabled or disabled based on specific conditions and more. We will take a look at the basics of creating menus using the Menu Designer, as well as looking at the code that is generated. It is sometimes desirable to create menus or menu options in your code, so it is helpful to understand the actual code that is used to work with menus.

A menu in dBASE is composed of a *menuBar* object which is the main container that appears in the appropriate location for a menuBar on a form or the application framewindow (typically directly under the titlebar of the form). The *menuBar* can contain *menu* objects and *menu* objects can contain other *menu* objects.

A menu can have whatever options you wish to place in it. It is important to note the following:

- In an MDI Application (multi-document interface), the menu is always placed in the application window's menuBar area (just below the titlebar of the main window), whether you use the form's *menuFile* property, or if you set the menu as part of the framewindow. (We will look at both options later in this chapter.)
- In an SDI Application (single-document interface), the menu will appear on the form itself if you use the form's *menuFile* property, otherwise if you set the menu as part of the framewindow for your application, it will appear in the menuBar area of the framewindow.

Basically this means that when designing menus, you have to determine if you want a main application menu used for all of your application; or if you want individual menus for each form, then whether you want the menu on the menubar of the framewindow or on the form.

There are advantages to each – you have to sort of puzzle through these options when designing your application.

The first menu we will look at is one for a form. For this example, I copied the form "SomeFish.wfm" from the code created in Chapter 15 and changed the form's *text* property to "Chapter 19 - Menu Examples".

To create a menu in dBASE using the Menu Designer, you need to click on the "Forms" tab of the Navigator, and then notice the third icon that says "(Untitled)". If you double-click this (or use one of the other options to create a new menu), the Menu Designer will appear. This looks like:

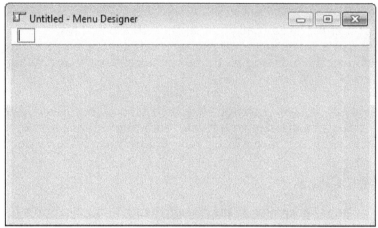

Figure 19-1

There is not a lot to look at – you have the actual design surface and the Inspector. That's all there is.

How do we use it? We type the text in that we wish to have displayed for the menu. For example, to create the "File" menu, we would type "File". Notice that this appears in the design surface as we type.

Normally menus have hotkeys – keystrokes that can be used to bring up that option, typically shown with an underscore. For example the word "File" might use the letter "F" (combined with some other key) to give focus to the File menu. To do that, we would have to enter an ampersand (&) before the letter we wish to be the hotkey. If you place the cursor before the letter "F", then type the ampersand, you should see: File in the menu when we move off of this menu item.

Before we move off of this item, however, you should assign a name to it. dBASE assigns what appear to be arbitrary names such as "MENU82" to a menu object, which is difficult to work with, to put it mildly. If you name this "File", then we can refer to it. We can refer to any sub-menu items that might be useful to have under it without having to figure out what the name of the menu is. To change the name click on the Inspector, make sure you are on the "Properties" tab and find the *name* property. Change the name to "FILE" (make sure you press the Enter key after typing this, or you may find the change lost).

This is what is often called a "Top Level" menu item, because it will appear on the *menuBar* directly. In most cases, the "Top Level" menu item does not actually execute any code if clicked on or selected. This means that for the most part, "Top Level" menu items do not have code associated with the menu object's *onClick()* event *(there are of course exceptions* *to any rule and if you **need** to have a top-level menu do something when clicked on, there is no real reason not to).*

We will now add a single item under the "File" menu, which is "Close". This is used, as it sounds, to close the form. To do this, press the down arrow key on your keyboard and notice that a new menu item is added under the File menu. Type: "&Close" *(without the quotes)* and change the *name* property of the menu item in the Inspector to "Close" as well. If you look at the Inspector, there is a property called *shortCut*. This is specific keys such as "Ctrl + W" used to execute the code for that menu option even if you do not actually select the menu. To add a shortcut to a menu, click on the Tool button for this property and you should see a dialog like:

Figure 19-2

If you want to use "Ctrl" and "W" *(the dBASE standard for closing a form)*, click the "Ctrl" radiobutton and then select "W" from the list on the right and click "OK". Notice that dBASE has placed "Ctrl+W" for the value of the property in the Inspector. It should be noted that many options available in this dialog do not appear to actually work. You should test these before deploying an application for your client(s).

How do we tell dBASE what to do when a menu item is selected? We use the Inspector and select the "Events" tab. The second item at the top of the list of event handlers is *onClick*. We will use a codeblock for this because it's a simple command. To get a codeblock, click on the "T" (for "Type") button, then select "Codeblock". Next, click the tool button (the one with the "wrench" on it), we get a dialog for building codeblocks. Enter: form.close() in the "body, and click on the "Command" radiobutton. This should look like:

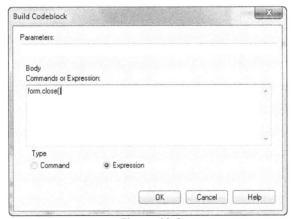

Figure 19-3

Click the "OK" button and in the inspector you should now see:

```
{; form.close()}.
```

If we want to add menu items to the right of the File menu, put focus back on that menu, then press the tab key. Note that a new menu item appears. The "Close" menu appears to have disappeared, but don't worry – it's still there. We don't need to add a cascading menu to the right, but the option is always there for all but the top-level menus. You can have cascading menus off of cascading menus if you need to.

Edit Menu Options

Most Windows based applications make use of standard "Edit" options, such as Copy, Cut, Paste, etc. You can create these menu options in dBASE easily. Because these are standardized, dBASE has the ability to insert them into a menu where you want.

To do this, select from the menu available in the Menu Designer, the option "Menu", then select "Insert "Edit" Menu. Notice that dBASE inserts the whole set of options for you!

Change the top level menu *name* property (text says "Edit") to "EDIT" (in the Inspector), but otherwise there is nothing else you need to do for this menu.

Continuing on ...

The next thing we want to do is add yet another top-level menu, this is one for navigating in the form's rowset. We are going to add options similar to those in the pushbuttons we created in an earlier chapter.

To add a new top-level menu item, tab to the right. Change the *text* property to "&Record" (without the quotes), and the *name* property to "Record". Using the down arrow key to add new menu items, add the following four under the Record Menu:

Text	Name	onClick Event
&First	First	{; form.rowset.first() }
&Previous	Previous	{; form.rowset.next(-1) }
&Next	Next	{; form.rowset.next() }
&Last	Last	{; form.rowset.last() }

We could add more, but this is just a sample. To save this, either use [Ctrl]+[S], or [Ctrl]+[W] (save and exit), and give it a name such as "FormMenu".

Attaching the Menu to a Form

Once you have a menu created, you can attach it to a form using the form's *menuFile* property. To do this, open a form, or create a new form in the Form Designer, select the Inspector window and find the *menuFile* property. Click the Tool button and find your .MNU file in the dialog provided. When you have done this, the *menuFile* property will be filled in when you view it in the Inspector and when you save the form, this property will be streamed out to the source code. When you run the form, the menu will appear:

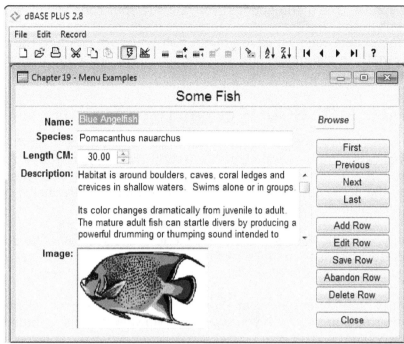

Figure 19-4

Notice that the menu will appear in the application's menu area until the form is closed!

In the case of form opened with the form's *open()* method, the menu should appear in the application menu area. If you run the form with the form's *readModal()* method instead, the menu appears *on* the actual form:

```
do somefish.wfm with true
```

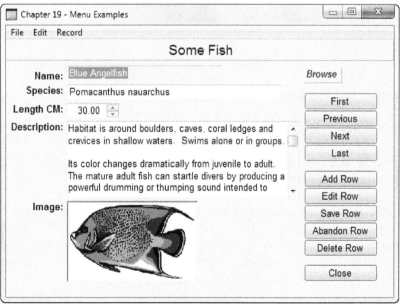

Figure 19-5

Notice with the modal form that *all* controls are shifted down to make room for the menu. If you wanted to use the menu in this way, you probably would want to do something different with the title text as shown in the image above (Figure 19-5).

In either case, if you use the menu options, you will see your code will execute. However, if you use the options in the "Record" menu, note that if you're at the first or last row, then try to navigate, the simple code we gave will not halt you from going to the *endOfSet*. You would most likely want to add more complex code like what is used in the pushbutton code we created in earlier chapters.

Creating an Application Menu

Many applications these days assign a menu with more functionality than the one we just created to the application framewindow directly, rather than requiring that forms use their own *menuFile* property. This has some benefits in that without any special effort all forms that open will use the same application menu, whether opened with *open()* or with *readModal()*, or a combination of both.

For such a menu, you might want to add more functionality, such as a Window menu (allowing you to select between multiple forms that are open, closing them, etc.), the ability to open individual forms from the "File" menu and possibly a "Help" menu.

For this we will need to add more functionality to the menu. I suggest copying the menu we created earlier ("FormMenu.mnu"). If you type the following in the Command Window, you will copy it to a new file:

```
copy file FormMenu.mnu to AppMenu.mnu
```

WARNING: This command does not rename the menu object contained in the source code, we need to do that manually.

```
modify command AppMenu.mnu
```

You should change the statements as noted below – the text that is bold needs to be modified to appear as shown in the Source Code Editor:

```
new AppMenuMENU(formObj, "root")
class AppMenuMENU(formObj, name) of MENUBAR(formObj, name)
```

(Change "FormMenu" to "AppMenu")

Save and exit the Source Code Editor with "[Ctrl]+[W]".

Next this menu needs to be modified in the Menu Designer, so double-click on it in the Navigator and the menu appears in the Menu Designer.

We are going to add some new options. To do this, we need to be able to insert menu items into the menu. For example, under "File", we need to insert an "Open" option. To do this, click on the "Close" menu option and press [Ctrl]+[N] to Insert a new menu item. Change the *name* property to "Open". Set the *shortCut* property to "Ctrl+O" similar to what we did for the "Close" menu, or type in the Inspector [Ctrl]+[O].

With the cursor still on the "Open" menu item, use the Tab key. Notice that you get a new option to the *right* of the current one – this is called a "cascading" menu. We can add many levels of menus, and this is the way to do it. At the moment we have only one form that we might want to open – for an application you most likely will have many forms that are options the user might wish to open.

For this new cascading menu, change the *text* to "Some Fish". Change the *name* property in the Inspector to "SomeFish" (no space). Click on the "Events" tab of the Inspector, and enter for the *onClick* event:

```
{; do SomeFish.wfm }
```

> **NOTE**
> There are many things that could be done here, including dealing with tracking what forms are open and setting top and left properties when new forms are open so that a form does not open on top of another form. To do that you would, among other things, need to open the form differently, along the lines of:
>
> ```
> set procedure to SomeFish.wfm additive
> f = new SomeFishForm()
> f.open()
> ```
>
> With other code in an application object, or perhaps in the custom form class, and more.
>
> The dBASE Tutorial and various sample applications that are available deal with these options. You may wish to take the time to examine them at your leisure … but we can't cover all contingencies in this book!
>
> Now that we have a menu option that can be used to open forms, we should add a menu option to close the application. We have one for closing the current form, but we might want to close the whole application from the menu.

Use the down arrow key to go past the "Close" option and create a new menu option:

Text	Name	ShortCut	onClick Event
E&xit	Exit	Alt+F4	use the *tool* button, we need more than a codeblock here

For the onClick event, enter the following code:

```
if "RUNTIME" $ upper( version(1) )
   quit
else
   // in the IDE
   close forms
   release object _app.rootMenu
   shell( true, true ) // reset shell
endif
```

What this does is check to see if the application is being run from the dBASE runtime (an executable application, which we haven't gotten to yet), if so simply issue a "Quit" command, otherwise to close all open forms and release the menu object. Finally we reset the shell to what it was before; otherwise we will be left with the menu up, with no ability to close the application! We will create the menu object reference that is being released in that code shortly, but not quite yet – you will have to keep reading to get to that!

Adding a Separator

If you look at the menu, it doesn't seem right to group all three of these menu items together. In most applications, the Exit menu option is always at the bottom of the File menu, but separated by a line. How do we add a separator?

With the cursor on the Exit menu item, press [Ctrl]+[N] to insert a new menu item. To make this into a separator, you just have to go to the Inspector, find the *separator* property which is currently *false* and set this to *true*. Notice that it changes to a line! If you want, you can leave the *name* property alone, but I tend to rename these to something like "Sep1" to note that this is a separator when I examine the source code.

Continuing On ...

Next we want to add a "Window" menu. This is very useful for MDI applications, but pointless for SDI applications. This menu gives you options to switch between windows and automatically keeps track of the current window. If your application is going to be all "modal" forms, then you do not need to do add a Window menu item to your menu, because you cannot switch between forms in the same way you can with an MDI application.

Click on the "File" menu, then use the Tab key to move to the right. Do this until you get an empty menu item. Rather than adding the "Window" menu manually, we can have dBASE do it for us – click on the "Menu" menu at the top of dBASE and select "Insert "Window" Menu". Notice that dBASE has done just that. Change the *name* property to Window.

Typically the Window menu has both a list of any open windows and a "Close All" option. We do not need to do *any* code to tell dBASE how to add or remove open windows from the Windows menu, but we do need to add the "Close All" option.

Use the down arrow key to add a new menu item. Enter "Close &All" for the *text* and change the *name* property in the Inspector to "CloseAll" (no space). This option does not need a *shortCut*, so all we have to do is tell dBASE what to do when it is clicked on. On the "Events" tab of the Inspector, select the *onClick* event and type the codeblock:

```
{; close forms }
```

For the time being, this is all we need for our menu. We could come back in and add options for Reports, Utilities, Help, whatever is needed for a full application, but for now we should be okay. Save the menu and close the Menu Designer ([Ctrl]+[W]).

Attaching a Menu to the Application Framewindow

This takes a bit more effort on your part, because you have to assign the menu properly and be able to remove it when the option to close your application is selected.

Assuming that the menu you wish to assign to the framewindow is the one we created earlier in the chapter, you might want to create some code such as a program named "start.prg":

```
set procedure to AppMenu.mnu additive
_app.rootMenu = new AppMenuMenu( _app.framewin, "Root" )
shell(false, true) // open the shell as an MDI shell ...
```

One thing that should be done is to remove the *menuFile* property of the form "SomeFish.wfm", because otherwise when we open that form, dBASE will change the menu to the other menu we created earlier. You can do this in the Form Designer, or you can do this by opening "SomeFish.wfm" in the Source Code Editor, and simply deleting the line:

```
menuFile = "FormMenu.mnu"
```

from the form's constructor code.

If you now run "start.prg" you will see the menu change, the Navigator and Command Windows go away and the toolbar change. If you select "File", then the "Open" menu, you can now open your form. If you click on the "File" then the "Exit" option, you should see the form close and the menu disappear.

Form and Rowset References

There is, however, one problem that now occurs. The "Record" menu options for navigation used code like "form.rowset.event". The problem is, the form is now opening in a way that does not assign the menu to the form and vice versa, so the menu doesn't actually have any way to reference the form, therefore cannot reference the form's rowset or the form's rowset events. Click on the "Cancel" or "Ignore" button if you have brought up an error, then use the menu's "File" "Exit" option to exit out of the menu.

How do we fix this? Well, it's basically a two-step fix. The first is to make a modification in the custom form class that we created in an earlier chapter, so we'll start there. In the Command Window, type:

```
modify form :MyCustomForms:Data.cfm
```

(This section of the chapter assumes that you did the follow-along parts of Chapter 17. If you have the sample code set up, this will still work. If not, note what is happening, but you won't be able to follow-along.)

The change we need to make is pretty simple, really. When a form gets focus (focus is a standard term that refers to when a form is the one that the user is currently interacting with), we want to assign a custom property to the application object (_app). In the Form Designer, go to the Inspector window and click on "Events". On this page of the Inspector, find the onGotFocus event. Enter this codeblock:

```
{; _app.CurrentForm = this}
```

What this codeblock does is create (if it doesn't exist) a custom property of the _app object and assigns an object reference ('this', meaning the current form) to the property. The property _app.CurrentForm will now be available when any form that is based on this custom form class is executed and gets focus.

Save the change you made, and close the Form Designer (`Ctrl`+`W`) .

The next thing to do is to modify the form itself.

If you double-click on "AppMenu.mnu" in the Navigator, this will bring the menu back into the Menu Designer. Click on the "Record" menu, then on the first menu item. We need to change the code currently assigned to the *onClick* event for the item, but the new code is going to be a little more complex than the codeblock. We can tell dBASE to change this from a codeblock by clicking on the "T" button and selecting "null". Next click on the tool button and in the Source Code Editor, enter:

```
function FIRST_onClick
    if type( "_app.CurrentForm" ) # "U" and;
       _app.CurrentForm.rowset # null

       _app.CurrentForm.rowset.first()

    endif
return
```

So, what is all this? We need to check and see if the _app.CurrentForm property actually exists (that is the check shown with the "type()" function, then checking for "U" – which means "undefined"). We also want to make sure that the form's *rowset* property has been assigned a rowset object. If this value is null, then we do not want to do anything but if both of those conditions are true, we want to call the rowset's *first()* method.

We need to do something similar for the other three menu items, the code will look like:

```
function LAST_onClick
    if type( "_app.CurrentForm" ) # "U" and;
       _app.CurrentForm.rowset # null

       _app.CurrentForm.rowset.last()
    endif
return

function NEXT_onClick
    if type( "_app.CurrentForm" ) # "U" and;
       _app.CurrentForm.rowset # null

       _app.CurrentForm.rowset.next()
    endif
return

function PREVIOUS_onClick
    if type( "_app.CurrentForm" ) # "U" and;
       _app.CurrentForm.rowset # null

       _app.CurrentForm.rowset.next(-1)
    endif
return
```

If you save the modified version of the menu and exit the Menu Designer (Ctrl + W), we can test it.

To test this, run the program we created earlier called "Start", select the "File" menu, then "Open". Select the "Some Fish" form and you will see something like:

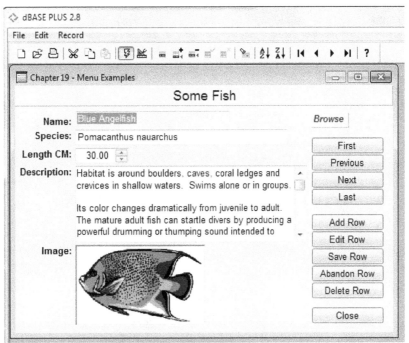

Figure 19-6

Even more fun, what happens if we open the form more than once? Try this (it helps to see a difference in the two forms).

Use the Next button on the form once, so we are not displaying the same fish, then move the form over to the left a little.

Now select "File", "Open" and select the form a second time. You should two forms (you may need to move one). You should see something like:

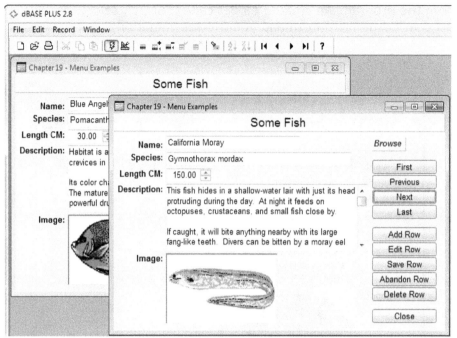

Figure 19-7

The question now is how does your menu know which form has focus? That should be fairly straight forward – we added code in the custom form's *onGotFocus* event and select the "Record" menu and navigate to the "Next" row, for example, the form on top should navigate. Try it ... Now click on the other form to give it focus, and do the same ("Record", "Next").

Now even more fun, look at the "Window" menu (click on it) and see what appears. It shows you the two forms and a checkmark by the one that has focus. You can switch between them using this menu. You can also close both of them using the "Close All" option.

One problem that might come up is that the last form (or instance of a form) that opened, left the custom property _app.currentForm set to that form's reference. This means that the menu code will now be assuming that a form is available. How do you fix that? The simple solution is to "null out" the custom property we assigned to the _app object ("null out" means to assign a value of "null" to the property) in the custom form's *onLostFocus* event.

Select the "File" menu and the "Exit" option, which if you left any forms open will close them.

Bring the custom form back into the Form Designer:

```
modify form :MyCustomForms:Data.cfm
```

And find the *onLostFocus* event. Enter the following in the Inspector (make sure you press the Enter key, or it will not be saved):

```
{; _app.CurrentForm = null}
```

Save the custom form and exit the Form Designer (⌃+Ⓦ).

> **📝 NOTE**
> The Menu Designer generates dBASE source code (dBL). This is important to understand, because there may be times when it is necessary to create a menu completely by code. This can be done and the simplest way to understand it is to examine the source code generated by the Menu Designer. While creating a menu "on the fly" could be useful, the topic of writing a program that generates a menu based on options *(for example, userid or something of that nature)* is complex enough that it would take many pages to try to explain here. Instead, I leave it as an exercise for the reader.

Creating Popup (Right-Click) Menus

So far we've looked at the "standard" menu used in most applications. However, if you work with a lot of different types of software, you may be used to the right mouse button being used to bring up options that are perhaps related to the current "place" in your application. In dBASE these are called "Popups" and they work the same way when a popup is assigned to a form. Right clicking with the mouse will cause the popup menu to appear, so you can then execute any code associated with the *onClick* event of the menu selections.

The Popup Menu Designer is accessed in much the same way as the regular Menu Designer is, but the Popup menu is the *fourth* "(Untitled)" icon under the "Forms" tab of the Navigator. If you double click on this icon, you should see something like:

Figure 19-8

This looks very familiar for a reason – the only difference visually between a Popup menu and a normal Menu is that there is no horizontal menuBar. Popup menus by definition are vertical, although you can have cascading menus to the side.

For the purposes of understanding popup menus, we will create a relatively simple one, that emulates some of what we have done elsewhere.

Because a popup menu is associated directly with a form, the problem encountered earlier in this chapter with the application menu will not be an issue. This will be important when looking at the code we associate with the menu options.

We're going to create a simple menu that allows us to Add and Delete data, as well as use the Copy, Cut and Paste options that use the Windows Clipboard.

With the cursor in the first menu position, type "&Add Row". In the Inspector, change the *name* property to "AddRow" (no spaces). On the "Events" tab of the Inspector, select the *onClick* event and click the tool button. In the Source Code Editor, type:

```
function ADDROW_onClick
   if form.rowset # null
      form.rowset.beginAppend()
   endif
return
```

This will place the rowset into append mode if there is a rowset property on the form. If we only ever assigned this popup menu to a form that had data, then checking for the form's *rowset* property would not be necessary.

We need to do something similar for a Delete option. Back on the Popup Menu Designer, use the down arrow key to add a new menu item. Type "&Delete Row" and in the Inspector, change the *name* property to "DeleteRow" (no spaces). On the "Events" tab of the Inspector, select the *onClick* event, click the tool button and in the Source Code Editor, type:

```
function DELETEROW_onClick
   if form.rowset # null
      if msgbox( "Delete this row?", "Delete Row?", 36 ) == 6
         form.rowset.delete()
      endif
   endif
return
```

As with some of the rest of what we have done elsewhere, these two bits of code could be more complex, but we're keeping things simple for the purpose of the example.

To separate sections of the menu, as we did with the regular Menu Designer add a separator – use the down arrow key to add a menu item. In the Inspector, find the *separator* property and change the value to *true*. I prefer to give a name to my separators, just to make sure I know what I'm looking at if I work with the source code, so change the *name* property to "Sep1".

The next thing we want to do is add the options for the clipboard to cut, copy and/or paste values to/from the Clipboard in Windows.

Use the down arrow key to add a new menu item. Type "Cu&t", change the *name* property to "Cut", then go to the "Events" tab on the Inspector and click the tool button for the *onClick* event. In the Source Code Editor, enter:

```
function CUT_onClick
   if type("form.ActiveControl.cut") == "FP"
      form.ActiveControl.cut()
   endif
return
```

> **NOTE**
> If an event handler does not exist for an event of a control on a form (or indeed for any object in dBASE), checking the "type" will return a value of null. If it evaluates to "FP", then we have a "Function Pointer", which is a fast way to see if this is defined.

We need to do something similar for the Copy and Paste options, providing code that looks like:

```
function COPY_onClick
   if type("form.ActiveControl.copy") == "FP"
      form.ActiveControl.copy()
   endif
return

function PASTE_onClick
   if type("form.ActiveControl.paste") == "FP"
      form.ActiveControl.paste()
   endif
return
```

The onInitMenu Event

We could also add code to check, when the popup menu opens, to see if the Active Control on the form has a cut event and if not, disable these three options. This can be done by clicking on the combobox at the top of the Inspector and selecting "form.root". The only event listed is *onInitMenu()*. Click the tool button for this and in the Source Code Editor, enter:

```
function ROOT_onInitMenu
   local bEnable
   bEnable = ( type("form.ActiveControl.cut") == "FP" )
   this.Cut.enabled := bEnable
   this.Copy.enabled := bEnable
   this.Paste.enabled := bEnable
return
```

This code creates a memory variable (bEnable) and assigns the value returned from a check to see if the *cut* event exists for the current control (the comparison must always return a *true* or *false* value, right?), then we assign the *enabled* property of each of the three menu items in question the value of the memory variable When the popup opens, either all three will be enabled, or all three will be disabled.

> **NOTE**
>
> The *onInitMenu()* event sort of "slipped in" here, and was not discussed in the section on menus. A regular menu can use the *onInitMenu()* as well, for much the same purpose being set here – to enable or disable specific items based on some criteria that you, the developer, have set, or might be set based on a user level value, or a variety of other criteria.
>
> The *onInitMenu()* event belongs to the menubar object (form.root). Under the Menu designer, the easiest way to select that object is through the combobox at the top of the Inspector – the very first item listed is the menubar object called "form.root".

With that done, save the popup menu and exit the Designer (Ctrl+W, call this "FormPopup").

Attaching a Popup Menu to a Form

Popup menus take a little more effort to actually assign to a form.

If we were creating a full application, we could make the decision to use this popup on all forms in the application, by doing the following in our custom form. For the time being, we are simply going to modify the one form we have available in our working folder.

Double-click on "SomeFish.wfm" in the Navigator to open it in the Form Designer.

Go to the Inspector and find the *onOpen()* event. Click on the tool button and in the Source Code Editor, type:

```
function form_onOpen
    set procedure to FormPopup.pop
    form.popupMenu := new FormPopupPopup( form, "MyPopup" )
    return
```

Popup menus must be opened and assigned differently than regular menus attached to a form. The code shown here will open the file containing the popup menu, then assign the popup menu to the form's *popupMenu* property, assigning a required name to the menu.

 NOTE
It should be noted that a popup menu can be attached to individual objects on a form, like a special menu for a grid or an editor, although this book is not going to explore that possibility. See the *dBulletin* article mentioned below for more details on ways you can use popup menus.

To see how this works, save the changes made, run the form, then right-click on various controls. In some versions of Windows, disabled popup items do not appear as if they were disabled (they should appear greyed out). I am not sure why this works this way, but there you are.

Now that we have done this, you have some idea of what can be done. There is a lot more, however, which has been written about quite well by other authors. Rather than try to duplicate their effort, if you need to know more about Popup Menus I suggest that you take a look at an article by David Stone in dBulletin, Issue 16 *(details on dBulletin can be found in the appendices of this book)*.

It is a good idea to close the form now.

Creating SpeedBars

What is a "speedBar?" A speedBar is a set of pushbuttons (we are not discussing the toolbutton class here) that have the *speedBar* property set to *true*, usually placed on a container so that they can be moved as a unit on a form.

If you followed through the examples in an earlier chapter of this book, then you have already done a lot of the work that would be involved in creating a speedBar. You created the pushbuttons, but you did not put them in a container and you did not set the *speedBar* property.

There are several advantages to creating this kind of a set of buttons:

● If you have a set sequence that you always use your pushbuttons in, placing them on a container means that you can just place the container on a form and move it to where you need to. The pushbuttons will always be in the same place in relationship to each other.

- If you set the *speedBar* property to *true*, your pushbuttons will not take focus away from the currently active control on the form. You may not see the benefit of this now, but trust me, it can save a lot of frustration down the road.

When it comes right down to it, dBASE already ships with a set of speedBars. If you open the Form Designer, by default on the Component Palette is the "Data Buttons" tab, which we looked at in an earlier chapter of this book. If you place your cursor over the first two items you should see "BarDataEdit" and "BarDataVCR". If you were to drag these to the design surface you would see a set of buttons that you can move around.

To understand how that works, we are going to create a version of these, using the buttons we created in an earlier exercise.

In the Command Window, type:

```
set procedure to :MyFormControls:MyPushButtons.cc
```

Then, create a new form in the Form Designer. Make sure you set the form's *metric* property to "6 - Pixels".

Now we want to drop a container object onto the form's design surface. This should look something like:

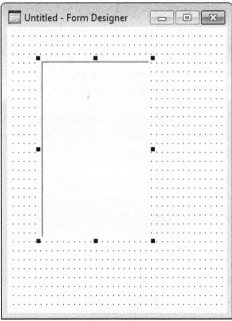

Figure 19-9

In the Inspector set the *name* property to "MySpeedBar" and the *metric* property to "6 - Pixels".

Next, on the Component Palette, click on the "Custom" tab (use the right arrow if necessary), you should see the pushbuttons we created. Drag them to the container, widen the container if needed and make it taller if needed. These should be in the same sequence that we have used them before (look at the "SomeFish" form images earlier in this chapter, if needed).

Spend a little time lining the buttons up and moving the border of the container around, so it looks nice in your eyes. You could even play with the *borderStyle* property of the container. Once you have something you like it should look like:

Figure 19-10

We need to do one more thing, that is to set the *speedBar* property for all of these buttons. This is done more easily than you might imagine – hold the [Ctrl] key down and click on each pushbutton. In the Inspector, find the *speedBar* property and set it to *true*.

To be able to use this, we need to save it somewhere. Make sure that the container object (named "MySpeedBar") has focus, select the "File" menu, then "Save As Custom ...". In the dialog that appears, make sure that the class is being saved to the file ""MyPushbuttons.cc" and uncheck the "Place in Component Palette" checkbox. Click "OK".

Close the form without saving it. The next thing we want to do is make a minor modification to the source code (remember we have been removing the "Name" parameter from our custom controls?). In the Command Window, type:

```
modify command :MyFormControls:MyPushbuttons.cc
```

Toward the bottom of this file you should see:

```
class MYSPEEDBAR(parentObj, name) of CONTAINER(parentObj, name) custom
```

Remove ", name" from the two places it exists here, so the statement looks like:

```
class MYSPEEDBAR(parentObj) of CONTAINER(parentObj) custom
```

Save and exit the Source Code Editor ([Ctrl]+[W]).

To see how this works, make a copy of the "SomeFish.wfm" file (in the Command Window type the following):

```
copy file SomeFish.wfm to SomeFishWithSpeedBar.wfm
```

If you bring the new form "SomeFishWithSpeedBar.wfm" to the Form Designer, we are now going to do something dramatic – we will remove the buttons that are currently on the form on the right side! To do that, hold the Ctrl key down and click on each – this will select all of the buttons.

Next, click the Del key. Notice that these buttons are now gone! We did do this intentionally. If you go to the "Custom" tab on the Component Palette, notice that there is now a container object there. If you hold the mouse over this, you will see "MySpeedBar". If you drag this to the form's surface, we can now place the speedbar where we want it.

Notice that you can move all of the pushbuttons at once! This is where container objects start to shine.

You should now see something like:

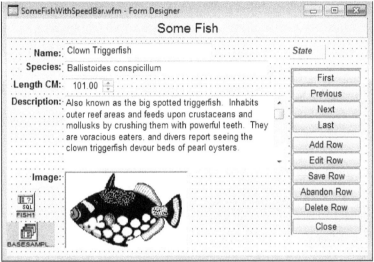

Figure 19-11

If you run the form, you should see it looking like:

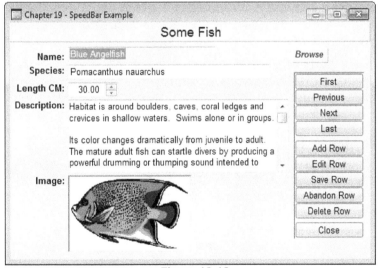

Figure 19-12

The most interesting thing is that if you click on a button, it doesn't actually take focus away from one of the controls on the form. So for example, in the image above (Figure 19-12) if you click on the "Edit Row" button, the Name entryfield would still have focus, where if we were using Pushbuttons that did *not* have the *speedBar* property set to true, clicking on the pushbutton would take focus away from the Name entryfield.

> **NOTE**
>
> In many cases, speedButtons tend to be image-only pushbuttons. We opted for this example to use pushbuttons that were previously defined, rather than creating a whole new set of pushbuttons. For your own applications, if you choose to use speedBars and speedButtons, you can certainly use images and no text, or a combination of text and images. This is completely subjective.
>
> An example of an image only speedbar:
>
>
>
> **Figure 19.13 - Speedbar with image-only pushbuttons**
> *(from the dUFLP – discussed in the appendices)*

This is a simple exercise, speedbars may not be what you want or need for your own application. Many developers are turning more and more to toolbars, as they have become a Windows standard. So instead of speedBars, you may wish to examine the use of toolbars (the rest of this chapter will be dedicated to them).

Creating Toolbars

An example of a toolbar is something you see all the time when you work with dBASE – at the top of the dBASE IDE screen, under the titlebar (the one that says "dBASE PLUS") and under the menus, are a series of pushbuttons – this is a toolbar.

A Toolbar in dBASE is a container with special properties:

- The only controls the toolbar can contain are toolButtons.
- The Toolbar can attach to a form
- The Toolbar can be a free-floating palette
- The Toolbar has a built in event – *onUpdate()* – which constantly "polls" the software, which you can use to check the state of the interface *(useful to determine if a button should be enabled or disabled)*.

As you work in different parts of the IDE, the content of the toolbar changes and some of the buttons are enabled or disabled based on what you are currently doing (for example, if you are in the source editor and you have not highlighted some text, the clipboard buttons are disabled).

How Do You Design a ToolBar?

Unfortunately, the developers of Visual dBASE 7 at Borland International did not give us a design surface for the toolbar class, and the R&D team at dBASE LLC. have not had time to create one yet which would make things much easier. However, given the nature of toolbars and the fact that their display is almost entirely automatic, this is not a serious drawback. If a toolbar is docked (the default), the only control you have on the display is the bitmaps on the buttons, the order the buttons appear and whether or not each button is enabled. If the toolbar is floating (not docked) you can also assign the title bar text and the toolbar's position.

At this time, the only way to design a toolbar is through code and a bit of trial and error.

NOTE

There is an article in dBulletin *(a free online newsletter about dBASE, details in the first appendix)* that describes creating and using a toolbar designer, if you really would prefer to design your toolbars visually. I have no direct experience with the application discussed in the article, but feel free to check it out.

To create a toolbar, you must define it as a subclass of the pre-defined toolbar class built in to dBASE (or your own subclass of the stock dBASE toolbar class):

```
class myToolbar of toolbar
   // properties go here

   // definition of toolbuttons go here

   // code (toolbutton onClick, toolbar onUpdate ...) goes here
endclass
```

In the dBASE samples directory is a toolbutton program called: CLIPBAR.PRG. Note that this is not in a .CC file, although you could create toolbuttons in a custom class file.)

We could use those exactly "as is", but the code gets a bit complicated, so we will simplify them a bit. In the early days at Borland, the Samples group tried to make these into "generic" toolbar classes which means that they can be used with a variety of applications. There are some drawbacks to that approach when trying to learn how they work, as a lot of extra code has been added to cover various contingencies that may not be necessary for your toolbars. We will examine simplified versions of these toolbars.

More Source Code Alias Stuff

As we discussed in Chapter 15, it is a good idea to create a source code alias to keep your toolbars in, so that you can have reusable code. To do this, create a new folder (using the Windows Explorer) called "MyToolBars" in the same place as your other source code library folders (if using the examples I gave, these would be something like: C:\MyCompany\MyFormControls):

```
C:\MyCompany\ToolBars
```

In dBASE PLUS itself, use the "Properties" menu and select "Desktop Properties" and click on the "Source Aliases" tab. Click the "Add" button, enter "MyToolbars" in the Alias entryfield, then click the tool button to select the folder, clicking "OK" to actually place that folder path in the Path entryfield. Click the "Add" button again, you now have a source code alias to store your toolbars in. (Click "OK" to close the "Desktop Properties" dialog.)

Putting Toolbuttons in the Toolbar

We need to take a look at the toolbutton class itself and how it works. Toolbuttons are the actual buttons that are placed in the toolbar container. These are related to the pushbutton class in dBASE, but are not true subclasses of the pushbutton. The only place you can use a toolbutton is on a toolbar – in otherwords, you cannot place a toolbutton object directly onto a form.

A simple toolbutton might be one that navigates in a table, perhaps a "top" button that always moves to the first row. For our sample, type the following in the Command Window:

```
modify command :MyToolbars:MyToolbar.cc
```

(If you decide not to use source code aliases, leave out the string ":MyToolbars:" from the command above.)

and in the Source Code Editor enter the following:

```
class myToolbar of toolbar
    // toolbar properties go here
    this.flat = true // flat buttons
    this.floating = false // make it a toolbar at the top
                          // of the application

    // definition of toolbuttons go here
    this.FirstToolButton = new ToolButton( this )
    with ( this.FirstToolButton )
        bitmap   := "RESOURCE TS_FIRST"
        speedTip := "First Row"
        onClick  := class::First_onClick
    endwith

    // you need to have code here for your onclick events:
    function First_onClick
    return ( this.parent.form.rowset.first() )

endclass
```

The code in the function "First_onClick" simply navigates in the rowset that is attached to the form. Note the syntax for this:

```
this.parent.form.rowset.first()
```

"this" refers to the toolbutton that called the code.

"parent" refers to the toolbar which is the container of the toolbutton.

"form" is the form that the toolbar is "attached" to *(we'll see how to attach a form to a toolbar later)*.

There are some possible problems here. The first is if you have this toolbar running and attached to a form that does not have a rowset assigned to the rowset property of the form. The second is that you don't really need to call this if you are already on the first row of the table. Using the toolbar's *onUpdate()* event we can actually deal with this fairly easily.

We need to add a new event handler for the toolBar class and specifically the *onUpdate()* event, which can go pretty much anywhere. For simplicity's sake we will put it below the definitions (the constructor code) of the buttons and above the *onClick()* event handlers for the buttons:

```
function onUpdate
    // check to see if there is a rowset on the form:
    if type( "this.form.rowset" ) # "O"
        this.FirstToolbutton.enabled = false
    else
        // check to see if we are already at the first
        // row:
        this.FirstToolbutton.enabled := ;
            NOT this.form.rowset.atFirst()
```

```
        endif
    return
```

The *onUpdate()* event will fire fairly constantly as long as there is no interaction with the toolbar. If the mouse is over the toolbar, or the user is clicking buttons, then the *onUpdate()* event is not firing – otherwise it will execute the code shown above quite often.

Making the Toolbar More Useful

Our sample toolbar is not very useful at the moment, because it only has a single toolbutton on it. We can build it up, which we will do a bit at a time.

To continue where we are now, let's finish the VCR part of the toolbar – the part used to navigate through the rows of a table on a form.

First, we need three more toolbuttons. These are going to do the "Previous", "Next" and "Last" settings that are common to most of this sort of toolbar. Note that the buttons will appear on the toolbar in the order they are defined in your source code.

The Bitmaps (Images)

The bitmaps being used in these examples have a resource name of "TS_xxxx" – the first two letters stand for "Toolbar Small", the underscore is a separator and the "xxxx" part is some descriptive name for the actual image.

These were created by the Samples and Art groups at Borland specifically for toolbars. There are also "TL_xxxx" which are the exact same images, but they are a touch larger, hence the "L" instead of "S" in the resource name.

To see what is in the standard RESOURCE.DLL file that can be used for your images for toolButtons, the simplest way is to go to the Command Window, and do the following:

```
t = new ToolBar()
t1 = new ToolButton( t )
inspect( t1 )
```

In the Inspector, click on the *bitmap* property, then click the tool button and a dialog will appear. In the combobox, select "Resource" (it will default to "Filename"), then on the right side of the dialog, click on the tool button again. You will see a new dialog and you can scroll through it until you find the image you want. Note it *(write it down)* – some images use numbers, some use text. If the image you want to use has text, then the string for your bitmap property will be:

```
"RESOURCE bitmapname"
```

If the image you want uses a number, then the string will be:

```
"RESOURCE #number"
```

The "#" sign is vital. Finally, if what you see has two images (the first set of images that are named "PS_something", for example) you have a SPLIT bitmap, and you need to modify the string so that the word "RESOURCE" is followed immediately by ":2", i.e.,

```
"RESOURCE:2 PS_FIRST"
```

In addition, you can use button images if you have bitmap files that are the right size. You can use images that are contained in files *(you can purchase or download collections of images that might give you what you need from various websites)*. To view them is a bit more difficult unless you create a form to do so. To use one, the bitmap property should read:

```
"FILENAME path\filename.bmp"
```

And if you happen to have a "split" bitmap, the statement would look like:

```
"FILENAME:2 path\filename.bmp"
```

Disabled Bitmaps

One difference between standard pushbuttons and toolbuttons is that toolbuttons only have one bitmap property called *bitmap*. Toolbuttons don't have a separate *upBitmap*, *focusBitmap*, *downBitmap*, and *disabledBitmap*. There are reasons for this. First, toolbuttons never get focus, so they don't need a *focusBitmap*. Second, dBASE automatically handles dimming the bitmap of disabled toolbuttons, so you don't need a *disabledBitmap*. The separate *downBitmap* is just not included because (I suppose) it's passé.

Continuing ...

Now that we've brought up the subject of dimming a toolbutton's bitmap, let's consider what happens to the bitmap when you disable a toolbutton. dBASE automatically interprets the colors of your bitmap to determine a dimmed representation of it. In doing so, one (and only one) color is seen to be transparent. With a 16 color bitmap, this color is rgb(128,0,128) which looks like a dark purple. Even using GIF files with a transparent color will not get around this limitation. GIF transparent colors appear to be ignored unless the color is set to the dBASE standard for transparent colors. If your bitmap does not contain the transparent color as a background, the background color will be interpreted as either light or dark and rendered accordingly. This may or may not provide the desired results. In any case, the user has control of the Windows color scheme and can change it at their whim. This means that your bitmap may not display correctly if the user changes colors. The bitmap will either display the background when not dimmed, or will not dim properly, or both. For best results it is recommended that you use a 16 color bitmap with the background set to dark purple (Red=128, Green=0, Blue=128) for your toolbuttons.

Add the following into MyToolbar:

```
this.PreviousToolButton = new ToolButton( this )
with ( this.PreviousToolButton )
    bitmap   := "RESOURCE TS_PREV"
    speedTip := "Previous Row"
    onClick  := class::Previous_onClick
endwith

this.NextToolButton = new ToolButton( this )
with ( this.NextToolButton )
    bitmap   := "RESOURCE TS_NEXT"
    speedTip := "Next Row"
    onClick  := class::Next_onClick
endwith

this.LastToolButton = new ToolButton( this )
with ( this.LastToolButton )
    bitmap   := "RESOURCE TS_LAST"
```

```
        speedTip := "Last Row"
        onClick  := class::Last_onClick
    endwith
```

And add the following onClick event handlers:

```
function Previous_onClick
    local bNext
    // navigate one row "back"
    bNext = this.parent.form.rowset.next(-1)
    // if that didn't work, we're at the endOfSet
    // and need to navigate back to where we were
    if ( not bNext )
        this.parent.form.rowset.next()
    endif
return

function Next_onClick
    local bNext
    bNext = this.parent.form.rowset.next()
    if ( not bNext )
        this.parent.form.rowset.next(-1)
    endif
return ( bNext )

function Last_onClick
return ( this.parent.form.rowset.last() )
```

And finally, we need to modify the *onUpdate()* event handler for the toolbar to include all the buttons (we don't want them enabled if there's no rowset, and we don't need the last button enabled if we're on the last row). We're going to make this a touch more complex. It is possible that during the processing of a form it may start with no rowset attached to the form's rowset property, but this may change. This adds a layer of complexity to the code below, but it makes it more flexible:

```
function onUpdate
    // check to see if there is a rowset on the form:
    local bRowset, bAtFirst, bAtLast
    bRowset = type( "this.form.rowset" ) == "O"
    if bRowset
        bAtFirst = this.form.rowset.atFirst()
        bAtLast  = this.form.rowset.atLast()
        this.FirstToolbutton.enabled    = NOT bAtFirst
        this.PreviousToolbutton.enabled = NOT bAtFirst
        this.NextToolbutton.enabled     = NOT bAtLast
        this.LastToolbutton.enabled     = NOT bAtLast
    else // No rowset ...
        this.FirstToolbutton.enabled    = false
        this.PreviousToolbutton.enabled = false
        this.NextToolbutton.enabled     = false
        this.LastToolbutton.enabled     = false
    endif
return
```

Now that we have all that, it is time to test it. Save your code and exit the source editor.

Testing Our Toolbar

To test this, first, we need a form that has a rowset on it. There are two ways a form may be opened (*open()* and *readmodal()*) and we will see how this works in both cases. We will use the form "SomeFish.wfm" that we've been using to test menus in this chapter. The first test is with a "modeless" form:

```
set procedure to SomeFish.wfm additive
set procedure to :MyToolbars:MyToolbar.cc additive
f = new SomeFishForm()
t = new MyToolbar()
t.attach( f )
f.open()
```

Note that when the form opens, the toolbar appears at the top of the screen (to the right of the "normal" toolbar – this is actually as designed, as we'll see later in this document), and if you are at the top of the rowset that the first two toolbuttons are not enabled. However, if you click on the buttons, you will see the form's rowset navigate as it should.

This should look like:

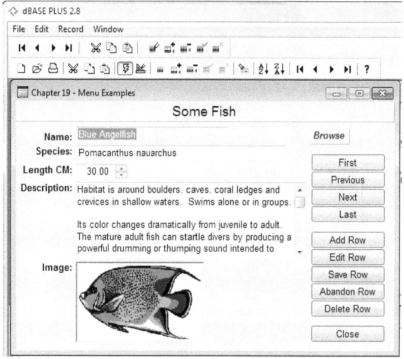

Figure 19-14

(The toolbar specific to this form is the top one in this example ...)

Once you are done experimenting, close the form and notice that the new toolbar is gone.

Now, let's try opening the same form with the *mdi* property set to *false* and we will see some differences:

```
t.detach( f )        // Detach the toolbar from the form
t=null               // "Null" the object pointer out
f.mdi := false
t=new MyToolbar()    // Re-instantiate the toolbar
t.attach( f )        // Re-attach the toolbar ...
```

```
f.open()
```

Notice that the toolbar is now on the form and that the form's objects have all shifted down to make room for it. (We'll talk about this later.) This should look like:

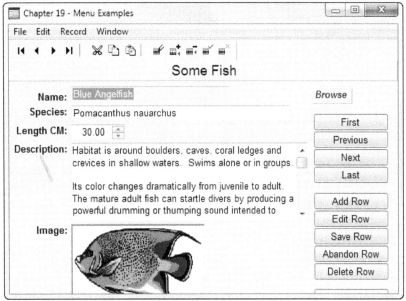

Figure 19-15

What happens if you want to do this on a completely modal form? (Close the form and do the following in the Command Window):

```
f.readModal()
```

The toolbuttons do not appear at all on the form!

Sequence of Property Assignments
There are some interesting behavioral problems in assigning specific values in specific sequences.

Gary White (a few years ago, in the dBASE newsgroups) spent a bit of time tinkering with this and has come up with the following when changing the *mdi* property of forms:

```
f=new SomeFishForm()
f.mdi = true
f.t = new MyToolbar()
f.t.attach(f)
f.open()
```

This works fine. Notice that the *mdi* property is being set before attaching the toolbar. In this case, the toolbar should appear on the application framewindow.

```
f=new SomeFishForm()
f.mdi=true // for test purposes
f.t = new MyToolbar()
f.t.attach(f)
f.mdi = false // <- Problem here
f.open()
```

In the above example, if you set the *mdi* property to *false* after attaching the toolbar, the toolbar appears attached to the application framewindow, rather than to the form, as you would expect for an SDI form. Now, before you go thinking "Cool! I can use that!" take a look at the last example. You'll see that this misdirection can be a source of instability problems and may cause you a great deal of grief later on.

```
f=new SomeFishForm()
f.mdi=false
f.t = new MyToolbar()
f.t.attach(f)
f.open()
```

This works as expected, because the *mdi* property is being set to *false* before attaching the toolbar – in this case, the toolbar will be attached to the form as it should be.

Finally, if the form is instantiated with *mdi* set to *false*, then you attach a toolbar and switch the *mdi* property to *true*, you will get a memory access violation error, or sometimes a GPF. (This is a particularly nasty one.)

```
f=new SomeFishForm()
f.mdi=false // for testing
f.t = new MyToolbar()
f.t.attach(f)
f.mdi=true   // this causes the gpf, but it won't
             // appear until you open the form
f.open()
```

Obviously it is quite important to get this sequence of statements just right. The important thing to remember is to set the *mdi* property before you attach the toolbar. If you need to change the *mdi* property after attaching a toolbar, you'll need to detach the toolbar and stub out the reference to it, then re-instantiate the toolbar in order to avoid problems. Assuming the previous example where f is the form, f.t is the toolbar and the form.mdi=false:

```
f.t.detach(f)         // detach the toolbar
f.t=null              // stub out the toolbar reference
f.mdi=true            // now change to mdi
f.t=new mytoolbar()   // re-create toolbar
f.t.attach(f)         // and re-attach
```

Adding Functionality to the ToolBar

We can add functionality in two ways – we can add more toolbars to the form, OR we can put a bunch of toolbuttons onto one toolbar.

The disadvantage to adding multiple toolbars, is that they sometimes stack up, one under the other. This may not be desirable (it's not for any application I develop).

The advantage is that each toolbar then can be pulled off the form or application as a floating palette by the user, or left where it is. This means that they can be independent of each other. Another advantage is easier reuse of code. All your toolbars won't need all the buttons. With them grouped into logical, smaller toolbars, you can simply add the functionality with an existing toolbar.

For our purposes, we'll simply be adding to the toolbar.

One thing that we might want to consider is putting a separator between the sections of the toolbar. It helps break up the purpose of the different parts of a toolbar if we do this. So, the first thing we should do is add a new toolbutton to our toolbar class. If you have the sample form open you should do the following – close the form, and in the Command Window:

```
t.detach(f)
t = null
```

Then to open the toolbar class file:

```
modify command :MyToolbars:MyToobar.cc
```

Add the following below the previous toolbuttons:

```
this.Separator1ToolButton = new ToolButton( this )
with ( this.Separator1ToolButton )
    separator = true
endwith
```

Note that the only property we need is the *separator* property.

The next thing we might want to add are the standard clipboard buttons used to cut, copy and paste text into/out of a control. The visual controls in dBASE that have the ability to use the Windows clipboard have methods built-in to handle these abilities, so we do not have to write any code to access the Windows clipboard.

What we do need to do is create the buttons and attach code in the *onClick()* events and the *onUpdate()* event for the toolbar.

Once again, we will be simplifying the code in the samples that ship with dBASE. First we'll add the following toolbuttons (after the separator we added above):

```
this.CutToolButton = new ToolButton( this )
with ( this.CutToolButton )
    bitmap    := "RESOURCE TS_CUT"
    speedTip := "Cut"
    onClick  := class::Cut_onClick
endwith

this.CopyToolButton = new ToolButton( this )
with ( this.CopyToolButton )
    bitmap    := "RESOURCE TS_COPY"
    speedTip := "Copy"
    onClick  := class::Copy_onClick
endwith

this.PasteToolButton = new ToolButton( this )
with ( this.PasteToolButton )
    bitmap    := "RESOURCE TS_PASTE"
    speedTip := "Paste"
    onClick  := class::Paste_onClick
endwith
```

We need the *onClick()* event code for these new toolbuttons:

```
function Cut_onClick
return ( this.parent.form.activeControl.cut() )

function Copy_onClick
return ( this.parent.form.activeControl.copy() )

function Paste_onClick
return ( this.parent.form.activeControl.paste() )
```

And we need to modify the *onUpdate()* event to determine if these should be enabled or not – the way we do that is to see if the *copy()* method is a "Function Pointer" for the form's active control (the current control). What should happen when the form is running is – as you (or your user) move through the controls on the form (tab, mouse, whatever), these toolbuttons will be enabled or disabled based on whether or not the control has a *copy()* method (which is built-in to the control).

```
this.LastToolbutton.enabled      = NOT bAtLast
// New Code:
bClip = ( TYPE("this.form.activeControl.copy") == "FP" )
this.CutToolButton.enabled       = bClip
this.CopyToolButton.enabled      = bClip
this.PasteToolButton.enabled     = bClip
```

And you can also add the code to check if there's no rowset on the form to disable these buttons. Unfortunately, dBASE does not surface a way to tell if any text is currently selected to provide more intelligent enabling/disabling of the cut and copy functions. If you find a way to get that using the API, please post a message in the dBASE newsgroups.

Another set of buttons which we'll add to our toolbar are ones that handle rowset editing operations – allowing us to edit the current row, add a new row, delete a row, save changes, cancel changes.

While I am using the EDITBAR program (in the dBASE Samples folder) as a basis for the following, the one button that is missing from that program is an EDIT toolbutton. This is useful if you have your rowset's *autoEdit* property set to false – this is how all of my applications work (without an Edit button there is no way for the user to actually modify a row).

```
this.Separator2ToolButton = new ToolButton( this )
with ( this.Separator2ToolButton )
   separator = true
endwith

this.EditToolbutton = new ToolButton( this )
with ( this.EditToolButton )
   bitmap   := "RESOURCE TS_EDIT"
   speedTip := "Edit Row"
   onClick  := class::Edit_onClick
endwith

this.AppendToolbutton = new ToolButton( this )
with ( this.AppendToolButton )
   bitmap   := "RESOURCE TS_APPEND"
   speedTip := "Add Row"
   onClick  := class::Append_onClick
endwith
```

```
this.DeleteToolButton = new ToolButton( this )
with ( this.DeleteToolButton )
   bitmap   := "RESOURCE TS_DELETE"
   speedTip := "Delete Row"
   onClick  := class::Delete_onClick
endwith

this.SaveToolButton = new ToolButton( this )
with ( this.SaveToolButton )
   bitmap   := "RESOURCE TS_SAVE"
   speedTip := "Save Row"
   onClick  := class::Save_onClick
endwith

this.AbandonToolButton = new ToolButton( this )
with ( this.AbandonToolButton )
   bitmap   := "RESOURCE TS_ABANDON"
   speedTip := "Abandon Row"
   onClick  := class::Abandon_onClick
endwith
And the following onClick() event code:
function Edit_onClick
return ( this.parent.form.rowset.beginEdit() )

function Append_onClick
return ( this.parent.form.rowset.beginAppend() )

function Delete_onClick
   local bDelete, bFirst
   bDelete = false
   bFirst  = false
   if ( not this.parent.form.rowset.endOfSet )
      if ( MSGBOX("You are about to delete the current row." ;
            + CHR(13) ;
            + "Click Yes to delete the current row.", ;
            "Alert", ;
            4) == 6 )
         bFirst  := this.parent.form.rowset.atFirst()
         bDelete := this.parent.form.rowset.delete()
         if ( not bFirst )
            this.parent.form.rowset.next(-1)
         endif
         if ( this.parent.form.rowset.endOfSet )
            this.parent.form.rowset.next()
         endif
      endif
   endif
return ( bDelete )
```

```
function Save_onClick
return ( this.parent.form.rowset.save() )

function Abandon_onClick
return ( this.parent.form.rowset.abandon() )
```

And this is how the toolbar's *onUpdate()* should look (this is the whole thing). The additional code in the first block checks to see if we are at the *endOfSet*, which would mean we can't edit or delete a row (therefore, we would disable those buttons) and the save and abandon buttons would only be enabled if a modification occurred to the row.

```
function MyToolBar_onUpdate
   // check to see if there is a rowset on the form:
   local bRowset, bAtFirst, bAtLast
   bRowset = type( "this.form.rowset" ) == "O"
   if bRowset
      bAtFirst = this.form.rowset.atFirst()
      bAtLast  = this.form.rowset.atLast()
      this.FirstToolbutton.enabled      := NOT bAtFirst
      this.PreviousToolbutton.enabled := NOT bAtFirst
      this.NextToolbutton.enabled       := NOT bAtLast
      this.LastToolbutton.enabled       := NOT bAtLast
      bClip = ( TYPE("this.form.activeControl.copy") == "FP" )
      this.CutToolButton.enabled        := bClip
      this.CopyToolButton.enabled       := bClip
      this.PasteToolButton.enabled      := bClip
      bEoF = this.form.rowset.endOfSet
      this.EditToolButton.enabled       := NOT bEof
      this.AppendToolButton.enabled     := true
      this.DeleteToolButton.enabled     := NOT bEoF
      bModified = this.form.rowset.modified
      this.SaveToolButton.enabled       := bModified
      this.AbandonToolButton.enabled    := bModified
   else // No rowset ...
      this.FirstToolbutton.enabled      := false
      this.PreviousToolbutton.enabled := false
      this.NextToolbutton.enabled       := false
      this.LastToolbutton.enabled       := false
      this.CutToolbutton.enabled        := false
      this.CopyToolbutton.enabled       := false
      this.PasteToolbutton.enabled      := false
      this.EditToolButton.enabled       := false
      this.AppendToolButton.enabled     := false
      this.DeleteToolButton.enabled     := false
      this.SaveToolButton.enabled       := false
      this.AbandonToolButton.enabled    := false
   endif
return
```

Things to Note

There are a few things you should consider for your own applications:

The dBASE Toolbar

If you have never done this before and you are working with an MDI application, you may be a bit annoyed to note that your toolbar appears to the right of the one that is normally in dBASE. For your application this would be ugly.

Don't despair, there is a simple solution – the application is an object in dBASE, with a name of "_app" and it has properties. One of those properties is *speedbar*, which has a logical value of *true* or *false,* that defaults to *true*. To turn the dBASE speedbar off, the command is:

```
_app.speedbar := false
```

Doing this, and using the samples we have so far if you typed the following in the Command Window:

```
_app.speedbar := false
set proc to :MyToolbars:MyToolbar.cc
set proc to somefish.wfm
f = new SomeFishForm()
t = new MyToolbar()
t.attach(f)
f.open()
```

You should see something like:

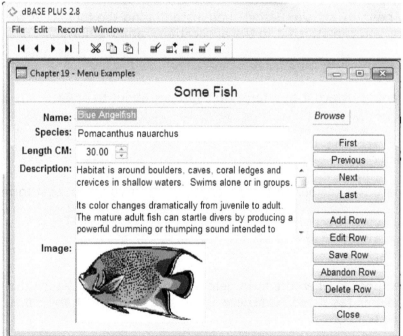

Figure 19-15

Don't forget to do the following once the form has been closed:

```
t.detach(f)
_app.speedbar := true
```

Detaching Toolbars

When you close your form, if you do not detach your toolbar, you may get some interesting results – the toolbar will be replicated the next time you run the same form *(you will have two or more of them)*. The simple solution is, when you close your form, in the *onClose()* event call the toolbar's detach method:

```
t.detach( this )
```

The problem with this particular assumption, however, is that the reference "t" is available to you at this time. You should consider perhaps creating an object reference to the toolbar in your form, when you instantiate the form:

```
f = new form()
f.toolbar = new MyToolBar()
f.toolbar.attach( f )
// etc.
```

This will allow you to detach the toolbar easily enough and even better, if you release the form, the toolbar reference is gone completely.

In addition, it gives you an easy method of accessing the toolbar itself during the form's execution, in case, for whatever reason, you wished to modify the toolbar, the reference to the toolbar is there, you can modify properties of individual toolButtons by just adding their reference to "f.toolbar".

Sharing ToolBars in an MDI Application

Another thing you may wish to consider is to have multiple forms (in an MDI application) sharing the same toolbar.

This turns out to be fairly simple. Rather than instantiating the toolbar as an object/property of a specific form, you can attach it to the application framewindow:

```
_app.ToolBar = new MyToolBar()
```

And when you want to attach it to a form that you are about to open:

```
fMyForm1 = new MyFormForm()
_app.ToolBar.attach( fMyForm1 )
fMyForm1.open()
```

If you want to share this toolbar with another form, when you open that form:

```
fMyForm2 = new MyFormForm2() // whatever the form is ...
_app.ToolBar.attach( fMyForm2 )
fMyForm1.Open()
```

One thing to remember is when the form gets closed, you should detach the toolbar, or you may run into problems (as noted elsewhere in this document, with the same toolbar appearing multiple times).

```
_app.ToolBar.detach( fMyForm2 )
```

The user who suggested this (Todd Kreuter, on the dBASE newsgroups) also suggested if you want to use multiple toolbars that you create an array to hold the object references for the toolbars, then attach the toolbars you wish to the individual forms:

```
_app.Toolbars = new Array()
_app.ToolBars[1] = new ToolBarClip()
_app.ToolBars[2] = new ToolBarEdit()
// etc.
fMyForm1 = new MyFormForm()
_app.ToolBars[1].attach( fMyForm1 )
_app.ToolBars[2].attach( fMyForm1 )
// etc.

// Do whatever you need to, and when the
// form closes:
_app.ToolBars[1].detach( fMyForm1 )
_app.ToolBars[2].detach( fMyForm1 )
// etc.
```

If you always want the toolbar to appear on the application framewindow, you could attach it to framewin, rather than to a form:

```
_app.ToolBars[1].attach( _app.FrameWin )
```

The problem with doing this, is that your code will need to be more complex. After some experimentation, you cannot do the obvious – attach a toolbar to both the framewin *and* a form (if you try it, you will get a dBASE error informing you that you cannot do this).

As noted, your code in a case like the above would need to be modified. The code attached to the toolbar and the toolbuttons will not have any idea what form to use. What this would mean is you would have to modify the code to look at an object reference for a "current" form, using a custom property attached to the toolbar, such as "currentForm":

```
_app.ToolBars[1].currentForm = fMyForm1
```

This means that you would need to be setting the *currentForm* property each time you open and close a form, using the form's *onGotFocus* event and when the form loses focus using the form's *onLostFocus* event and the form's *onClose* event you would need to set the property to NULL:

```
_app.ToolBars[1].currentForm = null
```

Don't forget when done to detach the toolbar(s) and so on.

As you can see, this does make the issue more complex – but it is doable. And through the use of custom forms, as noted in an earlier chapter, you could do most of the work once, then all derived forms would inherit that code.

Menu, Toolbar, and Popups In One Application

If you build an application with a main menu bar, a toolbar, and a popup menu, you may find that items on these three objects are duplicating functionality – like moving the row pointer on the form to the next row. You can create three distinct click events, one in each of the objects, to accomplish this task. That is effectively what we did in this chapter. But keep in mind that you could alternatively create a single method in your application that moves the row pointer and does any other checks that may be necessary. Then the *onClick* event handlers in the main menu, the popup menu and/or the toolbutton could call that method. You might, for example, add a "NextRow" method to the base custom form. Or you could create a custom class of methods and attach that object to the _app object. There are many possibilities and it is a good idea to avoid duplicating code wherever possible.

Toolbars and SDI Forms

If your form's *mdi* property is set to *false*, as noted elsewhere in this document, your toolbar will appear at the top of the form shifting everything on the form down to make room.

While it is handy that this is done automatically for you, the one problem that happens is that while the controls are moved down, the form is not resized to make room for the toolbar – which means that if you have controls at the bottom of the form, they are not necessarily visible anymore.

One solution is to always leave room at the bottom of the form for this to happen – the question is how to make sure you leave enough room. You don't see the toolbar on the form until you run it, so it's difficult to know exactly how much room to reserve. This becomes a bit of trial and error – I suggest you create a pushbutton which has the visible property set to false – its only purpose is to sit there and reserve room. Place it at the bottom of the form. Size it so that it takes close to the same amount of room as the toolbar, then tinker a bit. Run the form with the toolbar attached, see if you are close – set the text property of the pushbutton to something that will remind you what it's there for when you bring it back into the Form Designer.

One other problem I've noted is that toolbars do not have a bottom line when placed onto a form. This looks a bit unfinished to me. The simple solution is to use a rectangle *(since line objects do not allow you to set their appearance in the same way as rectangles)* and set the properties as follows:

```
left = 0
width = form.width
top = 0
height = 0.1
text = ""
```

The default border style (*borderStyle* property) is "etched-in" which will match the line at the top of the toolbar. The rectangle will be moved down with all the other controls when the toolbar is attached and will appear at the bottom of the toolbar. Of course, if you allow the form to be resized, you'll need to write the code to resize the width of the rectangle in the form's *onSize* event.

Floating Palettes versus Attached to Form

One user on the dBASE newsgroups noticed that even with the *floating* property of the toolbar set to *false*, the toolbar was able to be removed from the form and turned into a floating palette. This is actually "as designed".

If you really want your toolbar to stay attached to a form, you can force it by adding the following code to the *onUpdate* event of the toolbar:

```
if this.floating
   this.floating := false
endif
```

Which really just states that if the *floating* property has been changed (which it will do if the user attempts to drag it off the form), reset the *floating* property to *false*, which will snap the toolbar back to the form. *(This code example was provided by Bowen Moursund in the dBASE newsgroups.)*

Summary

This chapter discusses a lot of what you can do to enhance the user interface for your applications. What it doesn't do is discuss every single possible permutation of what can be done, although I have tried to cover the major ones. After you have worked with designing your own menus, popups, speedbars and toolbars, you can start to decide which works best for you, or even working with combinations of them. I suggest that at the very least you always use a menu for your applications and everything else is gravy.

NOTES:

Chapter 20: Reporting and Printing

One of the primary reasons for a database application is to be able to generate useful reports from the data. To that end, the following chapter is aimed at helping you get started with working with the Report Designer and the Report Engine in dBASE, creating useful reports and labels.

In order to work with the Report Designer and the dBASE report engine, you need to understand the report object and the objects that work specifically with reports.

Report Objects

Some of the following is based loosely on information in the Language Reference and is here to help understand what is going on in this powerful but sometimes confusing tool.

Like a form, a report is really a container for a bunch of objects, with some code of its own, since the report is an object with properties and methods (also just like a form). The report object hierarchy works something like the following:

- Report Object – which can contain:
  - Data Objects – these give access to data in tables:
    - Query objects
    - Database objects
    - Session objects

    Data Objects work much like they do on forms, except that a report does not have a primary rowset like a form does (you cannot refer to form.rowset).
  - Report Layout Objects – these determine the appearance of the page and where data is output (or streamed):
    - PageTemplate
    - StreamFrame

    A report contains at least one pageTemplate, and each pageTemplate contains at least one streamFrame.
  - Data stream objects – these read and organize the data from a rowset and stream it out to the report's *streamFrame* object(s):
    - StreamSource
    - Band (detailBand, group headerBand, group footerBand)
    - Group

    Each *streamSource* may have a *detailBand*, a group *headerBand* and/or a group *footerBand*. Each of these are subclassed from the Band object, and have all the properties of the band object. The Report Object itself has a group called the *reportGroup*, which has a *headerBand* and a *footerBand* – this will be discussed later in this chapter.
  - Visual Components – these are used to display the report's data:
    - Text
    - Line
    - Image
    - Rectangle
    - Shape
    - ActiveX
    - ReportViewer
    - Container (*not really visual, but used to contain other objects – note, however that containers do not work for band objects. The reason is that a container is a*

window object, and you cannot repeat window objects one for each detailBand (or other band object) like you can a text control – this information is straight from the original Borland development team.)

The primary method of displaying information in a report is through text objects.

How a Report is Rendered

A report gets rendered (or generated) by calling the report's *render()* method. The sequence of this generation is along these lines:

- The report's *firstPageTemplate* property is looked at to determine which *pageTemplate* (if there are multiple) is the first to be rendered (or generated).
- In the process of rendering the *pageTemplate*, all controls that are defined for that *pageTemplate* are rendered, in the order they are defined in the source code (this is also called the z-order). The important thing to note in this process is that it doesn't matter what order these controls appear on the report surface, but the order in which these controls appear in the source code.
- The *streamSource* is controlled by the data – your query (or queries), or more specifically, the rowset generated by the query. Most reports have only one *streamSource*, and the rowset for that *streamSource* controls the report.
- The *streamSource* controls how a *streamFrame* is rendered and for every row in the rowset referred to by the *streamSource* a *detailBand* is rendered inside the *streamFrame*.
- When a *streamFrame* is filled up, if there are still more rows to be rendered, these will be rendered in other *streamFrames* on the same *pageTemplate* – if any exist. (What this means is that you can have multiple *streamFrames* on a page – which is how labels are generated, as well as columnar reports.)
- If the current *streamFrame* is the last one on the *pageTemplate* (or the only one) and there are still more rows in the rowset to be rendered, then the *pageTemplate* looks at its *nextPageTemplate* property to determine where to go next. At that point a new *pageTemplate* gets scheduled, and the report's *onPage* event fires.
- The report will continue rendering until all rows in the rowset have been rendered.

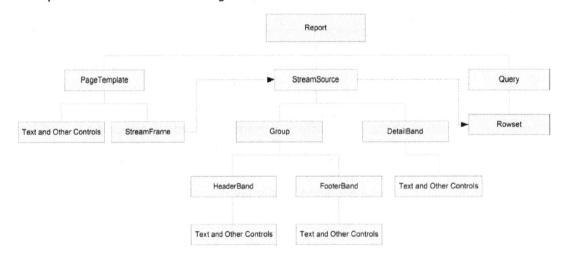

Figure 20-1
Based on a chart by Charles Overbeck

The Report Designer

When you are using the Report Designer, you will see a very busy screen, which can be a bit confusing at first – although if you've used the Form Designer you may be used to it, to an extent.

There are the palettes you've used in the Form Designer:

● The Inspector – used to inspect and change properties and events;
● The Component Palette – used to place specific controls onto your report;
● The Field Palette – one method of placing fields (columns from the rowset(s)) onto the report;
● The Format Toolbar – used to insert HTML formatting into your text controls.

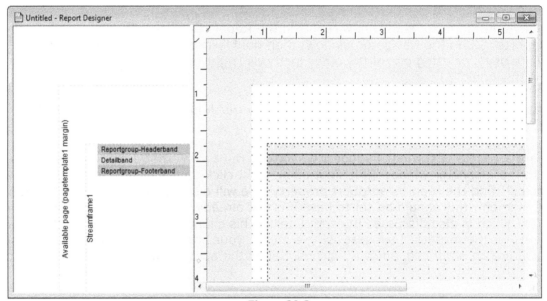

Figure 20-2

In addition, there is the report designer itself – this actually has two parts, although the default is to show just the report. These are called panes (it's a window) – the pane on the left is called the Group Pane and the pane on the right is the Report Pane. When you first open the Report Designer, there is a vertical bar on the left of the Report pane – if you drag this bar to the right, you will see the Group pane.

The Group Pane shows the hierarchy of objects in the report down to the bands (it does not show controls). The Report Pane shows the report appearance with the corresponding structures shown in the Group Pane – this uses live data. The Report Pane is where you will be working. The Group Pane has some use to show you what groups and bands you are working with, but it is not interactive and is not where you will do most of your work.

Metrics

The default metrics for the report designer are twips and there are 1440 twips to the inch (a twip is a "twentieth of a point"; there are 72 points per inch). This, for people used to thinking in inches, (or centimeters, or ...) can be a bit mind-boggling and trying to determine the width of a page, or how far from the left margin you wish to set an object, can be difficult at best. However, like the Form Designer, you can change the metrics for your reports.

If you think in inches, then by all means, change the metrics for your reports to inches. The *metric* property is found in the Inspector for the "form" – if you are designing a report, the form is the report – and if you click on it, you will see a combobox with several options: Chars; Twips (default); Points; Inches; Centimeters; Millimeters; Pixels. Most people don't think too clearly in anything but Inches, Centimeters or perhaps Millimeters – so you may want to get used to setting the metric property as soon as you start designing a report (just as with the Form Designer and forms, you could use a custom report that set this and any other properties you commonly change from the defaults for you – we will discuss this in the next chapter). Throughout this chapter, the examples use "inches" as the *metric* setting.

Creating a Simple Report

Before we get into creating custom reports and custom controls and – let's take a look at simply creating a simple report.

If you have not done so, start a new report in the Report Designer. This is done by going to the "Reports" tab in the Navigator window, then double-clicking on the first "(Untitled)" icon (the white one), or using one of the other methods (right click, etc.) discussed in other parts of this book.

The Report Designer should come up and look very much like Figure 20.2, although by default the Group Pane may not be showing.

There are a couple of settings I suggest we look at right away that are specific to the report itself. In the Inspector window (if it's not open, right click on the design surface and select "Inspector") find the report's *autoSort* property. We will discuss this in more detail later, but for the moment, this should be set to *false* if is not already. The other is the report's *metric* property, which is also discussed in depth later in this chapter. While you have the option to use pixels for the metrics, I suggest using a metric your brain can wrap itself around, such as *(if you are an American, anyway)* inches. Select the appropriate metric, and we'll move on.

A Quick Look at the Design Surface

When you look at the report design surface, you will see that you have the white area – this represents the printable area of the page – inside your margins and is called the *pageTemplate* – more on this later. You will see the yellow area – this represents the *streamFrame*, which is where the details from your data will be displayed/printed. You will see a pink or coral colored section, this is the *detailBand*, which is where the detail for your report goes. By default, you will see also a light green section, which represents the *reportGroup.headerBand* and a light purple or purplish-blue colored band which represents the *reportGroup.footerBand*. For this report, we will not be using these last two bands. If you select the *reportGroup.headerBand*, you will see that it has a height (if your report's *metric* is set to inches) of 0.17. If you change that to zero (0), the band will disappear. Do the same for the *reportGroup.footerBand*.

> **📋 NOTE**
>
> The *reportGroup.headerBand* and *reportGroup.footerBand* default height may change in later versions of dBASE. R&D is examining options – this is a change that was made in dBASE PLUS release 2.5, to give a default *height* to all band objects on a report. While this can be useful, it has caused a lot of developers to have to modify their reports so that the *height* is zero for these and sometimes other bands. While the *height* property is still set in release 2.6, if nothing is on these bands, they will not render. This means you do not have to change the *height* in dBASE Plus 2.6 and later.

The Report Design main window should look something like:

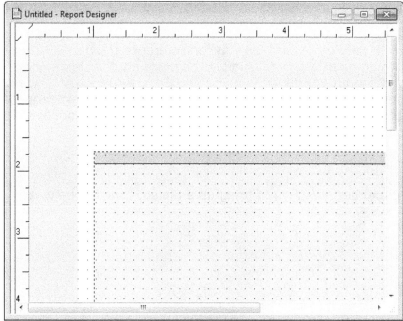

Figure 20-3

Report Headings

Before we get to placing controls on the *streamFrame* or *detailBand*, we should consider what we want to appear where. By definition, any control that is placed on the *pageTemplate* will appear on each page of the report. Therefore you should, as a general rule, never place fields from a table on the *pageTemplate*. This actually can confuse the report engine in dBASE and you may get some odd results.

However, you can place controls, text, images, etc., on the *pageTemplate*. This is a good place to put a report title, the date the report was printed, a page number if you want one, etc.

To get started, we're going to fall back on our default "Fish" table, let's put a text control on the *pageTemplate* at the top. Go to the Component Palette (if this window is not open, right click on the design surface, select "Component Palette") and on the "Standard" tab you will see the text control. Drag this to the white area at the top of the page.

Widen the text control by dragging the right side – make it a couple of inches (or something roughly equivalent) for the moment – it can be resized as needed.

Click on the text control and type "My Fish Report", replacing the word "Text1" that is the default text. Next, go to the Inspector and find the *fontSize* property, change the value to 14. Change the *name* property to "MainTitle".

You may wish to save this report, do so by pressing ⎗Ctrl+⎗S (or using the toolbar, etc.) and give it a name of "MyFishReport".

Move this control toward the very top of the *pageTemplate* (this is the printable area of the report, so you can go to the edge – it's not the edge of the paper). How do you center this? This is actually going to be easy – you make sure that the text control is selected, then choose the "Layout" menu, "Align" and "Center Horizontally in Window". This will center your text control within the margins of the *pageTemplate*. If you wish to be absolutely certain your text will be centered, you should also set the text control's *alignHorizontal* property to "1 - Center".

It is useful to have a date on reports, so you can reference the date it was printed. You might think this would be tricky, but it's not. Let's place another text control on the *pageTemplate,* and change the control's *name* property to "DateText". Again, I suggest widening the control a bit, make it an inch or two wide. Find the *text* property in the Inspector and click on the "Type" button (the letter "T"). Select "Codeblock" from the combobox. Notice that the text changes to:

```
{||"Text1"}
```

Next, click on the tool button. This will bring up a dialog. Change the text:

```
"Text1"
```

to read:

```
"Date: "+date()
```

and click the "OK" button. This has told dBASE that each time this codeblock is seen, to re-evaluate it so that the date function is called, and the current date is displayed.

Resize the text control a little, then center it on the page ("Layout" menu, etc. like we did with the title and again you may want to set the text control's *alignHorizontal* property to "1 - Center").

Adding a Page Number

When creating reports, it is also a good idea to have a page number appear, because even if the report is only one page long *now*, at some point, it is likely to get larger. Having page numbers is often useful (if the report is dropped, re-collating it will be difficult at best). How do we tell dBASE to place one on the page?

As it turns out, by default dBASE loads a custom text control that handles page numbering. I suggest that first you scroll down to the bottom of the page in the Report Designer, so that you can place this at the bottom, on the *pageTemplate*, under the *streamFrame* (not on it!).

If you move through the tabs of the Component Palette, you *should* see a tab that says "Paging". If you do not, you can get this to appear by going to the Command Window, then typing:

```
set procedure to :ReportControls:Report.cc
```

Clicking back on the Report Design surface and then on the Component Palette, you should now find the "Paging" tab.

This will have a single control, which appears as a number "1". Drag this to the bottom of the page. This already has the *alignHorizontal* property set, so all we need to do is tell the Report Designer to center it in the window as we did with the title text controls ("Layout" menu, etc.).

Add a Table

We need will a table to create a report. The simplest way to do this is to go to the Navigator, and click on the "Tables" tab. Select the "Look in:" combobox, and find the "DBASESAMPLES" database alias. Drag the "Fish" table from the Navigator window to the design surface.

You should see something like:

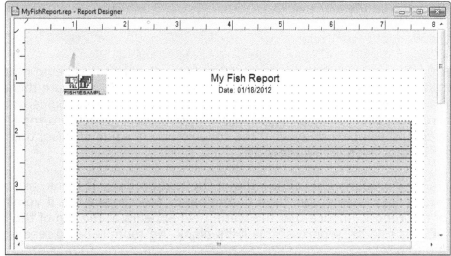

Figure 20-4

Notice that the Field Palette now shows the fields in the table.

Also notice that there are individual "bands" for each row in the table. These are the individual detailBands and as you will see when we start adding fields to the report, these will change for each row to show the actual data.

If you know you have an index you want to use for a report, a good time to set it is after you have dragged the table to the report design surface. We have an index tag on the Fish table that sorts the data by name, so we should use that.

Click on the icon for the query object ("FISH1") so that it has focus, then in the Inspector find the *rowset* property of the query object. Click on the inspect button ("I") which will drill down to the rowset for this table. Find the *indexName* property, and in the combobox for this property, select "NAME". That is all that is necessary to display the data in the correct sequence.

Place Fields on the Report

The next thing that we need to do is to tell dBASE to place fields from the table on the report surface. These will go in the *detailBand* of the report. For the time being we are going to use the Field Palette to place fields on the design surface.

Let's start with the "Name" field. If you look at the Field Palette, you should see a listing of the fields in your table. If you click on the "Name" field and drag it to the first band on the report (the first pink band), see what happens.

By default, dBASE places a heading control above the field! This can be useful, but it can also be a little disconcerting if you aren't expecting it *(this can be modified using the Customize Tool Windows option if you right click on the Field Palette).* If you are not seeing this behavior, perhaps you (or someone) modified the default settings – they should be reset for this exercise (the option is "Add field label" which should read "Above field").

We want to examine a couple of things here. The first is the title text that was placed on the report for you. If you click on this, using the Inspector note that the *suppressIfBlank* property has been set to *true* (the default is *false*) and that there is code assigned to the event handler for the *canRender* event:

```
{||this.parent.firstOnFrame}
```

This is a way of telling dBASE that if the *detailBand* (or other band) is being rendered for the first time on the current *streamFrame*, to display this text. To evaluate this a step further, the *canRender()* event is an event handler that must return a logical value of *true* or *false*. If there is an event handler associated with this event, which returns a value of *true*, then the control will be displayed. If the code returns a value of *false*, then the text control will not be displayed (or **rendered**).

The *suppressIfBlank* property tells dBASE that if the *text* property is blank, or if the control is not rendered, to not reserve room for it on the band. You can see this if you look at the other bands of the report – notice that the name field appears at the <u>top</u> of the band! That's because dBASE was told to "suppress" this if it's blank. No room is being reserved for it if there is nothing to print.

I suggest moving this so that the *top* and *left* properties are zero. You can do this either by moving the control yourself, or by going to the Inspector, finding these properties and set the value there.

Next, select the name text control in the first *detailBand*, set the left property to zero and adjust it so it is just below the title. If you are using "Inches" for your metric, this will be around 0.22 inches.

You should see something close to:

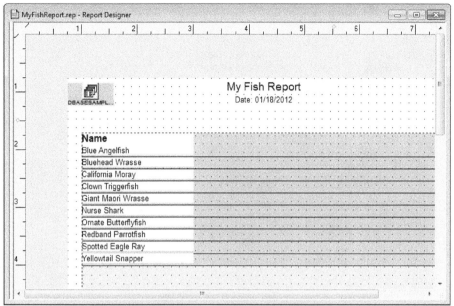

Figure 20-5

We will quickly step through the other fields – we're not placing them all on this report:

- Select "Species" from the Field Palette and drag it to the right of the Name field
- Select "Length CM" from the Field Palette and drag it to the right of the Species field

That pretty much uses all of the space on the report!

Next, line up the controls vertically and horizontally. You can do this using a combination of the Inspector and the align toolbar at the top of the screen.

Now, one problem that might come up is how to add more data? You can modify the *pageTemplate* margin properties, you can then widen the *streamFrame* so it fills the entire width of the *pageTemplate* and you can reduce the width of some of the columns you are displaying. If you change the *fontSize* property of individual text controls, you can reduce the widths further. Any combination of these will add more room for your report. However, for the moment, let's leave it as it is. This is just our first report and we're looking at the basics.

Save the report (Ctrl+S). At this point, you should have a report that looks something like:

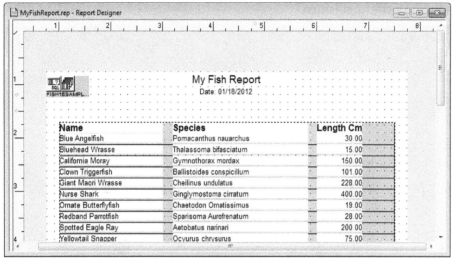

Figure 20-6

Of course, this is not really what it is going to look like once it has been run, or printed. For example, the colors used on the design surface to show the bands and the *streamFrame* will not be a part of the report.

To get an idea what this report will look like when printed, you can run it from here. Use the "Run Report" toolbutton in the toolbar (the one with the lightning bolt on it). You should see a preview window:

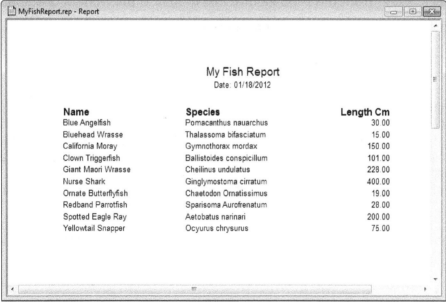

Figure 20-7

Multi-Table Reports

The next thing we need to examine are reports that work with multiple tables. If you wish to perform a follow-along, it is suggested that you copy the program in Chapter 8 used to create parent/child tables for this purpose. The program was called "MakeChapter8Tables.prg". If the program is available, run it, if not, enter it and run it. (Using the Navigator, click on the "Programs" tab, and double-click this program.) This will create two tables, one called ParentTest.dbf and the other called ChildTest.dbf.

When creating a report that works with more than one table, it is assumed that you will be using a parent/child type relationship. The reason for this is that the report's *streamSource* can really only handle a single table. By using a parent/child (or parent/child/grandchild, or similar structure) setup, you are actually creating what might be called a "virtual rowset" – this rowset consists of information from the tables in question, linked in the way you designate.

Start the Report

To get started, we need to create a new report. We're going to quickly run through a few settings, then get into the details of the report.

Click on the "Reports" tab of the Navigator window, then double-click the first "(Untitled)" icon. This will start the Report Designer. In the Report Designer set the following properties (in the Inspector):

metric	3 - Inches (or your preferred metric)
autoSort	false *(this may already be false, in which case leave it)*

Click on the reportGroup headerBand if it appears, set the *height* property to 0 in the Inspector, and do the same for the reportGroup footerBand.

Place a text control on the pageTemplate at the top of the report. Change these properties (in the Inspector):

fontSize	14
alignHorizontal	1 - Center

Change the text to read "Parent/Child Report" and adjust the width and height. Move this to the vertical position you wish, then use the "Layout" menu and select "Align", "Center Horizontally in Window".

Press Ctrl+S to save your work so far and name the report: "ParentChild.rep".

Add the Tables

Now comes the real interesting part. Rather than a single table, we need two. We could use dQuery and a data module, but we're starting simple. We are going to place the tables directly on the report using the Navigator window – dragging both tables to the Report Designer surface. Click on the Navigator (if you can't see it to click on it, use the "Window" menu, and select "Navigator"). Click on the "Tables" tab, then drag the two tables we need ("ChildTest.dbf" and "ParentTest.dbf") to the Design surface.

Notice that since we (most likely) dragged the "ChildTest" table to the surface first, that the Report Designer shows the number of detailBands that match the number of rows in the Child table. If the "ParentTest" table had been first on the Design surface, the number of detailBands shown would reflect the number of rows in that table.

We need to set properties on the "ChildTest" query's rowset object, using the Inspector. To do this, click on "ChildTest1" on the Design surface and find the *rowset* property in the Inspector. Click on the Inspect button (the "I" on the right side by that property) and drill down to the rowset object.

indexName	LinkField
masterRowset	parenttest1
masterFields	LinkField

You may notice the number of detailBands reduce on the design surface as we do this. Do not worry – all should be fine.

The detailBand

Normally with a parent/child type report, the detailBand is where the information from the child row is displayed. This is an important detail for designing your reports. The detailBand is for the detail, but what if you want to display information from the parent row? In most cases, you only want to do that once and you would place that in a group *headerBand* or *footerBand*. We will come back to these in a moment.

For this report, we want to display fields from the Child table. However, there is really only one field that has any data we need to display. I suggest dragging from the Field Palette the field "ChildData", to the pink (or coral) detailBand area.

The Group Object

The Group object is used to group data together and to display information at the beginning of the group, and/or at the end of the group.

To place a group object on a report, go to the Component Palette, then select the "Report" tab. With that selected, notice that there are only two items on this page of the Palette. Place your mouse over them and look at the speedTip. The one that says "Group" is what we want. Drag this to the streamFrame of the report.

Notice when you do this a green band appears with a text control that says "Header Text for Group 1".

To make groups work, you have to tell the Report Engine what field is being used to group the data. In this case, the field is "LinkField". You need to select the Inspector window and make sure you are pointing to the group object (the combobox should show: form.streamSource1.group1 – if it does not, then click on it and select "group1" in the dropdown).

Find the *groupBy* property and select "LinkField". It doesn't look like anything happened. That's okay.

The next thing we need to do is place a text control on the group headerBand for the data in the parent row. On the Field Palette, select the "ParentTest" tab, and drag the field "ParentData" to the (green) *headerBand*. At this point, you don't really need the default text "Header Text for Group 1", click on it and delete it. Move the text that says "Parent1" over to the left. You should have something that looks similar to:

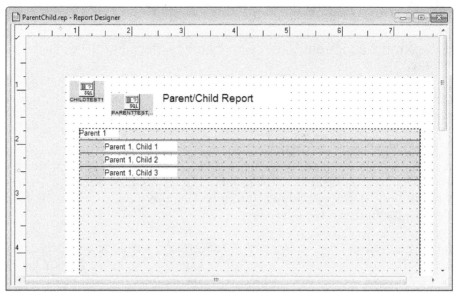

Figure 20-9

The problem is, where are all the other parent rows and all the child rows of those parent rows? What has happened is that dBASE is starting with the *child* row as the controlling rowset for this report, because it was the first row placed on the design surface. There may be times you want this to be the case, but as you can see, it causes some interesting results.

Change the Controlling Rowset

The controlling rowset is specified in the report's *streamSource* object's *rowset* property. You can get to this by going to the Inspector and selecting "streamSource1" from the combobox. Find the *rowset* property and click the "down arrow" (for a combobox) and select "parenttest1".

What a difference this makes! Notice that you now see all of the parent rows and all of their child rows!

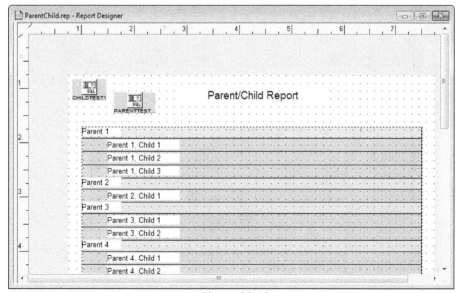

Figure 20-10

Granted, this is a pretty simple report – but it should give you the idea of how this works.

Why place the ChildTest table on the report first, when I knew this would happen? So that you could see it, too. It's important to have an idea how the controlling rowset actually controls the report.

You should save your report ([Ctrl]+[S]). We will do one more bit with this, which is to show you how to add some summary calculations (that are built in to dBASE).

Summary (Aggregate) Calculations

Reports often need to be able to show totals, sums, counts and averages, most often with reports like parent/child type reports. dBASE has built-in a set of aggregate functions that will do the work for you. Unfortunately with this report, we have no numeric fields, but there is one aggregate function we can use.

The first thing we need to do is give the group footerBand's *height* property a value that is greater than zero. To do that, find the group object in the Inspector (group1 in the combobox) and select the *footerBand* object. Use the Inspect button, then drill down to the footerBand object (you could also select the footerBand directly under group1 in the combobox of the Inspector). The *height* property is zero – set it to 0.17 (if using Inches as your report's metric). Notice that a light purple band has appeared.

This new band is the group's *footerBand*. We can place controls on this as easily as we can on the other bands of the report. We want to place a calculation here, but we don't want to do all the work ourselves. The Report Designer happens to have a handy wizard for this built in. Make sure the footerBand has focus, then select the "Layout" menu. At the bottom of the menu is an option labeled "Add Groups and Summaries ...". Select that and you should see something like:

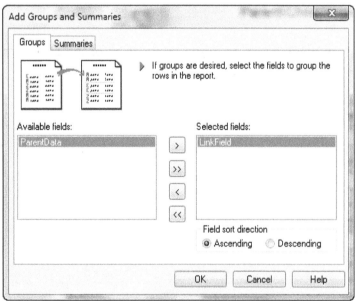

Figure 20-11

We want to look at "Summaries" (we already added the group "the hard way" earlier). If you click on the tab for this, you will see:

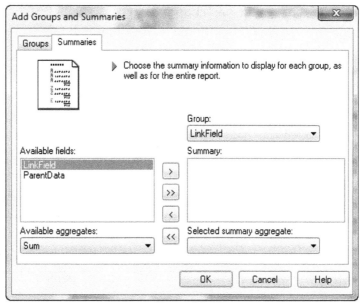

Figure 20-12

We want to do a count of the number of rows in the detailBand, so we can use the "LinkField" for our purposes. Under the "Available aggregates:" label is a combobox. Select "Count". Use the arrow at the top (the button that looks like ">"), and in the "Summary" list you should see: "Count of Linkfield":

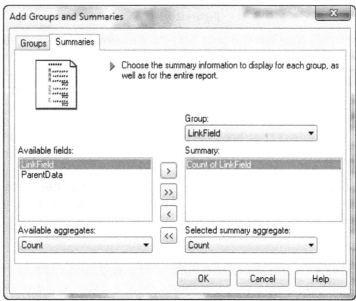

Figure 20-13

Click "OK", and notice that your report has changed:

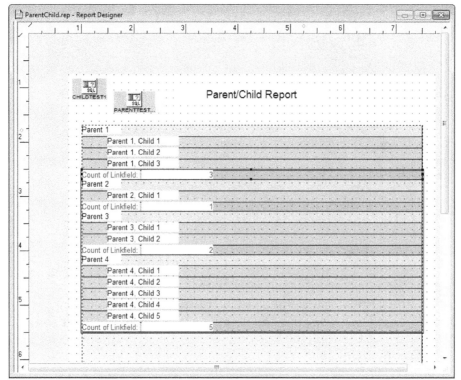

Figure 20-14

By default, the wizard uses blue for the text and as you can see the formatting is interesting. You may wish to change the color of the text to black for both of the controls that appear. This can be done by first using Ctrl and clicking on both controls, then going to the Inspector and setting the *colorNormal* property to "black" (rather than "b+" as appears in the Inspector – which stands for "bright blue").

I also suggest changing the text that has the count to display a smaller width. You can change the width by holding the Shift key and using the left (and right) arrow key.

You can also change properties such as *fontBold* and others to enhance the appearance of the report. The idea is to show you the basics of what can be done. With a bit of work you can do a lot more.

Group Report Hints

The following are suggestions that deal specifically with grouped reports (reports that use groups with headerBands and footerBands), based on my experience working with the Report Designer and the Report Engine in dBASE. Note that you can also nest groups, but your data needs to be correctly sorted. You could have multiple groups and break the data based on those different groups, perform various totals and other aggregate calculations, and more.

Sequence of Tables

As you can see, the sequence you place tables onto the design surface can make a huge difference as to how your report will render. Most of the time with a parent/child type report, you start with the top-level table, then the sequence the other tables are placed on the design surface shouldn't matter. What really matters is the first table you place on the design surface, because the Report Designer automatically assumes that this is to be assigned to the streamSource object's *rowset* property (very much like with the Form

Designer). However, if it turns out you placed the wrong table on the report first, there is no need to delete the query objects and put them back on in the right sequence, as we did in the exercise earlier, you can change the streamSource object's *rowset* property in the Inspector. Don't panic!

AutoSort

You may wish to set the value of the report object's *autoSort* property to *false* – this is something that I started you doing earlier in this chapter without much explanation – otherwise you may find your report sorting in ways you didn't expect. In current versions of dBASE Plus this is set to *false* automatically.

Autosort is used by the Report Designer to modify your query's SQL statement, so that the data "automatically sorts" the way you need it to. This can be useful in some cases, but in others can be confusing. What it does is add (or modify) the ORDER BY clause of the SQL SELECT statement of the query.

There are cases where you really need the report to use your index tag(s) and you would want to then turn *autoSort* off in your report. If you have a complex parent/child index tag that you need to use to get your data "just right" and *autoSort* is on, when you select the group object's *groupBy* property your index tag will be ignored and the Report Designer will create an ORDER BY clause that will only use the field selected for the *groupBy* property. Most of the time this is unnecessary.

group and group.headerBand Properties

There are a couple of properties of the group and group headerBand that I feel are important for you to know about.

The first is a property of the group object itself: *headerEveryFrame*. This property defaults to *false* but I almost always set it to *true* with my grouped reports. The reason? When you have a lot of data, going from page to page, sometimes a group of detail records gets broken up over more than one page (it might begin toward the bottom of one and flow to the top of the next). This is great, but when you look at the top of the next page, you aren't necessarily sure what the detail records are associated with. If you set this property to *true*, the group headerBand will display at the top of the page if necessary.

The other property I feel you need to be aware of is on the group headerBand: *beginNewFrame*. For the most part I don't use this one, leaving the value as *false*. However, this has its uses. You may need to have the report start a new page each time there is a break in the group field. In the example we did in this chapter on grouped reports, we might want a new page for each parent row. Setting this property (to *true*) would do that for you.

Repeating Data Grouping Incorrectly?

One confusing issue for many developers working with reports is that you can get some odd results with grouped reports. For example, a report that has two rows that are used to "break" the report such as:

> Group 1
> Group 1a

Logically these should be completely separate and you might expect your report to break when it sees "Group1a". However, what dBASE really sees is that "Group1" is contained in "Group1a" and it treats all rows associated as being in the same grouping. If you had a "Group 1b" that would be different from "Group 1a" and the group would break there.

The solution is to issue the following command before generating your report:

```
set exact on
```

When you generate the report you will see your groups have generated properly. If you need to change the setting of "EXACT", you may want to save the current setting, then when the report is done, reset it:

```
cExact = set("EXACT")
set exact on
// code to generate report - when your code is really done
// generating the report:
set exact &cExact.
```

More Than Two Tables?

This situation periodically comes up in the dBASE newsgroups. It is possible to link tables so that a parent row has a child rowset and the child rowset has a child rowset of its own. The problem is that the report engine in dBASE does not handle more than two tables *well*. This does not mean that it cannot handle it, but there does come a point where sometimes it is easier to just work around this and do things another way.

This requires creating a flat file table that has all of the fields you want to appear in the report, then then a program that loops through the data copying out the data as needed to fill the table. You would end up repeating information as needed for parent rows, to ensure that grouping works in the report. The time-consuming part of all of this is creating the program to create or empty the flat file table, then filling it with the data. Once you have it working it is often fairly fast.

Once you have the flat file table you will want to create an index on it that allows you to group the data the way you need to. If you need two groups, then make sure the data gets indexed on the field or fields needed in a single index tag, to sort properly.

Labels

One of the aspects of the Report Designer that is particularly useful is the ability to generate labels with very little effort. In addition, the technique used to generate labels can be used in other ways with reports.

The Report Designer has an option built in that allows it to create reports that use multiple streamFrames – one for each label. In the next chapter we will briefly look at this ability to have multiple streamFrames on one report, as it can be used to create a report with multiple columns! However, our focus at the moment is labels.

To create a label report (or label file), go to the Navigator window, then select the "Reports" tab. Notice that there are three icons labeled "(Untitled)". The first two are for reports and the last one is for labels. If you double-click on this icon, you will see the Report Designer, but it looks a little different than it has for reports we've created in the past:

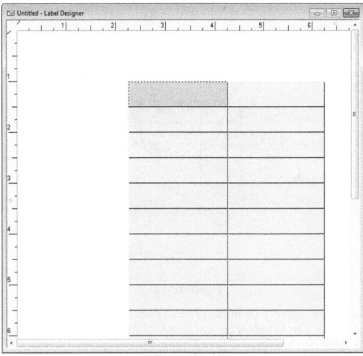

Figure 20-15

You should set your label's *metric* property as we did with reports earlier. The question now becomes "how do I define my labels?" As it turns out, you are not stuck with the default size labels that you see on the screen. You can use labels of varying sizes, numbers per page and so on.

The folk at dBASE worked with the Avery label company and updated the database of labels used by the Label Designer to give a closer match to what Avery currently sold at the time. While this database may not be 100% up to date with everything that is out there, the Avery label formats are an industry standard and they don't change a *lot*. Many other companies create labels using the same specifications because nearly all software that can create labels is designed to work with these.

To set your label size, select the "Layout" menu and notice the last option reads "Set Label Type ...". Select this and you should get a dialog that looks like:

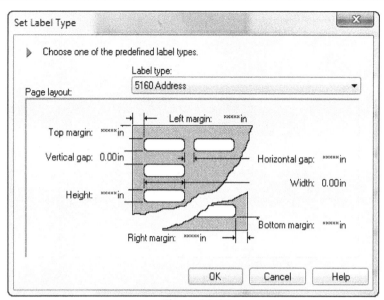

Figure 20-16

You can select from a large variety of label types. When deciding what label dimensions to use, check the package for the labels you have. All of the specifications should be given. This screen can be a little confusing.

I often use one of the more standard Avery label types, the Avery 5160 labels, which give me three columns of labels, 10 labels per column, or 30 labels per page. If you click on the combobox and scroll through it you can find "5160 Address". Select this and then click "OK".

Your Label Designer surface should now look like:

Figure 20-17

In all respects (except the ability to set groups) the Label Designer works like the Report Designer *(it really is the Report Designer with some minor changes)*.

Not having an address table handy for demonstration purposes, while we could create one, let's just use a table we've used in many other demonstrations, the dBASE Samples FISH table. To place a table on the design surface, select the Navigator window, then the "Tables" tab. In the "Look In:" combobox, select the "DBASESAMPLES" database and Drag the "Fish" table to the design surface. Notice that you now have a pink label for each row in the table (this is the detailBand for each row in the table).

If you look at the Field Palette, you should now see a list of the fields in this table. Select the "Name" field and drag it to the first label at the top left. Drag the "Species" and "Length CM" fields to the design surface as well. Spend a moment or two lining up the text so it looks "neat", then save your labels (call it something like "FishLabels"). dBASE will create a file called "FishLabels.lab" – the .lab extension tells us that this is a dBASE label file.

While this is, in a way, a silly exercise, it gives you the idea.

To see how this works, you could open the Source Code Editor (Press F12), and notice that there are 30 streamFrames in the file, each defined as the same size, but different positions. At the bottom of the label source code you will see something like (I truncated it as the lines look a lot alike):

```
this.firstPageTemplate = this.form.pagetemplate1
this.form.pagetemplate1.nextPageTemplate = this.form.pagetemplate1
this.form.pagetemplate1.streamframe1.streamSource = this.form.streamsource1
this.form.pagetemplate1.streamframe2.streamSource = this.form.streamsource1
this.form.pagetemplate1.streamframe3.streamSource = this.form.streamsource1
this.form.pagetemplate1.streamframe4.streamSource = this.form.streamsource1
this.form.pagetemplate1.streamframe5.streamSource = this.form.streamsource1
```

This code assigns to each streamFrame's *streamSource* property the label file's streamSource (if you opened the Source Code Editor, close it). You should probably save and close the label file.

If you run this, you will see that in this case, there's a lot of room left, but everything lines up nicely. If you were to print it on a sheet of labels, everything should line up precisely on the labels as shown in the designer.

Custom Label Sizes?

If you need to use a label size that is not listed in the table, there is a way to do it. This takes a bit of work, but you can add a new label definition to the table used by dBASE. This can be done manually by opening the table that is used in the folder (this assumes a default installation of dBASE) – the location will vary depending on what version of dBASE Plus and which operating system it is installed in. For Windows XP or for dBASE Plus versions before 2.7 the table will in this folder path:

```
C:\Program Files\dBASE\Plus\Designer\label
```

For current versions of dBASE on Windows Vista or later, the table will be in this folder path:

```
C:\Users\username\AppData\Local\dBASE\Plus\Designer\label
```

(See Chapter 2 for more details on file locations.)

The table is named "labe0009.db" (yes, it is a Paradox .DB table). However, there is a difficulty in entering the information if you do not know what all the fields are for, as some of the names of the fields are a bit confusing. In addition, the grid in dBASE does not recognize decimal settings in a Paradox .DB table unless you define a picture, which you cannot do when you simply double-click a table in the Navigator.

The following is a description of the fields:

description:	A description of the label. If it is your own custom one, you might want to make sure your name is included in the description.
topmargin:	Distance from the top of the page to the top of the first label.
bottommargin:	Distance from the bottom of the page to the bottom of the last label.
leftmargin:	Distance from the left of the page to the left of the first column.
rightmargin:	Distance from the right of the page to the right of the last column.
labelwidth:	Width of the label (left to right).
labelheight:	Height of the label (top to bottom).
horizontalgap:	Distance (left to right) between two labels.
verticalgap:	Distance (bottom of one label to top of the next) between two labels.
paperwidth:	Width of the page (left to right) – if using a tractorfeed printer, distance after the tear-off.
paperheight:	Height of the page (top to bottom).
metric:	Metric – defined by a numeric value:

      1 = Twips
      2 = Points
      3 = Inches
      4 = Centimeters
      5 = Millimeters
      6 = Pixels

To make this task easier, there is a form in the dUFLP *(discussed in the appendices)* called "CustLabl.wfm" that when run should allow you to see this information and it has appropriate pictures set for the entry of the numeric values. You can add or edit any label setting you wish.

You should note that if you do this, you may want to back up the "labe0009.db" table, so that if you install an update to dBASE, or your computer crashes, or some other thing happens that loses this information, you still have it.

Printing Reports

We have not really discussed printing the reports we have created. There are at least a couple of ways of printing a report. As you have noticed, if you run a report (or label) file, it appears in a preview window. This can be useful to get an idea what the report will look like when printed, but it does not actually send the report to the printer.

So, how do you actually print a report? The basic solution is that the report object itself has a property: *output*. The default value of this property is "3 - Default", which in this case is to a preview window that is opened by dBASE when you run the report.

Once the report is running, you can print from the preview window, using the "Print" button in the toolbar (it looks like a printer).

However, if you are developing a real application, there are other things you can *(and should)* do – some possible solutions are shown below.

Print from the Preview Window

You could just set up your application so that when a menu option is selected to generate a report, the code looks like:

```
do MyFishReport.rep
```

The user can preview it in the default window created by dBASE. This has the virtue of being very simple and no real coding is necessary on your part.

When they want to print it, they can use the default toolbutton, as mentioned above.

However, your application has *very* little control at this point and there are probably better ways to do what you need.

Print Using Code

One option is to use dBL code to generate the report, allowing you to send your report to the printer directly if so desired.

The code might look like:

```
set procedure to MyFishReport.rep
r = new MyFishReportReport()
r.outPut := 1 // Printer
r.render()
```

However, this will print to the default printer (what if there are several to choose from?) and what if your user decides after selecting this option that they do not wish to actually print the report?

Okay, we can take this a step further and *ask* the user if they want to print or preview the report using a *msgbox()* and/or we can bring up a *choosePrinter()* dialog (see below):

```
set procedure to MyFishReport.rep additive
r = new MyFishReportReport()
if msgbox( "Send report to Printer?", "Confirm", 4+32 ) == 6
                                                  // Yes
   r.output := 1 // Printer
   if r.printer.choosePrinter() // returns true or false
      r.render() // print it
   endif
else
   r.render() // send to default of a preview window
endif
```

Note that we used the report object's printer object and called the printer object's *choosePrinter()* method. This method returns either a *true* or *false* value, depending on whether or not the user clicked on the "OK" button or the "Cancel" button.

One important factor that you may wish to consider is that the application object (_app) has a printer object as well. You could use:

```
_app.printer.choosePrinter()
```

In the code shown above, rather than the report's printer object method of the same name. Why would you want to do that? The printer object associated with _app will set a default value for *all* reports in an application, which you may or may not wish to do. What this means is that if the user selects a printer using _app.printer.choosePrinter(), all subsequent reports will default to that printer, which may be useful, and may be confusing to the user. You could even combine these so that for some reports they use the default printer and others use the report object's printer object, which would affect just that one report.

Create a Preview Form Using a ReportViewer Object

You could create a form that lets the user see the report, then decide what to do from there with the report. This is a nice way to go but takes some work, learning how to use the ReportViewer object and how to control it.

There is an existing *free* report preview form available in the dBASE Users' Function Library Project, which is referenced in the appendix of this book, that handles displaying a report, allowing the user to determine number of copies, select starting and ending pages and more.

The following statement assumes you have the dUFLP set up and running, so unless you do, don't try the following:

```
do :dUFLP:Preview.wfm with "MyFishReport.rep"
```

Which would display your report in a window like:

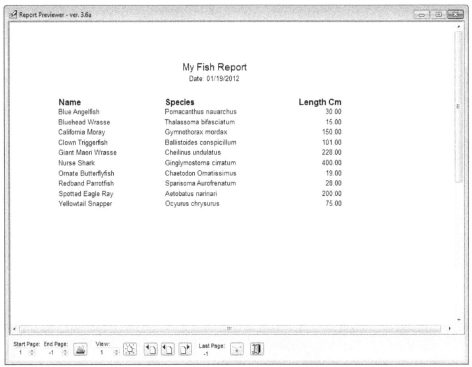

Figure 20-18

As noted, this is useful, as it allows you to print multiple copies and a lot more. The source code is available for you to examine as well, so if you wanted you could write your own version.

With a preview form of this sort, the user can view the report, then decide if it's what they need, close it, modify the data if necessary and then go back and examine it. They can move between pages, designate the number of copies to print, and more. This is very handy and allows for a lot more flexibility.

NOTE: If you have been following along, you should most likely go to the Command Window and type:

```
CLOSE DATABASE
```

to ensure that any database aliases that we opened are now closed. When you exit dBASE it will remember these and you may find some odd results, such as a new table ending up in the DBASESAMPLES alias, which will be confusing at best if you didn't mean to do that.

General Report Designer Hints

The more you work with the Report Designer, the more things you find that can make it easier to work with. The following are hints from various sources which may make designing your own reports easier.

Field Labels

When designing your report and dragging fields from the Field Palette, the Report Designer places labels for each field onto the report. The default is to place them above the field, however you can change this setting to the "left" or to simply not display them at all. Note that you get field labels in reports, but not when designing labels.

Some folks have discovered that it's easier when creating reports to turn these off, and to place your own labels where you need them. This can be done by right clicking on the Field Palette surface and then select the "Customize Tool Windows ..." item from the popup menu. In the dialog that appears, in the "Add field label" section, select "None".

The next time you drag a field from the Field Palette, no label will appear. You then can either place your own on the *pageTemplate* above the *streamFrame* or anywhere in the *detailBand*, if that is your desire.

Alignment Tools

When you are working in the design surface, getting your controls to line up can be bothersome. You can do it the hard way – going to the Inspector for one control, looking at the values and setting the same properties for other controls; or you can use the alignment tools.

When you are in the Report Designer, in the toolbar (in the "Align" menu you will find options that match the toolbar) are a set of toolbuttons designed to help you line up controls. To use these you need to select two or more controls that you wish to line up (use the Ctrl key and the mouse to select them) and then you can line them up on the left, right, top or bottom. (You can also make your controls the same size – height, width.)

In addition, you can center controls horizontally in the band you are working in (or the *pageTemplate*) by clicking on them and going to the Layout menu, selecting "Align" and then "Center Horizontally in Window". (In most cases you probably don't want to "Center Vertically in Window".)

Lines

If you want to place a line between *detailBands*, there are some options, but experimentation has shown that your best bet is to place the line at the top of the *detailBand*, not at the bottom, or in the group *headerBand* or *footerBand* (if you are using groups). This way, you always have the line at the top of the *detailBand* for each row that prints.

Large Tables

If you work with large tables in your reports, sometimes it takes a long time to make even the most simple changes – this is because the designer is making these changes for each instance of the *detailBand* that is generated for the report (remember, the Report Designer works with live data).

To make this a bit quicker, you may find that you need to use a little-known feature – the ability to only display a single row.

This can be done by right-clicking on the surface of the report and in the popup menu, selecting "Report Designer Properties". In the dialog that appears, you can then select the "One Row" radio button in the middle of the dialog and your report design can be sped up. Caveat: this affects all reports – so once you have completed your changes, you may wish to go back and reset this property to "All Rows".

Navigating In the Report Designer

If you are dealing with a large report, it is helpful to view data on various pages. As it turns out, in the designer, you can see the next page by pressing the PgDn key on the keyboard. Likewise, to see the previous page, you can press the PgUp key.

Null Fields

If you are using dBF7 tables, they use "true null" support. This means that a field that has not had a value entered into it contains a null value. This can be quite confusing when you try to generate a report, because the *isblank()* function is not going to return "true", but the field doesn't appear to contain a value. Note that *empty()* does return "true" in this case.

This isn't a real problem unless you are creating calculated fields in your reports that assume that there are values contained in the fields. If a null value is added to a character string, rather than getting the character plus the null value, you get simply a null value. This works for logical, numeric, date, and character fields.

The solution to this problem is to check for the null value. The following is assuming your calculation is contained in the text property of the text control:

```
{|| trim( ;
   iif( this.form.address1.rowset.fields["last name"].value ) == null, ;
      "", this.form.address1.rowset.fields["last name"].value ) ) +", "+;
   trim( ;
   iif( this.form.address1.rowset.fields["first name"].value ) == null, ;
      "", this.form.address1.rowset.fields["first name"].value ) ) }
```

Now, the above is a bit complex to store in the text property and you may want to use the *canRender* event to do this instead.

A more simple method of doing this is to pass the value of the field through the String class constructor (this converts nulls to empty strings), which has the added advantage of typing the long object reference only once:

```
{|| trim( new String( ;
    this.form.address1.rowset.fields["last name"].value ) )+;
   ", "+;
  trim( new String( ;
    this.form.address1.rowset.fields["first name"].value ) ) }
```

Displaying Numeric Values

Sometimes getting numeric values to display just the way you want them can be a bit tricky. You should consider using the picture clause or the transform() function to make sure that your numeric values line up just right in your report.

For example, if you have data that must display two digits on the right of the decimal, but in one calculation or field you have a value that has zeros for the digits to the right, you may end up seeing an integer value appear.

If you set a picture clause, you can get the value to always display two digits on the right of the decimal (999.99, for example).

In addition, in some cases, you may want to display percent (%) or other symbols – you may want to use *transform()* (see online help for details) to get everything to line up.

Summary

This chapter was aimed at getting you started working with the Report Designer. More details on working with reports can be found in my other book on dBASE, The dBASE Reports Book, available from AuthorHouse.

As you can see, the Report Designer in dBASE is a powerful tool and you can do a lot with it. This is good, because as you work more and more with application development, you will find that being able to do a *lot* with the report tool will be handy.

NOTES:

Part VI: Programming

A good programmer is worth his weight in gold or something like that. In chapters leading up to here, if you have followed the exercises, you have been doing at least some programming. While it has not been necessarily your own programs, you have been picking up on some of the ideas and techniques of programming. The following chapters will focus heavily on programming techniques in dBASE PLUS specifically, although many of the things you learn here could be used in other programming languages.

Chapter 21: Programming in dBASE PLUS

Up to this point, this book has focused heavily on some basic concepts and then working with the designers. Now we get to delve into dBASE's real power, the dBASE Programming Language, or dBL.

dBASE, from the very beginning, was based around a programming language from when Wayne Ratliff started working on Vulcan (the precursor to dBASE II) through all versions until now. Many people over the years have used this language whether they realized they were programming or not.

It started out pretty simply and of course, as software does, rapidly grew to be more complex but in the process has become much more powerful than most people even realize.

We will, in this and subsequent chapters of this book be examining many aspects of the language, but even so, we will not likely be able to delve into every single permutation of every single command, function, parameter, option, etc. The online help will assist if there are things you need to do that are not covered here. If you have not spent much time looking at it, you should definitely get familiar with it.

Using the Source Code Editor

The Source Code Editor in dBASE PLUS is a tool that we've already used to some extent, but we haven't really done a lot. We've mostly used it to make some minor modifications in some code generated by the designers and such. As we work more and more with dBASE PLUS and dBL specifically we will see that this tool is essential for working in dBASE.

While it is possible to use an external editor with dBASE (if you *really* wish to, see the "Properties" menu, then "Desktop Properties" – the dialog has a "Files" tab, on the right top is where you would specify the editor you wish to use instead of the one in dBASE), most dBASE developers have found that the dBASE PLUS Source Code Editor works quite well for their needs and feel no reason to rush out and find something else to use.

The Source Code Editor basically looks like:

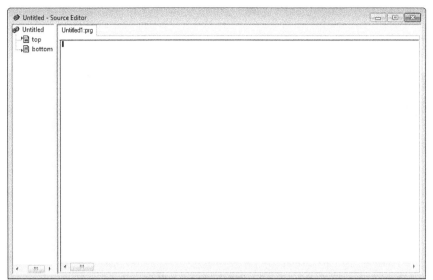

Figure 21-1

It has two "panes" to the window – the left "pane" has a treeview that shows objects and methods and such in the code. This is useful when you have a lot of code in a file – it allows you to move around between different parts of it. The right "pane" is the main editing area. If you notice, there is a tab at the top – you can have multiple files open and switch between them. You could open the same file twice and switch between views, but that can be confusing.

This doesn't look like much. However, if you were to open something that we had created before, such as a report from a previous chapter, you might see something like:

Figure 21-2

In the left pane you will see the treeview shows the objects and the methods in the report. The right pane shows the code, where we can edit the code.

Setting the Source Code Editor's Default Properties

The Source Code Editor has default properties that you can modify, which deal with the way it behaves. To see this, right click on the editor pane, and you will see a dialog like:

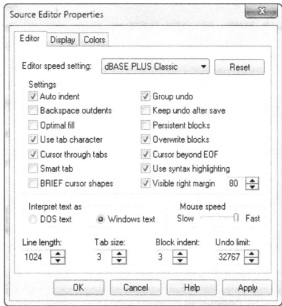

Figure 21-3

You can modify quite a bit about the way this works. It is not suggested that you change much, if anything, until you've gotten familiar with the editor and decide what kinds of things you would like to change. One thing you should note: Many or all of the changes made in the Source Editor Properties dialog will affect the way the Command Window works as well – this includes changing font sizes, colors, etc.

Using the Source Editor to Modify Your Forms, Reports, Labels and Other Source Code

If you've followed along with some of the exercises in earlier chapters of this book, you will have already worked with the Source Editor. You can open your forms, reports, labels, data modules, etc., in the Source Code Editor, because they are just dBL in files with very specific file extensions.

The simplest way to bring one of these files into the Source Code Editor, is to select it in the Navigator window and right click on it – the option to open it in the Source Code Editor will appear in the list. You can also go to the Command Window, and type:

```
modify command MyForm.wfm
```

and dBASE will open the file in the Source Code Editor for you.

There are always little things about a tool such as the Source Code Editor that may seem like tricks or hidden techniques until someone shows them to you. This is not really intentional, but this is a fairly sophisticated tool and it's hard to just write everything there is to know about it in any one place. Instead, as we work through this chapter and the next few, we will be using this tool and you will learn more about it and some of the perhaps not-very-obvious tricks that can make working with the source editor easier.

Getting Started

What is a program? It is a series of instructions or commands in a specific programming language. Since we are working with dBASE, the language is dBL. Many of the things discussed here might apply to C++, Visual BASIC, or any of the other hundreds of programming languages that are available out there. What it really boils down to is that a program is just a set of commands in a specific sequence.

The sequence is often very important. For example, if you want to increment the (numeric) value of a memory variable, you have to create the memory variable with a value to start with. If you jump in and write code like:

```
MyVar++ // increment
```

but "MyVar" has not yet been created, you will get an error when you try to execute the program. So the sequence of the commands in a program is usually very important.

Before we really delve into programming statements or commands, we should look at a few other things first.

Documenting Your Code

Why document your code? There was an old humor article being passed around in email for years that was based on the book "Real Men Don't Eat Quiche", called "Real Programmers Don't Do Documentation". The particular statement is "Real Programmers don't comment their code. If it was hard to write it should be hard to understand."

The problem with this concept is that *you* may be the person who has to come back and try to understand your own code – it may be a day from now, it may be 6 months from now, but it really helps *you* understand or remember what you were trying to accomplish with the code and why you wrote it the way you did, if you document it. You should also note that if you work in a larger company they may have their own documentation standards – you should check on that.

Comments

There are many ways to document your code and the first is by using comments in your programs. Comments are just ways of making notations through the code, they are ignored by dBASE. You can put anything you want to in a comment and dBASE won't care, because it has instructions that tell it not to. The question is how does it know?

Comments in dBL can be accomplished in several ways. In older versions of dBASE, the ways to comment code were:

```
* A comment
&& A comment
NOTE
      A Comment that can take multiple lines until dBASE
      sees the statement:
ENDNOTE
```

The first form of comment is the most common in dBASE/DOS and versions of dBASE up to Visual dBASE 7.0. The star (or asterisk) character at the beginning of a line tells dBASE to ignore everything after it and you can have multiple comments in a row.

The second form shown, with the double ampersand (&) characters at the beginning of the line is what is called an *inline comment*, meaning that while you could use it at the beginning of a statement, it was more useful at the end of one, such as:

```
do while .t. && loop until false
```

This allows you to document your code by adding comments with the commands themselves.

The NOTE/ENDNOTE construct allows for multiple line blocks of comments, for example if you wanted to put multiple lines in at the beginning of a file to explain how or why it works the way it does, or to tell dBASE to not execute some block of code if it fits between NOTE/ENDNOTE.

In the 32-bit versions of dBASE (starting with Visual dBASE 7.0 to current versions), the older forms of comments still work, which is particularly useful if you are migrating your older code to dBASE PLUS, but there are newer versions of two of the options given above.

The *inline comment* is more commonly done as:

```
do while true // loop until false
```

Rather than two ampersands, two slashes are used. *(The ampersands still work.)*

The *block comment* is now done in this fashion:

```
/*
   A comment that can take multiple lines until dBASE sees:
*/
```

This can be done in any combination – once dBASE sees the beginning of a block comment, it ignores everything until it sees the end. You could do:

```
/* A comment */
```

   Or

```
/* A comment
*/
```

or any variation that you can think of.

> ### NOTE
> Use of the block comment in your source code can sometimes cause some odd things to occur in the Source Code Editor. The following are ways to avoid these issues:
>
> - Character strings with special meanings such as "/*" should be entered as "/"+"*", which will create the appropriate string, but avoid the Source Code Editor thinking it is the beginning of a comment block. *(You should do the same with // or && inline comments – split the characters up.)*
> - /* should start on a new line, not be used as an inline comment or at the end of a programming statement.
> - Do not nest /* ... */ comment blocks within other comment blocks.

Naming Variables and Objects
The way you name your variables and objects is a way of documenting your code. Code that uses variables such as ...

```
x = 2
y = 3
z = 4
```

Is much harder to read and understand than:

```
nCounter1 = 2
nCounter2 = 3
nCounter3 = 4
```

By giving meaningful names to your variables, you or anyone reading your code will have a much better chance of understanding it. One coding convention for variables that is fairly common in the dBASE developer community suggests that you use a lower case letter (or letters) at the beginning of the name of the variable to suggest what the type of the variable is. So in the case of the examples above, "nCounter" tells us that it is numeric, because it starts with a lower-case "n". The capitalization is really up to you, as dBASE doesn't care (indeed, it would see "NCOUNTER" as being exactly the same variable as "nCounter" or "ncounter" or any variation). The difference in case is not one you can count on in other programming languages – some of them will see "nCounter" as being different from "NCOUNTER" or "ncounter", etc. and depending on your code, this could create three separate variables! In dBL this will not happen, but be warned if you program in other languages.

The following table contains some suggestions for naming conventions, which you can use or ignore:

Type	Prefix	Example
Character	c	cFirstName
Numeric	n	nCounter
Logical	l or b	lSubscribe or bSubscribe
Date	d	dBirthday
DateTime	dt	dtStartWork
Codeblock	cb	cbLastName
Function Pointer	fp	fpActivate
Object	o	oTestForm
Unknown/Varies	x	xTemp

The same concepts work for naming your objects. An object named:

```
ENTRYFIELD1
```

is not as useful if you come back and look at your code later on as:

```
FirstNameEntryfield
```

The concept of naming your variables and objects meaningfully is called *self-documenting code*.

The primary *(and frankly only)* drawback to documenting your code is that typically there is more typing to do, but in the long run, a well-documented program can save you a lot of effort.

Indenting Your Code

You may not realize it while you work on writing your code, but indenting code to show structure is a way to help make your code more readable. The following code is considered poor because you cannot tell at a glance where the if/endif structure ends:

```
n = 10
if n > 5
? n
else
? "n is not greater than 5"
endif
// do some more code
```

If you were to use more appropriate indentation in your code, this would be easier to read:

```
n = 10
if n > 5
    ? n
else
    ? "n is not greater than 5"
endif
// do some more code
```

While this does not seem like a big deal, the more complex your code is, the more that indenting will help readability. Any structure that has a beginning statement and an ending statement should always be indented and in some cases you may want to use even further indentation. This might include such things shown above with the if/else/endif, or a "do case" command, where the structure begins with the words "do case" and ends with "endcase", but between the two statements are further "case" statements, which should be indented and the code belonging to those should also be indented. As we look at the various structures, the examples throughout this book will show appropriate indentation.

Creating the Program File

So how do you create a program file? If you are not using the designers, then there are still at least a couple of ways to create a program file. The first is to go to the Navigator in dBASE and find the "Programs" tab. Double click the "(Untitled)" icon and the Source Code Editor will appear.

It should be noted that doing this will cause dBASE to assume that you are creating a file that will have ".PRG" as the file extension.

From there, you can start typing.

The other method is to go to the Command Window and type:

```
modify command MyProgram
```

If you do this, dBASE will assume that the file extension will be ".PRG", unless you add the extension at the time you type the command. This is useful if you wish to create, for example, a ".CC" (Custom Class) file, or perhaps a ".H" (header) file from the beginning. (You would type: "modify command MyCustomClass.cc")

As the command implies, if a file with that name exists, it will be opened in the Source Code Editor. If a file by the name you give does not exist, dBASE will, if you save the file, create a file by that name.

So, to create a program, go to the Command Window, and type:

```
modify command Hello1
```

This will bring up the Source Code Editor. Type the following and look at the screen as you type:

```
// A dBASE Program
? "Hello World!"
```

Notice that dBASE italicizes comments by default (unless you modified this in the Source Code Editor Properties dialog). This is useful as a way to see at a glance that the first line above is a comment.

After typing the first quote, notice that dBASE changed the quote to red – that's to show you that the string has been started, but not completed. When you typed the closing quote, it was changed to blue. This shows that a character string is here. These things can be useful when you get distracted and forget what you're looking at.

Testing Programs

So, what does this program do? Not a lot. If you were to run this, dBASE would display in the output pane of the Command Window:

```
Hello World!
```

You can run this program by clicking on the toolbutton at the top of the screen that says "Run" when you hold your mouse over it. If you look at the Command Window you should see something like:

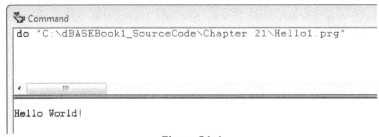

Figure 21-4

The Command Window, as you can see, shows output in the bottom pane (by default).

If you have been following along, you might want to close the Source Code Editor for the moment – we'll come back to it.

Working with the Command Window

One of the aspects of the dBASE IDE that very few other programming type software languages have is the Command Window. In dBASE, you will find that you can try out commands in the Command Window without having to run a complete program! This is really useful if you're trying to get that string manipulation *just right*, but don't want to run a 3,000 line program just to see if that one bit works properly.

Entering and Executing Commands

You can type commands directly into the Command Window, as noted above which is a very useful thing to be able to do. You can view output in the output pane of the Command Window, to see the results of what you are trying to do. The following is an example of something that can sometimes take a little work to get correct – extracting a string from inside another string, based on the location of, say, spaces in the string.

```
// find the middle initial in the name in variable cString,
// based on the location of the spaces around the middle
// initial:
cString = "Fred J. Smith"
? cString.indexOf( " " )
// 4 - the first space is the 4th character (we start from zero)
// Let's find the second space, we start the search from the 5th character
? cString.indexOf( " ", cString.indexOf( " " ) + 1 )
// 7 - the second space is the 7th character (we still start from zero)
// try to figure out how to get the string we want:
? cString.substring(cString.indexOf(" "),cString.indexOf("
",cString.indexOf(" ")+1))
// J. - that's it!
```

Whew! What just happened was a bunch of trial and error, one of the cornerstones of the way most people program. A bit of logic and perhaps some examination of the online help would show that the *indexOf()* method (of the string class – this will be discussed in a later chapter in more detail) will return the position of the space. But this is certainly a way to figure out what you will get using this and it means not trying to put all this into a program and then run the program, look at the results, open the program, find the place with the command we're working on, and so on.

There are some commands (some of which are shown later) that require multiple lines to operate, such as a for/next loop. The difficulty of testing these in the Command Window is that if you enter them one line at a time, you will get errors – you can resolve this for a quick test, however, by using the semicolon at the end of each statement and stack your statements in one line, such as:

```
for i = 1 to 5; ? "Number: "+i; next
```

While this is useful in the Command Window, it is hard to read. So when writing your programs, while this syntax works, it is not recommended in most situations (see the earlier section of this chapter on documenting your code).

Even better is that the Command Window is sort of a miniature version of the Source Code Editor in one aspect – you can move the arrow key up to the previous statement (or any previous statement that is in memory), select the whole statement, or part of the statement, copy it or just execute it again, modify it and execute it (by pressing Enter), etc.. You should experiment with this functionality. It is really useful.

Pasting Syntax from Help or Other Files

The online help often has code samples. You can copy code out of the online help, paste it directly into the Command Window and execute it. The same thing can be done with other files. For example, if someone posted some sample code in a newsgroup, you could copy this code to the Windows clipboard from the newsgroup reader you use, then go to the Command Window of dBASE and try it out by pasting this directly into the Command Window!

If you paste multiple lines of code, you will either have to highlight all of them and press the Enter key for the code to execute, or you will need to highlight or place the cursor over each line and press Enter for individual lines of code to execute.

The Command Window is a very useful tool for a developer and as such, you should take advantage of it as often as you can.

Functions and Procedures

Functions and Procedures are simply ways of grouping commands together in dBASE to perform a specific task. These can be used to handle events, as we have been using them in earlier chapters of this book. In older versions of dBASE (before Visual dBASE 7.0), a function was different from a procedure. A function used to be required to return a value of some sort, whereas a procedure usually did not. A function was called by using the name of the function followed by parentheses and if there were any parameters (we will discuss them later), they were placed in the parentheses, for example:

```
MyFunction( param1, param2 )
```

(When the parameters are enclosed in parentheses as above, they are considered to be local variables.)

A procedure was called with the word "DO" followed by the name of the procedure. If there were parameters, you had to use the keyword "WITH" followed by the parameters, like:

```
do MyProcedure with param1, param2
```

(When the parameters are called using the "with" keyword as shown above, they are considered to be "private" variables.)

While you can still use procedures and functions, dBL in all versions of dBASE from Visual dBASE 7.0 to current versions blur the line and procedures and functions are treated the same. You can call a procedure as if it were a function:

```
MyProcedure()
```

And you can call a function as if it were a procedure:

```
do MyFunction
```

The only difficulty with the latter is if you needed a value returned, in which case you would still want to use the normal syntax.

To that end, we will not be discussing procedures at all in the following pages. We will be using functions for all of our examples and event handlers for objects – it is more consistent and it is easier to remember only one form of syntax.

When you create functions, since they no longer require a RETURN statement to return a value, you could leave this statement out. I have found over the years that your code is more readable if you leave it in, even if there is no value returned from the function.

The example below is what is called a user-defined function or UDF. dBASE/dBL has a lot of functions that are built in to the language, some of which we have used in earlier chapters of this book and some of which will be discussed elsewhere in this book. Between the built-in dBL functions and the ability to create your own user-defined functions to extend dBASE's abilities, the language allows for some pretty powerful programming.

Example

The following is a simple function that calculates a person's age, returning a value based on their birthdate being passed to the function and the current date being used to calculate how old they are. Do not be worried if you do not understand the commands and functions used – we will discuss some of them here and the help for dBASE discusses many of these in much more depth than I can cover here.

In the Command Window, type:

```
modify command age
```

In the Source Code Editor, type:

```
/*
    Age( dBirthday )
    A simple function that returns the age of someone
    based on the birthday passed to it, and the current
    date.
*/
function Age( dBirth )
   local dReturn
   dReturn = ( floor( ( val( dtos( date() ) ) ) ;
                - val( dtos( dBirth ) ) ) / 10000 ) )
return dReturn
```

Save the program you created and exit the Source Code Editor ([Ctrl]+[W]).
In the Command Window, type:

```
? date()
? age( {10/23/1967} )
```

And you should see in the output pane something like:

```
03/22/2005
         37.00
```

The useful thing about functions in your own code is that you can create reusable code that can be called and used over and over again, without having to re-write the same code every time. We will be looking at and working with functions for various parts of this chapter.

Working with Memory Variables

What exactly is a memory variable? A memory variable or simply "variable" is a space in memory which is used to store a piece of information. In order to use that space in memory, we must assign a name to it so that we may reference it. As this information is stored in the RAM (Random Access Memory) of the computer, it is considered to be volatile – which means that if the computer is shut down, reboots, etc., the information stored in the memory variable is gone. All programming languages use variables and dBASE is a programming language (or perhaps more succinctly, dBL is a programming language). The name we use to reference the space in memory used by a memory variable cannot be changed, but the contents of that space in memory can be, hence the term "variable".

Memory variables can hold any "type" of value that dBASE can work with. One major difference between dBL and some languages – in dBASE the following is completely valid code and will not cause any difficulties:

```
cName = "John Smith"
cName = 2
cName = true
cName = date()
```

In some languages, once you have defined or declared a memory variable you cannot change the *type* of the value associated with the variable, without destroying it and re-defining it. That type of programming language is sometimes called "Strongly Typed". If that term is used, then dBL might be called "Weakly Typed" because dBL doesn't care. You can assign values on top of values. This is a great strength in some ways, but if you think about it, a careless programmer might destroy useful information rather easily, or accidentally change the purpose of the variable.

Variables are used to reference objects, as well as holding values. The following table shows the basic types of variables and the values returned by the function *type()*:

Type	Value Returned from type()	Example
Array	A	aColors = {"Red", "White", "Blue"}
Binary Field	B	(dBASE or Paradox table BLOB field)
Bookmark	BM	cName = "Fred Smith"
Codeblock	CB	cbSayHello = {; ? "Greetings" }
Date	D	dBirth = {01/05/1959}
DateTime	DT	dtCurrent = DateTime() (Any value returned by a TimeStamp or DateTime field as well)
Float	F	dBF Float field, or Paradox DB Numeric or Currency field
Function Pointer	FP	fpHowOld = Age
OLE/General	G	OLE field
Logical/Boolean	L	bApproved = true
Memo	M	DBF Memo field
Numeric	N	nTest = 34
Object (not Array)	O	oMyForm = new form()
Time	T	tCurrent = time()
Unknown	U	Unknown value – normally "not defined", may be "null"

Note that some of the values returned by the *type()* function are only used for specific field types. The function *type()* will be discussed in various places throughout this chapter. The maximum size of a memory variable in dBASE PLUS is pretty much limited to the amount of memory available to the computer. This means you can create some fairly large character strings as variables.

You can create three types of variables that are specific to programming and are not available to a table. These are *codeblocks*, *function pointers* and *objects*. We have discussed objects in earlier chapters, and we will continue to discuss them throughout this book. We should however take a brief look at Code Blocks and Function Pointers.

Codeblocks

A codeblock is a way of using at least one dBL programming statement without having to write a function. As an example, let us say you need to extract the last name from a customer you could create a small codeblock that did the work, such as:

```
cbLastName = {; return left( cName, at(",", cName) - 1) }
```

Then, if you had the name (you could store it to the variable "cName" from a field in a table, or obtain it in some fashion), you could get it by calling the code block. As a very simple example:

```
cName = "Smith, Fred"
? cName
? cbLastName()
```

You might see something like the following if you had entered all four lines shown into the Command Window:

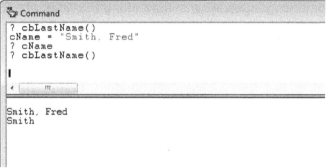

Figure 21-5

If we used the *type()* function on the variable that is used to reference the code block we created above:

```
? type( "cbLastName")
? cbLastName
```

We would see, in the output pane of the Command Window:

```
CB
{; return left( cName, at(",", cName) - 1) }
```

If you assign a codeblock to a variable name, as we did here, you can use a codeblock as any function in dBL.

Codeblocks are discussed in more detail in Chapter 6 of this book.

In addition to the example given here, code blocks are used for simple event handlers in forms, often with text controls in reports and throughout dBASE in many ways.

Function Pointers

A function pointer is a way to reference an existing function. However, you cannot use a function pointer to point to a function that is built in to dBASE, such as *UPPER()*. A function pointer can be used to point to an existing user-defined function.

You can use a function pointer the same way you can the actual function, so in most cases they are redundant. The only place that these serve a purpose that this author can see is when you get into working with the Windows API and you need a way to reference a function that is not actually built in to dBASE. We will come back to this concept in later chapters.

The Scope Commands

In dBL, like in many other languages, there are commands or operators that are *(optionally)* used to define the scope of memory variables. "Scope" refers to how available the memory variable is to code outside of the code that is currently being used. It should be noted that first, scope is not absolutely *required* by dBL – you do not have to define any scope at all for a variable. It should also be noted, that defining the scope of the variable does not actually define the variable. Some languages allow syntax along the lines of:

```
local cName = "Fred Smith"
```

In dBL, this would have to be split into two commands, but you should note that the LOCAL command must come first, because you cannot change or define the scope of a variable that has already been created:

```
local cName
cName = "Fred Smith"
```

So what exactly does the SCOPE do? It can make variables available to other parts of your application, or it can limit them to only be available to specific parts of the application.

What are the various means of scoping variables?

The examples given below will use functions, but they could just as well use programs.

By default, variables you initialize in the Command Window are *public* and those you initialize in programs without a scope declaration are *private* (see below).

Scope	Visible To	Duration
local	Only the function or program it was created in	Released when the function or program ends
parameters	The function or program created in, and any functions or programs called from the initial one	Released when the function or program in which the variable was created returns control to a prior function or program
private	The function or program that created it, and any functions or programs called from the initial one	Released when the function or program in which the variable was created returns control to a prior function or program

Scope	Visible To	Duration
public	All programs and/or functions	Released only by a specific RELEASE command, or CLEAR MEMORY, etc.
static	Only the function or program it was created in	Released by an explicit RELEASE command in the function or program it was created in. This is an obsolete command – see discussion below.

Local

Local variables are, as noted in the table above, only available to the function or program the variables are created in. The advantage to local variables is if you tend to use the same variable name for specific tasks throughout an application, because by declaring them as local, any called functions or programs cannot overwrite the value of the variable.

An example of how this works is shown in the following code. If you wish to see this yourself, in the Command Window, type:

```
modify command LocalTest
```

In the Source Code Editor, you would enter the code shown:

```
// A simple program to show the difference between
// variables declared as local and others not:
local cName
cName = "Smith, Fred"
cLast = ""
? "Before calling GetLast()"
? "Full name: "+cName
? "Last name: "+cLast
?

GetLast()

? "After calling GetLast()"
? "Full name: "+cName
? "Last name: "+cLast

function GetLast()
   cName = "Jones, George"
   cLast = left( cName, at(",", cName) - 1 )
return
```

If you were to run this, the output would look like:

```
Before calling GetLast()
Full name: Smith, Fred
Last name:

After calling GetLast()
Full name: Smith, Fred
Last name: Jones
```

When we returned from the GetLast() function, why is the full name not "Jones, George"? The reason is that the cName variable was declared as local. However, note that the cLast variable was not, so the value returned is the calculated value of the last name of the value assigned to cName in the function GetLast().

What this allows is for us to create variables of the same name in different places in our application, that do not affect or change the wrong instances of the variable name. Effectively when we called the GetLast function in the code above, since the variable cName was declared as local in the main program, when the GetLast function started to execute, it created a *new* variable named cName, and used that in the function.

The programming technique that often trips up many developers is when they use loops such as the FOR/NEXT loop *(discussed later in this chapter)* they tend to use the same variable name for the counter used in the loop. If the loop calls a function that also has a similar loop, the counter in the function could actually change the value in the counter in the main program – which will cause processing to jump to the wrong place, which can cause a real case of heartburn for me. If you use LOCAL to declare the variable before using it, you avoid that problem.

There is a coding technique in dBL called "macro substitution" which we will examine in more depth later. dBL does not allow LOCAL or STATIC (see below) variables as macros, so if you wish to use a variable as a macro, you would want to use PRIVATE, rather than LOCAL.

Parameters

Parameters are used to pass information between programs and functions in dBL. The Age function we created earlier in this chapter uses a single parameter, the birthdate, to determine the age. You can pass the value as a literal value, or as a variable.

It is generally considered bad form in a function to change the value of a parameter that is passed to it. Changing the value may alter data you did not mean to alter.

When you pass a variable to a function, you are using what is called "Passing by Reference". This allows the function to manipulate the variable. If you are using a function you did not write, and cannot tell if it will modify your parameter, you can pass the value as an expression. Functions cannot change the variables passed as an expression. The simplest way to turn a variable into an expression is to put parentheses around it. A simple example would be to create a function such as:

```
function ChangeValue( cValue )
   cValue = "After Change"
return
```

If you created this function, save it as "ChangeValue.prg". In the Command Window, you could then try:

```
cSaveMe = "Before Change"
ChangeValue( cSaveMe )
? cSaveMe // displays "After Change" in output pane
```

However, if you instead used an expression:

```
cSaveMe = "Before Change"
ChangeValue( (cSaveMe) )
? cSaveMe // displays "Before Change" in output pane
```

It should be noted that in dBL there is also a *parameters* statement for declaring parameters. This creates a parameter with private scoping (see below). If you wish local scoping, then you would use the parameter in the FUNCTION statement as shown here.

The *parameters* statement works like the following *very* simple example:

```
function MyFunction
   parameters nVar
   // display the value
   ? nVar
return
```

As noted, the parameter nVar would be treated as if it had been declared *private*, rather than *local*.

Functions to Work with Parameters

There are three functions that can be used with parameters as outlined here. These can assist you when working with code that has optional parameters.

pCount() and argCount()

Either of these functions can be used to determine the number of parameters passed to a function or a program. These two functions are interchangeable – they each do the exact same thing. Even better, they can be used in a situation where you do not have a parameters statement or have declared parameters in the function definition, to determine if any parameters and how many parameters were passed. For example:

```
function MyFunc
   ? pCount()
return
```

You could then call the function with:

```
MyFunc( "test", 123 )
```

And you would see the number 2 in the output pane of the Command Window.

A more useful test would be to see if a specified number of parameters were passed to a function *(or program).* If the correct number were not passed, either tell the user and halt the function, or you could do something such as change the value if needed.

```
function MyFunc( cParm1, nParm2 )
   if pCount() < 2
      msgbox( "You should have passed two parameters, "+;
              "a character and a numeric value!",;
              "MyFunc Error!", 16 )
      return
   endif
   ? "cParm1 = "+cParm1
   ? "nParm1 = "+nParm1
return
```

And of course you could get more elaborate.

argVector()

This function will return the value of a parameter passed to a function or program without needing a parameter declaration of any sort, which is a useful way of handling parameters on the fly. You must give a number to the function and if no parameter by that number is passed, the function will return a value of *false*. However, if no parameter is passed, you can also check for *empty()* and dBASE should return a value of *true* (meaning that the parameter is empty – or no value was passed). A simple example would be to display the value of all parameters passed to a function:

```
function MyFunc
   for i = 1 to argCount()
       ? argVector( i )
   next
return
```

Private

Private variables are used in situations where you wish to declare a variable in a function, but not have it accessible to the function or program that called it. What this means is that Private is sort of like Local, except that a Local variable is limited to the current function or program only. A Private variable is actually available to any functions or programs called from the code that created the variable, but is not available if that code was called from somewhere else. The easiest way to understand this is to take a look at the following sample. If you create this as a program and run it, save it as PrivateTest.prg:

```
// A test to see how Private variables work:
// execute function FirstFunc():
FirstFunc()

function FirstFunc
   cName = "Fred"
   SecondFunc()
   ? "First: "+cName
return

function SecondFunc
   private cName
   cName = "Jane"
   ThirdFunc()
   ? "Second: "+cName
return

function ThirdFunc
   cName = "John"
   ? "Third: "+cName
return
```

To understand this, it helps to actually step through it and see what happens:

- The function FirstFunc() is called, and the variable "cName" is created by assigning the name "Fred" to it. The function SecondFunc() is called, but until that occurs there is only one variable named cName.
- In the function SecondFunc(), because we used "private cName", this means that this function cannot overwrite the variable that currently exists by this name. Instead, dBASE creates a new variable named "cName" – there are now two of them. The one that is modified in this function is the second variable and contains the name "Jane". We then call the function ThirdFunc().

- In the function ThirdFunc(), we overwrote the variable "cName" with the name "John", then displayed the value in the command that begins with the question mark. Control is now returned to SecondFunc().
- Back in SecondFunc(), we output the value of cName, which rather than being "Jane" is now "John". We return control back to FirstFunc().
- When we return to "FirstFunc", the variable named "cName" that was created in SecondFunc() is now gone – it no longer exists, as it was released when the function returned control to the previous function. We then display the value of the first variable named "cName", which is still "Fred". Hence the output will look like:

```
Third: John
Second: John
First: Fred
```

The use of Private is interesting, and sometimes useful, but most of the time you will want to use LOCAL instead.

Public

Public variables, once created, always exist until they are explicitly released. The biggest problem with public variables is that any function or program may see and modify the value of the variable. Because of this, these should be avoided most of the time.

More importantly, a public variable will still remain in memory even if a RELEASE command is issued, which means that they are always there.

The online help suggests that if you really do need to make a variable "public" you should consider creating custom properties of the _app object (the application object), which is available at all times, but for the most part, global variables are generally a bad idea.

Static

Static variables can be created to give you variables that still exist in memory, but are not accessible outside of the function they are defined in. They only way to see the value or modify it is in the actual function. This might be useful if you needed, for example, a counter to see how often a function is called:

```
function CountIt
   static nCount = 0
   nCount++  // increment nCount
   ? "Function called: "+nCount+" times."
return (nCount)
```

Then in a program you could call this:

```
? CountIt()
? CountIt()
? type( "nCount" ) // returns "U"!
? CountIt()
```

The output for such a program would look like the following in the Command Window:

```
Function called: 1 times.
Function called: 2 times.
U
Function called: 3 times.
```

Note that the syntax for the STATIC command is different from the other scope commands in that you can assign a value to the variable at the time you define it as being static.

If you re-run the same program, the variable still exists and retains the last value assigned to it, unless you release the variable:

```
clear memory
```

(The dBL release command does not affect Static variables.)

Since properties of objects, which are scoped to the parent object, are visible *only* through the object and are persistent to the object, static variables are now irrelevant. Object properties might be considered to be "object-oriented static variables."

There are advantages to using custom properties of objects, including the fact that they are *enumerable* – meaning that you can loop through the properties and test them, which you cannot do with variables. *(See the enumerate() function in Online Help.)* You can also inspect properties using the inspector, which are inheritable (subclassed objects).

Assignment Operators

When you work with variables, you need to assign values to them. Just in this chapter alone we have already seen several ways of assigning values to a variable, so it's time we examined this.

When you create a memory variable, you must assign a value. If the variable does not exist, the only way to assign a value is with the equal sign (=). This would look like:

```
cName = "Fred Smith"
```

Once a variable has been created, we can assign new values to it either by using the equal sign, or by using the assignment operator ":=".

```
cName := "Jane Doe"
```

If you attempt to use the assignment operator on a variable name that has not previously been created, you will receive an error that looks like:

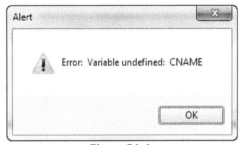

Figure 21-6

This particular piece of information is very useful when writing code. While of course you do not want to see errors, this can save you a lot of problems later on.

If you are writing a well-structured program and misspell a variable name, when you attempt to assign a value to it in your code all you are doing is creating a new variable:

```
cMame = "Joe Smith"
```

But if, rather than using the equal sign, the assignment operator were used:

```
cMame := "Joe Smith"
```

Then an error similar to that shown in Figure 21-6 would occur and you would know that you did something wrong, then come back and fix it. If you didn't use the assignment operator in this situation, you could spend a long time trying to find the problem in your code!

Very importantly, this ability works with assigning values to properties of objects, which again can save you a lot of trouble in your code. If you misspell the name of a property and use the "=" operator to assign a value, you will be creating a new custom property of the object. If, however, you use the assignment operator ":=" and the property does not exist, dBASE will return an error similar to the one shown above.

In addition to the = and := operators, there are some of mathematical assignment operators:

+=	A shortcut for adding a value to a variable. If you do not use this operator, to add a value to a variable you would use:
	
	`nVar = nVar + 5 // Add 5`
	`// or`
	`cVar = cVar + "A String"`
	
	Using the += operator, these same commands look like:
	
	`nVar += 5 // Add 5`
	`// or`
	`cVar += "A String"`

-=	Subtract a value from the variable:
	
	`nVar = 15`
	`nVar -= 5 // subtract 5 - returns 10`

*=	Multiply the value in the variable by another:
	
	`nVar = 4`
	`nVar *= 5 // multiply nVar by 5 - returns 20`

/=	Divide the value in the variable by another:
	
	`nVar = 8`
	`nVar /= 2 // divide nVar by 2 - returns 4`

%=	Modulus operator:
	
	`nVar = 50`
	`nVar %= 8 // returns 2 - the remainder after`
	`         // dividing 50 by 8`

Math

Standard mathematical operations may be performed on numeric values and we will take a look at some more complex built-in functions in dBASE later in this chapter. The basics are:

+	add two values, or concatenate two strings
-	subtract the second value from the first
*	multiply two values
/	divide two values
%	modulus
^ or **	exponentiation
++	increment a numeric value
--	decrement a numeric value

In older versions of dBASE, in order to increment a value, you had to issue a command such as:

```
nCount = nCount + 1
```

Now you can trim this down to:

```
nCount++
```

The same works for decrementing a value:

```
nCount--
```

If you need to work with the value at the same time you are incrementing or decrementing it, there are a couple of ways to do so:

```
n = 5      // Start with 5
? n++      // Get value (5), then increment
? n        // Now 6
? ++n      // Increment first, then get value (7)
? n        // Still 7
```

So it depends on what you need to do. By placing the operator first, you can cause the increment (or decrement) to occur first before you work with the value.

There is a bit more information in the Online Help for these operators as well.

One should always keep in mind the mathematical operator hierarchy. This affects the sequence in which math is performed in a statement. The basics are:

1. Exponentiation goes first
2. Any calculation contained in parentheses is executed
3. Multiplication and Division go next
4. Addition and Subtraction go last

For example:

? 4+5 * 2

You may assume that the addition would be performed first, however instead the multiplication is executed first, returning a value of 14. If instead, you did the following:

? (4+5) * 2

The value displayed would be 18. While this is a very simple example, it is an important concept when you start using math in your program code.

Some Basic Commands

The next part of this chapter will discuss some basic commands that are vital to any programmer. This will include a brief look at the uses of each. More commands will be discussed as we work through the rest of the chapter, but the following are some of the most vital to any programmer.

Display

One of the things you will see used throughout this book that has not really been discussed much is the question mark (?) being used as a command to display output. This literally is an output command and can be used to display information in the Command Window. Since you are creating Windows applications that most likely will not have a Command Window when the application is completed, we have not really talked about it much, but this can be quite useful when testing your programs, forms and other code, to display what is happening.

The syntax is pretty simple:

```
? "some value"
```

Where "some value" can be a variable (in which case you would see not the name of the variable, but the actual contents of the memory variable as stored in memory); it can be a literal string as shown here, the value of a field, the value of a property or a combination.

It is even possible to generate reports, as the ? command is used to create what is called "streaming" reports, but that's a topic we won't be getting into here. There is information in the online help about using the ? command, as well as related options, such as the ?? command, and some positioning techniques and a *style* option.

If you use the ? command to display output in the Output Pane of the Command Window, you should know about the command CLEAR which simply clears out the Output Pane – this is useful if you are doing a lot of testing and want to only see the current information.

There are other ways to display information. One common one is to use the built-in *msgbox()* function in dBASE. We discussed this a little in an earlier chapter, but it is worth a small "reminder".

The *msgbox()* function calls a dialog that can be used to show information on the screen and if you choose some of the options, allows the user to make a decision interactively. A simple dialog that only has an "OK" button on it might look like:

```
msgbox( "This is a simple msgbox() call" )
```

The actual msgbox would look like:

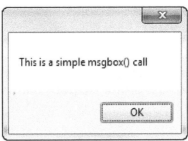

Figure 21-7

Text can be displayed in the titlebar by using the second parameter:

```
msgbox( "This is a simple msgbox() call", "A Message" )
```

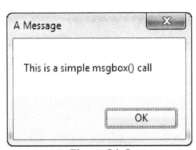

Figure 21-8

You can get fancier by adding an image which can take some getting used to, however. The online help for MSGBOX() will show you what the numbers are that can be used. You need to know what you want to do with the msgbox dialog – if you just want an "OK" button, the set of numbers by the graphics can be used by themselves. For example, if you wanted the "exclamation point" graphic, the command would look like:

```
msgbox( "This is a simple msgbox() call", "A Message", 64 )
```

Figure 21-9

If you wanted to change the buttons to something *other* than simply "OK" you have to add the numbers shown in the online help for the set of buttons you wish to use ("OK" has a numeric value of 0). So if you wanted to have the msgbox display Yes, No and Cancel buttons, it would look like:

```
msgbox( "This is a simple msgbox() call", "A Message", 64+3 )
    // or
msgbox( "This is a simple msgbox() call", "A Message", 67 )
```

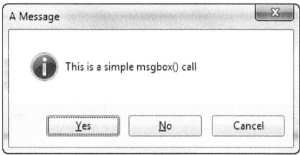

Figure 21-10

As shown in earlier chapters of the book, if you use a dialog that has buttons other than the "OK" button, you will most likely want to determine what to do with the results that are returned by the user clicking different buttons. In this case, the Yes button returns a numeric value of 6, the No button returns a numeric value of 7, and the Cancel button returns a numeric value of 2. To use this dialog, then, you might want to do something like:

```
nButton = msgbox( "This is a simple msgbox() call", "A Message", 64+3 )
if nButton == 2 // Cancel
    return
elseif nButton == 6 // Yes
    ? "You clicked the 'Yes' button"
else // last choice, 7 - No
    ? "You clicked the 'No' button"
endif
```

As you progress through the chapters on programming, you will most likely see examples of using *msgbox()* to communicate with the user. The *msgbox()* function is a good way to ask the user questions in your application. You can also create your own dialog forms as discussed in earlier chapters of this book.

Controlling Program Flow

One of the things programs do is compare values in order for the program to make decisions regarding what processing to perform. There are a couple of methods of comparing values that should be examined.

It should be noted here that in the sample code shown below I have inserted simply some comments that read things like "// do some processing". What exactly is meant by this? ANYTHING. You can do some processing right at that point, or call a function, program, or a method of a class. If you call other code, you need to understand that dBASE will return you, when the other code is completed, to where you were in the structure shown, and assume that the next statement needs to be processed.

IF/ENDIF

The IF statement is one of the most commonly used statement in programming, whether you program in dBL or in C++, or pretty much any programming language. It provides for some pretty basic branching and such.

The concept is that you start with the word "IF", followed by a comparison that must, in the final analysis return a value of true or false. The complexity of the comparison is up to the needs of the coder.

A simple IF statement might look like:

```
if nValue > 5
   // do some processing
endif
```

This is a nice and simple comparison – we are comparing the value referenced by the variable name nValue, and if it is greater than (>) 5, we want to perform some sort of processing. The "endif" statement is required for an "if" statement, so that dBASE knows that you have reached the end of the processing to do if the comparison returns a result of *true*.

If the comparison returns a result of *false* in this example, logic flow will move to any program statement <u>after</u> the "endif" statement and any code between those two statements will be ignored.

The IF statement structure is actually able to do a lot more than this. For example, you could have a set of conditions you wished to compare. You might need to do something along these lines:

```
if nValue > 5
   // do some processing
elseif nValue > 3
   // do some other processing
else // a catch all – if the other conditions are not met ...
      // do yet some more processing
endif
```

The "elseif" option is one that you should definitely be aware of – it basically says that if the first condition is *false*, let's look at another condition to see if it is *true*. If the second condition is *true*, then any processing that is to be performed for *that* condition will be done, until we reach either another "elseif", "else" or "endif" statement. Also note the "else" operator – this tells dBASE to do something if the other condition or conditions are not met, then continue until an "endif" is found.

This can get fairly complex, as well as more exciting, because you can "nest" the if/endif structures – in other words, you could have a condition inside of a condition and you can nest these pretty deeply. Much depends on what you need to do. You may want to start using some inline comments to make sure you can read the code:

```
if nValue > 5
   // do some processing
   if nValue == 7
      // do some special processing
   endif // nValue == 7
elseif nValue > 3
   // do some other processing
else // a catch all – if the other conditions are not met ...
   // do yet some more processing
endif // nValue > 5
```

Note the comment after the nested if/endif – this can help you when you figure out if you have enough "endif" statements to ensure you have ended your structure properly. Combined with proper indentation, your code can still be readable even if it is fairly complex.

DO CASE/ENDCASE

In addition to the IF/ELSE structure noted above, there is another structure that is used for comparisons – this can be particularly useful if you have a group of options you wish to perform in specific cases based on the same variable, for example:

```
do case
    case nValue == 1
        // do some processing
    case nValue == 2
        // do some processing
    case nValue == 5
        // do some processing
    otherwise
        // catchall - any condition not met above
endcase
```

This is basically the same as:

```
if nValue == 1
    // do some processing
elseif nValue == 2
    // do some processing
elseif nValue == 5
    // do some processing
else
    // catchall - any conditions not met above
endif
```

So why use the do case/endcase structure? More than anything it comes down to programming technique and/or programming styles. Personally I like the do case/endcase structure, but I know some developers do not. This structure requires a bit more typing, but otherwise I find it more readable than the if/endif structure for some situations.

Comparison Operators

The examples shown above show a couple of the operators used for comparisons in dBL. These are important to grasp so I will attempt to explain them here, starting with this table:

Comparison	Operator
Equal	= or ==
Less Than	<
Less Than or Equal	<= or =<
Greater Than	>
Greater Than or Equal	>= or =>
Not Equal	<> or #
Not	not or .not.
And	and or .and.
Or	or or .or.
Contained in	$

In some cases what you see in the "Operator" column shows two options – some of those are the same. However, the first operator, "Equal" shows two options that are not identical to each other. *(It should be noted that SQL can be very particular –using => may get you an error, where >= will not, but in dBL you can use either and get the same results.)*

The equal operator has two ways of determining if two values are equal. The first is simply "equal", the second is "exactly equal". To understand this, you have to understand the way dBL performs comparisons. With most types of data, these two comparisons are pretty much the same. However, when you compare character strings, these two are not the same. To see this, take a look at the following:

```
cFullName = "John Smith"
cFirst    = "John"
if cFullName = cFirst
    ? "Match found"
endif
```

In this example, you will actually get a match! This can be rather confusing to say the least. If you turn the statement around, you will not get a match:

```
if cFirst = cFullName
    ? "Match found"
endif
```

Now, why is that? Because by default, when comparing strings, dBL looks to see if the string on the LEFT of the equal sign begins with the string on the RIGHT. In the first example, the string "John" is at the beginning of the string "John Smith", so dBASE determines that there is a match. In the second example, the string "John Smith" is not at the beginning of the string "John", therefore there is no match.

There are at least three ways to deal with this. One is to change the expression to the second version. However you cannot always guarantee with your programs that this will do the trick.

The second solution then is to use the "==" or "Exactly Equal" comparison operator:

```
if cFullName == cFirst
    ? "Match found"
endif
```

Since the two strings are not identical, this will not return a match.

The third solution is to use the SET EXACT command. This is not normally recommended because it affects your whole application until you reset it. By default, this is set to "OFF", but you can change it:

```
set exact on
if cFullName = cFirst
    ? "Match found"
endif
set exact off
```

Note that I added the setting to return the state of "EXACT" matching to off.

The NOT operator is used to tell dBASE that the condition following must return a false result. This may seem confusing, as it is a form of "negative logic" that takes some getting used to.

```
if not cFullName = cFirst
```

is the same as:

```
if cFullName # cFirst
```

and this latter command is easier to read.

The AND and OR options are particularly useful when you have a more complex comparison. However, you can confuse yourself with these.

If you need two comparisons to return in a positive result, you would use AND:

```
if cFullName = cFirst AND nValue > 5
```

In this case, both conditions must evaluate to a result of *true*, for dBASE to consider the whole condition to be *true*.

If you need only one of two comparisons to return a positive result, you would use OR:

```
if cFullName = cFirst OR nValue > 5
```

In this case, if the first condition evaluates to *true*, it doesn't matter if the second one evaluates to *true* OR *false* and vice versa – if the second condition is *true*, the first can be *false*, in either case, the condition is met and dBASE will consider the whole to be *true*. The only way this will evaluate to *false* is if both conditions result in a value of *false*.

When using AND and OR in your conditions, it may be a good idea to use parentheses around them to make your code more readable, particularly if you start getting into some truly complex statements – this helps dBASE as well as yourself when trying to understand the code. By putting a comparison inside parentheses, dBASE will evaluate the condition inside the parentheses before evaluating anything outside of them. For example:

```
if cFullName = cFirst AND (nValue > 5 OR nValue == 3)
```

This is quite different from:

```
if cFullName = cFirst AND nValue > 5 OR nValue == 3
```

What dBASE will see here is that the first two conditions must be true, the last can be true or false, or vice versa, the last must be true and the first two may be false. By using parentheses you can guarantee that dBASE will group your comparisons the way you need them.

The last comparison operator in the table listed earlier in this chapter is the "Contained In" operator. This is useful to see if a string is contained in another string:

```
if cFirst $ cFullName
```

In the example above, you can check to see if the first name is contained in the full name.

A Few Notes
There are some things you should be aware of when performing comparisons that may not be intuitive, the following is based on information in the online help:

● If either operand is a numeric expression, the other operand is converted to a number:

- If a string contains a number only (leading spaces are OK), that number is used, otherwise it is interpreted as an invalid number.

```
? 123 = "123" // true
```

- The logical value *true* becomes one (1); *false* becomes zero (0).

```
? true = 1 // true
```

- All other data types are considered to be invalid numbers.
- All comparisons between a number and an invalid number result in *false*.

```
? 123 = "A123" // false
```

- If either operand is a string, the other operand is converted to its display representation:
  - Numbers become strings with no leading spaces. Integer values eight digits or less have no decimal point or decimal portion. Integer values larger than eight digits and non-integer values have as many decimals places as indicated by SET DECIMALS.

```
? "ABC" = 123 // false
```

  - The logical values *true* and *false* become the strings "true" and "false".

```
? "true" == true // true
```

  - Dates (primitive dates and Date objects) are converted using DTOC( ).

```
? "05/10/2005" == date() // false unless the value returned
                         // by date() is a match
```

  - Object references to arrays are converted to the word "array".

```
a = new array()
? a // "Array"
```

  - References to objects of all other classes are converted to the word "Object".

```
f = new form()
? f // "Object"
```

  - Function pointers take on the form "Function: " followed by the function name.
- All other comparisons between mismatched data types return false.
- When comparing dates, a blank date comes after (is greater than) a non-blank date. *(This can cause some serious consternation if you do not expect it, as this is opposite the way most comparisons occur.)*
- When comparing Date objects, the date/time they represent are compared; they may be earlier, later, or exactly the same. For all other objects, only the equality tests make sense. It tests whether two object references refer to the same object.
- String equality comparisons are case-sensitive, as well as following the setting of SET EXACT, unless you use the == (exactly equal) symbol.
  - You can get around the case-sensitivity if you wish (you may not wish to do so, depending on the needs of the application), by converting a string to either upper case or lower case:

```
if cFirst.toUpperCase() == cFullName.toUpperCase()
```

- For compatibility with earlier versions of dBASE, if the string on the right of the = operator is (or begins with) CHR(0) and SET EXACT is OFF, then the comparison always returns *true*. When checking for CHR(0), always use the == operator.

- The $ operator determines if one string is contained in, or is a substring of, another string. By definition, an empty string is not contained in another string.

Looping

Conditional statements allow us to perform some branching and perform specific operations/commands based on those conditions. Loops allow us to perform specific operations/commands until dBASE is told to stop. A loop inherently contains a condition that tells dBASE when to stop. You can nest loops, but you need to be very careful if you do so. It is very easy to create an infinite loop – one that will never meet the condition that causes the loop to stop. In the following pages we will take a brief look at the various types of looping structures built-in to dBASE.

DO WHILE/ENDO

Probably the most common looping structure is the DO WHILE loop. Like the conditional structures, there is an end statement that tells dBASE that you have reached the last statement in the loop and to go back to the top. This structure is sometimes called a "pre-test loop", because the statements inside the loop may never be executed if the terminating condition is *false* the first time it is tested. In this case it is "ENDDO". The basic structure of this statement is:

```
do while somecondition
   // perform statements needed
enddo
```

The condition must evaluate to *true* for the loop to process and once that condition evaluates to false, it will exit the loop. One of the more common uses of a loop such as this is to loop through the rows in a table and do something to or with the data, so you might do something like the following:

```
dSample = new database()
dSample.databaseName := "DBASESAMPLES"
dSample.active        := true

qFish = new query()
qFish.database := dSample
qFish.sql      := "select * from fish"
qFish.active   := true
// set the index:
qFish.rowset.indexName := "name"
// go to the first row:
qFish.rowset.first()

// loop until we reach the end of the rowset:
do while not qFish.rowset.endOfSet

   ? qFish.rowset.fields["Name"].value

   // very important: without this, we will
   // create an infinite loop, and only ever
   // display the value of the data from the
   // first row!
   qFish.rowset.next()
enddo

// some cleanup:
qFish.active := false
```

```
release object qFish
dSample.active := false
release object dSample
```

In the example shown, if you were to actually type this into a program and run it, you would simply loop through the Fish table and output the value of the Name field. Notice that if you do not have the statement:

```
qFish.rowset.next()
```

Your loop will become an infinite loop, as the comments note. This is a simple example and you can do a lot with it. As noted, you could insert another loop to do some special processing inside this loop, you could add some conditional statements and so on.

The Loop and Exit Commands

The *loop* and *exit* commands in dBL are special commands that can be used to alter the processing in a loop. These might be used in an IF structure to determine that you want to ignore the current row in a table (and skip processing it), or perhaps in some cases you might want to just exit out of a loop if a specific condition is met. These work along the following lines:

```
dSample = new database()
dSample.databaseName := "DBASESAMPLES"
dSample.active        := true

qFish = new query()
qFish.database := dSample
qFish.sql        := "select * from fish"
qFish.active    := true
// set the index:
qFish.rowset.indexName := "name"
// go to the first row:
qFish.rowset.first()

// loop until we reach the end of the rowset:
do while not qFish.rowset.endOfSet

    if "blue" $ qFish.rowset.fields["Name"].value.toLowerCase()
      ? qFish.rowset.fields["Name"].value
      qFish.rowset.next()
      loop
    else
      if "butterfly" $ qFish.rowset.fields["Name"].value.toLowerCase()
            exit
      endif // "butterfly" ...
    endif // "blue"
     // very important: without this, we will
    // create an infinite loop, and only ever
    // display the value of the data from the
    // first row!
    qFish.rowset.next()
enddo

// some cleanup:
qFish.active := false
release object qFish
```

```
dSample.active := false
release object dSample
```

In this example, if the word "blue" is contained in the current name field, then we tell dBASE to display it, navigate to the next row and then loop back to the top of the loop and if the word "butterfly" is contained in the field, we tell dBASE to exit the loop completely. In the case of the LOOP command, dBASE will loop back to the DO WHILE statement to check the condition and if the condition is now *true*, it will exit the loop, otherwise it will continue looping through the data. In the case of the EXIT command, control moves to the next command *after* the ENDDO statement.

📓 NOTE

If you are using XDML code to loop through a table, a special looping option was created for dBL, called the SCAN loop. This will process similar to the example shown above, but you do not need to give an ending condition. The following code does basically the same thing that the example for DO/WHILE does:

```
open database DBASESAMPLES
set database to DBASESAMPLES
use fish order name
go top
scan
    ? Name
endscan
use
close database DBASESAMPLES
```

Notice that no condition is necessary to get out of the loop and you do not need to tell dBASE to go to the next record. This *only* works for XDML and will not work with the database objects used in OODML.

DO/UNTIL

A less used and less known variant of the DO loop is the DO/UNTIL form. The primary difference between the two is that in the case of the DO WHILE loop, the condition used to exit the loop is at the beginning of the loop, whereas in the DO/UNTIL is at the end of the loop. This form of structure might be called a "post-test loop", because the condition is at the end of the loop, which means that the commands contained inside the loop will *always* be executed at least once.

```
do
    // some process
until somecondition
```

If we wanted to repeat some of the code shown in the DO WHILE loop, the code would look very similar:

```
dSample = new database()
dSample.databaseName := "DBASESAMPLES"
dSample.active       := true

qFish = new query()
qFish.database := dSample
qFish.sql      := "select * from fish"
qFish.active   := true
```

```
// set the index:
qFish.rowset.indexName := "name"
// go to the first row:
qFish.rowset.first()

// loop until we reach the end of the rowset:
do
    ? qFish.rowset.fields["Name"].value

    // very important: without this, we will
    // create an infinite loop, and only ever
    // display the value of the data from the
    // first row!
    qFish.rowset.next()
until qFish.rowset.endOfSet

// some cleanup:
qFish.active := false
release object qFish
dSample.active := false
release object dSample
```

In the example code above, if you wanted to use a LOOP command where would the logic go? Back to the *beginning* of the loop. This could be a potential problem – the condition is not checked until the *end* of the loop with the UNTIL statement! So you could actually be at the endOfSet and not have a way out, unless you planned for it (with perhaps right after the "do" command the following):

```
if qFish.rowset.endOfSet
    exit
endif
```

The EXIT command works the same way as it does in the example with the DO WHILE loop earlier.

FOR/NEXT

The FOR/NEXT loop is useful when processing a loop a known number of times, processing an array and so on. With a DO WHILE or DO UNTIL loop, you could simulate what is happening with a FOR/NEXT loop, but it means adding a counter variable. In the case of the FOR/NEXT loop, the counter variable is required anyway.

```
for variable = startvalue to endvalue step somevalue
    // do some processing
next // or endfor
```

The parts of this break down to:

variable   – the counter variable that increments (or decrements) each time through the loop

startvalue   – the starting point for the loop, often 1

endvalue   – the ending point for the loop – what does the value of the variable have to be to end the loop?

somevalue   – if you use the STEP option (it is optional, the default value is 1 – increment by 1), this will determine by how much to increment (or decrement) the value of the variable.

The end statement can be either the word NEXT or the word ENDFOR. Some programmers prefer the former, others the latter.

A simple loop that processed, say 7 times, would look like:

```
for i = 1 to 7
    ? i
next
```

You could tell dBASE to count backwards from 7 to 1 by adding the STEP option (and changing the start/stop values):

```
for i = 7 to 1 step -1
    ? i
next
```

You can nest this loop, so you could have a for/next loop contained inside another and the LOOP and EXIT commands also work for the FOR/NEXT loop structure.

There are many situations where this can be used. One example would be to obtain a list of fieldnames from a table:

```
dSample = new database()
dSample.databaseName := "DBASESAMPLES"
dSample.active        := true

qFish = new query()
qFish.database := dSample
qFish.sql        := "select * from fish"
qFish.active   := true
// set the index:
qFish.rowset.indexName := "name"
// go to the first row:
qFish.rowset.first()

// get a list of fieldnames:
local i
for i = 1 to qFish.rowset.fields.size
    ? qFish.rowset.fields[ i ].fieldName
next

// some cleanup:
qFish.active := false
release object qFish
dSample.active := false
release object dSample
```

Note the use of the LOCAL statement to ensure that if the processing in the loop called another program or function, that the code would not overwrite the value of the variable named "i" *(see discussion of LOCAL earlier in this chapter)*.

> **NOTE**
> The fields array that we used in this example is a subset of the array class built in to dBASE. This was discussed a little in earlier chapters on the database objects and when we get to the array object in a later chapter, some of what we did here will be easier to understand.

FOR loops are particularly useful when working with arrays. The following code will create an array, then populate it with information about the files in the current folder, loop through the array and display the names of the files:

```
aDir = new array()
aDir.dir()
for i = 1 to aDir.size/5 // 5 columns
    ? aDir[ i, 1 ]
next
```

> **NOTE**
> There are two primary types of looping structure discussed here, the DO type loop and the FOR type loop. Why use one or the other? The FOR type loop is useful when you know the number of iterations, or it can be obtained from a property of an object (for example, with arrays, you know how big the array is, because the array has a *size* property). For other situations where you don't know the number of iterations you should use a DO type loop. This is used a lot with tables as the number of rows in a table may vary each time your program processes the loop.

Working with Data Types

As noted earlier in this chapter data can be in various types, from character strings to numeric to logical. We will examine a few things you ought to know when working with some of these data types in the next section of this chapter.

Performing Financial Calculations

dBL has several financial calculations built in to the software. These are described in greater detail in the online help, but here is a brief description:

* FV()– Future Value – this function calculates the future value of a loan or investment given equal periodic payments at a fixed rate.
* Payment()– this function calculates the amount you would need to pay over time to repay a debt.
* PV()– Present Value – this function calculates the present value of an investment.

These functions return values based on the parameters passed, which are explained in depth in the online help, as well as details of what the actual "behind the scenes" calculations are. It should be noted that like the scientific and math formulas in the next section, the results returned will vary depending on the setting of SET DECIMALS, which we will examine shortly.

Computing Engineering and Scientific Formulas

In addition to the financial calculations that are built in to dBASE, there are also engineering and scientific calculations such as the trigonometric calculations shown below:

- ACOS() – The arc cosine of a number.
- ASIN() – The arc sine of a number.
- ATAN() – The arctangent of a number.
- ATN2() – The arctangent of a given point.
- COS() – The cosine of an angle.
- DTOR() – The radian value of an angle measured in degrees.
- RTOD() – The degree value of an angle measured in radians.
- SIN() – The sine of an angle.
- TAN() – The tangent of an angle.

There are also functions that deal with rounding or even truncating values:

- CEILING() – Returns the nearest integer that is greater than or equal to the specified number.
- FLOOR() – Returns the nearest integer that is less than or equal to a specified number.
- INT() – Returns the integer portion of a specified number, truncates the decimals.
- ROUND() – rounds a specified number to a specific number of decimal places.

The SET DECIMALS command affects the values displayed for your calculations.

Rounding

Many folk have noted that there are problems with rounding in dBASE, which can cause precision errors. To be fair to the developers at dBASE (and those who worked on the software before them) the problem is *not* specifically dBASE, but the underlying programming language of C or C++. These languages use floating point math.

The value that is actually used internally is often not what you might expect. For example:

```
set decimals to 18
x=2.01
? x                  // result 2.009999999999999787
x*=100
? x                  // result 200.999999999999971600
? int(x)             // result 200 - of course
```

(Note that the default setting in dBASE for SET DECIMALS is 2 – two digits to the right of the decimal. If you experiment and want to set things back to "normal" you may want to reset the value.)

Bowen Moursund (posting in the dBASE newsgroups) notes:

For round(), add a very small amount to the number-to-be-rounded before rounding.

For int(), round() to the significant decimal place first.

For comparisons, ensure that SET PRECISION is set low enough to eliminate the floating point difficulties. Usually SET PRECISION to 10 will do it.

The following was posted by Ken Chan in one of the many discussions in the dBASE newsgroups, and he details what happens with rounding using INT() and ROUND() quite well:

1. dBASE DOES NOT IMPLEMENT odd/even rounding . (Floating point errors may result in behavior that looks like it.) "Odd/even" rounding generally means that if a value is

"odd", such as 1.45, the rounding will go up, if it is even (such as 1.44), the rounding will go down – hence if you rounded to one decimal point:

```
? round( 1.45 ) // return 1.5
? round (1.44 ) // return 1.4
```

As noted, dBASE does not do this.

2. dBASE DOES NOT USE BCD (Binary Coded Decimal), which is why rounding "doesn't work" the way it "should".
3. With floating point, a number like 9.825 may actually be more accurately represented as 9.824999999999999999. (In other words, there is no 9.825, just like there is no accurate way to represent 1/3 in decimal notation [with a finite number of digits].)
4. You see the number 9.824999999999999999 as 9.825 because dBASE is rounding the results (the command window and Inspector use SET DECIMALS).
5. STR(),ROUND() and the way a number is displayed should have the same results. (There were/are bugs so that they don't, or they are implemented differently.)
6. The result of ROUND() is still a floating point number! For example, when you round 9.825 to two decimals places, you may actually be rounding 9.824999999999999999 to 9.819999999999999999 – because the internal representation is just under the half-way point, it is rounded down; the new value has no precise representation in floating point either.
7. The way to make rounding work the way we expect is to internally add a tiny amount, like 0.000000000000000002, because nobody ever wants to round 9.824999999999999999 on purpose; that is, they don't work with numbers with that much precision. In fact, the internal representations of a number should always have "extra digits" that cannot be manipulated from the language, to do calculations like this.

Note that trying to add 0.000000000000000001 won't work, because that value is too small – given the precision of the floating point number, you can either have 9.824999999999999999 or 9.825000000000000001; you can't have exactly 9.825, which was the problem to begin with.

Also note that the value of the adjustment depends on the magnitude of the number. For example, if the number was nine million something instead of nine something, then 0.000000000000000002 would be way too small to matter. (Because the numbers are binary (base 2), even nine and ninety are over three "places" apart, so the adjustment is very specific.)

One possible solution is to use a function like the following –written by Ken Chan and posted in the dBASE newsgroups (with a minor modification by Rich Muller to test for an empty argument):

```
function roundPrec( nArg, nPlace )
   if nPlace <= 0 or nArg == 0
      return round( nArg, nPlace )
   endif
   if empty(nArg)
      return 0.00
   endif
   local nAdj
   if (int( nArg * 10^nPlace ) + iif( nArg > 0, 0.5, -0.5 )) ;
      / 10^nPlace == nArg
      nReturn = round( nArg + sign( nArg )/10^(nPlace+1), nPlace)
   else
```

```
        nReturn = round( nArg, nPlace )
    endif
return nReturn
```

To use it, pass the numeric value to round as the first parameter (nArg) and the number of decimal places to round the value to as the second parameter. An example:

```
? roundPrec( 9.82532*2.234, 3 ) // returns: 21.95
```

Ken Chan notes "I seem to recall some cases which still do not behave as expected. It should be noted that it [the function roundPrec() above] relies on SET PRECISION, which – as always – should be as low as possible, but not lower than "nPlace" (although given the minimum PRECISION of 10, that's usually not a problem)."

Working with Date Data

Dates are used in a variety of ways and math can be performed on dates. In Visual dBASE 7.0 and all later versions of dBASE *(up to and including dBASE PLUS)* also have a Date class. We will discuss the date class in a later chapter of this book, but if you do a lot of work with dates, you should consider using the date class.

If you work with dates and simply need to do a calculation by number of days, you can do something like:

```
d = date()
? d
d++ // increment by one day
? d
```

Dates may be displayed in many formats, but the default is the date set in Windows itself. If you wish to change the date format you can do so either by using the SET DATE command, or by going to the "Properties" menu in dBASE and selecting the "Desktop Properties" dialog.

Figure 21-11

You can select the date format, the mark (separator character) and whether or not to display the full century (four digits, versus two digits) for the year portion of the date. It should be noted, that settings created here will not follow to your own applications and you will need to ensure that you use specific commands (detailed below) to make sure the date is formatted as you need it in your applications.

You can modify these same settings using various SET commands (discussed below).

Literal Dates

In various places in this book, you may have seen the use of a date placed inside curly braces ({}). This is what is called a literal date value. This might look like:

```
dBirth = {05/25/1956}
```

A literal date assumes the current date format, so if I am using the American default of MDY (Month Day Year), then 05 = the month, 25 = the day of the month and 1956 is the year. This is a useful way of working with dates where you know the date you need in your code. If you change the date format, you would need to move the values around.

The following list of functions and commands are specific to date handling in dBASE PLUS:

- DATE() – Returns the current date.
- CDOW() – Displays the day of the week as a word (Sunday, Monday ...).
- CMONTH() – Displays the month as a word (January, February ...).
- DATETIME() – Returns the current system date and time in the date format specified by the SET DATE, SET CENTURY and SET MARK settings, with the time as specified by SET HOURS.
- DAY() – Returns the day of the month as a numeric value.
- DMY() – Displays the date formatted as DDMMYY.
- DOW() – Displays the day of the week as a number. By default Sunday is 1.
- DTOS() – Returns a date in a character string displayed as YYYYMMDD. This is useful when creating an index on date values, so that the date is sorted by year, then month, then day.
- MONTH() – Displays the month as a number (1, 2 ...).
- MDY() – Displays the date formatted as MMDDYY.
- YEAR() – Displays the years of a date as a four-digit number.
- SET CENTURY – This determines if the date displays a four digit year (i.e., 2005) or a two digit year (i.e., 05). The syntax is SET CENTURY ON or SET CENTURY OFF. By default, dBASE PLUS assumes that this setting is ON.
- SET DATE – Determines the default formatting of dates:
  - AMERICAN – MM/DD/YY
  - ANSI – YY.MM.DD
  - BRITISH – DD/MM/YY
  - FRENCH – DD/MM/YY
  - GERMAN – DD.MM.YY
  - ITALIAN – DD-MM-YY
  - JAPAN – YY/MM/DD
  - USA – MM-DD-YY
  - MDY – MM/DD/YY
  - DMY – DD/MM/YY
  - YMD – YY/MM/DD
- SET EPOCH – Sets the base year for interpreting two-digit years in dates. The default base year is 1950, yielding years from 1950 to 2049. Use SET EPOCH to change how two-digit years are interpreted. This allows you to keep SET CENTURY OFF, while enabling entry of dates that cross a century boundary.
- SET MARK – Sets the separator character used between the day, month and year.

It should be noted that you can query the values associated with the commands that begin with SET:

```
? set("century")
? set("date")
? set("mark")
? set("epoch")
```

This gives you the ability in a program to save the current settings and change them temporarily, then reset them:

```
// save current settings:
cCentury = set("century")
cDate = set("date")
cMark = set("mark")
// change settings:
set century off // 2 year display
set date German // DD.MM.YY
set mark to "."
// display date:
? date()
// reset settings:
set century &cCentury.
set date &cDate.
set mark to cMark
// display date:
? date()
```

Working with Time Data

In dBASE you can work with Time to perform calculations. Normally time is displayed as HH:MM:SS, or Hours:Minutes:Seconds.

```
tTime = time() // current time
? tTime
```

The following functions allow you to work with time values:

- ELAPSED() – Displays the amount of time elapsed between two time periods.
- SECONDS() – Displays the number of elapsed seconds since midnight.
- TIME() – Returns the current time in a character string.
- TTIME() – Returns a value representing the current system time in the HH:MM:SS format. Note that this value is one that you can work with as a number, so you could add 60 to it, and increment the value by one minute.
- SET HOURS TO – Allows either 12 or 24 hour time.

An example to determine how long it takes to execute some code:

```
tStart = time()
// do some code
tEnd = time()
nDuration = elapsed( tEnd, tStart ) / 3600 // 3600 seconds in one hour
? nDuration
```

And finally in this category is a type called DateTime (in a dBF table, the field type is TIMESTAMP).

```
dtToday = DateTime()
? dtToday
```

This will return a value similar to: 03/24/2005 09:10:13 AM, based on your settings (such as the SET DATE and SET HOURS settings).

The TTIME() function displays the time with the AM/PM indicator. This returns its own type, which can be shown by using the *type()* function:

```
tT = TTime()
? type( 'tT')
```

This will return "T" for the value.

The actual value being used for the *TTime()* function is seconds.

You might want to convert to character and back using the *TtoC()* and *CtoT()* functions.

You can do math on the value returned by *TTime()*, which can be useful to find elapsed time values. For example:

```
tBeginTime = TTime()
// do some long process
tEndTime = TTime()

? "Elapsed time = " + (tEndTime - tBeginTime) + " seconds"
```

DateTime() And Related Functionality

In addition to the Date and Time features noted above, dBASE has some other date related features:

DateTime() is a function that shows the date and the time. It is its own type, which can be seen by using the *type()* function.

NOTE: *DateTime()* and "new date()" are almost identical; dBASE will do an on-the-fly conversion from one to the other when necessary. *("new date()" will create an instance of the Date object, which will be discussed in the next chapter.)*

```
dDT = DateTime()
? type( 'dDT')
```

Notice that the value that you get is "DT".

Internally, the value being stored is fractional days in scientific notation (i.e., 0.25 is six hours) – the only reason that this might be important is that you can attempt to perform math using the *DateTime()* function, but the values appear meaningless:

```
d1 = DateTime()
// Wait a minute or so ...
d2 = DateTime()
? d1 - d2
// In the output pane ...:
   -.92245370370436E-4
```

The *dateTime()* function can be useful if you wish to compare the date and time that some event occurs to another occurrence of the same event, however you should convert the values to something more useful than that shown above. This can be done by extracting the date and/or the time strings out of the returned value.

You can convert the value returned by the *DateTime()* function to character, using the function *DTtoC()* (DateTime to Character) and you can convert this back to a DateTime type by using the *CtoDT()* function (Character to DateTime).

If you are using the TimeStamp field in a dBF 7 table this is useful – you could store the current date and time to a field that was defined as a TimeStamp type:

```
queryName.rowset.fields["timestampfield"].value = DateTime()
```

This might be used for an audit trail or a variety of other situations.

NOTE: You can also use the date class to assign a value of this sort:

```
queryName.rowset.fields["timestampfield"].value = new Date()
```

Math on DateTime Values

In addition to all of the above, you can do math (if you know the values) on datetime values *(you can also use this functionality on Date Objects, which will be discussed in the next chapter)* along these lines:

```
dt = datetime()
? dt                          // current value of dt
? dt + 1                      // add a day
? dt + ( 1/24 )              // add an hour (24 hours/day)
? dt + ( 1/24/60)            // add a minute (1440 minutes/day)
? dt + ( 1/24/60/60 )        // add a second (86400 seconds/day)
d1 = CtoDT( "01/01/2000 10:00:00" )
d2 = CtoDT( "01/01/2000 10:01:01" ) // 1 minute, 1 second later
                                    // 61 seconds difference
? int( ( d2 - d1 ) * 86400 )        // should return 61 seconds
```

Working with Logical Data

Logical or Boolean data is simply a value that is either *true* or *false*. For compatibility with older versions of dBASE, you can also use *.true.* or *.false.* syntax, but the "dots" are not really needed anymore. The logical operators *and*, *or* and *not* can also use dots around them (*.and.*, *.or.* and *.not.*), but again the dots are not needed.

When working with a field in a dBF table (level 7), a logical field may also contain a value of *null* – this can cause some difficulties for some calculations or testing. This was covered in an earlier chapter of this book, as well as in other chapters, but it is worth reiterating.

Working with Character Data

Character strings have some interesting characteristics. We will take a look at the string *object* in a later chapter of this book, but one thing to note is that a character string can be treated as if it were a string object and you can use the various methods of the string object on a character string. For example, the following will output the string in upper case. :

```
? "John Smith".toUpperCase()
```

One of the more important and useful abilities in dBASE is to concatenate two (or more) strings together and as we will see in the next part of this chapter, to combine strings with other data types. You can concatenate two strings using the mathematical plus symbol (+) in dBL:

```
? "John"+" "+"Smith"
```

For example. This is a rather simple example, but we have actually used this ability throughout examples in earlier chapters of this book.

It should be noted that in SQL, the concatenation operator is different – it is "||" – two vertical bars or "pipes".

Delimiters

Character strings in dBL use delimiters to note the beginning and ending of a string. There are actually three different sets of delimiters – and you should not combine them – if you use one delimiter to start a string, you must use the same delimiter to end the string. The delimiters available are single quote ('), double quote (") or square brackets ([]). There are times when it is a good idea to use the latter, especially if a string may contain single or double quotes. In addition, for readability you may want to use the square brackets in some situations. For example, the rowset's filter property assumes single quotes around the literal value, so you could use double quotes for the complete string:

```
q.rowset.filter := "SomeField = 'SomeValue'"
```

But reading that is a bit tricky – the quotes can start to get mixed up in a complex string. The following is easier to read:

```
q.rowset.filter := [SomeField = 'SomeValue']
```

And it works just as well.

Converting Data Types

There are times when it is useful to be able to convert data from one type to another. Some functionality is built in to dBASE which we will discuss below.

Before we examine the functions that can be used to convert data, we should examine an ability that is in the 32-bit versions of dBASE (from Visual dBASE 7 on to present releases) called "AutoType". What this means is that if you want to output a date with some character values as well, dBASE will handle an automatic conversion to character for you. In older versions of dBASE you had to jump through some hoops sometimes to get a string such as *(these examples assume the date is set to American format)*:

```
dBirthday = { 05/27/1958 }
? "Birthday is: "+dtoc( dBirthday )
```

In current versions of dBASE, all you have to do is:

```
dBirthday = { 05/27/1958 }
? "Birthday is: "+dBirthday
```

This saves a bit of effort for the developer.

However, there may be times when the autotype capability isn't what you need and dBASE has the following functions built in to help convert between different types of data:

- CTOD() – Character to Date
- CTODT() – Character to DateTime

- CTOT() – Character to Time
- DTOC() – Date to Character
- DTOJ() or DTOH() – Displays the date in a character string format (JavaScript?), such as:
    Tuesday, April 05, 2005
    (These two function are not documented in the Online Help)
- DTOS() – Date to String (as noted earlier, YYYYMMDD)
- DTTOC() – DateTime to Character
- STR() – Number to Character
- TTOC() – Time to Character
- VAL() – Character to Number
- HTOI() – Hexidecimal to Integer
- ITOH() – Integer to Hexidecimal

The functions listed in this part of the book are a small fraction of what is available. Briefly noted elsewhere in this book is a freeware library of code called the dUFLP (dBASE Users' Function Library Project) which contains a huge amount of functions to enhance what is built in to dBASE, written by dBASE developers over the years and made available for your use so you do not need to reinvent the wheel. This will be discussed in the appendices, including where to get the most current version of this invaluable library of code.

Using Preprocessor Directives

When dBASE PLUS compiles a program file, that file is run through the preprocessor before it is actually compiled. The preprocessor is a separate built-in utility that processes the text of the program file to prepare it for compilation. The preprocessor handles quite a few tasks that the developer never really sees. A developer can take advantage of the preprocessor to do the following:

- Replace constants and "magic numbers" in your code with easy-to-read and easy-to-change identifiers
- Create macro-functions to replace complex expressions with parameters
- Use collections of constant identifiers and macro-functions in multiple program files
- Maintain separate versions of your programs, for example debug and production versions, in the same program files through conditional compilation

In order to do this sort of thing, dBASE has what are called Preprocessor Directives – special commands that are executed when the program is compiled. These commands all begin with a pound sign (#). The following is a listing of the preprocessor directives available:

- #DEFINE – Used to define a constant or a macro function.
- #ELSE – Part of the #IF structure, works like ELSE in an IF/ENDIF structure.
- #ENDIF – The end of the #IF structure.
- #IF – Used to compile some code, based on a condition.
- #IFDEF – If a constant or macro function is defined.
- #IFNDEF – If a constant or macro function is NOT defined.
- #INCLUDE – Inserts the contents of a file at the location of the #INCLUDE statement.
- #PRAGMA – Sets compiler options.
- #UNDEF – Undefines a constant or macro function.

As a coding convention these are normally shown in all upper case, but as with the rest of the programming language of dBL, the preprocessor doesn't really care.

A simple example of the use of some of the directives might be to conditionally compile parts of a program:

```
#DEFINE Shareware true
#IF Shareware
    // insert code that would be used in the case of a shareware
    // version of your program
#ELSE
    // insert different code that would be used if this was a full release
    // of the program.
#ENDIF
```

You could define constants that were used throughout a program:

```
#DEFINE Repeat 10000 // ten thousand
for i = 1 to Repeat
    // perform loop process
next
```

Because you used the #DEFINE statement, if you wanted to change the value while the program was running, you would not be able to. This would be a constant value throughout your program. This is a nice feature, because if your code attempted to change the value, it would not be able to.

If you wanted to have some setup code that you used at the beginning of more than one file, you could create what is called a "header" file and store, say, some definitions there, then use the #INCLUDE statement to include the header file in your program:

```
#INCLUDE <myheader.h>
```

One thing that should be noted – the Preprocessor in dBASE does not understand Source Code Aliases – what this means is that you either need to have the header file in the current folder, include the full path to the file, or place your header files in the folder provided by dBASE (the path below assumes a default installation of the current version dBASE PLUS, on a current version of Windows):

```
C:\Users\username\AppData\Local\dBASE\Plus\Include
```

Some of the other preprocessor functionality will be discussed in other places throughout later chapters of this book (specifically the sections on working with the Windows API). You can always find information on the preprocessor directives in the online help as well.

Using Source Aliases to Manage Your Code

If you have worked with earlier chapters of this book, you've delved into working with Source Code Aliases. This is an aspect of dBASE that can make your life much easier. You can create libraries of code, store them in specific locations, and when you need them, call them without having to remember the paths to the code. For example, earlier in this chapter mention was made of the dUFLP. By using a source code alias, all of the code in the dUFLP can be referenced by using the alias: :dUFLP:

This means that if you wanted to use the "DateEx.cc" class in the dUFLP, you could do so by using:

```
set procedure to :dUFLP:DateEx.cc
```

If you used a full path, then if at some point you moved the dUFLP to another folder on the hard drive, you would have to modify your source code to use the new path. A lot of effort can be saved by using the Source Code Alias. This is discussed in the chapters on working with custom forms, custom reports and toolbars. While it was discussed with parts of the book, it is also useful for *any* library of reusable code.

The definitions of Source Aliases are in the PLUS.INI file. Check information in Chapter 2 for the location of the PLUS.INI file that is actually being used by dBASE on your setup.

The SET PROCEDURE Command

The SET PROCEDURE command, which you have been using if you've been following the various exercises so far, is a very important one to a dBASE programmer.

The purpose is to open a file that contains code that you need to have available for execution at some point. This is very different from running a program, form, or report by simply either double-clicking on it in the Navigator, or using the DO command:

```
do MyProgram
```

When you have a file that has code contained in it that you want to be able to use at some point, you often want to just leave it open. Indeed, you may want to leave several (or even in a complex application many) procedure files open at once.

In all versions of dBASE prior to dBASE PLUS 2.5, you had to use the keyword "ADDITIVE" at the end of the statement. Why? Because if you use a command such as:

```
set procedure to MyFile.cc
```

Any procedures you may have opened before that will be closed.

This can be disconcerting, to put it mildly. What may happen is that some part of your code stops working for reasons that are far from obvious. You will get error messages that tell you that the file or function was not found. You will start searching, because you know it's there.

To avoid the problem, the keyword "ADDITIVE" is used to tell dBASE to open the file but to leave any previously opened procedure files open.

```
set procedure to MyFile.cc additive
```

While this book is focusing on dBASE PLUS 2.8, it is possible that some readers are using older versions of dBASE. However, the R&D team at dBASE have modified the way this works. The "ADDITIVE" keyword is assumed when you use the SET PROCEDURE command. This means that you do not really need it **IF** you are using dBASE PLUS 2.5 or a later release. It will not hurt anything, but it is not necessary either. Most or all of the examples in this book no longer use the "ADDITIVE" keyword.

In addition to the ADDITIVE keyword there is another keyword that not very many developers use as it is a relatively recent addition to the language, called "PERSISTENT". What this does is it leaves the procedure open, even if you issue a CLOSE PROCEDURE command. The only way to be sure to close a procedure that is opened with the PERSISTENT keyword is to either issue CLOSE PROCEDURE PERSISTENT, or specifically name a procedure file to be closed:

```
close procedure MyFile.cc
```

When you are "cleaning up" memory from some process, if you opened a procedure file, it is a good idea to close it. There is more information on these commands in the online help.

Debugging Your Programs

When you write code, you will introduce errors ... this is human nature. Errors, or bugs, that may occur in dBASE programs include the following:

- Compilation Errors – syntax errors in the code. These are usually typos – places where you typed the wrong thing, misspelled a command, left off a quote or parenthesis, etc. Some of these can be seen easily in the Source Code Editor, some of them may not be as obvious. When you try to compile or run your program, form, report, etc., an error dialog will occur, allowing you to fix the problem, ignore it, etc.
- Runtime Errors – These errors are usually cases where dBASE has been told to do something it cannot do, such as open a non-existent file.
- Logical Errors – These are sometimes the most perplexing to a developer, because they look okay in the Source Code Editor, the program compiles, but when you run them something does not work properly.

The last type of bug is the worst, because you can damage data by writing incorrect values.

dBASE comes with a full debugger. However, it has been found to be rather complex to use and have found that it has many flaws in it. There is quite a lot of useful information in the online help for working with the debugger and if you wish to do so, it is recommended spending some time looking at the help that comes up when you start the debugger itself. Unfortunately, I have never spent any time working with the debugger and as such, I am not providing any information on its use here.

There are other ways to debug your code. The simplest is to use the question mark (?) character for output. You can determine what is happening in your code fairly easily, by simply inserting statements like:

```
? "The value of 'n' before calling function MyFunc(): "+n
```

This kind of statement shows you exactly where you are in the code and the value of the variable at the time. You can use this for properties of objects, the value of a field and so on. You can insert this kind of statement all over the place, if you are not sure what is happening to some value and eventually track down the error. Some developers use calls to the *msgbox()* function, which is fine except that you have to interact with these, which is certainly an option. However be ready for the fact that they will pop up and you *have* to interact with them, where if you use the ? style of tracking values you do not.

One other means of debugging your code is to use the object Inspector in dBASE. You can insert a command such as:

```
inspect( MyObj )
```

Where "MyObj" is an object reference. This will display the Inspector and you can examine the properties of the object. For example, if you have an instance of a form called "myform", you might use the *findInstance()* function:

```
f = findInstance( "myform" )
```

```
inspect( f )
```

This would display the Inspector showing the properties of the object at the time. You can then drill down to any form objects (objects on the form), if needed, to see them.

Testing Methods, Fixing Program Errors

When you work on an application, you must do at least some testing yourself ... the more thorough the better. As a developer, you can find the most egregious errors, but it is a good idea to not rely on your own testing. One difficulty that many developers find themselves in is that since you wrote the code, you know how it should work and so you often don't think of some of the ways your user may try to work with your application. This can cause a lot of confusion.

Compiling the Code

One simple way to find errors is to compile your code. The compiler will find the most egregious problems – the typos, the missing quotes, etc. This can be done quite easily, you can do it from the Navigator, or from the Command Window. Using the Navigator, select the file to compile, right click, and select the "Compile" option. If you are using the Command Window, there is a command called "COMPILE":

```
compile MyForm.wfm
```

You can also call the compiler from within the Source Code Editor, by going to the "Build" menu, then selecting "Compile".

In any case, the compiler will bring up a dialog that tells you the number of lines, etc., if an error occurs it will tell you about that.

Visual Review

Visual Review is literally going over the code by hand and checking it for errors. The Source Code Editor can be useful with this, because some errors (such as a missing quote) will appear in red (by default – if you changed this in the editor properties it will appear however you defined it).

One aspect of Visual Review that many developers don't do is to have another developer read over their code. Sometimes errors, especially ones in logic, may jump out to another developer that you may not see right away. If you have to explain it to someone else, sometimes the logic falls into place and you can fix the problem.

Running Portions of the Application

Obviously running your application as you develop it will help you find problems. You can check results, you can run a form and make sure that the validation works properly, etc. However, as noted earlier, the developer can often be too close to his or her own code and so you may want to go to the next option.

Remember that with the Command Window you can also try out parts of the code without having to run everything. This can save you hours of debugging or testing.

Observing Others Running the Application

If this is possible, it is a good way to get a feel for how well the application works. You can watch how users or others actually interact with your application. They may tell you places where the interface does not make sense, or if they understand some aspect of the business that you are writing the application for better than you, they can tell you that your calculation is not correct and what is wrong with it.

Relying on others is sometimes hard for a developer to do, but it is a really great way to help you find those problems that are not obvious.

Using Code to Trap Errors

dBASE comes with some useful functionality to help you out when you need to be able to trap errors in your code and perhaps have your users contact you.

ON ERROR

This command, while left over from earlier days of dBASE, is still useful. It allows you to display an error, call a function, whatever you need to do. A fairly complex set of routines could be created to handle dealing with errors, including logging them (if you wanted to do the work), you could even set up the application so that it could email the information to you. For more information about this command, see the online help.

Application Object Error Handling

dBASE PLUS has some functionality that was added in a release of dB2K, that allows you to specify what dBASE should do if an error occurs in the code. This is quite handy, as you can actually have dBASE log information for you! This is done using the _app object, and the setting the following properties:

errorAction – This is the default action to be taken when an error is encountered. The options are:

- 0 – Quit – when an error occurs shut down.
- 1 – Send HTML Error & Quit – display an HTML error, then quit – this is useful for web applications.
- 2 – Log Error & Quit – store the error in a log file and then quit.
- 3 – Send HTML Error, Log Error & Quit – also aimed at web applications.
- 4 – Show Error Dialog (Default) – this is the default setting – it will show an error message.
- 5 – Log Error & Show Error Dialog – save the error in the log file, and show the error dialog for the user.

errorLogFile – Filename of the error log file to be used when the _app object's *errorAction* property is set to 2,3, or 5.

errorLogMaxSize – Approximate maximum size of the error log file (kilobytes)

errorHTMFile – Filename of an HTM file template (runtime web apps only). This can be useful, but some developers prefer more control than what is provided, or they prefer to store different information in the log file than what is stored by dBASE. However, this can be handled as well (see below).

In dBASE Plus 2.6, the developers added a new _app object property:
errorTrapFilter which can be used to limit what is trapped by the error handler. The default is "0 - Trap all errors"; the second is the reason the property was created. If you set this property to "1 - Ignore interpreter memory access violations", then some "crashes" caused for unknown reasons will not occur in a deployed (using the Runtime) application.

TRY/CATCH/ENDTRY

The TRY/CATCH/ENDTRY structure is very useful for catching errors. It uses a special class called an EXCEPTION class, designed to store information about an error. The basic syntax is:

```
try
   // some code
catch( EXCEPTION NameOfException )
   // do something if the error occurs
endtry
```

This is actually more complex as there is an optional section (FINALLY) and you can have more than one CATCH.

```
try
   // some code
catch( EXCEPTION NameOfException )
   // do something if the error occurs
catch( EXCEPTION secondException )
   // do something here
finally
   // do something no matter what happened with the errors
endtry
```

To understand this better, you need to understand the Exception class and the *throw* command.

The Exception Class

The Exception class is used to actually handle the error and has several properties that can be used. You should note that there are really two different Exception classes – the first is simply called Exception, the second is DBException, which can (should) be used if you are working with data and wish to specifically trap errors that might come from the database engine. The DBException class has a secondary class that it uses, called DBError, that actually contains the error information.

If you are working with the data classes of dBASE, you should use the DBException class, otherwise if you are just working in your code normally you should use the normal Exception class.

What can you do with these classes? At the most basic, you can display errors, or determine what to do if a specific error occurs. All errors in dBASE have an error number and an error message. You could do something like:

```
try
   // do some code
catch( Exception E )
   msgbox( "Error number: "+e.code+chr(13)+;
      "Message: "+e.message+chr(13)+;
      "Program: "+e.filename+chr(13)+;
      "Line: "+e.lineno,;
      "Unexpected Error!", 16 )
   return
endtry
```

This would display an error dialog on the screen for the user, showing the error code, the message, the program that the error occurred in and the line number. All of this could be used to have your user contact you with that information so you could try to find the problem.

You could get fancier and check for specific errors (using e.code, for example). I have had situations in my own applications where if one specific error occurs, I am fine and don't need to alert the user, but any other error I would want to know about. So I check for a specific error, and don't do anything, otherwise the code will display an error dialog.

The DBException Class

The DBException class is aimed at catching errors returned by the database engine and storing them in an array. This means that in order to use this class when trapping data errors, you cannot just use properties as shown, but must actually drill down one level in the object hierarchy to the array of dbError objects.

```
try
    form.database1.applyUpdates()
catch (DbException e)
    msgbox("Cached updates failed to post", "Fatal error", 16)
    local n
    for n = 1 to e.errors.size
        ? e.errors[ n ].nativeCode, e.errors[ n ].message
    next
endtry
```

THROW

You can also create your own exception classes, which might add their own properties, etc. The online help shows an example that we will use here. The example assumes you are working with some deeply nested code, and want a way out if some specific error occurs. You would define a custom exception class:

```
class JumpException of Exception
endclass
```

Then in the code, you create the JumpException object and THROW it if needed:

```
try

    local j
    j = new JumpException()
    // Lots of nested code
    // ...
                        if lItsNoGood
                            throw j // Deep in the code, you
                                    // want out
                        endif

catch (JumpException e)
    // Do nothing; JumpException is OK
catch (Exception e)
    // Normal error
    logError(new Date(), e.message) // Record error message
    // and continue
endtry
```

In the example above, the function logError() would be a custom function designed to write out the error message to a log file. What would happen is that when the code is executing, if the logical variable "lItsNoGood" is set to a value of *true*, your code would "throw" the exception – cause the exception to occur and kick you out of the nested code, without your needing to deal with, say, multiple EXIT statements or something.

With a bit of thought you could create a fairly elaborate set of your own custom exceptions and create a good set of error handling routines.

Shortcuts

Most dBL commands and many dBL functions, allow the use of a four-letter shortcut, such as:

```
modi comm MyProgram
```

instead of:

```
modify command MyProgram
```

I find that while this is possible (sometimes I use these in the Command Window), I do not tend to use the shortcuts in my code. I prefer, as noted very early in this chapter, self-documenting code – code that is readable to both me and to other developers.

This gets stickier when you get into working with methods and events, as you have to use the full name for those or dBASE will not find them and your code will generate errors.

I recommend against using the four-letter short cuts in the long run – they can lead to bad coding habits.

Built-In Functions and Other Commands

We have briefly looked at some of the built-in functions in dBASE, but we have only scratched the surface. There are a vast amount of functions and commands available to you as a developer that we have not even come close to covering because there is no way to include them all. The best thing that can be suggested is that as you start developing your applications, if you cannot find what you need in this book, you go straight to the online help – you might be surprised at what is there.

Summary

We covered a lot of material in this chapter, starting with basic programming concepts such as working with memory variables, all the way through trapping errors. There is a lot to absorb, but hopefully this chapter will help you get started with writing dBL programs. Further chapters will get into more complex topics, so if you are not real comfortable with some of what we have discussed, go over the examples and do some experimenting to be sure you understand it.

You can find more information about individual commands in the online help and in many cases, some sample code that might help you understand it as well. It should be noted that this chapter of the book does not cover every single function or dBL programming statement that you might need to use as a developer ... there is only so much space. If you examine the samples in the chapters of this book, work with the online help and Knowledgebase, you can figure out how to do just about anything.

A dBASE developer's best resource outside of this book and the OLH is the dBASE user groups provided by the developer. It is free and you can obtain a lot of useful advice and code there.

Chapter 22: dBASE's Non-Visual Objects

To this point we have discussed the visual classes used for forms and reports, the data classes used to manipulate data and the error exception classes. dBASE has quite a few other built-in classes that you, as a developer should be aware of and that is the focus of this chapter. We will be taking a look at arrays, associative arrays, the file class, date class, math class, string class, and timer class *(not necessarily in that order)*. These classes may be quite useful at some point as you start building your applications and deserve some of your attention.

Using Arrays

In the DOS versions of dBASE an array was not considered an object and in order to use it, a lot of functions were created to work with arrays. These functions still exist in dBL and they work with array objects but the array itself has matching methods built into it that can be used to manipulate the array. For the purposes of this book we will focus on the OOP methods of the array rather than the array functions, but if you are familiar with those they still work. Because arrays are as useful as they are, we will spend more time on them then on some of the other non-visual classes discussed in this chapter.

So what exactly *is* an array? An array object is a collection of variables that can be used to store information. It can be used as a "virtual table", or simply a bunch of data. An array allows you to use a single name for multiple memory locations. A simple array contains one "dimension" or column of information.

An array in dBASE is a "ragged" array – this means that you can store different types of data in the same array. One element might store a date, another a number, a third a character value – dBASE doesn't care – at least until you try to sort the data or search it – then you may have problems *(this is a hint that while you **can** store different types in a column, it is not a good idea to do so)*. A dBASE array can also store other arrays – there are two ways to do this – either storing an array as an element in another array; or as a multi-dimensional array – which is by definition, an array of arrays.

An array must have the following:

- An object reference variable, or name. Okay – most of the time an array requires a name – there is a special construct in dBASE called a "Literal Array", which will be examined in more detail later in this chapter which does not require a name.
- Elements –elements are the containers or perhaps you might say "cells", used to store the data in the array.
- Dimensions – Arrays can be single-dimension (Rows only (one column – see below)), two-dimensional (rows and columns) or even three or more dimensions. You can think of a three dimensional array as something like a three-dimensional tic-tac-toe board, with rows and columns on each level and the different levels being the third dimension. Another way to think of a three (or more) dimensional array is an "array of arrays". There is no easy way to visualize anything beyond "three-dimensional" arrays. For the purposes of this book we will not explore arrays with more than two dimensions.
- Rows – All arrays have rows. A row may contain any supported data type in dBASE, including another array (ragged arrays).

12

- Columns – All arrays have at least one column. If the array has only one column, it is considered to be a single-dimensional array. If you have two or more columns, it is at least a two-dimensional array. If you consider a two-dimensional array as being sort of like a table, each column is comparable to a field and each row is comparable to a record.
- Subscripts –subscripts are indexes to the elements in the array. If we have a single-column array with five rows in it, the subscript would point to each row. If we have a multi-column array, then one subscript refers to the row, another to the column. This is how we get to each element of the array. To differentiate an array from a function, we use square brackets (called in the Language Reference: Index Operators) around the subscript(s).

```
Example 1:
        Column 1
Row 1   San Francisco
Row 2   Los Angeles
Row 3   New York
Row 4   Miami
Row 5   Sydney
```

We would reference row 3 of an array defined like this with a subscript pointing to row three:

```
aCity[3]
Example 2:
        Column 1        Column 2
Row 1   San Francisco    4,000,000
Row 2   Los Angeles     10,000,000
Row 3   New York        25,000,000
Row 4   Miami            8,000,000
Row 5   Sydney           1,000,000
```

In a two (or more)-column array, to get to a specific element, we need to reference both the row and the column, so to point to the population of New York, we would use:

```
aCity[3,2]
```

The first subscript (3) points to the row, the second (2) to the column.

So, what's so great about arrays and why are they so useful?

As previously noted, by using an array you only have one name to worry about for a list. However, even better – an array can be quite dynamic – you can easily add or remove elements in the array, sort the contents of the array, and search an array to see if some value is contained within it. Try doing all of that with a list of memory variables as shown below:

```
City1 = "San Francisco"
City2 = "Los Angeles"
City3 = "New York"
City4 = "Miami"
City5 = "Sydney"
```

The following three lines of code can display all the city names from an array, which is much more efficient and compact code than needed to display each variable separately:

```
for i = 1 to ( aCity.size / aCity.dimensions )
    ? aCity[ i, 1 ]
next
```

If we used a variable for each individual city name, we would have to have a line of code to print each city name – three statements to do this are much better.

In addition, by storing the values in memory, processing a list is much faster than it is in a table.

You can use an array to emulate a table – if you use a two-dimensional array, the rows may be equivalent to records and the columns equivalent to fields. If you think of an array as similar to a spreadsheet, this may help as well. The fun part is, with modern spreadsheet software, you can create three-dimensional spreadsheets (multiple pages), which can be done with arrays in dBASE, as well.

How Do I Define An Array?

First off, you need to tell dBASE that you are going to use an array. This means you have to a) give a name; b) instantiate the array:

```
arrayname = NEW ARRAY()
```

If you wanted the array to start out with a specific size, you could state:

```
aCity = NEW ARRAY(5,2)
```

Which would start the array with 10 elements – five rows with two columns each.

There's one other method to create a one-dimensional array, but this assumes you already know what you want to put into it. This uses what is called a "Literal Array":

```
aCity = {"San Francisco","Los Angeles","New York","Miami","Sydney"}
```

A literal array uses braces and each element of the array is separated by a comma. *(We will come back to these later in this chapter.)*

Now You Have Defined The Array, How Do You Put Data In It?

An array is useless without data. One interesting bit is that if you do not populate the array, dBASE automatically places a logical value of *false* in each element that is not assigned another value – at least, this is what it appears as – in reality this is an empty cell and use of the *empty()* function will return a *true* value on a cell that has not been assigned a value. This can be useful and also be a bit annoying at times if you're trying to perform specific tasks (like sorting an array). For example, if you try to sort on character, numeric or date values and some of the elements have not been assigned values, or have been deleted (see below), you will get a "Data type mismatch" error.

Assigning values to an array can be as simple as typing in values:

```
aCity[1] = "San Francisco"    // requires you keep track of the
                              // subscript
```

or

```
aCity.Add("San Francisco")    // uses the object _method_ add()
```

or

```
aCity = {"San Francisco","Los Angeles","New York","Miami","Sydney"}
```

To place information in an array from a table you can use the XDML command COPY TO ARRAY (there is no OODML equivalent to this) and you can also create your own looping structure to loop through a table and add data to an array that way.

There are other methods of filling an array, as well. A lot depends on what you need to use the array for. For example, if you wanted to store two fields, such as first and last names in one array, you could store it as two columns, or as a single column. However, for a single column, you may want to store the name as "Last, First", for example *(so that when you sort the data it is sorted by last name)*.

There are two methods of loading data a table into an array that loop through the table, the first is a bit more complex and isn't really necessary – it is here to show the elegance of the second form (this code uses OODML):

```
q = new Query()
q.sql = "select * from mytable"
q.active=true
r = q.rowset
nMax = r.count()        // number of records in table
aNames = new array(nMax) // define array
for nRow = 1 to nMax // process table record-by-record
   // add name to the nRowth element of the array
   aNames[nRow] = trim( r.fields["last"].value )+;
                       r.fields["first"].value
   r.next()            // move to next row
next                   // end of loop
```

This will do the job. However, check out the simpler and more elegant method shown below:

```
q = new Query()
q.sql = "select * from mytable"
q.active=true
r = q.rowset
aNames = new Array()
r.first()
do while not r.endOfSet // process table ...
   // add name to new row of the array
   aNames.add( trim( r.fields["last"].value )+;
                   r.fields["first"].value )
   r.next()            // move to next row
enddo
```

There is no need to worry about a subscript, or to determine the size of the array before we add items to it. This is much simpler.

As you can see, arrays are quite flexible –the confusion some developers have with them stems from this flexibility!

Deleting Data in an Array

There are times when manipulating an array that you may want to delete an element, row, or column. There is a trick to this, because when you use the methods in dBASE to handle deleting one of these (element, row or column), dBASE moves the element/row/column to the end of the array and replaces the element(s)'s values with *false* (in reality, "empty" – see below). If you use the array sorting method in dBASE on an array in which you have deleted an element/row/column, you will get an error. The end of this section will show you how to avoid the error with the *resize()* method.

To delete an element in a single-dimensional array:

```
arrayname.Delete(element)
```

For example, in the aCity array, which looks like:

```
          Column 1
Row 1     San Francisco
Row 2     Los Angeles
Row 3     New York
Row 4     Miami
Row 5     Sydney
```

If we wanted to remove the second element:

```
aCity.delete(2)
```

The array would contain the following values after executing the command shown above:

```
          Column 1
Row 1     San Francisco
Row 2     New York
Row 3     Miami
Row 4     Sydney
Row 5     false
```

To delete a row (single or multiple dimensional array):

```
arrayname.Delete(nRow,1) // second parameter = row (1) or column (2)
```

Assuming a two column version of the aCity array that looked like:

```
          Column 1         Column 2
Row 1     San Francisco     4,000,000
Row 2     Los Angeles      10,000,000
Row 3     New York         25,000,000
Row 4     Miami             8,000,000
Row 5     Sydney            1,000,000
```

To delete the second row of this array, the command:

```
aCity.Delete(2,1)
```

Would leave the array looking like this:

```
        Column 1        Column 2
Row 1   San Francisco    4,000,000
Row 2   New York        25,000,000
Row 3   Miami            8,000,000
Row 4   Sydney           1,000,000
Row 5   false           false
```

To delete a column (multiple columnar array):

```
arrayname.Delete(nColumn,2) // second parameter = row (1) or col (2)
```

Assuming the aCity array looks like:

```
        Column 1        Column 2      Column 3
Row 1   San Francisco    4,000,000        678
Row 2   Los Angeles     10,000,000        123
Row 3   New York        25,000,000        456
Row 4   Miami            8,000,000        678
Row 5   Sydney           1,000,000       1234
```

The command to delete the second column would be:

```
aCity.Delete(2,2)   // first 2 is column, second tells dBASE it's
                    // a column you are deleting
```

Which would give us an array that looked like:

```
        Column 1        Column 2      Column 3
Row 1   San Francisco       678         false
Row 2   Los Angeles         123         false
Row 3   New York            456         false
Row 4   Miami               678         false
Row 5   Sydney             1234         false
```

In all three cases shown, the problem is, as noted, the element/row/column deleted will still exist in the array.

So, you then use the *resize()* method to remove the row or column:

```
arrayname.Resize(nNumRows,nNumCols) // number of rows/columns
                                    // the array will have after
                                    // execution
```

The following examples are combined code for the previous examples:

Removing an element from a single-dimension array:

```
aCity.Delete(2)
nRows = aCity.size
aCity.Resize(nRows-1)
```

Removing a row of a multi-column array (which removes all elements in the row):

```
aCity.Delete(2,1)
nRows = aCity.subscript( aCity.size,1)
aCity.Resize(nRows-1)
```

Removing a column from a multi-column array:

```
aCity.Delete(2,2)
nColumns = aCity.subscript( aCity.size,2)
nRows = aCity.subscript( aCity.size,1)
// Note, the ROWS parameter here must contain a value > 0
aCity.Resize(nRows,nColumns-1)
```

Referencing/Displaying Data in an Array

There are many ways to work with arrays. Once you have the data in the array, it is usually necessary to do something with that data, either using it for lookups, or whatever. So the question becomes "How do I reference the data in an array?"

The most important thing to remember is that you need to assign a subscript to the individual elements. If you are working with a multi-column array, you may want to use specific naming conventions for your subscript variables, such as "nRow" and "nColumn". This way you will not be as likely to get your subscripts confused. If you mix up your subscripts, you will either get an error ("subscript out of range" is most likely) or the wrong data. An easy way to get them mixed up is to use names like "x" and "y" to refer to them. (In a single column array, you can use any subscript reference you like, to point to the rows.)

So, how do you look at the elements of an array?

If you know the specific element you wish to look for, you can reference it with a number for the subscript. Assuming an array that looks like:

```
        Column 1
Row 1   San Francisco
Row 2   Los Angeles
Row 3   New York
Row 4   Miami
Row 5   Sydney

? aCity[2]
```

Will display "Los Angeles".

If the array aCity contains more than one column, however, you need to use another subscript to specify the column. Assuming the following array:

```
        Column 1        Column 2
Row 1   San Francisco    4,000,000
Row 2   Los Angeles     10,000,000
Row 3   New York        25,000,000
Row 4   Miami            8,000,000
Row 5   Sydney           1,000,000

? aCity[2,2]   // display contents of the element at
               // the second row, second column
```

This will display 10,000,000.

You can loop through an array to do some processing:

```
for nRow = 1 to aCity.size    // the size property is the number of
                              // elements in the array
   ? aCity[nRow]              // display the contents of the
                              // current element
next
```

This will display the contents of the array:

```
San Francisco
Los Angeles
New York
Miami
Sydney
```

Again, if you have multiple columns in the array, you will need to reference the column as well. If your array has three columns and you wanted to simply display the contents of the elements in all three columns for each row, you would want to nest a loop, along the following lines:

```
// the subscript method of the array returns
// either the number of rows or the number
// of columns ...:
nRows    = oArray.subscript( oArray.size, 1)
nColumns = oArray.subscript( oArray.size, 2)

for nRow = 1 to nRows
    for nColumn = 1 to nColumns
        ? aCity[nRow,nColumn]  // display the current element
    next  // nColumn
next  // nRow
```

This would display (assuming the example from earlier of a three-column array):

```
San Francisco
 4,000,000
       678
Los Angeles
10,000,000
       123
New York
25,000,000
       456
Miami
 8,000,000
       678
Sydney
 1,000,000
      1234
```

Not very pretty, but the contents are displayed. To make this more "pretty" you could write code along these lines, this example assumes that you are creating a "generic" printing routine to display in the Command Window the output of a multi-columnar array:

```
// ShowArray1.prg
parameter oArray
if type( "oArray" ) # "A"
```

```
   ? "Not an array!"
   return
endif

nRows    = oArray.subscript( oArray.size, 1)
nColumns = oArray.subscript( oArray.size, 2)
// display column headers
for nColumn = 1 to nColumns
    // assumes that each column will contain < 25 characters
    ?? "Column "+nColumn at (20*(nColumn-1))+7
next

// display items in each row for each column
for nRow = 1 to nRows
    // row header
    ? "Row "+nRow
    for nColumn = 1 to nColumns
        // actual element to be displayed
        ?? oArray[nRow,nColumn]  at (20*(nColumn-1))+7
    next
next
```

To use this with the aCity array:

```
do ShowArray with aCity
```

Which would list the data as:

```
        Column 1          Column 2          Column 3
Row 1   San Francisco     4,000,000              678
Row 2   Los Angeles       10,000,000             123
Row 3   New York          25,000,000             456
Row 4   Miami             8,000,000              678
Row 5   Sydney            1,000,000             1234
```

Sorting the Contents of an Array

Sometimes the data entered into an array is in a jumble, and you want it sorted (either for display purposes or other reasons).

The method to sort the data in an array is:

```
aCity.sort()
```

This sorts the array aCity on the first column. If there are more columns, the rows will all move with the elements in the first column.

Assume the following array before the sort:

```
        Column 1          Column 2
Row 1   San Francisco      4,000,000
Row 2   Los Angeles       10,000,000
Row 3   New York          25,000,000
Row 4   Miami              8,000,000
Row 5   Sydney             1,000,000
```

And after:

```
            Column 1          Column 2
Row 1    Los Angeles       10,000,000
Row 2    Miami              8,000,000
Row 3    New York          25,000,000
Row 4    San Francisco      4,000,000
Row 5    Sydney             1,000,000
```

To sort on the second column:

```
aCity.Sort(2)
```

Which would give us:

```
            Column 1          Column 2
Row 1    Sydney             1,000,000
Row 2    San Francisco      4,000,000
Row 3    Miami              8,000,000
Row 4    Los Angeles       10,000,000
Row 5    New York          25,000,000
```

A Couple of dBL Functions That Are Very Useful When Working With Arrays

The following two functions are quite useful when you are programming with arrays, but are not specific to arrays.

Type()

The *type()* function is used to determine if an object in dBASE is defined (if it isn't, this function returns a value of "U"), if it is an object (while an Array is an object, it's a special type) – this returns an "O", or other types (Character, etc.). If the object you are examining is an array, the function returns an "A". Example:

```
? type("aCity")
```

If this is an array, you should get: "A"

If this is a "normal" dBASE object, you should see: "O"

If the array (or object) has not been defined, you should see: "U"

In addition, this function can return the type of the contents of an element of an array. Example:

```
? type("aCity[1]")
```

Might return "C" for Character, "N" for Numeric, etc. *(See the previous chapter for more information.)*

Empty()

The *empty()* function can be used on elements of an array to determine if they are really empty (undefined), or contain a value of *false*.

Why is this important? dBL shows *false* if you print an element of an array that contains a logical *false* value, OR if the array element has not had any value assigned to it. This can be a bit confusing. So, to see if something is false, versus empty:

```
// check for _false_  and not empty()
if aCity[1] == false and not empty(aCity[1])
```

To see if it is empty:

```
if empty(aCity[1]) // returns true if empty, false if it has a value
```

Making an Array Larger

If you have a multi-columnar array, the *add()* method will not work properly. It will allow you to add items in the first column, but not any others. Instead, you should consider using the *grow()* method to handle this.

```
arrayname.Grow(<type>)
where <type>    =    1 for a row
                     2 for a column
```

Example — if we have this array:

```
           Column 1          Column 2
Row 1    San Francisco     4,000,000
Row 2    Los Angeles      10,000,000
Row 3    Miami             8,000,000
Row 4    New York         25,000,000
```

And we want to add elements to both columns:

```
aCity.Grow(1)     // add a row
aCity[5,1] = "Sydney"
aCity[5,2] = " 2,000,000"
```

Reminder – the *row* is the first part of the subscript and the *column* is the second. In a situation like this, if you do not know how many rows are currently in the array, you might want to use the *size* property or the *subscript()* method, to ensure you are in the correct row:

```
aCity.Grow(1) // add a row
// number of rows in array
nRow = aCity.subscript( aCity.size, 1)
aCity[nRow,1] = "Sydney"
aCity[nRow,2] = " 2,000,000"
```

Which would give us an array that looks like:

```
           Column 1          Column 2
Row 1    San Francisco     4,000,000
Row 2    Los Angeles      10,000,000
Row 3    Miami             8,000,000
Row 4    New York         25,000,000
Row 5    Sydney            2,000,000
```

The *grow()* method is useful as well if you wish to add a column to your array. Backing this up a step, if we had aCity defined as a single-column array:

```
        Column 1
Row 1   San Francisco
Row 2   Los Angeles
Row 3   Miami
Row 4   New York
Row 5   Sydney
```

and we wanted to add a second column:

```
aCity.Grow(2)   // add a column
```

Of course, at this point, the array would look like:

```
        Column 1        Column 2
Row 1   San Francisco     false
Row 2   Los Angeles       false
Row 3   Miami             false
Row 4   New York          false
Row 5   Sydney            false
```

Which means we would want to add data to the column. This could be done with:

```
aCity[1,2]  =  "4,000,000"
aCity[2,2]  =  "10,000,000"
aCity[3,2]  =  "8,000,000"
aCity[4,2]  =  "25,000,000"
aCity[5,2]  =  "2,000,000"
```

This will give us the array:

```
        Column 1         Column 2
Row 1   San Francisco     4,000,000
Row 2   Los Angeles      10,000,000
Row 3   Miami             8,000,000
Row 4   New York         25,000,000
Row 5   Sydney            2,000,000
```

The *insert()* Method

Sometimes it is desirable to add an element to an array at a location other than the end of the array. To do this, you would want to use the *insert()* method to place the element(s) into the array at the appropriate location(s).

```
arrayname.Insert(<position>[,<type>])
     where <position>   =    position you wish to insert at
                 <type> =    1 for a row (optional for a row)
                             2 for a column
```

Working with a single column array, assuming your array looked like the following:

```
            Column 1
Row  1     San Francisco
Row  2     Los Angeles
Row  3     New York
Row  4     Sydney
```

And you wanted to insert a row at 3, that contained "Miami":

```
aCity.Insert(3)
```

This will give you an array that looks like:

```
            Column 1
Row  1     San Francisco
Row  2     Los Angeles
Row  3     false
Row  4     New York
```

And then you would need to change the value of the element in row 3:

```
aCity[3] = "Miami"
```

NOTE: the last row now contains "New York", which is what you would expect to be the last row, "Sydney" is missing. This is because the *insert()* method literally inserts something into the current array, but does not resize it – this is as designed.

In order to make the array one row larger, as well as inserting a row into the array, you would need to use the *grow()* method *before* using the *insert()* method:

```
aCity.Grow(1)    // 1 for row, 2 for column
aCity.Insert(3) // new row at 3
aCity[3] = "Miami"
```

Which would produce:

```
            Column 1
Row  1     San Francisco
Row  2     Los Angeles
Row  3     Miami
Row  4     New York
Row  5     Sydney
```

If you are working with a multi-column array, you might wish to insert a new column into the array. This would be done in a similar fashion. If you had an array that looked like:

```
            Column 1          Column 2
Row  1     San Francisco      4,000,000
Row  2     Los Angeles       10,000,000
Row  3     Miami              8,000,000
Row  4     New York          25,000,000
Row  5     Sydney             2,000,000
```

And you wanted to shift column 2 to the right, making it column 3 and have a new column 2 that you could use for some other set of values:

```
aCity.Grow(2)       // add a new column
aCity.Insert(2,2) // insert a new column at column 2
```

This would give an array that looked like:

```
           Column 1        Column 2     Column 3
Row 1   San Francisco      false        4,000,000
Row 2   Los Angeles        false       10,000,000
Row 3   Miami              false        8,000,000
Row 4   New York           false       25,000,000
Row 5   Sydney             false        2,000,000
```

And again, you could replace the values in the new column:

```
aCity[1,2] = whatever
etc.
```

Adding Default Values Into An Array – *fill()*

Fill() is used to place values into an array – filling an array with default values, for example.

```
arrayname.Fill(<value>[,<start>[,<numelements>]])
          where  <value>              = value to fill the array with
                 <start>              = (optional) start position
                 <numelements>        = (optional) number of elements to fill
```

Example – If you were using an array to total some values, you might want to default everything in the array to 0:

```
aTotal = new array(20)
aTotal.Fill(0)
```

You can specify a starting location, so that if you only wanted the last 15 elements to be filled, you could specify:

```
aTotal.Fill(0,6)   // start at element six
```

You can also specify the number of elements to fill. If you wanted just the first five elements set to 0:

```
aTotal.Fill(0,1,5)
```

Directory Listings – *dir()* and *dirExt()*

For some situations, it is desirable to grab information from the directory. You may wish to give your user an option to open a specific table, for example. To do that, it is useful to give them a list of all tables in the directory.

This can be done with the dir() and dirExt() methods.

```
arrayname.Dir(<skeleton>)
          or
arrayname.DirExt(<skeleton>)
   where <skeleton> =       file skeleton – you can specify the
                            file type, for example, using standard
                            DOS wildcards (*, ?).
```

Example:

```
aTables = new array()
aTables.Dir("*.DBF")
```

Will get you all the .DBF files in the current directory. The only problem is, this will return the following columns:

1	2	3	4	5
Filename	Size	Date	Time	File Attributes (DOS)
Character	Numeric	Date	Character	Character

What if all you really wanted was the filenames?

One simple solution is to copy the elements from the first column to another array:

```
aTable1 = new array()
aTable1.Dir("*.DBF")
aTable2 = new Array()
                                    // number of rows in first array
for nRow = 1 to aTable1.subscript( aTable1.size,1)
   aTable2.Add(aTable1[nRow,1]) // add just the element in the
                               // first column
next
```

The second array will contain only the file names.

However, there is a shorter option and that is to use the *resize()* method to change the number of columns in the array.

```
aTable = new Array()
aTable.Dir("*.DBF")
// drop the table to one column - the first one
aTable.resize( aTable.subscript(aTable.size, 1) , 1, 1 )
```

You may wish to allow the user to see the "Short Filename". To get this information, instead of using the *dir()* method, use the *dirExt()* method:

```
aTable1.DirExt("*.DBF")
```

This will return an array with the same information as the DIR() method, but it will add additional columns to the right:

6	7	8	9
Filename "Alias"	Date Created	Time Created	Last Access Date
DOS Filename	Date	Character	Date
(Short name)			

The first column will hold the Windows "long" filename.

Storing the Records (or Certain Fields) in a Table Into an Array
NOTE: the following are XDML (XBase DML commands) – there is no equivalent for these using OODML.

```
COPY TO ARRAY <arrayname> [FIELDS <fieldlist>] [<scope>]
APPEND FROM ARRAY <arrayname>
REPLACE FROM ARRAY <arrayname>
```

These commands allow you to copy a record (or group of records) into an array for processing, then copy the contents of an array (back) to a table.

There are two ways to copy data from a table to an array. If you define an array that is one dimensional, you will only copy one record to the array – but you must define the number of fields to be copied – for example, if you wanted just the first five fields:

```
aMyArray = new array(5)
copy to array aMyArray
```

Will copy the first five fields of the current record to the array aMyArray. Note, that this effectively stores your record in a single column.

If you define an array that has two columns (or more, but only two will be used by this command), you must define the number of records (which equates to the number of rows in the array) and the number of fields (which equates to the number of columns in the array).

The commands:

```
aMyArray = new array(2,3)
copy to array aMyArray
```

will copy the first three fields of the current record and the next record in the table (two records). This is different than the first example, because dBASE actually stores the data in the array as if it were a table – the rows are the records, the columns are the fields (sort of like a grid in dBASE).

If you wanted to copy all records and all fields in a table, you might want to use a combination of the XDML *reccount()* and *fldcount()* functions with the instantiation of the array:

```
aMyArray = new array(reccount(),fldcount())
copy to array aMyArray
```

In addition, you can specify specific fields to copy:

```
aMyArray = new array(reccount(),1) // record count, 1 column
copy to array aMyArray fields FirstName
```

You can also specify a "scope" with the "NEXT" or "FOR" operators ...

There are quite a few options for this, check the Online Help for COPY TO ARRAY.

Coding Your Own
There are many ways to code a routine to fill an array. Below are some examples:

```
// each of these examples assumes that the table was opened
// using the new OODML syntax:
local aTable, r, i, nRows
aTable = new array()
r = queryname.rowset
```

```
r.first() // Make sure we're at the top of the table
nRows = r.count()
for i = 1 to nRows
    aTable.Add(r.fields["fieldname"].value)
    r.next()
next

    // or

local aTable, r
aTable = new array()
r = queryname.rowset
r.first() // Make sure we're at the top of the table
do while not r.endOfSet
    arrayname.Add(r.fields["fieldname"].value)
    r.next()
enddo

    // or (multiple columns)

local aTable, r, nRows, nColumns
aTable = new array( queryname.rowset.count(), queryname.rowset.fields.size
)
r = queryname.rowset
r.first() // Make sure we're at the top of the table
nRows = 0
// loop through the rows:
do while not r.endOfSet
    nRows++ // increment row counter
    // loop through the columns
    for nColumns = 1 to r.fields.size
        aTable[ nRows, nColumns ] = r.fields[ nColumns ].value
    next
    r.next()
enddo
```

Copying an Array

Sometimes it is useful to copy the contents of an array. With a little thought you can probably come up with a few situations where this would be useful, including, but not limited to, keeping a "backup" of the original, in case the user does something truly weird to the data.

The dBL function *aCopy()* is useful here, as it allows you to copy the contents of one array to another *(there is no array method to copy an array to another)*. The simplest way to do this is to ensure that the "target" array has been instantiated and is big enough to hold the contents of the first.

```
aCopy(<SourceArray>,<TargetArray>)
        where  <SourceArray> = the array you are copying from
                <TargetArray> = the array you are copying to
```

If you are copying a one-dimensional array:

```
nRows = aCity.subscript(aCity.size,1)
aBackup = new array(nRows)
aCopy(aCity,aBackup)
```

If you need to copy a multi-column array:

```
nRows = aCity.subscript(aCity.size,1) // row number
nCols = aCity.subscript(aCity.size,2) // column number
aBackup = new array(nRows,nCols)
aCopy(aCity,aBackup)
```

In some situations, you may want to only copy some of the data from one array to another. The *aCopy()* function has parameters to handle this (see the Language Reference for details). In addition, you may simply wish to code your own routine.

Searching An Array

The ability to search an array to find an element can be very useful. In dBL, this is done with the *scan()* method. Basically, this method returns the element of the item you are scanning for, if it is contained in the array.

```
arrayname.scan(<itemtofind>)
         where <itemtofind> = item being searched for.
```

For example, if you wanted to look in the (one-column version of the) aCity array for the city "Miami", the *scan()* method can tell you which row it is in:

```
nFoundRow = aCity.Scan("Miami")
? aCity[nFoundRow]
```

The *scan()* method is case-sensitive – this is quite important when searching character strings.

If you are using this with a multi-column array, it gets more complex, as you will be given the element number, not the row. To make this easier, you can combine the returned value with the *subscript()* method.

```
nElement = aCity.Scan("Miami")
nRow     = aCity.Subscript(nElement,1)
nColumn  = aCity.Subscript(nElement,2)
? aCity[nRow,nColumn]
```

It is important to note that the *scan()* method will return a value of zero if it does not find what you asked it to. You may want to add code to check and see if the value is zero:

```
nElement = aCity.Scan("Miami")
if nElement > 0
   nRow     = aCity.Subscript(nElement,1) // row number
   nColumn  = aCity.Subscript(nElement,2) // column number
   ? aCity[nRow,nColumn]
else
   ? "Not found"
endif
```

The *element()* Method

This method is useful to determine the element number of a specific element in an array.

```
arrayname.Element(<elementnumber/row>[,<column>])
         where  <elementnumber/row> = the element number, or the
                           row when using a multi-dimensional
```

```
                     array.
            <column> = (optional) column number
```

If you're working through an array in some form of processing, you could find the specific element with:

```
    nElement = aCity.Element(1)
```

In a one-dimensional array, the *element()* method is redundant – it's much more useful in a multi-dimensional array. The parameters allow you to specify subscripts – for example, in a two-column array, you could specify the row and the column:

```
    ?aCity.Element(3,2)   // row 3, column 2
```

This should return a value of 6, as this would be the sixth element in this array. If the array had more columns, the value returned would not be 6. For example, in a three column array, using the same command above would return a value of 8. This method is not really all that useful for most developers.

The *subscript()* Method

If you know the element number, you can determine the specific subscript for a multi-column (two-dimensional) array.

```
        arrayname.Subscript(<element>,<type>)
            where <element> =   element number you are looking for
                                the subscript for
                  <type> =      1 for row, 2 for column.
```

Example:

```
    ?aCity.Subscript(nElement,1) // row number
    ?aCity.Subscript(nElement,2) // column number
```

This will give you the actual subscript (row/column) information. You could, instead, display the contents of a specific element, which can be useful if you used the *scan()* method:

```
    nElement = aCity.Scan("25,000,000")
    nRow     = aCity.Subscript(nElement,1)
    nColumn  = aCity.Subscript(nElement,2)
    ? aCity[nRow,nColumn]
```

Using Arrays with dBASE User Interface Objects

In earlier chapters we looked at the various interface controls: comboboxes, listboxes, and tabboxes. Each of these needs to have a *datasource* property – this is where the lists come from. One option for a datasource is an array.

Comboboxes and Listboxes

Comboboxes and Listboxes can use arrays as the datasource.

One caveat – if you try to use a multi-dimensional or multi-column array, you may find your lists looking a bit strange. Example:

```
            Column 1         Column 2
    Row 1   Sydney           1,000,000
    Row 2   San Francisco    4,000,000
```

```
Row 3    Miami            8,000,000
Row 4    Los Angeles     10,000,000
Row 5    New York        25,000,000
```

If you set your datasource property to read: "ARRAY aCity", where "aCity" is an array that looks like the above, what you will get in your combobox or listbox display is:

```
Sydney
 1,000,000
San Francisco
 4,000,000
Miami
 8,000,000
Los Angeles
10,000,000
New York
25,000,000
```

The chances are, this is not what you wanted to happen. (One solution is to copy just the first column of the array into another array.)

In addition, one problem that sometimes drives developers a bit crazy is, "Where do you define your array so that the Form Designer doesn't remove it and it is available when you run the form?"

The reason this question comes up is that when you are designing a form, if the array does not exist, the Form Designer will allow you to continue. However, if you run the form without the array in memory, you will get an error.

So, Where Do You Want to Define Your Array?
A lot depends on where you are getting the data for the array. If the array is a hard-coded array (meaning that the values in it never change) and the only use you have for the array is the list (meaning you do not need to perform any lookups in the array in any other code in your form), you should use a literal array. If the array is coming from a field in a table, you should define this information when the form opens (using the *onOpen* event, or overwritten *open()* and/or *readModal()* methods).

The Literal Array
You can define your literal array either by hand, or by using the built-in visual array designer. To do it by hand, in the *dataSource* property, type:

```
ARRAY {"San Francisco","Los Angeles", etc.}
```

To use the visual array designer, click on the tool button by the *dataSource* Property in the Inspector. This will bring up the designer. This has been discussed in earlier chapters.

The one drawback to a literal array defined in this fashion is, there is NO name for the array. If, for any reason, you need to look at the contents, it will take some extra work on your part (one method is to actually have dBASE show the value of the datasource: form.combobox1.datasource – you can store this into a character memory variable and parse through it, but it's not the most efficient method of working with an array).

If you do need to use the datasource array elsewhere in your code, do NOT use a literal array.

Defining a DataSource Without Using a Literal Array

If you do not want to (or decide it is not in your best interests to) use a literal array, then where and how do you define your array for your datasource?

Two places immediately jump to mind:

1. In the Form's *open()* or *readModal()* method (you would need to overwrite them) or
2. In the Object's *open()* method

In either case, it is a good idea to make the array a custom property of either the form or the object. Otherwise, as soon as you leave the method, the array is no longer in scope (you will get errors that claim the array does not exist) – of course you could make the array public, but this causes problems such as remembering to release your array(s) when you close the form

To do this, when you instantiate the array, you simply add the object reference to the array. Remember – an array is just an object, but in this case, you can make the array a property of another object as well!

```
form.aCity = new array()
```

or

```
form.ComboBox1.aCity = new array()
```

The only drawback is that you must refer to the full "path" to the array any time you need to reference it. The advantage is that you do not need to make this a public array and do not need to worry about releasing the array from memory when you are done with it. When you close the form, the array object will disappear as well, since it is a property of the form (or object) – this makes managing memory a snap!

Once you have instantiated the array, you can then add elements to it as you need to:

```
form.aCity.Add("San Francisco")
form.aCity.Add("Los Angeles")
form.aCity.Add("Miami")
form.aCity.Add("New York")
form.aCity.Add("Sydney")
```

When you do this, do not set the datasource until after you have filled the array. Then add the statement:

```
form.Combobox1.dataSource = "ARRAY form.aCity"
```

or

```
form.Combobox1.dataSource = "ARRAY form.Combobox1.aCity"
```

What Happens If the Array Changes?

In some processing that takes place, the contents of an array may change. dBASE does not always display the changes, which can be rather confusing. The simple fix is to add the following statement after you have updated the contents of the array:

```
form.Combobox1.dataSource = form.Combobox1.dataSource
```

or

```
form.Combobox1.dataSource += ""
```

This forces dBASE to update the *datasource* itself and will cause the display to update as well (this is called "reasserting the datasource").

Array Size Limits

Arrays in dBASE PLUS use an unsigned 32-bit integer to track the total number of elements in an array. The theoretical limit on the total number of elements in an array is (2^{32}) - 1, or 4,294,967,295 elements. You may run out of memory faster than you will run out of the possible number of elements in an array.

Literal Arrays

Literal Arrays have been mentioned earlier in this chapter and there isn't a lot to add to them. A literal array is an array that is created directly by the developer using the curly braces, or is created by the design surfaces (such as the Form Designer) to use as a *dataSource* for a visual control.

The basic syntax is simply:

```
{ somevalue, another value }
```

Where the values shown are what you need to store in the array. By definition a literal array is a single column array, although it is possible to store an array inside of a literal array (including another literal array).

If you assign a literal array to an object reference variable, you can treat it as a normal array:

```
aCity = { "San Francisco", "Los Angeles", "Miami", "New York", "Sydney" }
? aCity[ 1 ]
// etc.
```

This is simply a convenient way to create an array as you write code. These do have their drawbacks – as noted they are single-column arrays; unless you assign an object reference variable to them, they are hard to work with later. If you use one as the *dataSource* for a control, referencing it is more difficult.

Associative Arrays

An Associative Array is an array, but pretty much everything you've learned about arrays in this chapter does not work for them. Associative Arrays are single-column arrays that store a name to reference a value – hence the term "Associative" – a string is used to associate some value with the string. This is similar to the way that items are stored in a .INI file – name/value pairs, where the item on the left is a name and the item on the right is a value.

In the case of an Associative Array, you have to instantiate it as you would a normal array, but there the similarities end. A simple example, based on the list of cities and some numeric value as done in the two column arrays earlier:

```
          Column 1        Column 2
Row 1     San Francisco    4,000,000
Row 2     Los Angeles     10,000,000
Row 3     New York        25,000,000
Row 4     Miami            8,000,000
Row 5     Sydney           1,000,000
```

In this example, an Associative Array would use the city as the key value and the second column as the actual value stored in the array. How do you do that?

```
aPopulation = new AssocArray()
aPopulation["San Francisco"] = "4,000,000"
aPopulation["Los Angeles"] = "10,000,000"
aPopulation["New York"] = "25,000,000"
aPopulation["Miami"] = "8,000,000"
aPopulation["Sydney"] = "1,000,000"
```

One of the most important things that should be noted right up front – the key in an associative array is case sensitive, so if you typed:

```
aPopulation["SAN Francisco"] = "4,000,000"
```

dBASE would see that as another value in the array, completely different from the first item shown.

Another aspect of an associative array that is often confusing the first few times you use them is that while you can add items in any sequence you wish, while looping through the array, the output may not be in the order in which they items were put in the array and there is no means to sort an associative array's elements. We will see that in a moment.

There are not a lot of methods or properties to an associative array, because there don't really need to be. Besides the *className* and *baseClassName* properties that all objects in dBASE have, the only property the associative array has is *firstKey*. This points to the first item in the array and is very useful when looping through an associative array.

The methods that are members of an associative array are *count()*, *isKey()*, *nextKey()*, *removeAll()* and *removeKey()*, pretty basic. The methods to remove elements are pretty straightforward, so we won't worry about them. Let's look at the others.

First is the *isKey()* method, because it is used to determine if a key exists in the associative array. You can check to see if a key exists by using:

```
? aPopulation.isKey( "San Francisco" )
```

This will return either a *true* or a *false* value – either the key exists or it doesn't. You could of course use this in an IF or CASE structure to determine if some code should be processed, add the key if it doesn't exist, etc.

The other important methods are *count()* which returns the number of elements in the array and *nextKey()* which is used to move from the current key to the next one. Both of these are useful when looping through an associative array:

```
cKey = aPopulation.firstKey
for i = 1 to aPopulation.count() // number of elements
    ? cKey + " - " + aPopulation[ cKey ]
```

```
        cKey = aPopulation.nextKey( cKey )
next
```

When run, this code (assuming the array was created and loaded as noted earlier) will produce:

```
Sydney - 1,000,000
San Francisco - 4,000,000
Los Angeles - 10,000,000
New York - 25,000,000
Miami - 8,000,000
```

Notice that this is not the sequence the elements were entered into the associative array. There is no way to sort these values unless you then copy them to a "normal" array class.

The associative array takes some getting used to, but once you start using this class, you may find it very useful. These are used extensively in the web class that ships with dBASE. The web class is a subclass of the associative array to which the developer added a lot of custom properties and custom methods.

The Timer Class

The timer class is used to execute code on a regular basis. This code may be used to determine if a user has interacted with a form, or simply to wait for a specific amount of time before performing some process. It can be used for such things as creating a text class that blinks on your form (changing color, or simply changing the state of the *visible* property, for example).

The one item that often trips up a developer using a timer object the first time is that when you are done, you *must* disable the timer (set the timer object's *enabled* property to *false*) or it will remain in memory and keep attempting to execute, even if you thought you had released it. This can cause some serious problems if the code it is attempting to execute involves an object that has been released from memory (such as a form).

The other important aspect is that the timer only functions during the idle time – meaning that it checks the time while nothing else is happening and only counts the interval (number of seconds) when nothing is happening. If your user is busy opening forms, navigating through rows in a table, etc., the application is not idle, the timer is not actually doing anything, it's not counting. Once the user stops interacting with the application, the timer starts counting.

So, how do you use a timer? Like all dBL objects, you must instantiate it:

```
t = new Timer()
```

Then you must tell it what you need it to do (set the event handler for the *onTimer()* event), at what *interval* (how often) - in seconds, then set the *enabled* property to *true*. This seems pretty basic. A very simple timer might look like:

```
t = new timer()
t.onTimer = {; ? "Timer Fired ..." } // event handler
t.interval = 2 // seconds
t.enabled := true // enable it
```

The difficulty is that this will go forever, because there isn't really a way to disable it *(while this code works in the Command Window from a program, it is not particularly useful – it is just an example)*. You could, if entering this from the Command Window, type:

```
t.enabled := false
```

If you did something like the above in a program, however, there might not be a way to get it to stop without shutting down your application and every 2 seconds it would output the text "Timer Fired ...". This code is not very useful in the Command Window or in a simple program. It is more useful in a form.

So you might want to do something in a more complex event handler. The following form uses a timer to increment the *value* of a progress bar, when it hits 10 it disables the timer and closes the form:

```
** END HEADER — do not remove this line
//
// Generated on 04/09/2005
//
parameter bModal
local f
f = new TimerExampleForm()
if (bModal)
   f.mdi = false // ensure not MDI
   f.readModal()
else
   f.open()
endif

class TimerExampleForm of FORM
   with (this)
      onOpen = class::FORM_ONOPEN
      metric = 6       // Pixels
      height = 191.0
      left = 350.0
      top = 0.0
      width = 280.0
      text = "Chapter 21 - Timer Example"
   endwith

   this.TEXT1 = new TEXT(this)
   with (this.TEXT1)
      height = 22.0
      left = 30.0
      top = 73.0
      width = 209.0
      text = "Timer Example ..."
   endwith

   this.TIMERPROGRESS = new PROGRESS(this)
   with (this.TIMERPROGRESS)
      height = 22.0
      left = 29.0
      top = 107.0
      width = 216.0
      value = 0
      rangeMin = 0
      rangeMax = 10
```

```
    endwith

    function form_onOpen
        // create an instance of a timer object as a property of
        // the form:
        form.t = new Timer()
        // when the timer interval is hit, do something:
        form.t.onTimer = class::TimeIt
        // set the interval to 2 seconds:
        form.t.interval := 2
        // create a reference to the form:
        form.t.parent = form
        // enable the timer:
        form.t.enabled := true
    return

    function TimeIt
        // event handler for the timer
        // when the interval is hit, we want
        // to increment the value of the progress
        // bar on the form.
        // when we hit 10, we want to disable the
        // timer and close the form
        this.parent.TimerProgress.value ++
        if this.parent.TimerProgress.value == 10
            this.enabled := false
            this.parent.close()
        endif
endclass
```

It should be noted that the timer object does not have a *parent* property, so the code in the form's *onOpen()* event handler that assigns this is creating a custom property called *parent* and giving a reference of the form itself. This allows us in the timer's code to be able to reference the form (as the timer does not know what a form is and the event handler does not understand the reference to a form).

The important part of the code is what is happening in the *TimeIt()* method, which is the event handler for the timer's *onTimer()* event. Also notice that the timer object's object reference variable was created as a property of the form, which means that when the form is released, the timer object is not left in memory.

This example will give you some ideas of what kinds of things you might wish to do with a timer object.

The File Class

The file class allows you to read from, create, and write to files other than tables, both binary files and ascii/ansi text files. Like some of the other non-visual classes, you can do a lot with this class – we could spend a lot of time on this. Instead, we will discuss some of the capabilities of the file class to get you started.

In order to use the file class, you need to create an instance of the object:

```
fMyFile = new File()
```

Now you have a file object, but there is no file open or being created – the object is now waiting to be told what you wish to do.

To Copy a File

Copying a file can be done in dBASE in several ways, including using the "COPY FILE" command. If you have a file object instantiated, you can copy a file simply by using:

```
fMyFile.copy( "somefile.ext", "somefile.bak" )
```

You can use memory variables to represent files and you can even use wildcards (i.e., "*.TXT") – if you use wildcards, dBASE will open the dialog used by the *getFile()* function.

If you store files in your executable (some developers like to "hide" files in the .EXE – this keeps the user from being able to mess with them), the copy() method will look for the file in the .EXE itself, then copy it out to disk from there. However, you cannot copy files into the .EXE – that is only done with the BUILD command.

If SAFETY is ON, dBASE will ask if you want to overwrite a file using this method.

If you use this method to copy tables, the auxillary files (.DBT, .MDX, etc.) are not automatically copied. You are better off using the *copyTable()* method of the database object, or the local SQL COPY TABLE command.

If a file is open for writing (i.e., it is not opened using the "R" attribute) you cannot copy it until it has been closed.

Rename a File

Renaming a file works very much like copying a file and the same comments noted above under the discussion of copying a file will hold true (you can't rename a file that is open, etc.).

```
fMyFile.rename( "somefile.ext", "somefile.bak" )
```

Deleting a File

Deleting a file is very straightforward:

```
fMyFile.delete( "somefile.ext" )
```

However, there is an optional parameter that allows you to send a file directly to the recycle bin (if you do not use this, it will not go to the recycle bin and will not be recoverable through that means). If you add *true* as a second parameter (see below) and if SAFETY is set to ON, you will be asked if the file should be sent to the recycle bin. If SAFETY is OFF, the file will be moved to the recycle bin without asking.

WARNING: If you do not use the recycle parameter (or if it is set to *false*), you (or your users) will not be asked about deleting a file, whether or not SAFETY is ON or OFF (i.e., SAFETY is ignored).

```
fMyFile.delete( "somefile.exe", true )
```

This method cannot delete an open file and will not automatically delete auxillary files for tables – if you need to delete a table you should use the database object's *dropTable()* method or the local SQL DROP TABLE command.

See If a File Exists

You can check to see if a file exists easily enough:

```
fMyFile.exists( "somefile.ext" )
```

This is the same as the dBL *file()* function.

To Check Attributes of a File

You can determine various file attributes using methods of the file class, most of these deal with dates and times, but not all:

- The *accessDate()* method returns the last date that a file was opened for read or write purposes.
- The *createDate()* method returns the date the file was created.
- The *createTime()* method returns the time on the date the file was created.
- The *date()* method returns the last date the file was modified.
- The *shortName()* method returns the DOS 8.3 character filename. You can use longer filenames in Windows 95 through NT versions. However, the operating system still tracks a shorter filename for DOS and in case the file needs to be used on an older operating system. You can find out what this is using this method.
- The *size()* method returns the size of a file in bytes (characters).
- The *time()* method returns the last time the file was modified on the date it was last modified.

Opening or Creating a File

Once you have an instance of a file object, you can then either create a new file with the *create()* method, or you can open an existing file with the *open()* method.

In either case, you need to determine the "access rights" for that file. Your options are:

Right	Meaning
R	Read-only text file
W	Write-only text file
A	Append-only text file
RW	Read and Write text file
RA	Read and Append text file
RB	Read-only binary file
WB	Write-only binary file
AB	Append-only binary file
RWB	Read and Write binary file

The access rights string is not case sensitive and the characters can be in any sequence (i.e., "RW" is the same as "WR").

As soon as you open the file, the *handle* property of the file object will change from "-1" to some numeric value representing the file handle. You don't really have to worry about tracking the file handle (you do if you use the low-level file *functions*) as the file object takes care of it for you.

A simple example would be to create or open a log file and store the current date and time to the file:

```
LOG_FILE = "AccessLog.txt"
f = new File()

if f.exists( LOG_FILE )
   f.open( LOG_FILE, "A" )
else
   f.create( LOG_FILE, "A" )
endif
f.puts( new Date().toLocaleString() )
f.close()
```

Basically this code checks to see if the log file exists and if so – opens it, if not – creates it. In both cases it only opens the file with "Append" rights (add data to the end). It stores the current date and time using the puts method, then closes the file.

Looping Through a File

You can loop through a file that you have opened as long as it is opened with read access rights. This can be handy if you need to skim through the file to find a specific item, or do some processing on the file.

The important thing is that you should always make sure you do not process past the end of the file. This is done by checking the value returned by the *eof()* method:

```
f = new file()
f.open( "ATextFile.TXT", "R" )
do while not f.eof()
   ? f.readLn()
enddo
f.close()
```

The code shown above loops through a file displaying each line.

You might want to, instead, store the value returned by the *readLn()* method to a variable so that you could parse it (scan it for some text, that kind of thing) – in which case the code might look like:

```
f = new file()
f.open( "ATextFile.TXT", "R" )
cLookFor = "Something to find"
do while not f.eof()
   cLine = f.readLn()
   if cLookFor $ cLine
      // do something
      ? "Found it!"
      exit
   endif
enddo
f.close()
```

The code shown above loops until it finds a specific character string in the line extracted from the file, if it does find it, exits the loop. Otherwise it continues until the item being looked for is found, or the end of file is reached.

Reading From a File

There are two methods of reading data from a file, the first we have already used, which is *readLn()* (*gets()* is identical to *readLn()* and is easier to type), the other is *read()*. The primary difference between them is that *readLn()* (and *gets()*) will read a line of text, which means it must end with standard "end of line" characters (Carriage Return/Line Feed).

You can, with the *readLn()* method, specify the number of characters to read, as well as an optional End of Line character to look for, but most of the time if you are using *readLn()* you will want to just read one line at a time. If the *readLn()* method does not find an end of line character it will read until it reaches the end of the file and return everything from where it started to that point (the maximum size of a character string in dBASE is, according to online help, approximately 1 billion characters, if you have enough virtual memory).

The *read()* method will read exactly the number of characters you tell it to. However and more importantly, if you are working with a file that is not a text file (i.e., a binary file) you will want to use the *read()* method.

Writing to a File

There are two methods to write to a file: *write()* and *writeLn()* (the *puts()* method is identical to *writeLn()*).

The major difference between these two methods is that *writeLn()* adds the EndOfLine character to the end of the line and *write()* does not. You would use *write()* to overwrite information in a file, or to work with binary files. If you wish to write a line at a time to your output file, then you would use the *writeLn()* method.

Both methods return the number of characters that were written to the file.

Example 1 - Strip Blank Lines From Text File

The first example will read a text file and strip blank lines out, by reading it one line at a time and writing every line that isn't blank to a copy of the file – for this, the *gets()* and *puts()* methods are the best way to handle it. Notice that to perform this task, two file objects are created.

```
n=0                                    // counter for blank lines
fReadIt = new File()
fReadIt.Open( "hasblanks.txt", "R" )  // open the file as read-only
fWriteIt = new File()
fWriteIt.create( "noblanks.txt" )     // create new file

do while not fReadIt.eof()            // loop
   cString = fReadIt.gets()           // read a line
   if not empty( cString )            // if not empty
      fWriteIt.puts( cString )        // write line to file
   else
      n++                             // increment blank line counter
   endif
enddo
fReadIt.close()                       // always close your files!
fWriteIt.close()
msgbox( n + " empty lines removed!" )
```

If you open the file "noblanks.txt" there should be no blank lines in it.

Example 2 - Changing "Unix" Style File to DOS/Windows Style

A textfile is normally formatted like this:

```
This is the first line of this file.CR/LF
This is the second line of this file.CR/LF
```

A line is by definition terminated by CR/LF (Carriage Return/Line Feed) in DOS and Windows. This is not always the case in other operating systems (like UNIX).

Unless you are operating on very special textfiles with paragraphs exceeding the maximum possible line length (which in dBASE is huge), *readLn()* or *gets()* is the way to go.

The following example will be using *gets()* to read lines of text out of a text file that is known to be a "Unix" file, then write out to a different file using *puts()* (which automatically writes the CR/LF characters to the file).

An important note on the first use of the *gets()* method is that if you do not specify some number of characters to read and the file needs to be "translated", then the *gets()* method will attempt to read the whole file. In the case of some files this is not an issue, but if you are trying to convert a six megabyte file, you will run out memory.

```
fReadIt = new File()
fReadIt.Open( "readme.unx", "R" )
fWriteIt = new File()
fWriteIt.Create( "readme.dos", "A" )

// Check to see how long the first line
// of the file is:
cString = fReadIt.gets( 1000 )
nLength = cString.length
fReadIt.seek( 0 ) // back to the top of the file
// if the first line is wider than 80 characters,
// we need to convert this file ...
nLines = 0
if nLength > 80
   do while not fReadIt.eof()          // loop
      // 10000 = an arbitrarily large value for the
      // number of characters to read
      // chr( 0x0A ) = the Line Feed character - information
      // for these is in online help
      cString = fReadIt.gets( 10000, chr( 0x0A ) )
                     // read a line to the Line Feed
                     // this places the position pointer
                     // on the next line ...
      // the puts() method writes out the CR/LF automatically:
      fWriteIt.puts( cString )
      nLines++
   enddo
else
   ? "No need to convert the file!"
endif
fReadIt.close()
fWriteIt.close()
? nLines+" lines converted to file 'readme.dos'"
```

Example 3 - "APPEND FROM" a File With Non-Standard Separators

One of the reasons I am somewhat familiar with low-level file handling is that I routinely receive (every couple of months) a fairly large file that uses a pipe (|) symbol as the separator between the fields.

This is a bit frustrating, to put it mildly, since the dBASE XDML *APPEND FROM* command does not have an option to use that symbol.

The data I normally receive is a lot more complex than what we'll look at here, but consider the following:

- The data may or may not contain all the fields for the table
- There are no delimiters (character values do not have quotes around them)
- If a field is missing in the "middle" of the data, there are simply two pipe characters next to each other (i.e., ||).

This can get a bit tricky to parse out.

The heavily documented code below will create a table, read the text file line-by-line, parse out the fields, then add new rows to the table, saving the appropriate fields. *(Do not try this unless you have a file formatted as noted to read, the code is here to show you what can be done.)*

```
// Delete table if it exists:
if file( "testconvert.dbf" )
   drop table testconvert
endif

// Create table:
create table "testConvert" ( ;
    "testConvert"."First Name"  character( 20 ),;
    "testConvert"."Last Name"   character( 20 ),;
    "testConvert"."Address1"    character( 30 ),;
    "testConvert"."Address2"    character( 30 ),;
    "testConvert"."City"        character( 20 ),;
    "testConvert"."State"       character( 2 ),;
    "testConvert"."PostalCode"  character( 10 ),;
    "testConvert"."Phone"       character( 14 ) )

// instantiate file object:
f = new File()
f.open( "somedata.txt", "R" )

// instantiate query:
q = new Query()
q.sql = "select * from testConvert"
q.active := true

// shortcut to fields array:
fFields = q.rowset.fields

// start the loop:
nRows = 0
do while not f.eof()
    // read a line:
```

```
cLine = f.gets()
q.rowset.beginAppend()

// start parsing ...
cString = ""
nPipe = 0 // number of pipes found
for i = 1 to cLine.length
    cChar = cLine.substring( i-1, i ) // current character
    // if it's not a pipe symbol and we're not at the
    // end of the line (the last field ...)
    if ( cChar # "|" ) and ( i < cLine.length )
        cString += cChar // add current character to string
    else // it IS a pipe symbol or last character in line
        if cChar # "|"    // it's the last character in the line
            cString += cChar // add to end of field
        endif
        nPipe++
        fFields[ nPipe ].value := cString
        cString = "" // blank it out again
    endif

next // end of parsing

// save the row:
q.rowset.save()
nRows++
enddo
f.close()
q.active := false

? nRows+" rows saved to table"
```

Hopefully between these examples and the discussion of some of the abilities of the file class, you have a starting point for what you might be able to do with them.

The Math Class

Not much is said about the Math Class in dBASE, largely because for the most part it is not really necessary. Why does this undocumented class exist? The history of dBASE is fairly large and extensive and includes a brief flirtation, via IntraBuilder (a Borland Product that did not sell very well), with JavaScript. The Math, Date, and String classes are based on JavaScript.

The math class is simply a class that has some basic mathematical functionality built into it, but you can actually use the equivalent functions built in to dBASE to perform the same calculations, without creating an instance of the math object to do so. If you really wish to experiment with this class, it is simple enough – you can create an instance of it as you do with any other object that is built into dBASE:

```
oMath = new math()
```

And to see what the methods are, simply use the object inspector:

```
inspect( oMath )
```

The one thing that might be useful is that some mathematical constants are set as properties of the class:

```
set decimals to 18
? oMath.pi
set decimals to 2 // reset
```

will return:

```
3.141592653589793116
```

And so on. So if you need these constants for your applications, they are available.

The Date Class

The Date Class, unlike the Math class, is very useful in dBASE. Yes, there are a lot of functions built directly into dBASE, but the date class encapsulates all of that and a lot more directly into one class, which includes the ability to ignore international date formatting and allow you a huge amount of control with dates. If your application works with dates more than just a little, it is suggested you work with the date class.

The simplest way to create a date object is the same as you do with most objects in dBASE:

```
d = new date()
```

Note that this is not the same as:

```
d = date()
```

In the first, you are creating an instance of the date object, in the second you are storing a date value to a memory variable. The date memory variable does not have access to the properties and methods of the date class.

If you create a date object with no parameters (as above), you are automatically setting the date and time to whatever the system date and time were at the instant that the object was instantiated.

It is possible to instantiate the date object with a specific value:

```
d = new Date( "01/01/2005" )
```

Note that the value is a character string – you can also include the time in this:

```
d = new Date( "01/01/2005 10:01:10" )
```

You can instantiate the date with a value that represents the number of milliseconds since January 1, 1970 00:00:00 GMT (GMT = Greenwich Mean Time):

```
d = new Date( 1112623200000.00 ) // March 4, 2005, 00:00:00 AM
```

Most people don't deal with this sort of value, but is available if you need it.

More importantly and very useful for internationalization of an application, you can instantiate the date with explicit values for the year, month, day and optionally hours, minutes, and seconds:

```
d = new Date( 2005, 2, 4, 10, 45, 42 ) // March 4, 2005, 10:45:42 AM
```

 NOTE

Probably the most confusing aspect of the date class is that the *month* property is zero-based. What this means is that the first month of the year – January – is zero. This means that in the example above, March is represented by the number 2, not 3 as you might expect. It also means when performing calculations that use the *month* property you have to add 1 to get a usable value for some situations. The *year*, *day* of the month and other properties are not zero-based, so you do not have to be concerned with those.

Date Math

It is always useful to be able to perform math on a date. There are some problems involved in performing math on a date object – if you treat the date object like a date memory variable, some of what you are used to doing will not function the same.

Example:

```
d = new Date()
? d+1
```

What you might expect to see is the current date plus one day – this is how it works if you use a date memory variable.

However, we have a date object. What happens if you do this?

This isn't all that bad – the math happened like you expected, but – the value displayed is not just the date, it is a value like:

```
3/05/2005 10:06:14 AM
```

This is not a date. It is the value returned as if you had typed:

```
? d.toLocaleString()
```

Interesting things can happen when you work with dates and times using the date object. The month, for example, is zero based – if you simply display:

```
? d.month // or ? d.getMonth()
// should display 2 if the month is March
```

This can be confusing if you're not ready for it, however, dBASE handles this stuff pretty well. For example, the *cmonth()* function (which is in dBASE) will read the date correctly:

```
? cMonth( d )
// should display: March
```

Note that the hard part is working with the year – while the year is calculated properly, the display of the year, if you simply query it, will display with two digits:

```
? d.year // or ? d.getYear()
// should display: 05 if the year is 2005
```

This is a bit of a problem as the *year()* function of dBASE will return the full four digits, if the CENTURY setting is ON:

```
? year( d )
// should display 1999 if the CENTURY setting is ON
```

International Issues

One of the best things about the date object is that you can use it to side-step issues involved in different operating systems, different locales, etc.. You can create methods that work perfectly for whatever language your users may be using.

You can create functions (a small example below) that bypass the international issues, because internally the date is stored in the same fashion, it is largely a matter of display.

If you instantiate a date object and then assign values to the date object's properties, you can perform math (see above) on the date (and time), then return a value that is in the same date format.

An example would be the *addMonths()* function shown below – this can be used to add months to a date:

```
function addmonths( dDate, nMonths )
   local dReturn, d
   d = new Date( dtoc( dDate ) )

   d.Month += nMonths

   // deal with century setting (either two digit or
   // four digit year)
   dReturn = CtoD( left( d.toLocaleString(), ;
                   iif( set("CENTURY") == "ON", 10, 8 ) ) )
return dReturn
```

Using a function like this is as simple as:

```
? addMonths( date(), 2 ) // add two months to current date
```

No matter what language drivers your users are using, this should return the current date plus two months set for whatever format their system is set to display the date in.

The statement that deals with extracting the actual date is important here – it extracts either 10 characters (if SET CENTURY is ON) or it extracts 8 characters (if SET CENTURY is OFF). The *toLocaleString()* method by itself would return a much larger string – including the time. For the purpose of this function we just wanted to manipulate the date.

The date class is useful for many things and there is an expanded or enhanced data class in the dUFLP *(the freeware library of code mentioned in the appendices)* which adds huge amounts of functionality to the date class itself.

The String Class

The last class we will discuss in this chapter is the String Class. This is a particularly useful class, because among other things, any string you create has access to the methods of the string class. Something as simple as the following:

```
cFirstName = "Fred"
? cFirstName.toUpperCase()
// outputs FRED
```

To create an instance of a string object:

```
sMyString = new String()
sMyString.string = "Some Text Here"

// or
sMyString = new String( "Some Text Here" )
```

Methods That Operate on The String

Most of the methods shown here have direct equivalents in dBL functions from older versions of dBASE, some going all the way back to the beginning of dBASE (dBASE II). We will not examine every single method associated with the string class, because there are many, some not as useful as others. Some are specific to working with the Windows API, such as *getByte()* and *setByte()*, and can be rather confusing. All of these are detailed in the online help, as well.

charAt()

The *charAt()* method returns the character at a specific position in the string. This can be useful if you need to parse a string and find a specific character and manipulate the string based on that character.

Note that this is zero-based – it means that the first character is actually zero and if you need to work through the string one character at a time, you would want to check for the stringObj.length-1. If you attempt to go beyond the end of the string no error occurs, but no value is returned.

Example:

```
sMyString = new String( "This is some text" )
? sMyString.charAt( 3 )
```

This example would return a lower case "s" (the fourth character in the string ...).

indexOf()

This method is used to find the location of a string within the actual string object. Keep in mind that the positions are zero based (the first character is zero, the last character is the length of the string - 1). This method is very similar to the *at()* function in dBASE. The search is case-sensitive, so you may want to use *toUpperCase()* or *toLowerCase()* to deal with case insensitive searches. See also *lastIndexOf()*.

Examples:

```
sMyString = new String( "This is some text" )
? sMyString.toUpperCase().indexOf( "IS" )
```

Will return a numeric 2 (remember that we start counting at zero – the characters 'is' start at the third position).

If you wanted to start looking at a position other than zero, you can use an optional parameter:

```
sMyString = new String( "This is some text" )
? sMyString.toUpperCase().indexOf( "IS", 4 )
```

This tells the *indexOf()* method to start at position four (the fifth character), which should return the numeric value of 5.

If the return value is negative one, then one of the following has occurred:

* The search string isn't found
* Either the search or target strings are empty
* The search string is longer than the target string.

(The "Target" is the string you are looking in ...)

isAlpha()
This returns a true if the first character of the string is alphanumeric. This is equivalent to the dBASE *IsAlpha()* function.

Example:

```
sMyString = new String( "This is some text" )
? sMyString.isAlpha()
```

This should return a value of *true*.

isLower()
This returns a true if the first character of the string is a lower case (alphabetic) character. This is equivalent to the dBASE *IsLower()* function.

Example:

```
sMyString = new String( "This is some text" )
? sMyString.isLower()
```

This should return a value of *false*.

isUpper()
This returns a true if the first character of the string is an upper case (alphabetic) character. This is equivalent to the dBASE *IsUpper()* function.

Example:

```
sMyString = new String( "This is some text" )
? sMyString.isUpper()
```

This should return a value of *true*.

lastIndexOf()

This method is used to find the location of a string within the actual string object. Keep in mind that the positions are zero based (the first character is zero, the last character is the length of the string - 1). This method is the opposite of the *indexOf()* method, in that it starts the search at the right side of the string. This method is very similar to the *rat()* function in dBASE. The search is case-sensitive, so you may want to use *toUpperCase()* or *toLowerCase()* to deal with case insensitive searches. See also *indexOf()*.

Examples:

```
sMyString = new String( "This is some text" )
? sMyString.toUpperCase().lastIndexOf( "IS" )
```

Will return a numeric 5 (remember that we start counting at zero – the first occurrence of the characters "is" are at position 5, if you start counting from the right).

If you wanted to start looking at a position other than zero, you can use an optional parameter:

```
sMyString = new String( "This is some text" )
? sMyString.toUpperCase().lastIndexOf( "IS", 4 )
```

This tells the *lastIndexOf()* method to start at position four (the fifth character) and should return the numeric value of 2.

If the return value is negative one, then one of the following has occurred:

- The search string isn't found
- Either the search or target strings are empty
- The search string is longer than the target string.

(The "Target" is the string you are looking in ...)

left()

The *left()* method returns "n" characters from the left side of the string, where "n" is a number you supply to the method. This is the equivalent of the dBASE *left()* function.

Example:

```
sMyString = new String( "This is some text" )
? sMyString.left( 6 )
```

This would return the characters:

```
This i
```

leftTrim()

The *leftTrim()* method removes spaces on the left of a character string. This can be useful for situations where, perhaps, you have built up a string through some process and want to display it now without the extra spaces.

Example:

```
sMyString = new String( "     This is some text" )
```

```
? sMyString.leftTrim()
```

Without the use of the *leftTrim()* method, we would see:

```
       This is some text
```

With the use of it, we see:

```
This is some text
```

right()
The *right()* method returns "n" characters from the right side of the string, where "n" is a number you supply to the method. This is the equivalent of the dBASE *right()* function.

Example:

```
sMyString = new String( "This is some text" )
? sMyString.right( 6 )
```

This would return the characters:

```
e text
```

rightTrim()
The *rightTrim()* method removes spaces on the right of a character string. If you store or reference values from fields in a .DBF, these fields will be padded with spaces which can be easily removed. This is equivalent to the dBASE *trim()* function.

Example:
```
? queryName.rowset.fields["first name"].value.rightTrim()+;
    " "+ queryName.rowset.fields["last name"].value
```

This would trim the spaces from the first name field, add (concatenate) a single space, then concatenate the last name field to the end of that.

stuff()
The *stuff()* method is used to replace some characters in a string with other characters. This method is nearly identical with the dBASE *stuff()* function, but remember character strings are zero based.

Example:

```
sMyString = new String( "This is some text" )
? sMyString.stuff( 8, 4, "more" )
```

This replaces the word "some" with the word "more", and you should see:

```
This is more text
```

substring()
The *substring()* method is used to extract a number of characters from inside the string. You must specify the beginning position and the ending position of the characters to extract. It is important to remember that this is zero based, so the first character is zero, and the

last is string.length-1. This is similar to the dBASE *substr()* function, but is not exactly the same.

Examples:

```
sMyString = new String( "This is some text" )
// three characters starting at the fourth one:
? sMyString.substring( 3, 6 )
```

Should return:

```
s i
```

The *substring()* parameters might be defined as the first is the beginning of the character string you wish to extract and is zero based; the second is the end of the string you wish to extract (the last character) and is one based. In the example above, the first parameter is the fourth character in the string, but you use "3" because it is zero based. The last character is the sixth character in the string and you use "6" because the second parameter is one based.

toLowerCase()
This returns the lower case equivalent of the character string. This is exactly the same as the dBASE *lower()*function.

Example:

```
sMyString = new String( "This is some text" )
? sMyString.toLowerCase()
```

This would return the characters:

```
this is some text
```

toProperCase()
This returns the proper case equivalent of the character string. This is exactly the same as the dBASE *proper()* function.

Example:

```
sMyString = new String( "This is some text" )
? sMyString.toProperCase()
```

This would return the characters:

```
This Is Some Text
```

toUpperCase()
This returns the upper case equivalent of the character string. This is exactly the same as the dBASE *upper()* function.

Example:

```
sMyString = new String( "This is some text" )
? sMyString.toUpperCase()
```

This would return the characters:

```
THIS IS SOME TEXT
```

Methods That Wrap the String in HTML Tags

These can be useful if you want to generate HTML, either for text objects in forms or reports, or if you wanted to actually create an HTML page (using the file object, for example.). These tags may also work in the editor control if the editor's *evalTags* property is set to true.

In all cases, the HTML tags have beginning and ending tags associated with them. In some cases you have to pass a parameter to the method, in others you do not. Rather than listing all of them with examples, you should simply be aware that they are available to you. Details on their use can be found in the online help.

Using the String Object's Methods

Ok, now that you know what many of the methods are, there are a couple of other things that it doesn't hurt to know.

First, any string can use the string object methods. Take a look at the following examples:

```
sMyString = new String( "This is some text" )
? sMyString.toUpperCase()

? "test text".toUpperCase()

c = "Another test string"
? c.toUpperCase()
```

In all three cases, we displayed the upper case version of the text. The first is a string object defined as a dBASE object is normally defined. The second is a literal string and the last is a memory variable.

This gives you a ton of functionality at your fingertips, because this means that any string in your application can automatically use these methods – you can do the same thing with a rowset's field:

```
? queryName.rowset.fields["somefield"].value.toUpperCase()
```

As long as the value of the field is of type character, this will work.

Can you use the string methods on non-string values? Well, yes and no. You can't do directly, but dBASE has a feature called "AutoCasting" – it means that if you combine values of different types, dBASE will sort them out. You couldn't, for example, use the it *right()* method on a date, but you could autocast the date to a string and use the *right()* method on that:

```
? d.right( date()+"", 4 )
```

This would print the right four characters of the date. You can do the same type of thing with numeric values, and more.

Stacking Methods

As shown in other sections of this chapter, it is possible to "stack" methods, or use methods to affect the returned value of other methods. You might want to combine some HTML and other features:

```
? "this is some text".toProperCase().bold().italics()
```

This should actually display:

```
<I><B>This Is Some Text</B></I>
```

And when actually displayed either in a text control (on a form or report), an editor control, or an HTML file, you would see:

This Is Some Text

Working Character-by-Character Through String

Something you may need to do is search through a string for a specific character. You can use code along the following lines to do this:

```
c = "Some character string * with a star in it"
for i = 1 to c.length // length of string
    // check character at 'i-1' — remember, we have
    // to start counting at zero ... see if it's the
    // character we need:
    if c.charAt( i-1 ) == "*"
        // do something
        ? "Found a star"
    endif
next
```

Strings and Nulls

If you attempt to concatenate any type of value with a value that evaluates to a null value, the returned value will always become null. (This is sort of like multiplying by zero.) Example: a field, by default, is null – if the user does not enter a value, then the value contained in the field is null (unless the developer changes it in the table definition or in some other fashion).

This can be problematic, particularly if you are trying to create reports. The last thing you want is to put together a calculated expression and end up with nothing displaying on the report.

You can actually get around this situation *(this is a feature of dBASE "works-as-designed")* by using the string class. If you pass a string through the String class constructor, which evaluates to null, the string class will return an empty string.

For example, suppose you are combining, first name, middle initial, and last name. The middle initial field may be null. You can safely combine the three like this:

```
fullName = firstName + " " + new String( middleInitial + " " ) + ;
          lastName
```

If the middle initial is null, adding a space to it results in null and the String object will return an empty string. If the middle initial is not null, adding a space will result in a space between the middle initial and the last name.

Summary

As you can see, the non-visual and non-database classes that are built into dBASE have a lot of functionality that any developer will find quite useful when writing applications. You should spend some time working with these beyond anything discussed here, then experimenting to see if you can find specific uses for them. You may be surprised!

Part VII: Working With the Outside World

When working with dBASE applications it is often necessary, or at least a good idea, to be able to work with software other than dBASE. Sometimes this is just a case of communicating with some other software, passing data back and forth, or communicating with the Windows Operating System. This section of the book will focus on such things as OLE (Object Linking and Embedding), WSH (Windows Script Host), the Windows API (Application Programming Interface) and working with ActiveX controls.

Chapter 23: OLE and WSH

When you need to communicate with software other than dBASE from within a dBASE application, one of the most common means is by using OLE – or Object Linking and Embedding. Through the use of the OLEAutoClient object in dBASE, you can access many software packages and we will look at some of what can be done. You can also have your application access the Windows Script Host (WSH) server that is installed with Windows itself, and access aspects of the operating system.

Object Linking and Embedding (OLE)

Object Linking and Embedding or OLE, is the ability to link to and control another software package. There is another aspect – embedding – which we will look at shortly, when we discuss working with fields in dBF tables.

OLE allows us to communicate with and control other software, such as Microsoft's Word or Excel, by setting up that software as an OLE automation server. dBASE would be an OLE automation client, meaning that it can use the application that is the OLE automation server. One of the most important things to note is that when you use OLE automation to communicate with another software package, you are communicating with it in its own language, not with dBL. You are using dBL to do the work, but the actual information must be passed to the automation server in a way that it understands.

OLE2 Automation Support

In order to actually set dBASE to be an OLE automation client, all you have to do is to create an instance of the OLEAutoClient class:

```
oAuto = new OLEAutoClient("theOLEAutoServer")
```

The parameter is the important part of this code – it tells dBASE what the server is and it looks it up in the operating systems registry to find it. For example, if you wanted to hook up to Microsoft's Word, provided it was installed on the machine, you could do so with:

```
oWord = new OLEAutoClient("word.application")
```

Once you have done this, you can examine the properties, events and methods available to you by using the Inspector:

```
inspect( oWord )
```

Doing so will give you something that looks like:

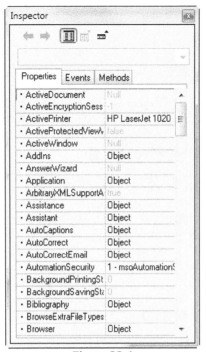

Figure 23-1

The difficulty with looking at this is that you could probably guess what some of the properties, events and methods do, but it isn't that easy sometimes to know exactly what to use when and so on.

The best bet with Word is to try looking at the Word Visual Basic help file – all of the properties, events and methods are defined there and you can learn a lot from them.

Of course, Visual Basic does not translate directly into dBL, but if you try you can work a lot of it out. One suggestion is to try using the Macro Recorder in Word, execute the commands you wish, then try to translate the Macro that is saved to dBL. The following code was created to open a file in Word by inserting it, which would deal with some formatting issues *(HTML does not translate directly to standard Windows formatting)*, then copy it to the Windows clipboard, which would allow the text to be pasted into some other software. This leaves the original file alone and all of this is done from inside of a form *(this is just an example – do not try it unless you have a file named "LP_TEMP.HTM" in the folder you are trying to run this code in ...)*:

```
oWord = new oleAutoclient("word.application")
oWord.Application.displayAlerts = false
oWord.Documents.Add()
// set the file to be inserted into Word:
wdFile = set("dire")+"\LP_Temp.htm"
oWord.Selection.InsertFile(wdFile)
// Copy it to the clipboard - copy the whole text, this
// allows us to continue using the current
// version of oWord
oWord.Selection.Start := 1 // set first character
oWord.Selection.Copy()     // to clipboard
// Cause this background copy of Word to quit
oWord.quit(0)
// Release the object
release object oWord
```

```
// and wipe out the reference to it
oWord = null
```

When this code is executed, you could take the text that was in the file selected which is now in the Windows clipboard and put it somewhere else.

You can do other interesting things, such as opening a file in Word and printing it:

```
oWord = new oleAutoclient("word.application")
oWord.documents.open( "C:\My Documents\Doc1.doc", false, true )
oWord.activeDocument.printOut()
oWord.quit( 0 )
oWord = null
```

You can do more, including such things as performing a mail merge with form letters and so on. For more information on working with OLE Automation and Word, you might want to read the article in dBulletin issue 16 by Gary White titled "Using Word Under dBASE".

Communicating with Excel

Microsoft Excel™ is a popular software package that works with data in a way that looks like a table – it is displayed in rows and columns like a grid object in dBASE. It is possible to read and write data to Excel spreadsheets using OLE Automation.

Like Word, Excel uses Visual Basic as its underlying programming language for manipulating the spreadsheet(s) in Macros and such. If you use the macro recorder in Excel you will still need to try to figure out what is needed in your dBL code to communicate with the software.

The following are some excerpts from code that I wrote some time ago, to import some data from Excel and to export some data to Excel. This is simplified a little, however. The following assumes a simple spreadsheet with data in cells A1 through E7 of the spreadsheet.

```
// open a spreadsheet, and load data within a range
// of cells into an array:
try
   oExcel = new OLEAutoClient( "excel.application" )
catch( Exception E )
   ? "Cannot open Excel"
   return
endtry
oExcel.DisplayAlerts=false
try
   oExcel.workbooks.open(set("dire")+"\TestSpreadsheet.xls")
catch( Exception E )
   ? e.message
   return
endtry

// Get Start Row and Column
cStartRange = "A1"
cEndRange = "E7"
oExcel.Range( cStartRange ).Select()
nStartCol = oExcel.activecell.column
nStartRow = oExcel.activeCell.row
oExcel.Range( cEndRange ).Select()
nEndCol = oExcel.activecell.column
```

```
nEndRow = oExcel.activeCell.row
// need to know the number of rows ...
nEndRow = ( nEndRow - nStartRow + 1 )
// Load the array:
aExcel = new array( 7, 5 ) // 7 rows, 5 columns
for i = nStartRow to nEndRow
    for j = nStartCol to nEndCol
        // 64+1 = 65 = "A"
        cCell = chr(j+64)+ltrim(str(i))
        aExcel[ i, j ] = oExcel.Range( cCell ).value
    next
next

// display the array (simply, not real pretty):
for i = 1 to 7 // rows
    ? "Row: "+I
    for j = 1 to 5 // columns
        ?? aExcel[ i, j ]
    next
next

// cleanup
oExcel = null
```

This next example goes the other way, storing data to an Excel spreadsheet:

```
// Export some data to an Excel Spreadsheet:
// instantiate Excel object
oExcel = new oleAutoclient("excel.application")
// create new workbook
oWorkBook = oExcel.workbooks.add()

// open DBASESAMPLES database, and Fish table:
dData = new database()
dData.databaseName := "DBASESAMPLES"
dData.active        := true
qFish = new query()
qFish.database := dData
qFish.sql        := "select * from fish"
qFish.active    := true
qFish.rowset.indexName := "Name"
qFish.rowset.first()

// Loop through the rows of the table:
nRows = 0
do while not qFish.rowset.endOfSet
    nRows++ // increment row counter
    // Loop through the fields (columns) of the table,
    // but not the image field which is the last one:
    for nCols = 1 to qFish.rowset.fields.size - 1
        // get the value:
        xValue = qFish.rowset.fields[ nCols ].value
        // get the new cell to add data to:
        oCell = oExcel.ActiveSheet.cells( nRows, nCols )
        // assign value to the cell:
        oCell.formula = xValue
        // from Gary White's Xldef.h —
```

```
        // set the vertical alignment to the top:
        oCell.verticalAlignment := -4160
      next // field

      // Next row:
      qFish.rowset.next()
   enddo

   // size the columns to fit
   oExcel.ActiveSheet.Columns.AutoFit()

   // save to disk
   oWorkBook.SaveAs(set("dire")+"\TestExcelExport.xls")

   // close Excel
   oExcel.quit()

   // cleanup:
   oExcel = null
   qFish.active := false
   release object qFish
   dData.active := false
   release object dData
```

As with the Word example shown earlier, there is much more that can be done. There is an excellent article by Gary White in the dBASE Knowledgebase (under Advanced Topics) that goes into more depth on working with Excel.

Some Fun – The Sound API in Windows

I thought it might be fun to discuss something that was brought to the attention of dBASE developers by Jim Sare on the newsgroups. While this is the Sound API (Application Programming Interface), it appears that you can access it through dBASE using the OleAutoClient object. Windows ships with at least one "voice" and the ability to pass a character string to it and have it attempt to pronounce it. *(The code and examples here are used with Jim's permission.)* The simple form of this is something like:

```
   oSound = new OleAutoClient( "sapi.SPVoice" )
   inspect( oSound )
```

The call to the Inspector in dBASE will show what properties, events and methods are available.

To get this to actually work, try:

```
   ? oSound.speak( "Hello, Ken" )
   ? oSound.speak( "How are you today?" )
   ? oSound.speak( "I am fine." )
   ? oSound.speak( "How about a nice game of chess?" )
```

A simple program that will loop through the letters of the alphabet and the digits 0 to 9 (by Jim Sare):

```
   // Test the Sound API, looping through the alphabet and
   // digits:
   oSound = new OLEAutoClient( "SAPI.SPVoice" )
   for i = asc("a") to asc("z")
```

```
      ? oSound.speak( chr(i) )
      sleep .1
   next

   for i = asc("0") to asc("9")
      ? oSound.speak( chr(i) )
      sleep .1
   next
```

A more complex program that will let you hear any voices that are installed on your computer *(by default there is only one, but it is possible to download more from the Microsoft website)* is:

```
// A program by Jim Sare to show what voices are installed
// on your computer using the Windows Sound API:
oSound = new OLEAutoClient( "SAPI.SPVoice" )
cString = "Hello <emp>d</emp>BASE Users!"
? cString // display it in the Output Pane
_app.executeMessages() // clear message queue
oSound.speak( cString, 8 ) // 8 means the text contains XML SAPI Tags
// Change the string, and use the getDescription() method
// to list the name of the voice:
cString = [This is spoken by the default voice which is ]+;
         oSound.voice.getDescription()
? cString
_app.executeMessages() // clear message queue
oSound.speak( cString )
// create object to store list of voices
oVoices = oSound.getVoices()
// loop through list of voices:
for i = 0 to oVoices.count - 1
   oVoice = oVoices.item( i )
   // if not the default:
   if oVoice.getDescription() # oSound.voice.getDescription()
      cString = [<voice required="Name=] +;
            oVoice.getDescription()
      cString += [">This is spoken by ]+;
            oVoice.getDescription()+;
            [</voice>]
      ? cString
      _app.executeMessages() // clear message queue
      try
         oSound.speak( c )
      catch( Exception E )
      endtry
   endif
next
```

You can learn more about the Sound API by going to the Windows website, download the full SAPI developer's kit and there is a link to other voices. Go to this page (this is one long URL and should be entered as a single line):

```
http://www.microsoft.com/downloads/details.aspx?FamilyID=5e86ec97-40a7-
453f-b0ee-6583171b4530&DisplayLang=en
```

Or search for SAPI on the Microsoft website.

Working with OLE Data and Fields

When you work with OLE data in a field of a dBASE table, you should be able to edit the data by using an OLE server. Linking a field to an OLE object is similar to inserting a file into a binary field.

Windows ships with several OLE servers, such as Paint and if you have installed a copy of Microsoft Office, then you also have access to Word, Excel, etc.

If you have a field in a table that is an OLE type field, you can double-click on it (if it is in a grid) and the OLE viewer will be displayed. To see this, you might wish to run the following code, which will create a simple table with an OLE type field (save it to a program such as "MakeTestOLETable.prg", then run it):

```
create table TestOle (;
       CharField char(10),;
       OLEField blob(10, 4 ) )
use TestOle
append blank
replace CharField with "Test1"
use
```

Once you have done this, double-click on the table in the Navigator (click on the "Tables" tab and it should be there). You should see something like:

Figure 23-2

If you double-click on the empty OLE Field, you should see the OLE Viewer:

Figure 23-3

Now if you right-click on the viewer and select "Insert Object ...", you will be shown the Insert Object dialog:

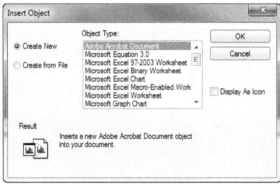

Figure 23-4

You can add an OLE object from here. If you had an Excel Worksheet you could actually store either a link to it or a copy of the file in your table. Storing the Link would take less disk space in the table, storing the file would be Embedding it and store the file actually in the table (in the .DBT file) – changes to the version in the table will not be reflected in the version outside of the table.

You can also create a new object. The default action is "Create New" as can be seen by the dialog. If you have Microsoft Excel installed on your computer, you might try selecting "Microsoft Excel Worksheet" from the dialog. Before you click "OK", check the "Display As Icon" checkbox. This will tell dBASE to display an appropriate icon in the table. Click "OK". When you do, dBASE will bring up Excel with an empty worksheet.

If you type something in the spreadsheet, and then close Excel ("File" menu, "Close and Return to OLE Field"), it will be saved in the field. Now notice that the OLE Viewer looks like:

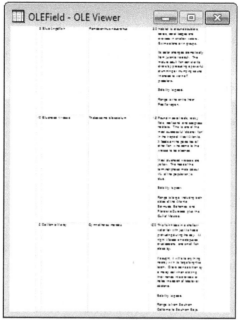

Figure 23-5

If you close this viewer, you will see in the table:

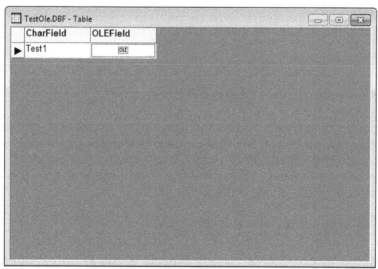

Figure 23-6

You can go back to this field at any time and double-click on it, etc. You can bring up Excel and modify the worksheet.

What we did here was to embed the object in the table. This stores it in the .DBT file that is associated with the table (if you create a Binary field or a Memo field, a .DBT file is created to store this information).

Alternatively, we could have created a Link to an existing object. To do this, you must go to the OLE Server software, such as in this case Microsoft Excel and copy an object to the Windows Clipboard. If you wanted to copy a worksheet to the clipboard, you would highlight the cells you wish to store the link to and use Ctrl+C to copy them to the clipboard. Then you would go back to dBASE and on the OLE Viewer window right click and select "Paste Link". This will store the link and you can work with the object as you would if you had embedded it.

The differences between the two can seem a bit confusing; let's attempt to clear things up. Linking as noted earlier takes less disk space in the table. Embedding makes a copy of an existing file, or if creating a new object the object is stored in the table. Considerations:

- Embedding – should be used if the table will be distributed to different users on different computers that are not networked together.
- If the object is going to be updated by various users at the same time, you should use a Link instead.
- If disk space is an issue, you should use a Link instead. If a Link is used, the original file exists on the hard drive and can be updated either from the field in the table, or from the (OLE) application directly *(in the example here, Excel)*. If it is embedded, it can only be updated from a user of the table.
- Linking is a better approach if you want to retain data integrity. An embedded OLE object is stored in the .DBT file associated with the .DBF. If this file gets corrupted (or accidentally deleted), then your OLE objects are no longer accessible. If you use linking, the original file will still remain on the hard drive even if corruption or deletion of the .DBT file occurs.

There are some odd issues that occur with OLE fields. For example, the *empty()* function returns *false* even if there is nothing in the field *(if this function returns "false", it means that the field is **not** empty, which in this case is wrong)*. There does not appear to be a way to empty the field, either.

The following XDML command allows you to store a value to an OLE field:

```
REPLACE OLE <OLE field name> FROM <filename> [LINK]
```

The keyword "LINK" is optional, but if used will create a link.

The OODML method of doing this is to use the field object's *replaceFromFile()* method, but this method currently has no option to create a Link to the file, it will only embed it. You may also be able to use the field object's *copyToFile()* method to create a copy of the embedded object – testing however shows the file to be unreadable in the appropriate software. It is not a good idea to rely on this method.

Windows Script Host (WSH)

Microsoft has created a way to access various aspects of the Windows operating system through Visual Basic and Microsoft's Jscript. This is detailed at the website linked to here (part of the Microsoft library):

```
http://support.microsoft.com/kb/188135
```

According to Microsoft:

> "Microsoft® Windows® Script Host (WSH) is a language-independent scripting host for Windows Script compatible scripting engines. It brings simple, powerful and flexible scripting to the Windows 32-bit platform, allowing you to run scripts from both the Windows desktop and the command prompt."

It is important to note that if you have users who are working with Windows 98 and you use WSH in your application, they will need to go to the Microsoft website and download WSH.

You can also make sure you have the most current version of WSH by going to their website:

```
http://msdn.microsoft.com/library/default.asp?url=/downloads/list/webdev.asp
```

Another useful website that discusses Windows Script Host is at:

```
http://www.devguru.com/Technologies/wsh/quickref/wsh_intro.html
```

(Also keep in mind that the URLs provided here may change over time, as the owners of the websites in question may move things around on their sites.)

Although the author of the website noted above assumes that you can only use Visual Basic or Microsoft's Jscript to run programs that use WSH, he discusses it in some depth. There are other websites and the information out there can either overwhelm you or if you are ready for it, give you exactly what you need. In all cases you will have to try to work through the fact that the sample code is not dBL and while similar there are some major differences.

What does this mean to you, as a dBASE developer? It means that through the use of Ole Automation, you can work directly with various aspects of the Windows operating system. Some of this is pretty simple and of course like anything, can get more complex fairly quickly. We will look at the simple stuff and anything beyond that is an exercise for the reader.

It is possible that WSH may not be available in Windows 8. We will soon see.

> **NOTE**
> There are some concerns about just using WSH in your application:
>
> - Some organizations turn off WSH because a clever virus writer can use it to do some bad things to your hard drive. According to the Windows help for Security, there is a signature verification policy that affects WSH that allows the administrator user to set scripts to run only if by a trusted signature, to prompt the user if the script is untrusted, or to run all scripts. One user's testing *(Ivar B. Jessen)* shows that it didn't seem to matter what he set the registry key to, the scripts he tried all seemed to run with no prompts. The registry key is located in the registry at:
>
> ```
> \HKEY_CURRENT_USER\SOFTWARE\Microsoft\Windows Script
> Host\Settings\Trust\Policy
> ```
>
>   And the registry key can have one of these three values:
>   0   Run all scripts
>   1   Prompt if script is untested
>   2   Run only trusted scripts
>   It should be noted that under Windows XP Home, this key does not exist by default and "Windows Script Host" is simply "Windows Script".
> - You should check the documentation on the Microsoft website, or in a book to be sure you understand exactly what you are doing, what the parameters are, and any issues to look for when using a specific method. There may be implications to the code that you are unaware of.
> - Some might claim that the Windows Script Host adds more overhead than using the Windows API. However, there is strong advantage, in that the WSH script will generally be shorter, and usually easier to read.
>
> Because of some these issues, you may want to use the Windows API (next chapter) to do the same sorts of things, instead.

To understand some of what is possible with WSH, from inside dBASE, you need to know what kinds of objects are available.

This is a bit tricky, because it appears that the way you instantiate these objects does not match the exact descriptions on the Microsoft web pages (the examples there are most likely for Visual Basic or other software).

The following will create an object reference to the WSH FileSystemObject, which you can then use to manipulate files and the File System.

```
oWSH = new OleAutoClient( "Scripting.FileSystemObject" )
```

One way to get some idea of what you can do is to use the Inspector:

```
inspect( oWSH )
```

The following examples are from code that has been posted in the dBASE newsgroups by various developers.

The first example will get the size of a file. If you read the chapter that dealt with the non-visual classes in dBASE, you will know that the File object already has that ability built in to it, so why should we go to WSH? The dBASE File object has a problem with files that are really large – if you try to get the size of a file that is larger than 2 gigabytes in size, you will get an unreliable value. However, by going straight to Windows itself, you can get this value easily. This code was created by Roland Wingerter, although I expanded it out to multiple lines:

```
function GetFileSize( cFile )
   local oWSH, nSize
   oWSH = new oleautoclient("Scripting.FileSystemObject")
   nSize = oWSH.getFile(cFile).size
return nSize
```

The Script object is the "FileSystemObject" and the code calls the object's *getFile()* method, then checks the *size* property of the object. This looks a lot like dBASE code, doesn't it? To use it, you would call this function by passing the path and name of the file you want to obtain the size of:

```
? GetFileSize( "C:\dBASETest\MyFile.txt" )
```

If you wanted to have your application open the Windows Explorer at a specific location for whatever purpose, you could do something like the following (code by Rich Muller):

```
function OpenExplorerAt( cPath )
   local sh
   sh = new oleAutoClient( "Shell.Application" )
   sh.Explore( cPath )
return
```

You would call this function as:

```
OpenExplorerAt( "C:\dBASETest" )
```

Or to open the Explorer in the folder that dBASE (or your application) is currently looking at:

```
OpenExplorerAt( set("dire") )
```

The following is useful because there is no simple way in dBASE to determine how much disk space is used by all the files in a folder. This was created by Ivar B. Jessen, and posted on the newsgroups:

```
function FolderSize( cPath )
   private fso, nSize
   fso = new oleautoclient("Scripting.FileSystemObject")
   try
      nSize = fso.GetFolder( cPath ).size
   catch( Exception E )
      msgbox( "Error: "+e.code+" – "+e.message+chr(13)+;
              "(Make sure path is correct!)",;
              "FolderSize error", 48 )
      nSize = 0
   endtry
return nSize
```

These various bits of code will give you some idea what can be done, but you may want to take this further and explore the subject on your own.

In the dUFLP (dBASE Users' Function Library Project – described in the Appendices) is a set of sample code in the file MiscWSH.prg. If you are interested in seeing more of what is possible, this is a good place to start.

Summary

We have just started to take a look at some of what can be done to communicate with other software using dBASE. As you can see, dBASE can be extended quite well through the use of OLE and WSH. But this is just a start.

Chapter 24: The Windows API and DLLs

Overview

The Windows operating system provides the capability to dynamically link program modules which allows for code reusability, smaller memory footprints and extended functionality. Through its support of dynamic linking, dBASE greatly improves its capability to extend functionality far beyond that which is offered in the dBASE product itself. Using dynamic linking, it is possible to tap the power and functionality that already exists in thousands of software modules that are already written and tested. The Windows NT-based operating systems (NT, 2000, and XP) and 9x-based operating systems (95, 98, and ME) directly support dynamic linking to their functions through an interface known as the Windows 32-bit Application Programming Interface, or Win32 API.

> **NOTE:**
> This chapter has not been updated for Windows 64-bit, or Windows 8. The author of the chapter, Jim Sare, has been incommunicado with the dBASE community for some time, and this does not appear to be something that is going to change. If your applications run on Windows 64-bit operating systems it is possible some of the code samples may need modification. However, I have tested all the sample code on Windows 7 64-bit, and they work.

We will cover the basics of API programming using dBASE. The information presented is the same for all versions of dBASE from Visual dBASE 7.00 through dB2K and dBASE SE and PLUS. We will see the techniques for function prototyping, data and prototype conversion between languages and working with data structures to exchange information with external functions. Approaches to bundling API code in dBASE applications will also be covered.

Although this information focuses on using the Win32 API, the basics presented here are also fully applicable to using any other API library in dBASE. The third-party market is flooded with all sorts of API libraries providing very powerful functionality such as communications, image acquisition, image processing, credit card processing, audio/video multimedia, instrument data collection, you name it. Any binary module (.dll, .drv, .exe, etc) which exports functions that can be dynamically linked can be used in dBASE using the information presented here.

The Right Documentation

The very first thing we will need to work with the Win32 API or any third-party API is authoritative reference documentation which covers the functions we will be using. There are many reference books available which cover the Win32 API. Some are excellent references, some are not. The best primary reference documentation for the Win32 API as well as all of the associated extensions to Win32 is provided for free by Microsoft and is on the web at:

```
http://msdn.microsoft.com/library
```

Why is it the best primary reference? Simple answer; Microsoft is the author of Win32. Who better to document it than those who own, develop and maintain the source code.

The MSDN Library might seem daunting and confusing at first. But hang in there. After you've used it for some time and become familiar with the Win32 API and some of the associated extension APIs, MSDN will most likely become your lifeline ... you'll find it difficult to envision working without it.

Also don't ignore the many third-party books available. There are some good reference books as well as 'how to' style books which can be very helpful in learning about the Win32 API and learning how to accomplish various tasks.

MSDN is primarily aimed at C/C++ programmers. Third-party books are mostly aimed at C/C++, Pascal (Delphi), or Visual Basic programmers. If you're experienced in any of those languages, the choice is obvious. If you're not experienced in any of those languages, books aimed at Visual Basic will most likely be the easiest to work with because Visual Basic most closely 'maps' with dBASE in its approach and facilities for accessing external API's and its syntax is probably the easiest to follow.

But whatever you do, don't even try working with a single function from any API, whether the Win32 API or other third-party API library, without the appropriate reference documentation. Trying to work without the right reference will guarantee application crashes and other instabilities and bugs, all of which might be highly intermittent or solid. And all of which will lead to subsequent high frustration levels.

Header Files

Header files are almost always as necessary as having good reference documentation, whether working with an API in dBASE or any other development environment. When working with any API, there is almost always one, if not multiple associated header files. Header files contain function definitions, data type definitions, and data constants that are used by the compiler when the API module is compiled. Typically the module vendor will use #define statements to define data constants (data values) and to map the names of data types from meaningful names for use in the module's source code to the compiler's native data types. Then in the reference documentation, the vendor will document the parameters for the functions in the module using the data constant names and data type names which are #defined in the header file. A couple of lines that #define data constants from a header file might look something like this:

```
#define WM_SETTEXT          0x000C
#define WM_GETTEXT          0x000D
```

The data constants are typically associated with one or more functions in the particular API. The vendor's API reference documentation will refer to data constants such as WM_SETTEXT and WM_GETTEXT when discussing acceptable values for a function parameter instead of referring to the actual numeric values 0x000C and 0x000D. Either you will need to know what values WM_SETTEXT and WM_GETTEXT represent when calling the associated function so that you can pass the values directly. Or more acceptable, copy/paste the #define statements into the dBL source code so that you can use the WM_SETTEXT and WM_GETTEXT constants when calling the function.

For Win32, the associated header files are contained in the Windows Software Development Kit (SDK) supplied by Microsoft. The Windows SDK has been available for download from MSDN. For third-party APIs the appropriate header files are usually included with the API's development package. If you have a Windows-compatible C++ compiler, then you most likely have some version of the Windows SDK available. In the \include folder of the dBASE root install folder are a number of header files that were installed with dBASE and contain extracts from the Windows SDK. These header files represent a small fraction of all the header file content of the full Windows SDK. Also, the majority of the content of these header files only covers some of the constants used in the core of Windows. They include very little of the constants defined by the extensions to the Win32 API and none of the constants for Windows extension technologies released over the past 6-7 years *(at the time Jim Sare wrote this)*.

The EXTERN Statement

The EXTERN statement is used in dBASE to establish the link between dBASE and the external module containing the function we want to use. Although the name EXTERN is appropriate because the function is external to dBASE, you could think of it as 'DynamicLinkTo' instead, because that is what EXTERN does. It dynamically establishes the link from dBASE to the function contained in the external module.

When establishing the link using EXTERN, we also need to do some translation, the same as if we were trying to help 2 individuals speaking 2 different languages to communicate. In this case, the 2 individuals are dBASE and an external function that was written in an entirely different language. In dBASE, variables occupy a certain defined amount of space (bytes) in memory. These variables may and in most cases do occupy an entirely different memory size in the external function.

```
EXTERN [<calling convention>] <return type> <function name |
alias>([<parameter type list>]) <module filename | module alias> [FROM
<function name>]
```

As you can see, the EXTERN statement allows us to define the calling convention, the data type of the return value, the function name that we want to use to call the function, the data types of any arguments required by the function and the software module containing the function. The FROM option allows us to specify the original name of the function contained in the binary executable module.

Typical EXTERN Statement

```
extern CLOGICAL IsWindow(CHANDLE) user32.dll
```

This EXTERN statement dynamically links a function named IsWindow contained in the module filename referenced as User32.DLL to dBASE. This tells dBASE the name of the function and how to reference the module that contains the function. The specific purpose of the IsWindow function is not important at this time.

Referencing the module properly is the important point here. Modules can be referenced in 1 of 2 ways; either with the module's filename as in the example shown above, or with the module's alias name. In many cases, the module alias is the same as the module filename without the file extension. For example, the alias for the module contained in USER32.DLL is 'User32'. And the alias for the module contained in GDI32.DLL is 'GDI32'.

Calling Convention

Executable modules such as DLLs can be developed using different languages. For this and other reasons, functions contained in executable modules require the arguments to be passed in a specific sequence, may or may not require a specific number of arguments, may enforce case sensitivity for function names and may require that function names are prefaced with the underscore character. This is the 'calling convention' required by the executable module. Following is a chart listing the calling conventions supported by dBASE:

	C	Pascal	Standard Call
dBASE Keyword	cdecl	Pascal	stdcall
Fixed # of Parms	N	Y	Y
Function Name Case	Fixed	Upper	Fixed
Parameter Seq.	R to L	L to R	R to L
Prefix Underscore	Y	N	N
Stack Restoration	Caller	Caller	Called Function

You can see from the chart above that there is some detail involved in calling a function that is contained in an external module. However, as the programmer, all you need to know is the calling convention that is required by the module and then specify the appropriate calling convention keyword in the EXTERN statement. dBASE defaults to the Standard Call convention as does Win32. Therefore, when working with the Win32 API (and most third-party APIs) using dBASE, you can omit the calling convention keyword in almost all cases. The calling convention should be noted in the Win32 API (or other API) reference documentation.

The above chart also signals another significant item. The Win16 API uses the Pascal calling convention in which all function names are specified using upper case characters. The previous 16-bit versions of dBASE masked this for the programmer by automatically converting to uppercase the function names of all functions EXTERNed with the Pascal convention. Therefore, in the previous 16-bit versions of dBASE, the case mix of the function name was not critical in the EXTERN statement.

The Win32 API uses the Standard Call convention in which all function names are case sensitive. When specifying a Win32 API function name in the EXTERN statement, you must use upper/lower case exactly as it is specified in the Win32 API reference documentation. A function name specified in the wrong character case within the EXTERN statement will result in a 'Procedure not found' error, the same as if the function name was spelled incorrectly. After the function has been prototyped using EXTERN, it can be called without regard to case sensitivity.

Mapping Data Types

Let's look again at our typical EXTERN statement but from now on, we will be using the module alias User32 instead of the module filename User32.DLL:

```
extern CLOGICAL IsWindow(CHANDLE) user32
```

Here is the corresponding C prototype for the IsWindow function:

```
BOOL IsWindow(HWND hWND)
```

When referencing documentation for the Win32 API, most likely you will encounter the functions prototyped in C as above. We will need to know how to convert the C data types to the appropriate dBASE data types to successfully pass data between dBASE and external functions.

A logical boolean value is stored in C compiled for 32-bit as a 32-bit integer. A logical in dBASE is represented with true and false to represent true and false values respectively. However, Windows does not understand what true and false are intended to represent.

There needs to be a means to tell dBASE how to translate different internal dBASE data types into data types that are recognized by the function we are linking to. This is done using keywords associated with the EXTERN command.

Here is an expanded data type mapping table which is similar to the table contained in the dBASE online help documentation for EXTERN which defines the associated keywords and their corresponding types in C and Basic:

Data Type Mapping

dBASE Keyword	As Pointer	Data Type (1)	Data Size	C	Basic (2)
Parameters or return values:					
CINT	CPTR CINT	Numeric	32 bits	int	Long
CLONG	CPTR CLONG	Numeric	32 bits	LONG	Long
CSHORT	CPTR CSHORT	Numeric	16 bits	short	Integer
CWORD		Numeric	16 bits	WORD short int	Integer
CCHAR		String	8 bits	Char	Byte
	CSTRING	String	32 bits (address)	LPSTR/ LPCSTR char *	String
CUINT	CPTR CUINT	Numeric	32 bits	UINT	Long
CULONG	CPTR CULONG	Numeric	32 bits	DWORD/ unsigned long	Long
CUSHORT	CPTR CUSHORT	Numeric	16 bits	unsigned short	Integer
CUCHAR		String	8 bits	unsigned char	Byte
	CSTRING	String	32 bits (address)	LPSTR/ LPCSTR char *	String
CFLOAT	CPTR CFLOAT	Numeric	32 bits	float	Single
CDOUBLE	CPTR CDOUBLE	Numeric	64 bits	double	Double
CLDOUBLE	CPTR CLDOUBLE	Numeric	80 bits	Long double	
CLOGICAL	CPTR CLOGICAL	Numeric	32 bits	BOOL	Long
CHANDLE	CPTR CUINT	Numeric	32 bits	Handle, hWnd, hPen, hDC, etc.	Long
CVOID (Only needed as return type)	N/A	N/A	N/A	void	Procedure
Parameters only:					
CPTR	N/A	Numeric	32 bits (address)	void * lp<somevalue>	

Note 1: *This column represents the actual size, in bits, of the data passed. Notice that CSTRING and CPTR do not pass the actual data, but instead pass a 32-bit memory address (pointer) to the data.*

Note 2: *The data types for the BASIC programming language are also included in this chart for use when mapping functions documented in the BASIC language. The current dBASE documentation does not include the BASIC data types.*

Using the data type mapping table, we can see that the single parameter (CHANDLE) passed to IsWindow will be passed as a 32-bit (4 bytes) value. All handles to objects in Win32 are assumed to be 32-bit integers. dBASE internally stores numeric values with a much larger number of bits. CHANDLE tells dBASE to convert the number passed in the parameter to IsWindow from the dBASE internal numeric format to a 32-bit value. Proper conversion or mapping of data types is essential. Without it, we would have at best, erroneous results and at worst (and most likely) corruption of the memory stack which will almost always result in a nearly instantaneous General Protection Fault (GPF).

From the syntax template shown earlier for the EXTERN statement, we know that the first word after EXTERN and the optional calling convention keyword is the function's return type. Using the Data Type Mapping table, we can also see that the dBASE CLOGICAL keyword would result in the return value of true or false on return from the IsWindow function. Logicals at the machine level are actually represented as 1 for true and 0 for false. The CLOGICAL keyword tells dBASE to interpret (translate) the 1 and 0 values returned from IsWindow as the dBASE logicals true and false respectively. Now we can easily test whether a window handle is valid or not as seen by the Windows operating system:

```
extern CLOGICAL IsWindow(CHANDLE) user32
? IsWindow(_app.FrameWin.hWND)   // Result: true
```

But what if we made an error when we prototyped IsWindow using EXTERN?

If the function has already been called, chances are that the system memory stack is now corrupt. In this case, exit dBASE and Windows and reboot the system, even if a GPF has not yet occurred.

If we have not yet called IsWindow, we could do 1 of 2 things. Issue another EXTERN statement with the correct prototype specifications. Or we could use the RELEASE DLL command to cancel the EXTERN:

```
RELEASE DLL User32
```

RELEASE DLL cancels the function definitions of all prototyped functions that are contained in the specified module. Therefore, if we had already used EXTERN to prototype other functions exported from the User32 module, we would no longer have access to those functions until we repeated their respective EXTERN statements.

After a function is prototyped using EXTERN, the function is a valid Function Pointer (FP) dBASE data type. We can subsequently call the function in exactly the same manner as we would call any of the native dBASE functions.

```
? type("IsWindow")                // Result: U (Undefined)
extern CLOGICAL IsWindow(CHANDLE) user32
? type("IsWindow")                // Result: FP (Function Pointer)
? IsWindow(_app.FrameWin.hWND)    // Result: true
```

We can see from the Data Type Mapping chart and the original C prototype for IsWindow that the BOOL data type is passed as 32 bits. As a result, we can change our EXTERN statement so that the call to IsWindow actually returns a numeric value:

```
extern CINT IsWindow(CHANDLE) user32
? IsWindow(_app.FrameWin.hWND)   // Result: 1
```

188

Notice that all we did was change the return type in the EXTERN statement from CLOGICAL to CINT. This tells dBASE to map the 32-bit return value to a dBASE numeric value instead of a dBASE logical value.

Taking Advantage of Module Aliases

A module alias is not always the same as the module filename without the file extension. A vendor of a given module could release an updated version of the module with a different filename. However, the vendor would normally specify the same alias name for the new module as existed in the old module. By using the module alias name within EXTERN statements, it is rarely ever necessary to change the EXTERN declarations to accommodate a new version of the module. If using the LOAD DLL statement in dBASE to load the module, you only need to change a single LOAD DLL statement to load the module by its new filename into memory. After the DLL file is loaded into memory, all of the EXTERN statements for functions in the module can use the module alias.

In the case of Windows and the core Win32 API, this becomes even simpler. Whenever dBASE is running, Windows is running. All of the modules that comprise the core Win32 API functionality are already loaded into memory. And whenever Windows is running, the 3 core Windows module files USER32.DLL, GDI32.DLL, and KERNEL32.DLL are already loaded into memory and can be referenced by their alias names. To cross-reference the 3 core Window modules to their alias names:

Filename	Alias
USER32.DLL	User32
GDI32.DLL	GDI32
KERNEL32.DLL	Kernel32

When we want to use a function contained in the USER32 module such as IsWindow, we can dynamically link to it with:

```
extern CLOGICAL IsWindow(CHANDLE) user32
```

As I previously mentioned, a module alias may not be the same as the module filename without the file extension. If you attempt to EXTERN a function using an assumed alias, if the assumed alias is incorrect, dBASE will most likely display an "Error loading DLL" error message. To determine the correct alias to use for any module, find the module file using Windows Explorer, right-click the file, select 'Properties', select the 'Version' tab, then click 'Internal Name'. The module's alias is the module's internal name.

Aliasing Function Names

The generally accepted practice is to map a function as closely as possible to its C (or BASIC or Pascal) prototype as shown in the reference documentation for the API. If the function is mapped differently, it should be identified differently. The EXTERN statement allows for this with the FROM clause which allows specifying a different name (alias) for the function.

It's important to make a distinction here. We were just previously discussing module aliases, which are static and are assigned to the module when the module is compiled and linked by the module vendor. Here, we are discussing the dynamic assignment of an alias when referring to a function from within dBASE.

Here's some example code showing how one might use function aliasing:

```
release dll user32            // Cancel previous prototypes
```

```
? type("IsWindow")                    // Result: U
? type("nIsWindow")                   // Result: U
extern CINT nIsWindow(CHANDLE) user32 from "IsWindow"
? type("nIsWindow")                   // Result: FP
? type("IsWindow")                    // Result: U
? nIsWindow(_app.FrameWin.hWND)       // Result: 1
extern CLOGICAL IsWindow(CHANDLE) user32
? type("nIsWindow")                   // Result: FP
? type("IsWindow")                    // Result: FP
? IsWindow(_app.FrameWin.hWND)        // Result: true
? nIsWindow(_app.FrameWin.hWND)       // Result: 1
? IsWindow(0)                         // Result: false
? nIsWindow(0)                        // Result: 0
```

We now have IsWindow and a function called nIsWindow available to us. Note that the type of IsWindow was still undefined until an explicit EXTERN was issued to prototype it.

There are many reasons why it might be advantageous or even necessary to alias function names. An example of necessity would be a possible situation (although remote) which used a function from 2 different DLLs and both functions had the same function name.

```
extern CWORD SomeFunc1(CWORD) My1st.DLL from "SomeFunc"
extern CLONG SomeFunc2(CINT, CINT) My2nd.DLL from "SomeFunc"
```

Notice that the original exported names of the functions in both DLLs are the same (SomeFunc). However, with aliasing, we can prototype both functions and reference them with different alias names.

In another situation, a function may have different behavior or produce different results depending on the parameter type and value passed to the function. For example, the Windows API function SendMessage is used to send messages to an actual window or windowed control to change a characteristic of a window or control, or to exchange information with it. In fact, the newer Common Controls in all 32-bit Windows versions such as the TreeView, ListView, RichEdit, and NoteBook are heavily based on using messages. Here is the C++ prototype for SendMessage:

```
LRESULT SendMessage(HWND hWnd, UINT Msg, WPARAM wParam, LPARAM lParam);
```

Translating the above to a more common EXTERN that you might see in various dBL code fragments that are floating around:

```
extern CLONG SendMessage(CHANDLE, CUINT, CLONG, CLONG) user32;
        from "SendMessageA"
```

The above would be used to send numeric values to a window using SendMessage. An example of use might be:

```
SendMessage(hLV, LVM_SETCOLUMNWIDTH, nCol, nWidth)
```

This call to SendMessage would cause a message to be sent to a ListView window represented by the numeric window handle contained in the variable hLV to tell the ListView to set a column width. The third parameter indicates the number of the column and the fourth parameter indicates the width of the column in pixels.

Notice the second parameter value LVM_SETCOLUMNWIDTH. This is a constant numeric value which is #defined in a header file which is included in the Windows SDK. Rather than trying to remember numeric values, it is much easier to remember LVM_SETCOLUMNWIDTH to scroll the ListView window. It's also more self-documenting. Now you can see why having the proper header files is important.

Here's another example. This time we will use the LVM_GETSTRINGWIDTH message to retrieve the width of a specified string in pixels using the current font set in the ListView window. In this case, we would need to develop a different EXTERN prototyping statement:

```
extern CLONG SendMessageC4(CHANDLE, CUINT, CLONG, CSTRING) user32;
        from "SendMessageA"
```

Notice that we have changed the alias name from SendMessage to SendMessageC4 and we've changed the fourth parameter type from CLONG to CSTRING. An example of use might be:

```
nWidth = SendMessageC4(hLV, LVM_GETSTRINGWIDTH, 0, "ListItem Text")
```

As you can see, function aliasing allows us to use a multi-personality function such as SendMessage in many ways within the same code string without having to repeatedly execute EXTERN statements each time we need to use one variation or another.

Working with Win32 Character-Based Functions

The Win32 API encompasses 2 primary operating systems that are quite different in many respects. WinNT (NT/2000/XP) is the native base operating system for Win32. Win9x (95/98/ME) actually implements a subset of the full Win32 functionality. Another area where these 2 operating systems differ dramatically is that of internal handling of character data. Windows NT uses Unicode as its native character set. Unicode uses a multi-byte code to represent characters. Win9x uses the ANSI single-byte code to represent characters. To confuse things more, dBASE internally uses double-byte characters and supports passing character strings using either the CSTRING or CPTR options of EXTERN. Sounds confusing but we'll clear that up.

Dealing with Character Data

The character-based functions in the Win32 API are available in 2 flavors distinguished by a suffix letter added to the end of the function name for the functions that work with character strings. The letter 'A' represents the ANSI version of the function, the letter 'W' represents the 'wide' Unicode version of the function. Therefore the function GetWindowsDirectory is actually available as GetWindowsDirectoryA and GetWindowsDirectoryW in the Win32 API. The WinNT platform (NT/2000/XP) implements both functions whereas the Win9x platform (95/98/ME) only implements the ANSI ('A') version of the function. Under Win9x, the wide version of the function can usually be prototyped successfully with EXTERN. However, when the function is called, it always returns zero indicating that the function failed because the function is not internally fully implemented, but instead does nothing but arbitrarily return a failure indication. An example under Win 9x/ME:

```
extern CINT GetWindowsDirectory(CSTRING, CINT) kernel32;
      from "GetWindowsDirectoryA" // ANSI version
cBuff = space(41)          // Allocate buffer to receive pathname
? GetWindowsDirectory(cBuff, 40)   // Length of directory pathname
? cBuff                    // C:\WINDOWS
extern CINT GetWindowsDirectory(CPTR, CINT) kernel32;
```

```
                from "GetWindowsDirectoryW"  // Wide version
  cBuff = space(41)                          // Clear the buffer
  ? GetWindowsDirectory(cBuff, 40)           // Zero if running under Win9x/ME
  ? cBuff                                    // Blank
```

Because the basic character data type in dBASE is a double-byte character type and because the ANSI character functions are supported by both Windows 9x/ME and Windows NT/2K/XP, code written in dBASE should normally use the ANSI version of the character-based functions to ensure compatibility across both platforms. This can be best accomplished by aliasing the function name as done in the above code example for GetWindowsDirectoryA which is aliased as GetWindowsDirectory. Internally, WinNT (including 2K/XP) stores character information in Unicode. When GetWindowsDirectory (aliased from the ANSI version) is called in WinNT, WinNT does the conversion from its internal Unicode character format to ANSI and stores the ANSI characters in the buffer specified in the first parameter. When GetWindowsDirectory is called in Win9x, Win9x simply stores the ANSI characters in the specified buffer.

That's all good that both the NT and 9x platforms can give us a consistent character mapping to work with, the ANSI single-byte characters. But wait a minute. Remember that dBASE internally uses double-byte characters. How will dBASE correctly interpret the ANSI characters returned by the GetWindowsDirectory function call?

The answer is the CSTRING parameter type option of EXTERN. CSTRING tells dBASE that it should handle the string parameter as an ANSI single-byte string. When a string is being passed to a function and it is prototyped using CSTRING, dBASE automatically converts the passed string from the dBASE internal double-byte representation to a string containing ANSI single-byte characters for the function's use. On return from the function call, dBASE automatically converts the ANSI single-byte string back to double-byte for regular internal string storage and manipulation within dBASE.

In the previous 16-bit versions of dBASE, it is more reliable and almost as easy to use CPTR instead of CSTRING for passing character strings. In all 32-bit versions of dBASE, with the differences in the way the NT and 9x platforms handle strings and the automatic conversion between ANSI and double-byte that dBASE performs when using the CSTRING keyword, it is usually more reliable and much easier to use CSTRING when exchanging actual string text data with external 32-bit ANSI function APIs.

As previously mentioned, EXTERN allows passing strings using either CSTRING or CPTR. If using CPTR, dBASE does not do automatic character conversion from/to ANSI. If your code is targeted only for NT/2K/XP systems, you might want to use CPTR instead with the W version of the character-based functions. This will provide slightly faster performance because the automatic character conversion is not performed.

The Windows API consists of the 3 main core binary modules; kernel32, user32, and gdi32. But it also consists of many more extension APIs that support access to other facilities and technologies provided by the operating system. Examples are the Windows Shell facility, internet access (WinInet), Windows Sockets (WinSock) and multimedia (WinMM), among many others. Many of the extension APIs have been available with all 32-bit versions of Windows since Windows NT and Windows 95. The extension APIs are generally consistent with all of the information presented here.

In some cases, the newest extension APIs have departed from supporting both ANSI and wide versions of functions. An example is GDI+. GDI+ is a new output rendering technology that provides better performance and much greater functionality than the old GDI engine.

In GDI+, all functions that accept string data parameters expect the strings to be in the wide character format. ANSI character strings are not supported by the GDI+ functions. Also, some third-party DLLs only support wide character strings. In these cases, you would use CPTR instead of CSTRING to pass the character strings. When CPTR is used, dBASE does not perform any character conversions with the strings. The strings are passed to and received from the functions unmodified by dBASE.

To receive a string, all you need to do is EXTERN the function, pre-allocate a buffer to receive the string to the size of the anticipated string + 1 for the null (this is for insurance as some functions allow the NULL to extend past the specified length), then make the call:

```
extern CLONG GetWindowText(CHANDLE, CSTRING, CINT) user32;
       from "GetWindowTextA"
cText = Space(81)  // Allocate 1 more byte than expected for length
GetWindowText(_app.frameWin.hWND, cText, 80) // Up to 80 chars + 1 null
? cText
```

Data Structures 101

In the vocabulary of some who have attempted Windows API programming, the term Data Structure appears on a list about 10 steps below root canal. This is because data structures can be confusing and can be rather tedious to work with. However once the handling of data structures is understood, it really isn't as difficult as it first appears.

Using a Simple Data Structure

Let's take what we now know regarding EXTERN to develop a simple routine using a simple data structure. The purpose of the routine is to determine the client width and height of a form in pixels so that the number of pixels per form unit in the horizontal and vertical directions can be calculated. Before we start, we need to pull a few facts into scope.

- The width and height of a dBASE form as registered in the width and height form properties are the width and height of the client area of the form, in the form's current metric units.
- The client area is the form's window area excluding the titlebar and any frame drawn around the window.
- Windows measures everything on the screen in terms of pixels. Windows has no idea that dBASE can use 6 different scaling factors as determined by the form's metric property to determine form size, position and control size and position.
- If we want to talk to Windows about dBASE forms and controls using the Win32 API, we need to be able to convert form units to pixels.

Knowing these facts will help us to determine the best and easiest way to design the procedure we need. It will also help us to verify the results of our routine.

If we could find a Windows API function that will retrieve the client area width and height of a form in pixels, we can use that to calculate the pixels per unit. This would be simpler than any other approach because there are no other extraneous variables to take into account.

According to the Windows API documentation, there is a function called GetClientRect which is made to order for this. Here is the description from the Borland C++Builder Win32 API help file:

The GetClientRect function retrieves the coordinates of a window's client area. The client coordinates specify the upper-left and lower-right corners of the client area. Because client coordinates are relative to the upper-left corner of a window's client area, the coordinates of the upper-left corner are (0,0).

```
BOOL GetClientRect(
    HWND hWnd,    // handle of window
    LPRECT lpRect // address of structure for client coordinates
    );
```

Parameters:
hWnd - Identifies the window whose client coordinates are to be retrieved.
lpRect - Points to a RECT structure that receives the client coordinates.
The left and top members are zero. The right and bottom members contain the width and height of the window.
Return Values:
If the function succeeds, the return value is nonzero.
If the function fails, the return value is zero.

Referring to the Data Type Mapping table, we see that BOOL translates to CLOGICAL for the return value. In other words, the function will return a numeric non-zero or zero value depending on whether it succeeds or fails. hWND translates to CHANDLE for the first parameter.

What's this lpRect stuff all about? Again referring to the Data Type Mapping table, we see that lp<somevalue> equates to a 32-bit memory address that is typecast as CPTR. So lpRect is actually a memory pointer to a RECT data structure as defined in the Windows API. So the third parameter is CPTR. Now we can build the EXTERN statement for GetClientRect.

```
extern CLOGICAL GetClientRect(CHANDLE, CPTR) user32
```

That was pretty easy ... and the more you work with it, the easier Windows API programming becomes.

If you remember when we were talking about string parameters and API functions, I mentioned that CPTR tells dBASE to pass the specified string as-is with no automatic conversions to/from double-byte and ANSI. This is a good thing because we will be using dBASE character strings to create our data structure and we certainly don't want dBASE to change the content of our data structure.

Retrieving Data from a Structure

Now to build the RECT data structure. Here is a portion of the description of the RECT data structure from the Borland C++Builder Win32 API help file:

The RECT structure is defined by the Windows API to hold the coordinates of the upper-left and lower-right corners of a rectangle.

```
typedef struct _RECT {
    LONG left;
    LONG top;
    LONG right;
    LONG bottom;
} RECT;
```

Members:
left - Specifies the x-coordinate of the upper-left corner of the rectangle.
top - Specifies the y-coordinate of the upper-left corner of the rectangle.
right - Specifies the x-coordinate of the lower-right corner of the rectangle.
bottom - Specifies the y-coordinate of the lower-right corner of the rectangle.

We need to build a memory buffer to receive data from GetClientRect that is the size of a RECT data structure that holds 4 32-bit LONG values. So all we need to do is tell dBASE to set aside a piece of memory large enough to hold the data structure. We know that dBASE internally uses double-byte characters. So a character memory variable in dBASE occupies 2 bytes of memory for each character in the character string. And the total memory space occupied by the character variable is contiguous.

```
xRECT = space(8)
```

We now have a 16-byte memory buffer set aside which is the same size as we need for the RECT data structure which holds 4 32-bit integers (4 * (32 / 8)). In this case, we don't care what the actual contents of the memory buffer are because GetClientRect is going to write the client coordinates into the memory buffer replacing whatever was there previously. We only care that the memory buffer is protected which is accomplished by assigning an 8-character value (16 bytes) to our memory variable named xRECT. We could have just as easily declared the memory buffer using REPLICATE:

```
xRECT = replicate(chr(0), 8)
```

In this case, our RECT data structure pointed to by xRECT is now filled with zeros. It makes no difference to GetClientRect what the specific contents of the buffer are. GetClientRect is simply going to overwrite the contents of the buffer with the client coordinates.

Type each line into the Command window (without the comments) and let's see if this will fly.

```
extern CLOGICAL GetClientRect(CHANDLE, CPTR) user32
f = new Form()                    // Instantiate a form
f.left = 0                        // Move it out of the way
? f.hWND                          // Result: 0 (not a valid window)
f.open()                          // Make it a valid window
? f.hWND                          // Result: # 0
xRECT = replicate(chr(0), 8)      // Create RECT data structure
GetClientRect(f.hWND, xRECT)
```

Note the emphasis on the value of the form's hWND property. Whenever you are calling an API function that requires a window handle, the handle usually cannot be zero. Or in other words, to use an API function with a dBASE form or with a form-contained object, the form must be opened. Opening the form creates the window objects for the form and the form's controls and assigns a valid hWND value to the form's and controls' hWND property. The actual value of a form's or control's hWND property is assigned by Windows and the hWND value will always be unique. This is how Windows identifies which specific window the API function should target.

We now have the client coordinates of the window in the RECT data structure referenced as xRECT. So now, all we have to do is ? xRECT and read the 4 long (32-bit) values from the result window, right?

```
? xRECT
```

Well, maybe not. This is because the values are stored in the memory buffer for the RECT structure (dBASE character string) as natural binary values. Let's consider the makeup of the RECT data structure for a moment. It is 4 32-bit values stored contiguously in memory. Each value would look like this in memory:

```
[Left-lsb][Left-nsb][Left-nsb][Left-msb][Top-lsb][Top-nsb][Top-nsb]Top[msb]...etc.
```

In words, each 32-bit value is stored to the RECT structure in Least Significant Byte (LSB) - Most Significant Byte (MSB) order. What we need to do is extract the values in byte quads and combine the quads of bytes to obtain the 32-bit value for each of the 4 long values.

dBASE provides the functionality to do what we need in native dBL using the getByte method of the String class and the bitLShift function. Remember that dBASE thinks that xRECT is a 16-byte character string (8-characters). So we can use the getByte method to extract each individual byte. Then we apply BitLShift to properly align the 4 individual byte values and combine the values numerically.

Making Structures Easy with OOP

To make things easier, we'll take advantage of OOP to create a reusable class called StrBaseStruct that is subclassed from the String class and has methods to handle storing and retrieving signed and unsigned 16-bit and 32-bit values in data structures. And we'll create a subclass of the StrBaseStruct class called strRECT that will be the RECT data structure as defined in the Win32 API.

```
// Structs.CC
CLASS StrBaseStruct(nSize) of String

    this.sizeOf =                 0

    if not empty(nSize)
       this.zero(nSize)    // Structure size = nSize
    else
       this.zero(2048)     // Default structure size to 2k
    endIf

    // PROTECTed stock properties
    PROTECT anchor, big, blink, bold, fixed, fontcolor,;
           fontsize, italics, link, small, strike, sup
    // PROTECTed stock methods
    PROTECT asc, charAt, chr, indexOf, isAlpha, isLower, isUpper,;
           lastIndexOf, left, leftTrim, replicate, right, rightTrim,;
           space, stuff, sub, subString, toLowerCase, toProperCase,;
           toUpperCase
```

```
PROCEDURE Zero(nLen)

   if pCount() # 0
      this.sizeOf := nLen
   endIf
   this.string := replicate(chr(0), ceiling(this.sizeOf / 2))

FUNCTION GetU16(nIndex)

   RETURN int(this.getByte(nIndex) +;
           bitLShift(this.getByte(nIndex + 1), 8))

FUNCTION Get16(nIndex)
   LOCAL n

   n = this.getU16(nIndex)
   RETURN iIf(n < 0x8000, n, -0x10000 + n)

FUNCTION GetU32(nIndex)

   RETURN int(this.getByte(nIndex) +;
           bitLShift(this.getByte(nIndex + 1),  8) +;
           bitLShift(this.getByte(nIndex + 2), 16) +;
           bitLShift(this.getByte(nIndex + 3), 24))

FUNCTION Get32(nIndex)
   LOCAL n

   n = this.getU32(nIndex)
   RETURN iIf(n < 0x80000000, n, -0x100000000 + n)

PROCEDURE SetU16(nIndex, nVal)

   this.setByte(nIndex, bitAnd(nVal, 255))
   this.setByte(nIndex + 1, bitAnd(bitRShift(nVal,  8), 255))

PROCEDURE Set16(nIndex, nVal)

   this.setU16(nIndex, iIf(nVal >= 0, nVal, 0x10000 + nVal))

PROCEDURE SetU32(nIndex, nVal)

   this.setByte(nIndex, bitAnd(nVal, 255))
   this.setByte(nIndex + 1, bitAnd(bitRShift(nVal,  8), 255))
   this.setByte(nIndex + 2, bitAnd(bitRShift(nVal, 16), 255))
   this.setByte(nIndex + 3, bitAnd(bitRShift(nVal, 24), 255))

PROCEDURE Set32(nIndex, nVal)

  this.setU32(nIndex, iIf(nVal >= 0, nVal, 0x100000000 + nVal))

PROCEDURE Logout(lHex)

   ? "————— Begin Logout —————"
   ? "Structure: " + this.ClassName +;
     " - Size: " + int(this.sizeOf) +;
                "/0x" + iToH(this.sizeOf, 4)
```

```
         if type("this.logoutData") $ "CB|FP"
            this.logoutData()
         else
            ? "Formatted member data logout is not available."
         endIf
         if lHex
            this.logoutHex(this.sizeOf)
         endIf
         ? "————— End Logout —————"

      PROCEDURE LogoutHex(nLen)
         LOCAL n, x, xStr, cAscStr, nChr

         ? "————————— Begin Dump"
         ?? " —————————————"
         ? "        00 01 02 03 04 05 06 07  08 09 0A 0B 0C 0D 0E 0F"
         ?? "   01234567 89ABCDEF"
         ? "        ————————————————"
         ? "————————"
         ? " 0000|"
         n = iIf(pCount() # 0, nLen, this.length * 2)
         x = 1
         xStr = this.string
         cAscStr = "  "
         do
            nChr = this.getByte(x - 1)
           cAscStr += iIf((nChr < 32) or (nChr > 127), ".", chr(nChr))
            ?? " " + iToH(nChr, 2)
            if x % 8 = 0
               ?? " "
               cAscStr += " "
            endIf
            if (x % 16 = 0) or (x >= n)
               ?? cAscStr At 55
               if x < n
                  ? " " + iToH(x, 4) + "|"
               endIf
               cAscStr = "  "
            endIf
         until ++ x > n
         ? "————————— End Dump"
         ?? " —————————————"

   ENDCLASS  // StrBaseStruct of String

   CLASS strRECT of StrBaseStruct(16)

      FUNCTION left(n)

         if pCount() > 0
            this.set32(0, n)
         endIf
         RETURN this.get32(0)

      FUNCTION top(n)

         if pCount() > 0
            this.set32(4, n)
```

```
        endIf
        RETURN this.get32(4)

    FUNCTION right(n)

        if pCount() > 0
            this.set32(8, n)
        endIf
        RETURN this.get32(8)

    FUNCTION bottom(n)

        if pCount() > 0
            this.set32(12, n)
        endIf
        RETURN this.get32(12)

    PROCEDURE LogoutData

        ? "left:   " + "0x" + iToH(this.left(), 8)
        ? "top:    " + "0x" + iToH(this.top(), 8)
        ? "right:  " + "0x" + iToH(this.right(), 8)
        ? "bottom: " + "0x" + iToH(this.bottom(), 8)

ENDCLASS  // strRECT of StrBaseStruct

// EOF: Structs.CC
```

One of the strongest features of dBASE is the Command window. Everything we have done to this point except for creating the structure classes has been from the Command window. The Command window and dBASE's elegant EXTERN system provides the basis for a rather powerful Windows API prototyping tool. It is, in effect, a Windows API interpreter which immediately executes anything we need to test. This combination makes for a very easy learning tool and development prototyping tool for working with the Windows API.

Here is the same code that we ran from the Command window, but modified to use the new structure classes we created:

```
// Test1-1.PRG
set procedure to Structs.CC additive
if type("GetClientRect") # "FP"
   extern CLOGICAL GetClientRect(CHANDLE, CPTR) user32
endIf
xRECT = new StrRECT()                  // Instantiate a RECT data structure
f = new Form()                         // Instantiate a form
f.left = 0                             // Move it out of the way
? f.hWND                               // Result: 0 (not a valid window)
f.open()                               // Make it a valid window
? f.hWND                               // Result: <> 0
GetClientRect(f.hWND, xRECT)           // Get client area size in pixels
? xRECT.left()                         // Result: 0
? xRECT.top()                          // Result: 0
? xRECT.right()                        // Result: > 0
? xRECT.bottom()                       // Result: > 0
nPPUX = xRECT.right() / f.Width        // Calculate pixels/horz form unit
nPPUY = xRECT.bottom() / f.Height      // Calculate pixels/vert form unit
? nPPUX                                // Result:  7
? nPPUY                                // Result: 22
xRECT.logout(true)                     // View structure contents
```

We have now calculated the number of pixels per horizontal and vertical form unit. These values could be used to much benefit in subsequent Win32 API work in dBASE to further manipulate dBASE forms and form-contained windowed controls.

The values that were displayed on your system for nPPUX and nPPUY might not be the same as the values shown above, but the values that were displayed on your system are correct. The values are dependent on the system's display settings for small fonts/large fonts, etc, and they are dependent upon the form's current metric property setting. And if using a metric property setting of 0 – Chars, then the values are also dependent upon the settings of the form's scaleFontName, scaleFontSize, and scaleFontBold properties.

More About Structures

The StrBaseStruct class could serve as a base for deriving many other structure classes other than the RECT structure. You could expand the StrBaseStruct class to include methods for storing and retrieving 8-bit signed values, 24-bit unsigned values, and 64-bit signed and unsigned values, as well as floats and doubles. You would also need to add methods to handle storing and retrieving ANSI strings and most likely multi-byte character strings.

The RECT data structure is a very simple data structure consisting of only 4 32-bit signed data members. In reality, a majority of the data structures used by Win32 and third-party APIs are more complex, having more members and the data types of the members will not all be the same, but rather mixed. The StrBaseStruct class was kept as simple as possible for simplicity's sake for the discussions here.

Note also that the approach taken with the example data structures includes methods for logout of the data structure contents in both formatted member format and hex dump format. This is to aid in debugging while developing code that uses structures. To obtain the formatted member logout of the RECT data structure, simply add this line in the code:

```
xRECT.logout()
```

This will display the structure member names and member values in the Command result window. To obtain the formatted member logout and the hex dump, add this line in the code:

```
xRECT.logout(true)
```

This will display the formatted members and a hex dump of the structure's current contents. This significantly aids learning and understanding structures, and makes debugging much easier.

All versions of the dBASE 32-bit product shipped with a set of files for handling structures. The files are in the \Samples folder as Structure.prg, StructAPI.prg, Strucmem.dll and a sample form in the Win32api.wfm file as well as the related header files in the \Include folder. This set of files takes an entirely different approach to handling data structures. I've found it to be much more cumbersome to work with and I haven't yet encountered a data structure that I needed a special .DLL to work with the structure. I've also found the approach to be slower in terms of performance, so I can't recommend using that approach. However that alternative is available for exploration. Comments are included in the prg and wfm files to explain how to use it.

When to EXTERN

You'll notice one other addition in the previous code sample. There is the addition of an *if...endIf* construct around the EXTERN statement. This is to bring another important point to light. After a function has been prototyped using EXTERN in a dBASE session, it remains available to us in its current mapping until 1 of 3 things happens:

- RELEASE DLL <the DLL containing the function>
- EXTERN <return value> <the same function name>...
- Quitting dBASE

Therefore, repeated EXTERNs of the same function are unnecessary and in fact will negatively impact performance. EXTERN takes a considerable amount of time to execute due to the overhead in Windows involved with managing reference counts for loaded modules and the overhead involved with locating the particular function in the module and laying out an internal memory map to the function within dBASE. Using *if...endIf* constructs to avoid reEXTERNing a function which has already been prototyped will produce faster performance because the *if...endIf* construct executes faster than the actual EXTERN statement.

Generally, the best way to implement EXTERN is to enclose each and every EXTERN for each individual function within an *if...endif* construct like this:

```
if type("GetClientRect") # "FP"
   extern CLOGICAL GetClientRect(CHANDLE, CPTR) user32
endIf
```

Or better, if you can place all of the EXTERN statements required for an application in the application's startup code where it will only execute once, do that and forget the *if...endIf* construct. The disadvantage in doing this is that it confuses things considerably when building custom control classes that use the Windows API.

In the case of custom control classes, the best place to EXTERN is in the class constructor code with *if...endIf*. In this manner, you are assured of picking up all of the required EXTERNs when you first use the custom class. In addition, if you use the custom class multiple times in the same application, you gain the benefit of the *if...endIf* construct to improve performance by not repeatedly executing the EXTERNs for the custom class.

dBASE ships with a header file, WINAPI.H, which contains EXTERN statements for many of the common functions in the Windows API and #DEFINE statements for the associated constant values required. This header file is located in the.\include folder under the dBASE root install path. WINAPI.H (and the associated header files it uses) serves as a good starting point for developing Windows API code. However, each function is prototyped only once, using the most commonly used data type mappings. As previously discussed, you may need to use an entirely different data type mapping to achieve the results you need.

When using EXTERN statements from WINAPI.H, don't #INCLUDE WINAPI.H in your program. You will typically only use a handful of Windows API calls. Including the entire WINAPI.H in this manner consumes significant memory to hold all of the function mappings and will take a noticeable amount of time to run. Instead, copy the specific EXTERN statements that you need to use to the clipboard and paste them into your source code. Or better yet, write your own EXTERN statements for the functions you need. After you've done it a few times, you might find it easier to do than copy/paste from WINAPI.H.

There are many more functions in the Win32 API that are not contained in WINAPI.H. This should not be construed to mean that the functions not contained in WINAPI.H are not usable in dBASE. In fact, almost all of the functions defined in the Win32 API are usable in dBASE.

Placing Data in Structures

Creating a data structure for passing data to Windows or any third-party API is really the reverse of extracting data from a structure. To extract data from a structure, we used the getByte method of the string class and the bitLShift function. To place data in specific fields of a structure, we simply reverse that to use the setByte method and the bitRShift function. The code for this can be seen in the setU32 method of the StrBaseStruct class.

In our next example, we create a RECT data structure. The RECT data structure will specify an area within which we will draw some text. The structure is filled using real-time data based on the form's size to draw text within a rectangle that is within 20 pixels of the form's borders.

We'll also use a few other Windows API functions to dress it up slightly. The background color of the text is set to transparent using the SetBkMode Windows API function so that the text appears to be drawn directly on the form surface. And finally, we'll draw a line under the bottom of the block of text.

```
// Test1-2.PRG
LOCAL f, xRECT, nPixWidth, nPixHeight, cText, hDC, nHeight
set procedure to Structs.CC additive
if type("DrawText") # "FP"
    extern CINT DrawText(CHANDLE, CSTRING, CINT, CPTR, CUINT) user32;
        from "DrawTextA"
endIf
    #define DT_WORDBREAK 0x0010
if type("GetClientRect") # "FP"
    extern CLOGICAL GetClientRect(CHANDLE, CPTR) user32
endIf
if type("GetDC") # "FP"
    extern CHANDLE GetDC(CHANDLE) user32
endIf
if type("LineTo") # "FP"
    extern CLOGICAL LineTo(CHANDLE, CINT, CINT) gdi32
endIf
if type("MoveToEx") # "FP"
    extern CLONG MoveToEx(CHANDLE, CINT, CINT, CPTR) gdi32
endIf
if type("ReleaseDC") # "FP"
    extern CLOGICAL ReleaseDC(CHANDLE, CHANDLE) user32
endIf
if type("SetBkMode") # "FP"
    extern CINT SetBkMode(CHANDLE, CINT) gdi32
endIf
    #define TRANSPARENT 1
    #define OPAQUE      2
f = new Form()                       // Instantiate a form
f.left = 0                           // Move it out of the way
f.Width = 50                         // Adjust width for wrap effect
f.open()                             // Make it a valid window
xRECT = new StrRECT()                // Instantiate RECT structure
GetClientRect(f.hWND, xRECT)         // Fill RECT with client dimensions
nPixWidth = xRECT.right()            // Get client area width in pixels
nPixHeight = xRECT.bottom()          // Get client area height in pixels
xRECT.left(20)
xRECT.top(20)
xRECT.right(nPixWidth - 20)
xRECT.bottom(nPixHeight - 20)
cText = "This is a simple test of the DrawText function in the " +;
        "Windows API." + chr(13) + chr(13) +;
        "Notice how these lines are wrapped within the rectangle " +;
        "specified in the RECT data structure contained in the " +;
```

```
        "character variable xRECT." + chr(13) + chr(13) +;
        "Left:    " + xRECT.left() + chr(13) +;
        "Top:     " + xRECT.top() + chr(13) +;
        "Right:   " + xRECT.right() + chr(13) +;
        "Bottom: " + xRECT.bottom() + chr(13) + chr(13) +;
        "dBASE and the Windows API are positively great fun." +;
        chr(13) + chr(13) + "That's all folks!!!"
hDC = GetDC(f.hWNDClient)        // Default device context for window
SetBkMode(hDC, TRANSPARENT)      // Text background color = form color
nHeight = DrawText(hDC, cText, -1, xRECT, DT_WORDBREAK) // Display text
MoveToEx(hDC, 20, nHeight + 20, null) // Set line starting position
LineTo(hDC, nPixWidth - 20, nHeight + 20) // Draw line
ReleaseDC(f.hWND, hDC)           // Always release DC when done with it
```

The DrawText API function that was used is similar to the dBASE built-in Text class with an alignHorizontal property setting of 0 – Left, alignVertical property setting of 0 – Top, and wrap property setting of true. DrawText accepts various parameter values for text formatting. We used the predefined Windows API constant DT_WORDBREAK to cause the text to be wrapped. There are other predefined Windows API constants for centering the text, right-alignment, etc.

Upon closer examination, you will probably realize that some of the built-in classes in dBASE such as Text and Editor are nothing more than OOP wrappers that transform the DrawText API function into reusable built-in classes that have additional features added to draw the borders, change the font, change text alignment and such.

SetBkMode was used to change the default text drawing mode of the form to transparent. The default mode established for the window by dBASE is OPAQUE. The default text background color is white. If we commented the SetBkMode line, the text would have been drawn with a white background.

Because we have no way to trigger a redraw of the text at the appropriate times, if this window is overlaid by another window and then that window is moved away, the text will be erased in the overlay area. Similarly, if the form was minimized and then restored, the form would be redrawn in its restored position and size without the text. If the Form class had an onPaint event, we could use code similar to the code in Test1-2.prg to redraw the text at the appropriate times. A way around this would be to use a PaintBox that fills the form's client area and tie into the PaintBox's onPaint event.

Summary

This chapter examined the significant basic concepts of using the Windows API in dBASE. Particularly, some of the types of functions available in the Windows API, the basic concepts needed to use the Windows API or any third-party API in dBASE and a detailed breakdown of the handling of data structures was given.

It should be noted that for the 3rd edition of this book this chapter is largely "untouched" – except for formatting to match the new layout. The sample code has been tested under dBASE Plus 2.8 on Windows 7 and works as expected.

NOTES

Part VIII: Putting an Application Together

When you find that you are building an application, there are a lot of things to think about. Will the application be MDI (Multiple Document Interface), will it be SDI (Single Document Interface), will you use menus, popups, toolbars? Do you want to use the Application Frame Window? *(This will affect your menus and toolbars.)* Once you have those questions worked out, you will then need to decide if the application will use Dynamic External Objects (DEO), or if you will compile everything into one .EXE file. Learn how to use the Project Manager to build your application, work with the .INI file and determine what you need to do with it (if anything) and prepare your application for deployment. But even that has questions – will it be deployed in a network situation or a standalone computer? Etc.

Another thing to consider is whether or not your application will work with Windows Vista or Windows 7/8 and the User Account Control (UAC). When developers using dBASE first encountered the UAC, we worked around the UAC, instead of working with it. Starting with dBASE Plus 2.7 (March 2011), the software is more tolerant of the UAC. The chapters that follow have been, in some cases, completely re-written to help you build a UAC compliant application, if you need it.

The following chapters are aimed at helping you examine the pros and cons of various aspects of application design and completion and get you well on the way to completing your application and preparing it for deployment to your users.

Chapter 25: Some Application Design Concepts

This chapter is aimed at raising some questions that you need to think about when designing your application and help you make the right decision for how your application is deployed.

There are other issues that deal with deploying your application discussed both in Chapter 2, and in later chapters. These deal with the Windows UAC and designing your application to work with it. Some of that discussion will be continued here.

You will find that in many cases there is no "one right way" to design an application. Many applications use the application framewindow as the background; other developers never use the application framewindow as a background for their applications, and there are still more who do for one application and don't for another. There are a lot of things to consider.

The Application Framework

dBASE has an application object built in called _app. This has been discussed briefly in the past, but as you get to a certain point it is important to understand what this is and how it works.

The _app object is an object that is always available, either in the development environment (IDE) or in the runtime (your applications). The _app object is a way to make available custom properties (treated as if they were public variables), custom objects affect the application across the board.

If you have an object that you need to make available to your whole application for the duration of the application, rather than creating an instance this way:

```
public oMyObj
oMyObj = new MyClass()
```

You can create an instance this way:

```
_app.oMyObj = new MyClass()
```

These are effectively the same, but by tying the object to the application framework, you avoid some of the issues that may occur with a public object reference variable while still being available anywhere in your application.

In addition, the _app object has some properties and methods associated with it that you should be aware of. You can see these by going to the Command Window and typing:

```
inspect( _app )
```

And of course if you go to the online help, the _app object is described there. There are a lot of useful properties (30 or so) available to this object in dBASE Plus 2.8.

_app Properties

We won't discuss all of the properties of the _app object – some of them have been discussed in earlier chapters and some of them we don't need to get into in any detail. The following are ones that as a developer you should be aware of. The following were in versions of dBASE prior to 2.7 – there will be a discussion of some newer properties later in this chapter.

allowDEOExeOverride

This property defaults to *true*. It affects whether or not Dynamic External Objects (DEO) will affect your executable. If this is true, when your executable sees a call to an object such as a form, it does the following (in this order):

1. It looks in the folder that the EXE is in to see if the object (.WFO, for example) is in that folder and if it is, uses that object.
2. It looks in the .INI file to see if any DEO folders have been defined (we will discuss this in detail later) and if so, checks those folders for the object.
3. It then looks inside the EXE file to see if the object is contained in the executable.

This property, if set to *false* will tell dBASE to go straight to option 3 and ignore options 1 and 2.

This is particularly useful if you are testing the executable in the folder that your source code (and the object files) are in. For example, if you update a form file because you are testing something you may not want to see the changes appear when running the executable. There will be further discussion of this topic *(bundling the objects into the executable versus leaving them as external objects, and the advantages of both in later chapters)*.

If you wish your application to be a DEO application, leave this property alone.

allowYieldOnMsg

This property tells dBASE to allow a Windows message to come through while your application is processing a long process. The property defaults to *false*, but this one is a good idea if your application has long processes in it and you want to update the screen. If you leave this *false*, you may see during a long process that the screen does not update properly, or if you go to another program (as an example you might want to check your email while your program is doing its task), then return – your screen may appear partially white, or have other odd distortions. Setting this property to *true* can solve many of these issues. It should be noted that this can slow down a long process by a tiny amount, but with computers getting faster and faster it is likely you won't notice. You should also look at the _app.executeMessages() method discussed below.

databases

The *databases* property is an object reference to an array of databases. For the most part I don't recommend using it to store references to your own database objects, because it can be confusing. It is useful in that the default database object in dBASE (and your applications) – the current folder, can be accessed from here:

```
_app.databases[1].someMethod()
```

So if you need to empty a table, or use other methods of the database object and the table is in the same folder as your executable, you can use it. But for the most part trying to add your own database objects to this array and work with them is not really worth the trouble.

detailNavigationOverride

This property allows your application an application-wide way to affect all rowsets in master/detail relationships. This setting is not really recommended – don't use it unless you are sure. The default setting is "0 - Use rowset's detail settings". The other settings will affect all rowsets in your application even if you have set specific properties such as *navigateByMaster* or *navigateMaster*. This was added to dBASE for use by dQuery *(see Chapter 9)*, but you can create havoc in your application unless you really are sure you know what you will be affecting and how.

exeName

You might think this would not be all that useful, as it is the path and name of the executable. However, if you wish to write some "generic" code that works in more than one executable, this particular property can be quite handy. It returns the full path and name of the executable:

```
cMyEXE = _app.exeName
```

The property is read-only, meaning that you cannot change it, but you may be surprised at how useful it can be. If you want to know the path that your executable is stored in you can, using this and a combination of string methods and functions, return that information:

```
? _app.exeName.left( rat( "\", _app.exeName ) )
```

This may be useful in cases where your application changes the working folder using the SET DIRECTORY command, or perhaps to make sure if you are using a .INI file that it is in the correct folder (since the .INI file must be in the same folder as the executable).

frameWin

The *frameWin* property is another object reference that is assigned to the _app object. This particular object is very important to any dBASE developer if they wish to use the *frameWin* in the first place for an MDI application. It is affected by the *shell()* function which we will discuss shortly in more depth.

iniFile

The *iniFile* property points to the location of the .INI file being used by your application. This is automatically set by the executable, although your code *could* change it (this property is not read-only). If you have code that reads/writes to the .INI file (there is a class in the dUFLP that allows for this), then being able to pass the contents of this property to that code can save a lot of effort on your part.

insert

This property allows you to affect the state of the Insert key on your keyboard. It defaults to whatever state that this key is in and changing it is as easy as:

```
_app.insert := false // turn off the Insert key
```

It is interesting to note that this does not appear to affect the Windows setting – it is not quite the same as pressing the Insert key to change its state, because all Windows applications are affected by that. This only affects your executable.

language

The *language* property is a read-only property that is used to identify the language used in the design and runtime environments. This is affected by the language DLL being loaded by dBASE or by your own application, which is determined by a setting in the INI file for dBASE or the executable.

lDriver

This property is also read-only and is loaded by looking at either a setting in the .INI file, or by looking at the default driver in the BDE.

printer

The *printer* property is an object reference to a printer object that can be used to affect your whole application – you can set a default printer driver, for example:

```
_app.printer.printerName := "HP LaserJet 5L"
```

This can also be done with the *printer* object's *choosePrinter()* method:

```
_app.printer.choosePrinter()
```

By using this, all reports in an application can be sent to the same printer without the user having to select the printer each time.

There are other properties of the *printer* object – you should examine these.

It should be noted that the default printer object does not always allow specific settings to work for specific reports. You may need to use the printer object associated with a report (myreport.printer.choosePrinter()) to modify specific properties, such as *duplex*.

session

The *session* property is an object reference to the default session in your application. If you need to use a session's properties without creating your own session, it is possible to do so this way. This might be useful for a multi-user application for example. This has already been discussed in some depth in an earlier chapter of this book.

sourceAliases

This property is another object reference to an Associative Array of the source code aliases you have defined. This is only useful inside the IDE – it is not useful in your own deployed application, because source code aliases are not recognized by the runtime engine (use DEO instead).

speedBar, statusBar

These two properties default to *true* and allow the developer to turn the default dBASE toolbar and statusbar on or off for their own applications.

_app Events

There is only one event handler that a developer can "hook" into:

onInitiate()

This event is fired when a client application requests a DDE link with dBASE Plus as the server, and no DDETopic object for the specified topic exists in memory. *(For more details, see the OLH.)*

_app Methods

There are only three methods of the _app object, but they all have their uses:

addToMRU()

This was created specifically to be used by dQuery, but you can use it yourself to add a file to an MRU entry in the menu for your application. "MRU" stands for "Most Recently Used".

executeMessages()

This method is handy when you are working a complex loop in your code and you have a form that displays to show the status, or you have another application running, etc. The method, if placed inside the loop, will execute any Windows messages that may have built up in the queue, including refreshing screens, mouse clicks, etc.. It is used this way:

```
do while not qQueryName.rowset.endOfSet
   fMessage.progress1.value ++ // move a progress bar
   _app.executeMessages()
   // do some processing
   qQueryName.rowset.next()
enddo
```

themeState()

This returns a value (0 to 2 – see below) detailing whether Windows themes are being used in your application. The following are the return values and a description of what they mean (taken from the online help for dBASE):

0 – themes are not available (older version of Windows, no manifest files, or themes are disabled in some fashion).
1 – themes are enabled, but with the old theme (the user has chosen to use "Windows Classic").
2 – themes are enabled and a newer theme is active.

Individual form-based objects have a property called *systemTheme*, which is part of what the *themeState* method is used for – to let you know if this property is useful in your applications.

User Account Control (UAC)

In addition to the properties of the application object noted earlier, in release 2.7 of dBASE we have some new properties and methods specifically designed to work with the UAC:

useUACPaths

If this property is set to *true* (the default setting), dBASE (or an application) should follow the UAC rules, if it is *false*, the application will act as if developed in earlier versions of dBASE. For this book we are assuming this property is set to *true*.

currentUserPath

This is the full path to the users' private dBASE or application folder. When using the IDE (developer's environment), this shows the dBASE folder. When using an executable, this points to a path similar to one of these:

1) In Windows XP, the private user folders are located under:

   ```
   C:\Documents and Settings\yourapplication
   ```

2) On later versions of Windows (Vista, Windows 7, etc.):

   ```
   C:\Users\<username>\AppData\Local\yourapplication
   ```

Where *yourapplication* is the path structure of your .exe from either the main drive, or the Program Files folder structure of Windows.

allUsersPath

This property contains the full path to the shared folder where shared files or folders may be located for dBASE Plus or for your application. Within the IDE, this defaults to the dBASE BIN folder. Inside your own application:

1) On Windows XP,

   ```
   C:\Documents and Settings\All Users\Application Data\yourapplication
   ```

2) On newer versions of Windows, this folder defaults to:

   ```
   C:\ProgramData\yourapplication
   ```

Where *yourapplication* is the path structure of your .exe from either the main drive, or the Program Files folder structure of Windows.

roamingUsersPath

This is the full path for the current users' roaming folder, where you can choose to store data for an application that will roam from one workstation to another if a network hosting an application is configured to support roaming users.

1) In Windows XP, the roaming user profile folders are located under:

   ```
   C:\Documents and Settings\<username>\application data\
   ```

2) In newer versions of Windows, roaming user profile folders are located under:

   ```
   C:\Users\<username>\AppData\Roaming\
   ```

This gets fairly involved and there is a lot of information on setting up an application to handle roaming users in the OLH.

_app.session.addAlias()

This method adds User BDE Aliases to the default BDE session. This is useful to create a temporary alias, for example to create/modify some temporary table (or tables) for your application. Assuming the path exists, you would do this by using:

```
_app.session.addAlias( <aliasname>, <driver>, [<options>] )
```

The alias name would be something like "TempData", the driver depends on the actual data type you are using. If you are working with dBASE tables, then this would be "DBASE". The options are important if the path is not in the same folder as your exe (for UAC applications this should not be done – see Chapter 2). Assuming a temporary database path in the ProgramData folders:

```
_app.session.addAlias( "TempData", "DBASE", "PATH:C:\ProgramData\TempData" )
```

There is more information on this Chapter 2, 5 and 10, as well as in the OLH.

_app.session.deleteAlias()

This allows you to remove a User BDE Alias from the current BDE session (other than the default session).

The Application Framewindow

The object referenced by _app.framewin is quite important to a dBASE developer. If you wish to use this in your application, it is the background – a menu or toolbar object will be placed on it, and by default all forms are contained by it. It is possible to use it, or not use it, as you desire for your MDI application.

When you create a .exe, there is a function called *shell()* that is used to tell dBASE what to do with the framewindow.

By default, when dBASE starts, the framewindow is on and visible. This is because the Command Window, Navigator, and so on are MDI windows and must have a parent form to contain them. dQuery is also displayed inside the framewindow, so if you have dBASE configured so that dQuery always starts with dBASE, you will see that dQuery is contained inside the application's framewindow.

When you create an executable, the opposite is true – the framewindow is assumed to be off, *unless* your application uses an MDI form. If an MDI form is opened, the framewindow must be available to contain it. In addition, if your application assigns a menu to the _app.framewin object, the framewindow must be displayed.

If your application is SDI – you can do away with the framewindow, if you so desire.

An example that ships with dBASE that does this is the Contax example. To see this, using the Navigator window, and click the folder button on the right of the "Look in" combobox, find the Contax folder *(see below)* – select this folder (and click OK). The location of this folder can be found with current versions of dBASE Plus in one of the following:

1) Windows XP:

    C:\Program Files\dBASE\Plus\Samples\Contax

2) Current versions of Windows:

    C:\Users\<username>\AppData\Local\dBASE\Plus\Samples\Contax

Figure 25-1

Then click on the "Programs" tab and double-click the file "Contax.prg". This will show you the main startup screen of the Contax application – notice that the application framewindow does not exist:

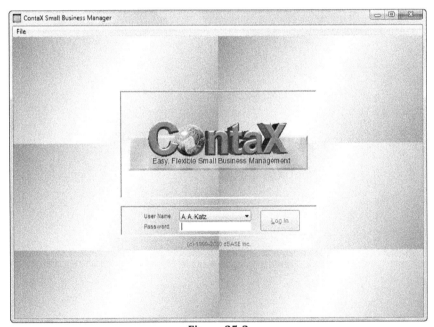

Figure 25-2

Typing the letters "CEO" in the password field and clicking the Login button, you will see a new form:

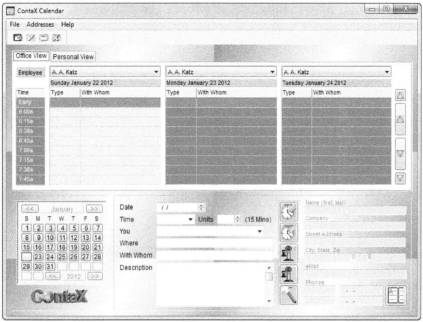

Figure 25-3

The full application works without the application framewindow. This is done in the startup program (in this case the file "Contax.prg") by executing the *shell()* function this way:

```
shell( false )
```

If you wish your application to use the application framewindow, you would use:

```
shell( true )
```

📋 **NOTE**

If you choose to use the framewindow with your application, there are a few interesting things you can do with it to enhance the appearance of the application. The following code (provided by Gerald Lightsey) can be used to add a gradient background to your form:

```
set procedure to gradient.cc addi
_app.gradient = new gradient()
_app.SpeedBar = false
_app.StatusBar = false

_app.gradient.Color2 = _app.gradient.rgb(200,200,200)
_app.gradient.Color1 = _app.gradient.rgb(100,100,200)
_app.gradient.dir = 1   // vertical, if you want
                        // horizontal, use any other number
_app.gradient.Open()
```

The code necessary for "gradient.cc" is in the dUFLP (see the appendices) in "gradient.zip". This can be used to add a picture to the background instead of a gradient.

There is a second parameter that tells dBASE to force the MDI shell – in other words to make sure it is there even if no menu is assigned to _app.framewin, and forms are contained within the framewindow:

```
shell( true, true )
```

By default the second parameter is assumed to be *false* and if the first parameter is *false*, there is no need to use the second one. You may see in some applications (if you examine the source code):

```
shell( true, false )
```

But the second parameter is not really necessary. You can examine the code for this application at your pleasure. You may learn a few things ...

The Application Framewindow's Properties, Events, and Methods

The framewindow does not have a lot of properties that you can directly affect, however the following is a listing of what you can change:

text
This property is what is displayed in the titlebar of the application framewindow. You can change it within dBASE directly:

```
cOldText = _app.framewin.text
_app.framewin.text := "My Application"
```

The text in the titlebar has now changed:

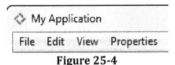

Figure 25-4

You can reset it using the code shown above:

```
_app.framewin.text := cOldText
```

systemTheme
This allows you to specify whether to apply the *systemTheme* property for your application and is assumed to be *true* or *false* for form controls. The default setting is *true*. This sets an application default, and individual controls that have the *systemTheme* property can be modified individually as needed in your application.

visible
By default the framewindow is visible, so this property defaults to *true*. You can set it to *false*, but you might have some difficulties if you forget to set it back to *true*.

windowState
This determines if the framewindow is "maximized", "minimized" or "normal" (neither) and can be used in your startup code. You would need to determine the status of the framewindow when the application is closed and save this to a .INI file, then when you next start the application you can reset it to the previous state.

onClose()
This is the only event handler that you can work with, but it is useful one. This was added in recent versions of dBASE to allow the developer to handle the user clicking the close button

(the 'x') in the titleBar of your application. This allows you to set up code that can close an application gracefully. Many applications in the past have disabled the 'x' button in the titlebar because there was no way to handle closing the application properly from there.

hasHScrollBar() and *hasVScrollBar()*

These two methods can be used to determine if the framewindow is displaying scrollbars (horizontal and/or vertical). These methods return a value of *true* if a scrollbar is currently displayed and *false* if not. These are useful for determining the amount of screen "real-estate" available for your forms.

That's all there really is. Developers have asked for the ability to change the background color, or to set an image in the framewindow. Currently to do these things one must use Windows API calls, which are a bit beyond the scope of what is being covered here *(although some of this is available from code in the dUFLP, specifically "gradient.zip" by Vic McClung)*.

Creating an Application Object

As a developer there are many ways to build and control an application. One option that has been around since early in the days of dBASE Plus is to create an object that is used to open, close and perhaps store code that is used by all aspects of your application. This might include such things as navigation in rowsets – rather than storing code that navigates in multiple places (menu, toolbar, etc.), you could place it in the application object and call it from there.

This is a very object-oriented way of thinking and while this may still be a new concept for some developers, it can make your application easier to work with. If it is created well, you might be able to re-use the application object for multiple applications with only minor changes.

The following is a trimmed down version of an application object I use for some of my applications. It does things such as initialize the menu, set the text in the titlebar, etc.. When the application is closed, the code for that resets some things and ensures forms, tables and databases are closed, etc. You can add code as needed and permission is granted to use this in your own applications if you wish. After this sample code listing, we will discuss two programs that are used with this, Start.prg, and Setup.prg.

```
/*
   SampleApp.cc.prg
   A sample dBL program from
   The dBASE Book
   by Kenneth J. Mayer.
   Program copyright ©2005-2012
   Permission granted for use as a learning tool for dBASE Plus.

   This has been updated for dBASE Plus 2.8 and later versions.

   Sample from: Chapter 25
   This is the application object used to start/close an application,
   trimmed down from work done on a recent project by myself.

   Dependencies: Setup.prg
                 MainMenu.mnu
                 :dUFLP:Ini.cc
```

```
      To see this work properly, you should download the dUFLP
      from the author's website, install it as designed, and
      then the code should work ... otherwise the custom class
      "ini.cc" will not exist, and will cause problems.
*/
#define APP_VERSION "1.0"
#define APP_NAME    "A Sample Application"

class SampleApp

   // Set up procedures in memory -- calling the SETUP.PRG file:
   if not setup()
      release object this
      return
   endif

   // assign the instance of this class
   // as an object reference off the _app object:
   _app.Sample = this

   /*-------------------------------------------------
      This method handles opening the application
   -------------------------------------------------*/
   function open

      // set the menu:
      set procedure to MainMenu.mnu
      this.rootMenu = new MainMenuMenu( _app.framewin, "Root" )

      // You could insert code to load a toolbar here.

      // Set Shell
      shell( false, true )

      // Save titlebar text:
      this.OldTitleText = _app.Framewin.text

      // set the speedbar/statusbar off
      _app.Speedbar  := false // turn it off
      _app.StatusBar := false // same

      // if you save specific settings into a .INI file,
      // this might be a good place to read them, using
      // a file object, or a .ini class (such as the
      // one in the dBASE Users' Function Library Project),
      // or code similar to what is used in the chapter
      // of the book dealing with Windows API calls.
      // use .INI file to check for a couple of user preferences:
      set procedure to :dUFLP:INI.cc

      // are we in the runtime, or are we
      // in the IDE?
      // RUNTIME first:
      if ("runtime" $ lower( version(1) ))
          // we are in the runtime, use the default
          // .INI file which should be in the same
          // folder the executable is in:
          _app.ini = new ini( _app.IniFile )
```

```
   else
      // otherwise we are in the IDE
      // We are working with "SampleApp", so need
      // that as the name of the executable:
      _app.ini = new ini( set("directory")+"\SampleApp.ini" )
   endif

   // set speedtip preference:
   cSection = "Preferences"
   cEntry   = "ShowSpeedTips"
   // if it doesn't exist, create it with default:
   if empty( _app.ini.getValue( cSection, cEntry ) )
      _app.ini.setValue( cSection, cEntry, "true" )
   endif
   // get value, and set (convert string to logical)
   this.ShowSpeedTips = ;
         iif( _app.ini.getValue( cSection, cEntry ) == "true",;
                              true, false )
   // Note about code shown above -- it was written
   // for an application that allows the user, through the
   // use of a menu option and a dialog form, to set
   // this preference. The menu option does not exist
   // in this smaller sample application. It is here as
   // an example of how it works.

   /*
      disable the 'x' for _app ONLY if we're
      in runtime. This forces the user to use
      the "File" menu to exit the application.
   */
   if "RUNTIME" $ upper( version(1) )
      sysClose( _app.Framewin, false ) // disable
   endif

   // display version and text in titlebar ....
   _app.FrameWin.text := APP_NAME + " -- " + APP_VERSION

   // make sure application is "on top"
   if type('BringWindowToTop') # 'FP'
      extern clogical BringWindowToTop( cHandle ) user32
   endif
   BringWindowToTop( _app.framewin.hWnd )

return


/*------------------------------------------------
   Shutdown
------------------------------------------------*/
function close

   // close anything we may have left open:
   close forms

   // close any open data:
   close tables
   close databases
```

```
            // reset titlebar:
            _app.Framewin.text := this.OldTitleText
            this.OldTitleText  := null

            // Save any settings to the application's .ini file
            // such as user preferences here.

            // release menu
            m = this.rootMenu
            release object m
            release m

            // if you loaded a toolbar in the open() method,
            // it would be prudent to detach it here, and release
            // the object reference.

            // release application object
            release object this
            _app.Sample := null

            // restore _app.framewin ...
            shell( true, true )

            // issue 'quit' only if we're in RUNTIME, otherwise
            // testing gets really annoying ...

            // If you don't issue the 'quit', then the shell
            // gets left on screen, which is weird, to say the least.
            if "RUNTIME" $ upper( version(1) )
                quit
            else
                // reset:
                _app.speedbar  := true
                _app.statusbar := true
                sysClose( _app.Framewin, true ) // enable close button
                keyboard('{ctrl+tab}')
            endif
        return

    endclass

    /*
        --------------------------------------------------------------
        Enables or disables the "close" item on the system menu as well
        as the Win95 X.

            Syntax:     sysClose( oForm, lEnabled )
            Example:    sysClose( _app.FrameWin, false ) // disable
                        sysClose( _app.FrameWin, true )  // ensable

        Posted by Gary White in the VdBASE newsgroups
        7/3/1998

        Returns the previous state of the menu item.
        --------------------------------------------------------------
    */
    function sysClose
    parameters oForm, lEnabled
```

```
local hMenu, lRetVal
#define MF_ENABLED       0x00000000
#define MF_GRAYED        0x00000001
#define SC_CLOSE         0xF060

   if argCount() # 2 or ;
       type("oForm.hWnd") # "N" ;
       or type("lEnabled") # "L"
     msgbox( "Correct syntax is:  sysClose( oForm, lEnabled )",;
        "Error", 16 )
      return
   endif
   if empty( oForm.hWnd )
      msgbox( "Form is not open", "Error", 16 )
      return
   endif

   if type( "GetSystemMenu" ) # "FP"
     extern cint GetSystemMenu( cHandle, cInt ) USER32
   endif
   if type( "EnableMenuItem" ) # "FP"
      extern CLOGICAL EnableMenuItem( cHandle, cInt, cInt) user32
   endif
   hMenu = GetSystemMenu( oForm.hWnd, 0 )
   if lEnabled
      lRetVal = EnableMenuItem( hMenu, SC_CLOSE, MF_ENABLED )
   else
      lRetVal = EnableMenuItem( hMenu, SC_CLOSE, MF_GRAYED )
   endif
return not lRetVal
```

That looks complicated, but it's not really. One important aspect of this code is the use of the Windows API function to disable the "x" in the titlebar. This is because dBASE applications have no way to fire an event if the user clicks on that "x", so you cannot manage the closing of the application that way. By disabling this, the only way a user can close the application is from the menu used by the application, or if you have code that fires from a form, toolbar, etc. This will allow you to properly shut down the application and process any code you feel is needed when the application closes.

Unfortunately while the framewin object has an *onClose* event, this currently does not work and the developers at dBASE are not sure if they can get it to work. This event (if working) would fire by clicking the 'x' button on the title bar, then by using your own event handler; create specific code to close the application gracefully.

There are some places that have comments that say "You could ..." and such in there. These are sort of place holders. If you wanted to open a toolbar with your application, there is a spot that it is recommended in the *open()* method above to do so. There is also a note in the *close()* method where you should detach and release it. If you wanted to insert some code that reads from and/or writes to the .INI file there are some comments (and some sample code in the *open()* method that uses a custom class in the dBASE Users' Function Library project) to do so. This is all a skeleton – you can add and remove code as you need to for your own applications.

Next let's look at the startup program. This program is used to start an application. In this case its primary purpose is to create an instance of the application object and call the object's *open()* method.

```
/*
   Start.prg
   A sample dBL program from
   The dBASE Book
   by Kenneth J. Mayer.
   Program copyright ©2005-2012.
   Permission granted for use as a learning tool for dBASE Plus.

   Sample from: Chapter 25
   Startup program for sample application.

   Dependencies: SampleApp.cc
*/

close all
clear all
release all

set procedure to SampleApp.cc addi

// instantiate a new class, defined in SampleApp.cc
// which is the application itself:
_app.Sample = new SampleApp()

RETURN ( _app.Sample.Open() )
```

This program quite literally just creates an instance of the application object, setting the object reference variable as a property of the _app object (_app.Sample), then calls the application object's *open()* method. That's it.

The Setup program, which is called from the SampleApp object's *open()* method is used to do things such as open any procedure files that are used throughout the application, do any necessary setup that isn't done elsewhere and so on. I often use the setup program to perform any setup I need when I am developing an application.

For example, in some of my applications there are functions in procedure files that are used in reports. If I do not open those procedure files before working on the reports, errors may occur. If I run the setup program *first*, then the files are available and I can work on the reports without the errors. By writing the code properly, you can make this code work in both the IDE when developing, and executing the application's executable.

```
/*
   Setup.prg
   A sample dBL program from
   The dBASE Book
   by Kenneth J. Mayer.
   Program copyright ©2005-2012.
   Permission granted for use as a learning tool for dBASE Plus.

   Sample from: Chapter 25
   This is a program that can be used by a coder who wants to
   work on modifications to this application, and
   it can be called as a basic "setup" for the
   application from the Start program.
```

```
    It makes sure the environment that the developer
    is working in is okay, and any setup that might
    be done has been completed.

    Dependencies: Start.prg
                  mainmenu.mnu
*/
clear

// if we're not in the runtime environment,
// make sure the application's speedbar
// and statusbar are available:
if NOT "runtime" $ lower(version(1))
    _app.speedbar   := true
    _app.statusbar  := true
endif


// ----------------------------------------------------------
// set procedures:
try
    set procedure to program(0)
    set procedure to start
catch( exception e )
   msgbox( "Unexpected error occurred in program setup."+chr(13)+chr(13)+;
           "Error: "+e.code+" -- "+e.message+chr(13)+chr(13)+;
           "Program: "+e.filename+chr(13)+;
           "Line: "+e.lineno,;
           "Setup Error!", 16 )
endtry

// ----------------------------------------------------------
set epoch to 1950

// whatever else gets stuffed in here
set century on

return true

// end of main routine, we can store any functions here that we
// might want to use for multiple parts of the application ...:

/*
    End of SETUP.PRG
*/
```

Note the "generic" error trap shown – it is mean to deal with unexpected situations, and let you know where the error occurred.

The only thing left would be a menu – the application object's *open()* method uses "mainmenu.mnu". For our purposes, if you wanted to copy the following you would have a very simple menu to use. This one literally only has a "File" option, which has an "Exit" option in it. But you could copy this and expand it as needed:

```
/*
    MainMenu.mnu
    A sample dBL menu from
```

```
    The dBASE Book
    by Kenneth J. Mayer.
    Program copyright ©2005-2012.
    Permission granted for use as a learning tool for dBASE Plus.

    Sample from: Chapter 25
    A basic menu for use when building an application.
*/


** END HEADER -- do not remove this line
//
// Generated on 04/13/2005
//
parameter formObj
new MainMenuMENU(formObj, "root")

class MainMenuMENU(formObj, name) of MENUBAR(formObj, name)
   this.FILE = new MENU(this)
   with (this.FILE)
      text = "&File"
   endwith

   this.FILE.EXIT = new MENU(this.FILE)
   with (this.FILE.EXIT)
      onClick = class::EXIT_ONCLICK
      text = "E&xit"
   endwith

   function EXIT_onClick
      // when the user selects this option,
      // call the application object's
      // close method:
      _app.Sample.close()
   return

   endclass
```

If you have all that code in a folder, you can test it by running the Start.prg file. You should see something similar to:

Figure 25-5

In a compiled application the "x" in the titlebar on the right is greyed out (not shown above) which is disabled. The text is as we defined in the SampleApp.cc class, the menu is up with just the "File" option, etc. If you select the "File" option, then the "Exit" menu option, this will all return to the way it was, including the text.

It is important to note that the environment should be returned to the state it was in before you tested your application ... the sample code here does that.

Issues for Setup of Your Application

The developers at dBASE have provided some program code that may be able to help you set up your application for your end-users.

These two programs are described below with some examples of how they might be used. You would need to decide if you want to use them at all, and if so, if you wanted to use them in your application class, your setup program, etc. In both cases, the developers have provided the *source code*, so that you can open the files and view the code, the comments, and see more details than what may be provided here.

InitNewUser.prg

If you are using current versions of dBASE on current versions of Windows, this file will be found in this path structure:

```
C:\Users\<username>\AppData\Local\dBASE\Plus\dBLClasses\Startup
```

If you are using Windows XP, this will be in:

```
C:\Program Files\dBASE\Plus\dBLClasses\Startup
```

In either case, you should be able to view the source code by typing something along these lines in the Command Window:

```
// This is one statement:
cPath=left(_app.currentUserPath,len(_app.currentUserPath )-
3)+"\dBLClasses\Startup"
// This is another statement:
modify command cPath+"\InitNewUser"
```

One of the first things to note is that in the comments at the beginning you are given permission to copy and alter the code. So for your own application you might have your own copy of "InitNewUser.prg", and deploy it with the application, doing just the things you need it to do.

This program code is used by dBASE Plus itself to set up the folders needed for dBASE under a full UAC enabled installation and the User BDE Aliases used by dBASE.

You should also note the list of dependencies – these are other program files used or referenced by this one. So if you chose to include this with your application you would want to make sure you include the other files as part of your application.

What does this program do?
In dBASE Plus, this program does the following things:

1) It creates an object (oSettings) based on the class UserSettings contained in the file.
2) The oSettings object creates a list of folders to be copied to the appropriate user folder path structure (CSIDL_LOCAL_APPDATA or CSIDL_APPDATA) as appropriate (see Chapter 2 for definitions of these).
3) It checks to see if the current user is a new user by looking for the user folder structure.
4) If this is a new user *(the user folder structure does not exist)* it creates the folder structure, copies folders of files into it, and sets up the User BDE Aliases that should be stored in Plus.INI based on those folder structures.

If you want to use this for your own application(s) you will want to copy the file and make the necessary changes for it to work for your application (list of folders to be copied, User BDE Aliases to be created, etc.).

qBDEMgr.cc
If you are using current versions of dBASE on current versions of Windows, this file will be found in this path structure:

```
C:\Users\<username>\AppData\Local\dBASE\Plus\dBLClasses\NonVisual
```

If you are using Windows XP, this will be in:

```
C:\Program Files\dBASE\Plus\dBLClasses\NonVisual
```

This file should be easier to find and modify, as there is a Source Code Alias set up in dBASE to help.

```
modi comm :NonVisual:qBDEMgr.cc
```

What does the program do?
Well, first – this is not a program file *per se*. It is a custom class file with a set of classes defined to help work with User BDE Aliases.

The primary purpose for you as a developer is to be able to extract information about BDE Aliases, create them as needed, and so on.

This is a large and complex set up code, which you can see if you examine it a bit in the Source Code Editor.

Some basic useful information:

```
set procedure to :NonVisual:qBDEMgr.cc
// create an instance of the qBDEManager class:
oBDE = new qBDEManager()
// obtain the description of a BDE Alias:
oDBDesc = oBDE.GetAliasDesc("SomeAlias")
? oDBDesc.szName()    // BDE Alias Name
? oDBDesc.szText()    // returns any description of the database
? oDBDesc.szPhyName()   // returns the Path assigned to the BDE Alias
? oDBDesc.szDBType()  // returns "STANDARD" or SQL Link Driver
                      // Name, or ODBC Driver Name
```

With this information, you could create a new User BDE Alias for a session object, if needed (an example is shown in a previous chapter of this book), if you need to know, in your code, the path to the database so you can do some special processing, this will return that path. And so on.

There are other methods of creating User BDE Aliases, described elsewhere in this book.

Other things that might be useful:

The GetAutoInc() and SetAutoInc() Methods

This method of the qBDEManager class can be used with a level 7 .DBF table to change the value of an autoIncrement field in the table to whatever you need it to be. The code below assumes a query object has been created with a table loaded that has an AutoInc field:

```
set procedure to :NonVisual:qBDEMgr.cc
// create an instance of the qBDEManager class:
oBDE = new qBDEManager()

// obtain the next value to be used by the AutoInc field:
? "Next AutoInc value: "+oBDE.GetAutoInc( qTest.rowset.handle )

// change it to some other value:
oBDE.SetAutoInc( qTest.rowset..handle, 10 )
```

Why would you need this? If you have emptied a table out, you may want the autoIncrement to start at 1. Other examples might include loading data from a table through the XDML "APPEND FROM" command – this command does not update the autoInc value in the table. By using this code you could set the next autoincrement value to what you needed it to be. For example if you know you added 300 records to a table, you may want to start the next number to 301, this would allow you to do that.

There is similar code in the dBASE Users' Function Library Project (dUFLP), and if all you needed was this ability, you might want to go there. However, these two methods are just a part of what is available to a developer.

Other Methods in This Class

There are many other methods of this class that you may want to examine, including the ability to delete BDE Aliases, check to see if BDE Aliases exist, obtain lists of tables contained in specific database aliases, find the Primary Key in a table, and a lot more. If you wish to use this class with your own applications, dBASE has provided the code. You should examine it to decide what you might need.

Some of these are available in classes in the dUFLP, but having them in one place may be very useful for your own applications.

SDI vs. MDI Style Applications

One of the biggest decisions to make is whether or not your application will be SDI (Single-Document Interface) or MDI (Multiple-Document Interface). You may decide that one application is SDI and another MDI. However, combining the two is a way to create havoc. So you should decide on one or the other.

This is not to state that an MDI application cannot have a form that is opened with the *readModal()* method (this is particularly useful for dialogs), but that the overall architecture of the application should be either MDI or SDI.

When you create an SDI application, there should be a starting form and everything must be form driven. For example, if you close a form without opening another first, your application may end. One option would be to have a main form and everything else would be called as a dialog.

Issues with SDI applications:

- Windows has to create a taskbar button for each form although you can set the form.showTaskBarButton property to *false* if you do not want to display a button on the taskbar
- Windows *(and your application)* has to expend more GDI (Graphics Design Interface) resources in order to create and paint additional menus, separate toolbars, etc.

However, SDI applications are easier to create.

Issues with MDI applications:

- Windows must "fight" for the topmost position, especially when mixing SDI (e.g. modal dialogs) and MDI forms.
- If an application loses focus, sometimes getting focus back to the form that *should* have it requires more effort.
- Tracking forms that are open is a necessary aspect of your application, as well as determining if a form may be opened more than once, also becomes an issue.
- If you wish to allow a user to open a form that interacts with data more than once, and that form uses a database, you may need to use session objects, which can add a layer of complexity to the form's code.

However, MDI applications are more "Windows-like", even if they do take more work to set up and create.

The difference between these was discussed early in the chapter on forms. Rather than be redundant and cover the material again, you should go back and re-read the chapter on Forms.

Menus, Toolbars, Popup Menus – Should You Use Them?

This question affects the overall architecture of your application as much as the SDI/MDI question.

If your application uses menus, will you use a system-wide menu or will you have menus that change as you perform specific tasks? Or will have you have specific menus, if required, for each form being displayed?

Likewise, if your application uses Toolbars, will you again have system-wide toolbars or have different toolbars to be used with different forms? There are advantages to going either way. You can even have toolbars that are used for all aspects of the application and add smaller toolbars that are used for specific forms that are then removed (detached) when done. But you should think about this before creating the application.

Will your application use popup menus? If so, you need to examine these issues. Popups add another layer of complication in your code, but are a very common Windows element.

Passing Parameters to an Application

You may want to set up your dBASE executable (we will discuss building an executable in a later chapter) to accept parameters. For example, you might want to call it as:

```
myApp abcd efgh 123
```

This would pass three parameters – they would all be considered to be character strings, so you would need to convert the last one using the *val()* function to a numeric value in the startup program.

To deal with these, the startup program in your application would need to be set to accept parameters. You could test this in dBASE in the Command Window by creating this program:

```
// StartWithParams.prg -- to test parameters
parameter cVar1, cVar2, nVar3
msgbox( "Number of parameters passed: "+argCount() )
if argCount() > 0
   msgbox( "Type of cVar1: "+type( "cVar1" ) )
endif
if argCount() > 1
   msgbox( "Type of cVar2: "+type( "cVar2" ) )
endif
if argCount() > 2
   nVar3 = val( nVar3 )
   msgbox( "Type of nVar3: "+type( "nVar3" ) )
endif
msgbox( "Done" )
if "runtime" $ version(1)
   quit
endif
```

Save the program, and then type in the Command Window:

```
compile startWithParams
build startwithparams.pro to testparams
```

This will make sure startwithparams.pro has been compiled, then build an executable from that program. To test the program:

```
run( true, "testparams abc def 123" )
```

This will run the program with the three parameters. The program will tell you how many parameters were passed using *argCount()* (you could use *pCount()* as well) then shows the type of each. When it gets to the third parameter it uses the *val()* function to convert the value to a numeric from a character string. The list "if" statement checks to see if we're in the runtime, if so will close down the .EXE properly.

Summary

This chapter was aimed at getting you starting to think about the overall picture when developing an application and to present options that you should consider. While some specific code was given, it can be ignored, modified, etc. Every application has its own needs and every application developer is different and thinks differently. There are seldom cases when developing an application in dBASE that there is only one "right way" to do something.

Chapter 26: Using the Project Explorer/Building Your Executable

Any developer who needs to finish their application is going to run into the fact that the process of Compiling and/or Deploying their application is not well documented in the manuals or online help (although this process is better documented in dBASE PLUS than in previous versions). This chapter spends a lot of time on the Project Explorer, but toward the end I show other methods of building your executable. Deployment of your application is covered in Chapter 28.

This process is actually pretty simple, but it may not appear that way the first time you try it. While you could build a "Response File" (.RSP) and "BUILD" (using the BUILD command) from there, it is simpler to use the Project Explorer that ships with dBASE PLUS which is designed to be a front-end for the these options. This is discussed later in this chapter.

It may take a bit of work, but in the long run you are ensured that everything is set the way it should be, especially when you start looking at the DEO *(Dynamic External Object)* settings.

Following along you should be able, when done, to create a project file and build/compile your application and be ready to deploy it.

The Difference between Non-DEO and DEO Applications

This issue can easily confuse a developer. A Non-DEO application is one where all of the object files (compiled forms, programs, etc. – files with an extension ending in "o" such as .WFO, .PRO, .REO, .CO, etc.) are built into the .EXE itself. If these files are contained in the .EXE then the application does not need to look elsewhere to find them.

A DEO application is a .EXE that does not have all (or even most) of the object files contained internally ("Dynamic **External** Objects"). This gives the developer the ability to update a single object, such as a form, send it to the end user, and not have to re-deploy the application. The external objects may be in the same folder as the .EXE, or they may be stored in another folder (or several folders), based on information stored in the application's .INI file.

There is also the possibility of a "hybrid" application – one that has the object files build into it as a Non-DEO application, but if you place an object file in the folder with the .EXE (or in the paths referenced in the .INI file as DEO object paths) the new object file will be used instead of the one built into the .EXE.

A dBASE Plus application follows the following instructions when it looks for any compiled object:

1) It looks in the folder with the .EXE (the "home" folder) for the object – if found, it executes it and stops looking for it anywhere else;
2) If it does not find it in the "home" folder, it then looks in the .INI file for the DEO object path entries (discussed later in this chapter) – if found, it executes the object file and stops looking;
3) It looks internally – in the .EXE file to find the compiled object and if found, executes it. If not found, an error occurs, telling you (or your user) that the object file cannot be found.

This hopefully will help as we discuss the DEO and Non-DEO application aspects of building the executable throughout this chapter.

Security of Your Source Code

One concern that often comes up for a developer is the security of the intellectual property that is the source code. The developer has put a lot of time and effort into that and either the developer, the client, or the company they work for owns that source code. Deploying the source code could mean not having control over that intellectual property.

When you build an executable (as will be shown in this chapter), or even if you test your files (run a form, a program, a report ...) in dBASE itself, dBASE compiles those files into object files (a .WFM is compiled into a .WFO file, etc.).

dBASE compiled objects cannot be "uncompiled" – in other words, if you have a .PRO file, you cannot open it in an editor and see/steal/borrow the code, it is encrypted in such a way that this has not proven possible. Security of your source code is not an issue with dBASE applications, as long as you do not deploy it with your application *(something you would have to intentionally do)*.

BDE Aliases

For this chapter, as well as Chapter 28, we will be using User BDE Aliases for the sample code. I am focus on these because with modern operating systems, the BDE configuration is harder to set up when deploying an application than User BDE Aliases *(due to rights issues)*, and your application will work with User BDE Aliases as if they were the older style "hard-coded" BDE Aliases. User BDE Aliases are discussed throughout the book starting in Chapter 2 if you need more information.

User BDE Aliases will require additional code pointing to where the data resides on the computer. As discussed throughout this book, User BDE Aliases default to being temporary, which means that they disappear from memory when the application or dBASE closes. In most cases this should not present a problem.

We will be using code similar to:

```
_app.session.addAlias( "DBASEFISH", "DBASE", ;
       "PATH:"+" C:\dBASEBook1_SourceCode\Tables")
```

(You may remember that in earlier chapters we copied the Fish table to the "Tables" folder ...)

For your own application obviously we would need to set a path to a different location as you most likely will not be deploying the dBASE Samples tables. For the time-being we will default to these.

Starting a New Project

Starting a new project is quite easy with the Project Explorer. Just like other design tools in dBASE, in the Navigator, click on the "Projects" tab and you will find an option "(Untitled)". If you double-click this the Project Explorer will open with a brand new and completely empty Project.

When the Project Explorer screen comes up, you may have to widen the form a little, to see everything that is on it. For example, I have found the checkbox that belongs to the text "Build as UAC app?" is very far to the right and you need to widen the screen to view it.

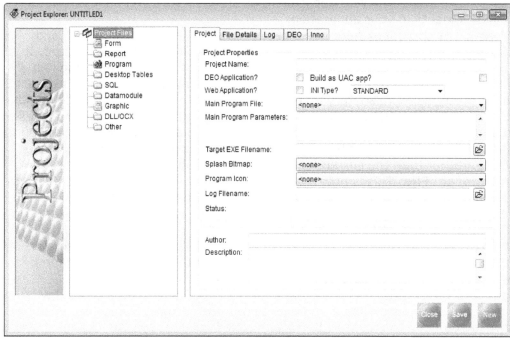

Figure 26-1

On the left is a TreeView that shows the different types of files. If we already had files in the project, the folders would be open and displaying the files contained in them.

On the right is a notebook with several tabs – we will briefly discuss each of them. Please note, these are just very short and quick discussions – more detail will be provided as the chapter progresses and you are walked through the process of building an executable.

The *Project* Tab

This is an important page of the project as it defines a variety of things that are important for how your application is built.

- **Project Name:** This is just an internal name that you will use for your project. It will be the default name of your executable. In other words, if you type "MyApplication" in this entryfield when you move focus off this entryfield you will see "MyApplication.exe" in the "Target EXE Filename:" entryfield.
- **DEO Application?** This is used if you want your complete application to be a Dynamic External Object based application. For more details on this concept see the discussion of DEO later in this chapter and also see "DEO" in the online help for dBASE PLUS. NOTE: If you only want some of your files to be treated as DEO, do NOT use this checkbox. *(It is possible to create what might be called a "hybrid" application, partially DEO and partially not – we will look at this later.)* The checkbox is a bit far to the right from the text and appears to belong to the text "Build as UAC app?", but it doesn't. I have been told by the developers this will be fixed in a future release of dBASE.
- **Build as UAC App?** Checking this box tells the Project Explorer, when you build the executable that the runtime will use the (default) UAC settings for dBASE Plus 2.7 or later applications. This was discussed at some length in Chapter 2. Note the checkbox is very far to the right … do not use the checkbox to the left of the prompt, that belongs to "DEO Application?"

- **Web Application?** This tells the Project Explorer, when you build the executable to add the "WEB" option. It tells the dBASE Runtime to not load the elements used for user-interface (such as forms, etc.), which speeds up loading the runtime. Do not check this unless you are creating a web application, or are very sure you have absolutely no user-interface elements in your application.
- **INI Type:** The combobox here has three options: "STANDARD", "NONE" and "ROAMING". Standard is the default setting, because it is ... well ... standard. It is the usual way a Windows application works, there is a .INI file with the same name as the executable (i.e., MyApp.exe would have a .INI file named MyApp.INI). The "NONE" option is pretty self-explanatory – your application does not use a .INI file and has no need of one. The last option is for applications on a network server where users may login at different workstations. This is mostly handled automatically, but the option here tells the dBASE runtime that the .INI file will be in the roaming users' file folder structure, rather than the current user file structure on the computer.
- **Main Program File:** This is not really optional. However, it can be set either here after you have added files to the project (see below), or when adding files and setting it there. This is the program file that is initially run when your application starts up – such as "Start.prg" or "MainForm.wfm", etc.
- **Main Program Parameters:** This is only used if you are requiring parameters for startup of the application. There is an explanation and an example in Chapter 25 *(toward the end of the chapter)*.
- **Target EXE Filename:** This is the name of the executable that is created when you select "Build". It is auto-filled if you type text in the "Project Name" entryfield, but otherwise you need to create it. If it is auto-filled for you, you can change it and the Project Explorer should remember it.
- **Splash Bitmap:** The name of the bitmap to be used for the splash screen of your application. The file must be in the project file list. *(A splash screen is an image that displays as your application is loading ... many developers don't use them as much these days, as the load time for executables has gotten shorter.)*
- **Program Icon:** The name of the icon file to be used for the titlebar of your application. This is also the icon that will appear on the desktop if you set a shortcut to the executable, and various other places in Windows, to represent your executable. The file must be in the project file list.
- **Log Filename:** This is a text file (default extension of .txt). This is written to while the application is being built (or re-built) using the "Build" menu options. Any errors or warnings will be displayed here. It is a good idea to use this.
- **Status:** Shows the last date/time the file was created or modified.
- **Author:** What it sounds like: the author(s) of the program.
- **Description:** Describe the program.

The *File Details* Tab

This option is only allowable if a file is selected in the listing on the left of the screen. Since the project shown above is empty, you would not be able to select this item. This will be discussed below under "Adding Files to The Project".

The *Log* Tab

When you select the option(s) to build or rebuild the executable from the "Build" menu, a log file is used to store errors and/or warnings that are generated in the process. It is displayed on this page of the form and will be discussed when we look at building an executable.

The *DEO* Tab

This is where you specify the folders used for a DEO application. We will discuss this in more depth under the section of this paper titled: "Creating a DEO Application".

The *Inno* Tab

This tab brings up a series of pages *(a notebook control)* that allows you to define how to deploy your application. It assumes you have installed the free deployment software package called "Inno Setup" (by Jordon Russel) – a copy should be on your dBASE PLUS CD. NOTE that this option is only available in dBASE PLUS 2.5 or later in the Project Explorer, but all versions of dBASE PLUS should have a version of "Inno Setup" on the CD. We will explore this option in Chapter 28.

Adding Files to the Project

There are several ways to add files to the Project:

- Right click on the treeView or one of the specific categories (list of folders) on the left part of the screen and select "Add files to Project";
- Drag files from the dBASE Navigator to the treeview;
- Select files in the Windows Explorer and drag them to the treeview.

For each file you add to the project there are some questions you need to examine, many of which are defined on the "File Details" page of this form. These will be discussed later in this chapter as we take a look at the process.

Now we have examined the basic parts of the Project Explorer we will perform a step-by-step walk through the creation of an executable using the sample applications in this book.

Creating a "Basic" (Non-DEO) Application

For the examples that follow, we will be looking at a fairly simple application, using some files from the previous chapter (the Start.prg, Setup.prg, MainMenu.mnu *(slightly modified)* and SampleApp.cc files) and also copying from an earlier chapter's exercise, the "SomeFish.wfm" file. The SomeFish.wfm file relies on a custom form, as well as some custom classes, so we will need to include those as well. We may want an application icon and perhaps a splash screen.

A "basic" dBASE application is a snap to do with the Project Explorer, once you have all your files loaded. So the first thing to do is to add the files that you need into the project. For this demonstration we will be creating a project from scratch, adding all the files and establishing any specific settings.

If you have not done so, start the Project Explorer. The simplest way is to go to the "Project" tab of the Navigator in dBASE PLUS and double-click on "(Untitled)". This will bring up the screen shown in the example earlier in this chapter.

📝 **NOTE**

In the sample code for this chapter the form *SomeFish.wfm* has been modified to use the database alias "DBASEFISH", as described at the beginning of the chapter. The file *SampleApp.cc* includes code to create the User BDE Alias as needed. The code only does this for use inside the IDE. This is because with a deployed application you can specify the User BDE Alias in the .INI file for the executable. This will be discussed in detail in Chapter 28. If you wish to test this, you will want to open SampleApp.cc and make changes to the path for the sample tables. See the comments in the code that explain what to change and where.

Getting Started

Once you have the Project Explorer form displayed there are a few things you should do. Enter a "Project Name:". In this case, since this is going to use the SomeFish form, call it "My Fish". When you tab off this entryfield, note that the "Target EXE Filename" has been filled in. You may want to remove the space between "My" and "Fish" – I find that if you name an executable with a space in it, it can cause a lot of problems.

Since this edition of the book is focusing heavily on making your applications Windows compliant, you should check the "UAC Application?" checkbox.

Just going down the "Project" tab items, you would need to know various things, such as "Is this a DEO Application?", in this case it is not, so leave that unchecked. It is not a "Web Application", so leave that unchecked. "Main Program File" – We haven't added any files to the project yet so leave that alone. We are not passing any parameters to the executable when it is run, so we are leaving that alone. The "Splash Bitmap" and "Program Icon" entries cannot be worked with until those files are added to the Project, so we will come back to them. The "Log Filename" is a useful thing to have, so that the Project Explorer can display any warnings or errors that occur when building the application. Call this "FishLog.txt". For the "Author" use your name and the description can be long or short ... it's not used for anything outside of the Project Explorer.

At this point it is a good idea to save the project. Click the "Save" button, or press ⌘Ctrl⌘+⌘S⌘ and name this "Fish1".

The Project should look like the following – Figure 26-2 *(be sure you examine the blue note earlier about the paths to the tables)*:

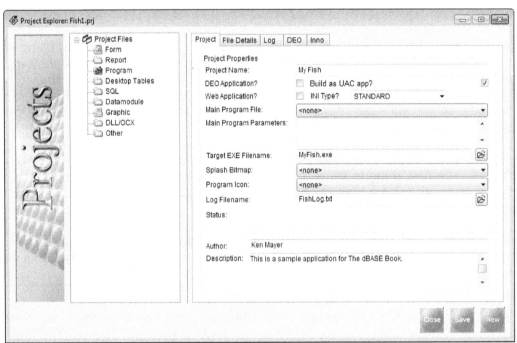

Figure 26-2

Add Files

The next step is to add the files to the Project that need to be there. Determining what needs to be in the Project is not always easy. One option is to simply add everything. Anything that the PE doesn't know what to do with will end up in the "Other" section. You should include all files related to your application, including forms (.WFM and .CFM), custom controls (.CC usually, although they might be in .PRGs), program files (.PRGs), and so on. This should also include tables, images, ActiveX controls, .DLL files ...

There are a couple of ways to add files, one is just to grab everything you want in the Project and add it at once *(from where you have them on your system/hard drive(s))*, the other is a bit more orderly. It's completely up to you.

If you right-click on the main folder that says "Project Files", you will see only two options enabled: "New" or "Add files to Project". The "New" option allows you to go to the appropriate design surface and create a new file of the type selected which will then be added to the Project. We're going to assume for now that all the files we need have already been created.

You can also go to individual folders *(treeItems)*, right click on them and see the same thing. However, if you select, for example: "Form", right click and then select "Add files to Project", you will be limited to only adding forms (.WFM), custom forms (.CFM), compiled forms (.WFO) or compiled custom forms (.CFO) and several others for menus, popups ..., or you can select the "All" option, which will list all files in the folder. You will see similar selection options for each of the other folders or *treeItems*.

For the purpose of this demonstration, the files will be added for each folder (forms, reports, etc.) one folder at a time. This is really just a preference on my part, you should use what works for you.

Make sure when you add forms to include any Custom forms that might be required *(if your form is based on a custom form, be sure to include it, if your custom form is based on another custom form, you need to include that as well)*.

One other thing to note, if you use files that are in other folders, you will have to navigate to them. While dBASE, LLC, intends to add the ability to use Source Aliases in the future, this is not currently an option *(the current version I am working with will recognize a source alias, but does not stream them out)*.

For the moment, select "SomeFish.wfm" and "MainMenu.mnu". If you click on "SomeFish.wfm" you will see the Project Explorer now shows the "File Details" page. This page will look something like:

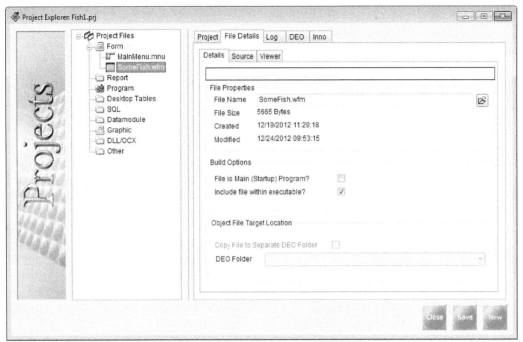

Figure 26-3

If you click on the "Source" tab, you will see the Source Code and if you click on the "Viewer" tab you will see the form displayed. It is *not* interactive – you cannot modify code, navigate, etc. The only purpose is to show you what it looks like.

Make sure you are on the "Details" tab and note that this displays the full path to the file, how big it is, date created and more. Below that are some "Build Options" and more but we will come back to these.

For the SomeFish form to work there are some other files that need to be added, because we used a custom form class, some custom form controls and custom pushbuttons. If we do not include these with our application, dBASE will not be able to find them. If you click on the "Source" tab, you can view the source code and note the names of the files we need, which in this case are all listed at the top of the code. We need the custom form class named "Data.cfm", the custom class files "MyPushbuttons.cc" and "MyFormControls.cc". You will want to right click on the folder and select the appropriate options, using the dialog to go find those particular files (look in the sample folders for MyCompany\Forms and MyCompany\FormControls).

You may not recall (it was a few chapters ago) but "Data.cfm" also needs "Base.cfm", so you should ensure you include that file as well.

You will also need to add the following files:

```
start.prg
setup.prg
SampleApp.cc
```

And from the dBASE Users' Function Library (dUFLP) you will need:

```
ini.cc
setproc.prg
stringex.cc
```

With all of these files loaded, the Project Explorer should look like Figure 26-4:

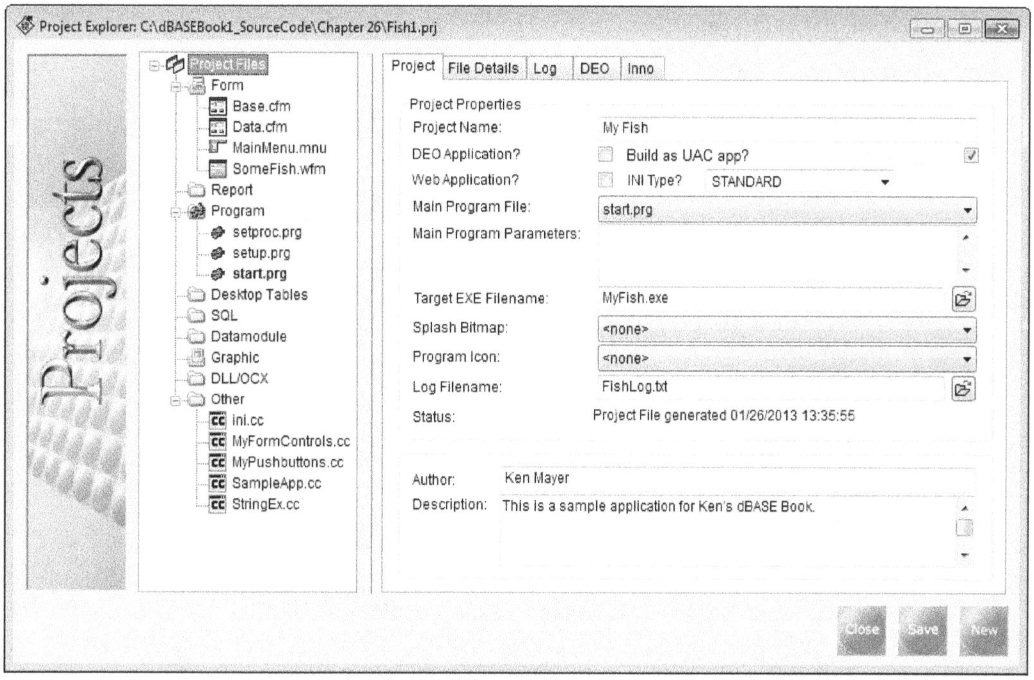

Figure 26-4

We have not dealt with an icon or splash file, but we can come back and deal with those later.

If you are adding the Source Code for a file, you do NOT need to add the compiled object for that file *(in other words, for "MyProg.prg: – you do not need to include "MyProg.pro")*. If you add tables to a project, you do not need to add the auxiliary files (for DBFs, the .MDX and/or .DBT files; for Paradox (.DB) tables, all the various extensions that may be needed for a table), just the table itself. The only reason to add a dBASE object file is if you do not have, or do not wish to use, the source code for that file.

As files are added to the project you will see that the last file added will appear with the "File Details" tab on the project showing and on that page of the Project, the "Details" tab will be set. This allows you to modify how the file is dealt with by the Project. We are going to use the default options for now.

> **📝 NOTE**
>
> With some experimentation, if you use any of the code provided by dBASE, LLC in the folders installed with dBASE, be careful which versions you place into your project. If you are on a Windows computer with UAC enabled, a copy of these files is placed in the users folder structure (CSIDL_LOCAL_APPDATA):
>
> ```
> C:\Users\username\AppData\Local\dBASE\PLUS\dBLClasses
> ```
>
> for example. You should use this version in the Project Explorer. I discovered this building an application using SEEKER.CC which is in the "FormControls" folder. I used the version under "C:\ProgramData ..." and when I tried to build the executable. It could not compile the file (the folders are by default read-only), then the reference to SEEKER.CC was removed from my project. Changing the path used to that shown above allowed the PE to compile the program and everything completed properly.

Start Program

There needs to be one program that is loaded when you start the application. This is called the "Main (Startup Program)". You should find this and click on it in the treeview listing on the left of the screen. In this case the startup program is called "Start.prg".

If you click on that file, you can set this as the "Main" program by either checking the checkbox that says "File is Main (Startup) Program?", or by right clicking and selecting "Set as Main". This should now look like Figure 26-5:

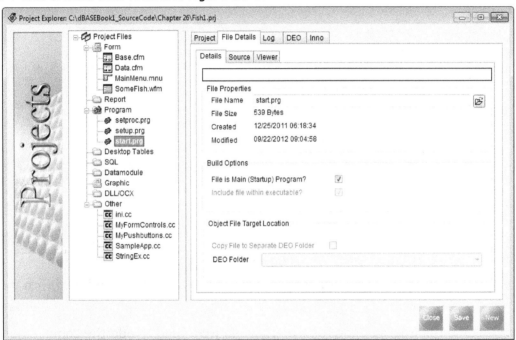

Figure 26-5

It should be noted that the startup program is shown in bold in the treeview listing. Your startup program does not have to be a .PRG file – it can be a form, report or whatever you need. Most developers use a .PRG as it allows a lot of non-UI code to be handled in the background. It all depends on your needs.

Finishing Touches

At this point all the files needed for the application should be loaded into the Project and all the settings should be made. There is no need to do much more, but there are some minor finishing touches you might want to consider.

If you go back to the "Project" tab of the project you can set the last properties needed. Note that since we have set the start program, the combobox for "Main Program File:" is now filled in for us.

If you want a splash screen to appear when your application loads you will need to select that from the images that are in the project. If you did not load any images, you should add the image you wish as your Splash bitmap (for whatever reason these must be .BMP files, as no other file format is acceptable).

You will want to do the same for the "Program Icon" and again the icon file (.ICO) needs to be included in the project.

For this example, an icon file that will work to represent this executable exists in the dBASE PLUS samples folder, so you can right click on the "Graphic" folder and select "Add files to Project ...", and then find the file in the folder

```
C:\Users\username\AppData\Local\dBASE\Plus\Samples
```

called "Fish.ico". Once you have selected that file, click on the "Project" tab, then in the combobox titled "Program Icon", select "Fish.ico" and you will be set. *(As specified in other chapters of this book, the folder will be different if using older versions of dBASE or Windows XP – in this case, the folder would be under the Program Files path structure of Windows.)*

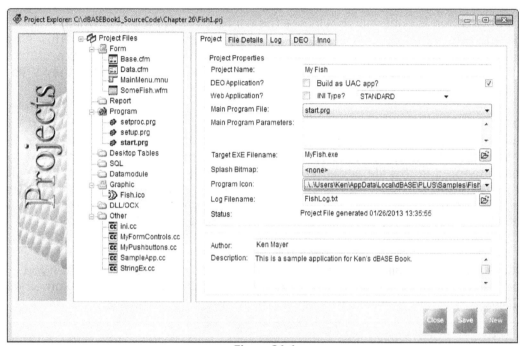

Figure 26-6

Now What?

At this point the Project is "ready to go". You can look at files and the source code in the "File Details" part of the project. You can add files, remove them if you realize you don't need them in your project and more. You can go to the appropriate design surface by right clicking on any individual file and modify the file if you need to. This is a handy place to get your application ready to roll, but it is also a handy place (and some developers may prefer this) to work from, meaning that you can modify and update the application directly from the Project Explorer.

Compiling and Building the Application

Ultimately of course, the goal is to compile the application and get it ready for deployment to your customers or users *(again, deployment is covered in Chapter 28 – this chapter is all about creating your executable, not getting it to the customer(s))*.

Once you have the options set this should be as simple as using the "Build" menu and selecting either "Build" or "Rebuild All".

The differences between "Build" and "Rebuild All" were noted earlier in this chapter, but to summarize: "Build" assumes that all of your object files exist; "Rebuild All" will recompile all your source files into object files, then build the executable.

It should be noted that when you "Build" or "Rebuild All", for a "non-DEO" application, all of the object files are built *into* the executable – meaning that your whole application is a single package or .EXE file, and when the executable is run by your users, there is no need for it to find or use any compiled objects such as a .PRO, .WFO, etc.

I prefer to just use "Rebuild All" as this will recompile all the source code in my application and then build the executable. You should experiment to find what works best for you.

Once the application is built you should see the contents of the log file, which includes warnings and errors that occur while compiling and building the executable. This is useful if something doesn't work properly, or if you get an error that says that the executable was not built. If you view the log, you can pin things down faster in most cases than if you just experiment.

NOTE

It should be noted that building or rebuilding the application multiple times appends information to the end of the Log file. The issue that comes up is that there is a *lot* of information stored in this file and after it reaches a fairly large size the Project Explorer gets very slow and has been known to freeze up on some developers. It is a good idea to periodically use the "Empty Log" button in the upper right corner ... as a matter of fact, I tend to *always* use it before clicking the "Build" or "Rebuild" button.

When you are done compiling and building your executable, if successful, after you acknowledge a message that says the executable was built, you should see something like Figure 26-7:

Figure 26-7

You can scroll down through the log and see any warnings that may have occurred. If the build failed, you can see any errors (and their location) that might have occurred.

You can now test-run your compiled application, either by going to the "Build" menu and selecting "Execute MyFish.exe", or using Windows Explorer and going to the folder that contains the executable, and double-clicking the file there.

The .INI File

There should be a .INI file for your application. There may be items that should be included in the .INI file. This application is using the "DBASESAMPLES" BDE Alias that is installed with dBASE to access the Fish table, so there isn't a lot that needs to be placed in the .INI file.

If this application is set up as a UAC application (which it should be if you followed my instructions), the runtime engine will create (if it cannot find one) a .INI file in a different location than you might expect. For example, working on this book I have a folder structure for the sample code of:

```
C:\dBASEBook1_SourceCode\Chapter 26
```

The difficulty is that the runtime will expect to find the .INI file in a completely different folder structure (and it will create the folders and the .INI file if needed):

```
C:\Users\username\AppData\Local\dBASEBook1_SourceCode\Chapter 26
```

It is interesting that the executable expects to find the .INI file in the folder from where it is being run *if* the file cannot be found in a path such as that shown above. The runtime engine will create this folder structure and a .INI file in that place, even if your executable is not being run there.

What is important is that there is a .INI file that is used by the application whether your code specifically reads or writes to it. In a UAC compliant application this file will be in the Users folder structure as shown above.

Note that in the process of deploying the application, you do not have to explicitly place the .INI file in the users folder structure as shown above, it will be done for you automatically. Any code in your application that reads from and writes to a .INI file will automatically use the one in that folder structure.

More details on .INI files can be found in Chapter 27.

Testing Your Executable

For the purpose of testing your executable, you will need to add the User BDE Alias to the .INI file. If you open MyFish.INI and add the following at the end, you will be able to run the executable and test it:

```
[UserBDEAliases]
0=DBASEFISH

[DBASEFISH]
Driver=DBASE
Options=PATH:"C:\Users\Ken\AppData\Local\dBASE\Plus\Samples"
```

Change the username "Ken" to your own when you test. When you deploy the application you will copy the table (or tables) to an appropriate location and the path to them will be different than shown here. This is only so that you can ensure your program works.

Running the Executable in the Same Folder as the Source

In the case of a non-DEO application, if you try to run the executable (.EXE) file in the same folder as the source code, you may find yourself with some odd surprises, especially if you modify a form or program and have not built it into the executable. You might not expect there to be any changes in your code, however the executable by default uses DEO. This means that if you modify something and run it in the IDE, then run your executable, it has been compiled and the executable will see it and use the modified version – even if you don't want it to. *(See discussion at the beginning of this chapter ...)*

There is a solution, however. Add to your start program this programming statement to set the _app object's *allowDEOEXEOverride* – this will tell the runtime engine to ignore the objects in the folder and only use what is in the executable or in the DEO folder structure you defined (and in the .INI file as described later in this chapter).

```
_app.allowDEOExeOverride := false
```

If you then rebuild your executable, any changes made to your source code will not appear in the .exe again until you rebuild it in the future with those changes. This allows for testing the executable without having errors occur because of changes in the source code.

Creating a DEO Application

Creating an application that relies on Dynamic External Objects is pretty easy to do using the current version of the Project Explorer.

Dynamic External Objects, or DEO, is a really useful way to deploy an application. What it means is that your executable will typically contain a single object such as the Start program. Everything else will be stored outside the executable as object files and can be easily used or updated.

The advantage to this type of application really is obvious when you update a single part of an application. If you use the previous method, where all the objects are stored in the application's .exe file, any updates will require that you redistribute the complete executable to your users. If you have a lot of users, this can be tedious. If the application is on the network, it would require a lot of extra work to be sure everyone has the same version of the executable.

By using DEO, if you update a single form, all that you have to do is deploy a copy of the .WFO file (or the appropriate object file for a custom class, etc.) and your users will all see the changes without having to deploy or download a full .exe file. In addition – on a network if you have a folder on the network drive that contains your objects, you don't have to do anything other than update the specific object and all of your users will be able to use these changes.

NOTE:
One suggestion from one of my editors is that when using a client/server network using Win2008/2012 for the server, a better approach might be to deploy updates to the server (Client_Apps) and have the server set to automatically update the clients on the next user login. I am not able to verify/test this and so leave this as an exercise for the reader.

DEO requires that the object files either be in the same folder as the executable, or in a folder (or folders) specified by settings in the .INI file.

The following information assumes that you have a project that has the files that you wish to use for your application already loaded (see the previous section).

Once you have all the files set up for your application you can make the application a DEO application in a few steps. For this example, we'll assume the MyFish (sample) application as it was seen just before selecting the option to Build the executable. If you wish to follow along, open (if it is closed) the "Fish1.prj" file that was created in the previous part of this chapter (or go and create it now). Then go to the file menu and save this as "Fish2.prj" (make sure you save it in the same folder as your original "Fish1.prj" or things may get confused). I recommend also changing the name of the executable to "MyFishDEO.exe" and the name of the log file to "DEOFishLog.txt".

If you wish to change this application to a DEO application the first thing you will want to do is to check the "DEO Application?" checkbox on the main project page (click the "Project" tab). When you do, you will see this dialog (Figure 26-8). Click "Yes" if you really wish to change this to a DEO application:

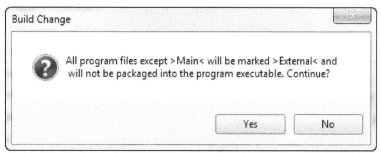

Figure 26-8

The question now becomes "How do you tell the Project Explorer where to place the object files for my DEO application?" It will take some time as you have to set the information for each file in the application, but it's pretty simple.

DEO Folders

The first thing to do is decide what folders will be used and what the path is. This is what the "DEO" tab on the main part of the form is all about.

Select that tab, which should appear as:

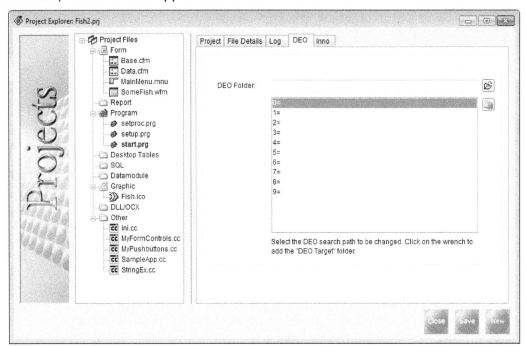

Figure 26-9

If you have existing folders that you wish to use for your DEO deployment, you can select them by clicking on the "tool" button. This will bring up a standard dBASE dialog allowing you to select a folder.

If you wish to create new folders type the **full** path into the entryfield and press the ENTER key. The Project Explorer will create the folder.

For this example, let's create a single DEO folder (you might want several – you can have up to 10, numbered 0 to 9).

To create the folder:

- Select the item in the list you wish to modify, for example "0=" in the listbox.
- Click on the "DEO Folder" entryfield.
- Type the folder path. If you do not give a path, it will be placed under the current working folder. For example, this application is being created under "C:\dBASEBook1_SourceCode\Chapter 26". If I simply typed "DEOSample", the path would be "C:\dBASEBook1_SourceCode\Chapter 26\DEOSample". This may or may not be what you want. If you want the folder off the main drive, you would need to type: "C:\DEOSample" instead. If you want the folder to be on a network drive, you will need to use that path.
- You will be asked if you want to create the folder. Select "Yes" if you do.

Basically you would repeat this for each folder you wish to add, selecting the item in the listbox you wish to change first. If you add a second folder, then select "1=" (the second item in the list), when you add a third folder, select "2=", etc.

You can remove an item from the list if you decide you don't want it by clicking on it and selecting the "-" button on the right.

Once done selecting the folders you wish to use you should see something like Figure 26-10:

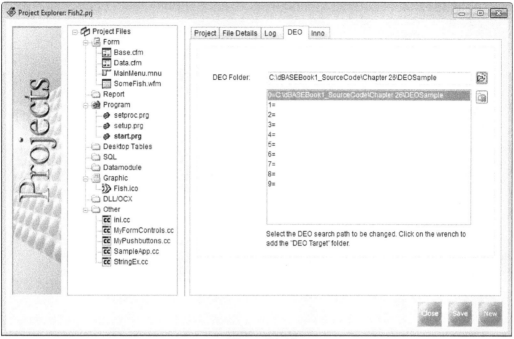

Figure 26-10

Selecting the DEO Folder for Each File

Once you have set up the folder(s) you wish to use, you now need to tell the Project Explorer where to place each of the files.

Select the first file in the treeview and look at the "Details" tab (if not selected, click on "File Details", then "Details").

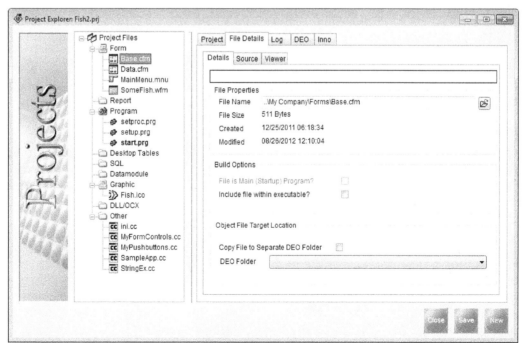

Figure 26-11

Note that the checkbox "Include file within executable?" is unchecked which is correct if you're creating a DEO application. Next you need to check the checkbox that says: "Copy File to Separate DEO Folder". When you do that, the "DEO Folder" combobox is now available to you and you can select the folder where you want the object file located.

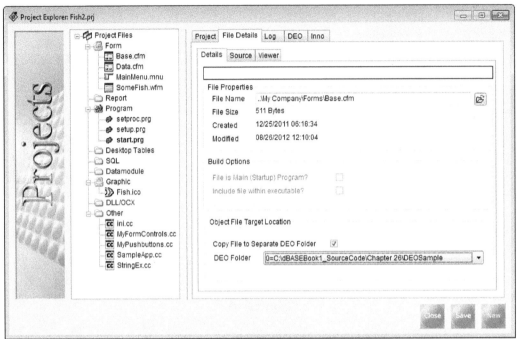

Figure 26-12

You have to do this for each file that can be compiled (forms, programs, reports, menus, etc.). There are files you do not really need to worry about for the application. If you have multiple DEO folders, the only difficulty is deciding which folder to have the files placed in.

You should note when you get to the program you have marked as the startup program ("Start.prg"), the Project Explorer will not allow you to set the DEO Location ... this is proper behavior. The application must have that file compiled and built into the executable itself.

The file "Fish.ico" has only one purpose for this application, to appear in the titlebar. You may want to check the "Include file within executable?" checkbox for this one and not worry about DEO.

The Application's INI File

You should create a .INI file for your application that has any specific settings you need (such as User BDE Aliases, and anything else – see earlier chapters). In addition, the Project Explorer will add any DEO paths you needed it to create. In this particular example:

```
[ObjectPath]
objPath0=C:\dBASEBook1_SourceCode\Chapter 26\DEOSample
```

It is important that a copy of the .INI file in this case be IN THE SAME FOLDER as the executable. Testing shows that if it is not, then even if a .INI file in another folder location is found by the runtime, the DEO Object Path (*as shown above*) does not work properly. The .INI file should be in the same folder as your .EXE file. When you deploy the application the runtime engine will copy the .INI file to the Users folder structure as discussed earlier in this chapter.

> **⚠ WARNING**
> The requirement to place a copy of the .INI file in the same folder as the .EXE appears to be a bug in the software. However, we have been told that this bug, while known, will not be fixed until the next full release of dBASE. As such, you will need to follow the suggestions above. When this is fixed, you should only need to deploy the .INI to the C:\Users\... folder structure.

Compile and Build the Application

The last step is to actually compile and build the executable. You need to use the "Build" menu / "Rebuild All" option (or the "Rebuild All" tool button). Why this option instead of "Build?" Because among other things, "Rebuild All" will copy the object files to the appropriate DEO folders as specified in the Project. If you choose to do this, then you will (unless there are errors) get a dialog telling you that the application has been built, then the Log file page of the project will be displayed.

For each file you specified a DEO folder the log shows you that the Project Explorer copied the object to that location.

At this point you should probably test the application. Make sure if/when you copy the .exe file that you also copy the .INI file. In order to test this, especially because this is a DEO application, you may want to copy the .exe and .INI files to a new folder on the hard drive – one that does not contain the object files for the application. For testing, you might create a folder:

```
C:\DEOTest
```

And copy the files "MyFishDEO.exe" and "MyFishDEO.INI" to that folder. Then, as noted above, copy "MyFishDEO.INI" to the correct path in the Users folder structure:

```
C:\Users\Ken\AppData\Local\DEOTest
```

If you then run "MyFishDEO.exe" from that folder and you did everything correctly it should start up and work. The .INI file in the "C:\DEOTest" folder is effectively a "read-only" file, even if the folder is not set with those rights. Any code in the application that modifies the .INI file will modify the one in the "C:\Users ..." folder structure.

DEO and NON-DEO?

One thing you might want to do is make part of the application DEO and the rest "non DEO". What this means is that you could opt to have more than just the startup program in the executable, and only some of the files be handled as DEO. To do that, simply uncheck the "DEO Application" checkbox, then for individual files either select the "Include file within executable?" checkbox or the "Copy File to Separate DEO Folder" checkbox (and don't forget to select the appropriate DEO folder). When you chose the "Build" menu, then use "Rebuild All", the DEO files will be copied to the appropriate location(s), and the others will be compiled and built into the executable.

In addition, if you update a form, for example the MyFish.wfm form shown here, you could simply compile it (right click in the Navigator and select "Compile"), then copy the file MyFish.wfo to either the same folder where the executable is located, or a folder referenced by the DEO entries in the .INI file.

As with a lot of aspects of dBASE, you can also create an application where some files are referenced (as noted) in a DEO location, and others stored in the same folder as the .EXE.

Some developers work this way. What I'm really saying here is that there is no "one true way", as it were.

.INI Files

There are often a few settings saved into the .INI file for dBASE that most people don't even think about. This will be discussed in chapter 27 in detail.

Other aspects of .INI files have been discussed in this chapter, including the location of the .INI that is being used to store values that you can read from and write to in your application.

ActiveX and DLL Controls

ActiveX and some DLL Controls usually require some registry settings. The problem is that it's not 100% automatic in most cases. In earlier versions of this book I gave some examples, but current versions of Windows have changed a lot and I don't have any handy .OCX files to test with. Modifying the registry under current versions of Windows is not a good idea in general unless you do it "just right", and for an application to modify the registry requires running the application "As Administrator", because by default your application will not have the correct permissions to alter the registry. This can get complicated.

As it turns out the install program that comes with dBASE (Inno Setup) has simple options for installing ActiveX controls. The only time this might be a problem would be if your ActiveX requires specific registry keys. In this case you may need to create a special installer or a dBASE application with elevated privileges. This will be discussed in Chapter 28.

Network Deployment

Network deployment is a two-step process. You must install the program and the data files as well as any object files for your application on the network.

It is suggested that you build one install program that does not include any shared tables. The tables that will reside on a shared network drive would be placed there by a separate install program.

This will be discussed in chapter 28 (deploying applications).

Being Sure Your Application Is Set Up Correctly

A developer should always be concerned about the application being set up with all the files in the appropriate locations. This chapter, as well as Chapter 28, discusses these topics in more detail.

The developers at dBASE, LLC created a program that you may have noticed the first time you ran dBASE (if you have been working with dBASE Plus 2.7 or later) that is actually used for this purpose.

The program is "INITNEWUSER.PRG". This file is in several locations with your installation. However, if you read the comments in the code at the very beginning of the program you will see that the developers at dBASE, LLC have granted us the option to copy and use this program for our own applications.

This is a fairly complex set of code and you will want to modify how it runs for each application you deploy.

I recommend copying it from:

```
C:\ProgramData\dBASE\Plus\dBLClasses\Startup\InitNewUser.prg
```

to your source code for your own application.

The INITNEWUSER program also depends on several other files, so if you wish to use this in your application you would want to deploy those files (put them into the Project Explorer, and make sure when you deploy the application they are distributed with your other files).

The code does the following things:

1) It starts with the init() method:
    a. This sets up paths to folders that need to be copied to the Users folder structure,
    b. It also sets up User BDE Aliases with paths and some instructions.
2) It then calls the IsNewUser() method, which determines if one of the folders in the folder list exists and if not sets a flag that this is a new user (for example, if the folder exists, this is **not** a new user ...).
3) If the method IsNewUser() returns a value of *true*, then the code in the method SetupNewUser() is called. This sets up the folders and User BDE Aliases in the application's .INI file.

This is fairly involved. The code you would want to modify is specifically in the init() method, because this is where the paths for folders and User BDE aliases are defined.

It is possible to do what is needed as well using Inno Setup, which will be discussed in Chapter 28. The use of INITNEWUSER would be an "after installation" operation. This is an interesting technique however and should not be dismissed out of hand.

Other Ways to Build Your Executable

We have looked at the automated ways of building your executable, but let's take a look at the fact that there is really something going on behind the scenes. There is a command built into dBASE called BUILD that actually is used to build the executable, whether you use the Project Explorer or if you want to build your executables yourself.

You could do nearly everything that was done with the Project Explorer earlier in this chapter, but do it manually. The two things that the BUILD command will not do is compile your source code (you would need to use the COMPILE command for that) and it will not copy files to the DEO locations specified (the Project Explorer is most likely using COPY FILE commands to copy the files to where the DEO folders are specified, and your own deployment would use Inno Setup or some other install program to put the files where they need to be).

The BUILD command can also use a file called a "response" file, one that is a text file listing files to be built into the executable. It typically uses an extension of .RSP. The BUILD command can also use a project file as is created by the Project Explorer, as we discussed in this chapter.

The Project Explorer creates a .RSP file for you, so if you want to see how this works, you can open "Fish1.RSP" in the command window by typing:

```
modify command Fish1.rsp
```

You should see something similar to:

```
FILES
    C:\dBASEBook1_SourceCode\Chapter 26\start.prO
    C:\dBASEBook1_SourceCode\Chapter 26\SomeFish.wfO
    C:\dBASEBook1_SourceCode\Chapter 26\MainMenu.mnO
    C:\dBASEBook1_SourceCode\My Company\Forms\Base.cfO
    C:\dBASEBook1_SourceCode\My Company\Forms\Data.cfO
    C:\dBASEBook1_SourceCode\My Company\FormControls\MyFormControls.cO
    C:\dBASEBook1_SourceCode\My Company\FormControls\MyPushbuttons.cO
    C:\dBASEBook1_SourceCode\Chapter 26\SampleApp.cO
    C:\dBASEBook1_SourceCode\Chapter 26\setup.prO
    C:\dUFLP Current\ini.cO
    C:\dUFLP Current\setproc.prO
    C:\dUFLP Current\StringEx.cO
TO C:\dBASEBook1_SourceCode\Chapter 26\MyFish.exe
ICON C:\Users\Ken\AppData\Local\dBASE\PLUS\Samples\Fish.ico
WEBAPPLICATION False
```

More information on the BUILD command can be found in the dBASE Plus Help file.

When you build the executable you are storing files INTO a .EXE file. This is a way of bundling things into one place. At the very least, you must have a single program (form, etc.) that is called when the program starts and if your application is fully DEO, the rest of the files can reside outside of the executable. If your application stores everything needed, is not a DEO executable. Most importantly if it has the *allowDEOEXEOverride* property of the _app object set to *false*, your application must have all of the required files built into of the executable.

If you use the Project Explorer, all of the work is done for you. This is a nice feature, but if you really need the control, you can use the BUILD command directly.

There is a huge amount of information on this command in the online help. It is mentioned here because it can be useful if you want to do a quick test. For example, in an earlier chapter we discussed the case where parameters are used with an executable and we did a quick test, building an executable that checked for parameters and converted one to numeric.

Running a dBASE PLUS Executable

When you create your executable, there *must* be a startup program, whether you use DEO or whether you put everything into one executable. This is the first program that dBASE will attempt to run when your executable starts. But what is really happening?

When you run an executable program created by dBASE you are not actually loading dBASE itself which includes the full IDE (Integrated Development Environment). Instead your executable will call what is called the dBASE Runtime Library. This is the file called

PLUSrun.exe and is in the dBASE\PLUS\Runtime folder on your hard drive, along with PLUSr_en.dll *(where "en" is for "English" – if you are using dBASE in German, this will be PLUSr_de.dll and for other languages the two letters will also be different)*, and a copy of Resource.dll.

Those three files are absolutely vital to being able to run a dBASE PLUS executable. When you install dBASE PLUS to your computer, a registry key is added to Windows to allow it to know where the runtime files are located and your application executable has some code created by dBASE in its own startup routine that tells it to look for these runtime files. If they are not available, your application will fail. This is discussed in more detail in Chapter 28.

Using an Alternate INI File

You can, as noted elsewhere, pass parameters to a dBASE PLUS executable. One optional parameter that has not been discussed is the ability to use a.INI file that does not have the same name as your executable. By default, a .INI file must have the same name as the .exe. For example, if your .exe is named MyApp.exe, then you would need a .INI file named MyApp.INI.

If you wanted to use a different name for your application's .INI file, it is completely possible by calling your application in a completely different way.
You can pass your application name to the PLUSrun.exe file:

```
PLUSrun.exe -cSomeIni.INI SomeApp.exe param1 param2
```

There does not appear to be a way to get an alternate .INI file to be recognized without using the syntax as shown here.

Running an Executable with Startup Parameters

This topic is discussed in detail toward the end of Chapter 25, and it seems silly to discuss it again here. If you need to do this, please see that chapter.

Summary

This chapter and the examples created here can hopefully help you through the process of preparing your application(s) for deployment. You have learned how to build the executable here. In Chapter 27 we will discuss the ins and outs of working with the .INI file, and in Chapter 28 we will get to the last stage – deploying the application to your customer(s).

NOTES:

Chapter 27: The .INI File

The .INI file has been a source of much confusion for dBASE developers, so this is an attempt to explain how the .INI file works and briefly look at the PLUS.INI file used by dBASE. This will also give us some insight for how to work with our own applications and the .INI file used for them. This chapter is broken down into three basic areas – Initialization files in general, the dBASE Plus .INI file, and .INI files for your applications.

Initialization Files in General

What Exactly Is a .INI File?
The letters "INI" are short for "Initialization". An initialization file is used to contain information for an application and is often (but not always) read during the startup of the application. Sometimes the .INI file is checked while the application is open – a lot depends on the needs of the application and how the developer wrote the code.

When starting dBASE, a specific .INI file is used, if it doesn't exist, it is re-created with a set of default settings. If the .INI file exists, but specific settings are not there, dBASE will re-create those settings.

The same thing happens for an application created by dBASE – if a .INI file does not exist, it is created *(or re-created)*, and even if it does exist, if some settings are missing they are created with default values.

What Are the Names of the .INI file?
For the most part, these are the names of the .exe file. So, for dBASE PLUS the .exe is named "Plus.exe", therefore the .INI file is named "Plus.ini". For an application you created (a .EXE used with the dBASE runtime), the name of the .INI should be the name of the executable (i.e., "MyApp.exe" would have "MyApp.ini").

Finally, a .INI file is simply a DOS Text file which can be opened in the Source Editor of dBASE, it can be opened with WordPad, Notepad and any other application that can read and write text files. It can be manipulated in dBL either by using a file object, the Windows API, or by using a special custom class called ini.cc (which uses the Windows API) to manipulate it (INI.cc can be found in the dBASE Users' Function Library – dUFLP for short).

Be careful when modifying the .INI file for dBASE PLUS – if you change something you didn't mean to, you may get some odd results (in most cases, if you delete the entry, dBASE will re-create it).

Note that as you make changes in the properties dialog, or in other parts of the IDE, that dBASE will be updating the Plus.INI file – this is so that it can remember the last place the inspector was in the designers, for example. dBASE writes to the .INI file in different ways depending on the tools being used – when you exit dBASE for example, some items may be updated, but when using the Properties dialog they may be updated as soon as you close the dialog (or click the "Apply" button in some cases).

How Do I Find Things in My .INI File?
In a .INI file, each line is called an entry. There are two kinds of entries – section headings and name/value pairs.

A section heading is a title with square brackets around it. It might look like:

```
[CommandSettings]
```

The name/value pairs are specific things that the application looks for under a section heading by name, followed by an equal sign (=) and then by the value. Note that since this is a text file, all values appear as character strings and if you use code to read these values, they will be returned as character strings (more on that later). A typical name/value pair might look like:

```
SEPARATOR=,
```

Note that the string is not in quotes – this is not necessary and can actually cause some difficulties. A value is assumed to be a string, if it is not then in your own code you have to deal with modifying it as you save it or read it back to use it. If you need the value to be numeric, then you would want to use the *val()* function, for example.

Locations of .INI Files

One of the difficult (for the developer) aspects of working with Windows is the whole UAC issue, which has been discussed throughout this book. The biggest concern is the location of the .INI file for an application, as there may be multiple copies – which is the one being used by the application?

There is a fairly complete discussion of this topic in Chapter 2 (Vol. 1) of this book. Rather than going back over this in detail here, please reference that chapter or the quick summary of the topic at the end of this chapter.

More Information on .INI Files?

If you need more details on .INI files that are not covered here there is an excellent article on Wikipedia that may be of use:

```
http://en.wikipedia.org/wiki/Ini_file
```

The dBASE PLUS .INI File

We will take a short look at the basics of the PLUS.INI file for dBASE. Earlier versions of this book included *all* sections in my own PLUS.INI file, but as the software evolves what is stored in this file changes. To understand how it works, it is not truly necessary to examine all options. There are bound to be different keys depending on whether you have dBASE installed as a UAC application or a non-UAC application.

Install

The Install section is created when you install dBASE. It contains just some basic information that you fill in when you run the installer. Some of this information appears in the "Help | About dBASE" dialog.

A typical "install" section looks like:

```
[Install]
Username=Ken Mayer
Company=Golden Stag Productions
CustomerNumber=000 000
```

(I'm not giving you my customer number.) For your own applications, you probably do not need this section, unless you intend to do something similar to what dBASE does (read this and use it for the Help | About dialog).

Custom Classes

This section is used to load specific custom classes into memory when dBASE PLUS loads and is used for the design surfaces. As the design surfaces in dBASE are not available to your end-users, this section is not necessary for your application.

If you find that when you load dBASE it gives an error about a custom class that it cannot find, then this is where you can fix this problem. Simply find the entry for that file and delete it.

How do custom controls get added to this list? There are a couple of ways – the first is to double-click on one in the dBASE Navigator. This automatically places it in the .INI file. The other is to use the File menu when in the form or report designer and select to save a custom control when done designing it. There is a checkbox in the save dialog to place it on the Component Palette. You can also add custom controls with the "Setup Custom Control" dialog. If you click the Checkbox it will be placed in the .INI file in the list below. *(All of this is covered in some detail in a previous chapter of this book.)*

```
[CustomClasses]
CC0=:FormControls:\DATABUTTONS.CC
CC1=:FormControls:\SEEKER.CC
CC2=:FormControls:\Splitter.cc
CC3=:ReportControls:\REPORT.CC
```

Toolbars

The toolbars section is used to define information about specific toolbars used in the IDE (Integrated Development Environment), including whether they are available (turned on), "float", etc. For your own application this section is not necessary.

In the case of many of these options, the choice is simply 1 or 0 – 1 means "on", zero or 0 means "off". In some cases zero (0) means "use the default" and one (1) means do something other than the default.

Position entries: The entries that have four numbers with spaces between them are used to define the following – position of the left side of the toolbar from the left of the screen, position of the top side of the toolbar from the top of the screen, position of the right side of the toolbar from the left side of the screen and position of the bottom of the toolbar from the top of the screen. What this means is if you see the following:

```
StandardPosition=0 38 222 69
```

It means that the toolbar has the following coordinates:

Left: zero pixels from the left of the screen
Top: 38 pixels from the top of the screen
Right: the right side of the toolbar is 222 pixels from the left side of the screen
Bottom: the bottom side of the toolbar is 69 pixels from the top of the screen.

Note that if a position given is REALLY large or has a negative value, you may find that this is the reason you cannot see something – one way to reset this is to delete the entry from outside of dBASE (with dBASE not running), then run dBASE again and the entry will be re-created with a more rational setting.

The question then becomes "what do each of these entries stand for?" In many cases this is pretty straightforward, but I will attempt to explain in some detail:

```
[Toolbars]
Standard=1
StandardFloat=0
StandardStyle=0
StandardPosition=0 38 222 69
```

The standard toolbar is the one that is normally docked at the top of the screen in the IDE. The first entry means that it is on – in other words, when you start dBASE it appears. *(This is affected by _app.speedBar.)*

StandardFloat references whether or not it is a floating toolbar – in other words, is it docked or not? If it is floating it appears as a palette or window. This defaults to zero (0) or "off", meaning it is NOT a floating toolbar.

StandardStyle? (I have no idea what this means – obviously the standard toolbar, but I cannot find an explanation of what the style options are.)

StandardPosition – see the discussion on "Position entries" above.

There may be quite a few entries under the toolbars. The only one you might be concerned with for an application is the Format toolbar and you might want a section such as the following if you do not wish it to appear in your application:

```
[Toolbars]
Format=0
```

CommandSettings

Many or most of these can be located and changed or modified from either the Desktop Properties dialog, or from commands in dBASE (SET or SET TO commands – check online help).

```
[CommandSettings]
LDRIVER=Windows
EDITOR=
PATH=
ALTERNATE=
SEPARATOR=,
POINT=.
CURRENCY=$
DATE=MDY
MARK=/
REFRESH=0
REPROCESS=0
DBTYPE=DBASE
IBLOCK=1
MBLOCK=8
TYPEAHEAD=49
BELL=512,50
EPOCH=1950
```

```
DECIMALS=2
PRECISION=10
MARGIN=0
Language=EN
```

When preparing an application for deployment, you should check to see if these commands are ones you need to have in the .INI file for your application. If these are not in the .INI file the user may get defaults that don't match, many of these mismatches are the cause of differences that developers experience between their application running in the IDE and a separate executable on a user's machine.

Startup Program?

Some programmers like to set up a program that will execute when they start dBASE to configure settings, and so on. If you would like to set something like that up, you can have dBASE run this program by adding an entry in the [CommandSettings] group:

```
[CommandSettings]
command=do <path\programname.prg>
```

(Replace the path and name of program appropriately.) When you next start dBASE, it will run this program ...

OnOffCommandSettings

Nearly all of these, if not all, can be modified through SET commands (i.e., "set century on" and/or they can be modified through the Desktop Properties dialog. Check the online help for details about these specific entries (SET CURRENCY, for example).

```
[OnOffCommandSettings]
CURRENCY=LEFT
CENTURY=ON
LDCHECK=OFF
LOCK=ON
EXCLUSIVE=OFF
AUTONULLFIELDS=ON
AUTOSAVE=OFF
DELETED=ON
EXACT=OFF
NEAR=OFF
ENCRYPTION=ON
CONFIRM=ON
CUAENTER=ON
ESCAPE=ON
BELL=ON
FULLPATH=OFF
SPACE=ON
COVERAGE=OFF
DEVELOPMENT=ON
DESIGN=ON
SAFETY=ON
TALK=OFF
TITLE=OFF
HEADINGS=ON
```

When preparing an application for deployment, you should check to see if these commands are ones you need to have in the .INI file for your application. If these are not in the .INI file the user may get defaults that don't match, many of these mismatches are the cause of differences that developers experience between their application running in the IDE and a separate executable on a user's machine.

ErrorHandling

The given *errorHandling* options match up with the options in the Desktop Properties dialog and with the _app properties of the same name. Check online help for details on how these work.

```
[ErrorHandling]
ErrorAction=4
ErrorLogFile=PLUSErr.log
ErrorLogMaxSize=100
ErrorHtmFile=error.htm
```

You may want to use these for your own applications – particularly the options for Web Applications, but the others can be quite useful as well if you want to create error logs, etc.

Keeping in mind the requirements of UAC applications, your error log should be in a location other than the one that the executable is in. So using the example above, you might want to use a path like:

```
ErrorLogFile=C:\Users\username\AppData\Local\MyCompany\MyApp\PLUSErr.log
```

ComponentTypes

These options can be located in several places when working in the IDE, including from the Desktop Properties dialog (Table tab, "Associate Component Types" button), to specify what the default component types are for specific field types.

```
[ComponentTypes]
ComponentTypeNumeric=1
ComponentTypeDate=1
ComponentTypeLogical=0
ComponentTypeMemo=0
ComponentTypeBinary=0
ComponentTypeOLE=0
ComponentTypeNumericForTables=1
ComponentTypeDateForTables=1
ComponentTypeLogicalForTables=0
ComponentTypeMemoForTables=0
ComponentTypeBinaryForTables=0
ComponentTypeOLEForTables=0
```

For a deployed object it may be useful to include this section from your own application – in some cases, specifically grids, if you have modified these settings you may see incorrect settings on your forms.

.INI Files For Your Applications

The rest of this chapter will focus on setting up and using a .INI file for your dBASE Plus applications.

This includes recommended sections and name/value pairs and methods that can be used to read from and write to your application's .INI file.

Custom BDE .CFG File

When deploying an application that uses a custom .CFG file, you need a special set of entries:

```
[IDAPI]
CONFIGFILE01=mycustom.cfg
```

The name of the .CFG file, as well as the path, if it is not in the folder of the application should be included.

Encrypted Tables

If you are working with encrypted tables (using the dBASE PROTECT command to do so), you will need to deploy the DBSYSTEM.DB file, but you also need to have an entry in your .INI that looks like:

```
[CommandSettings]
DBSYSTEM=D:\PATH
```

Where "D:\PATH" is the path to the directory where you are deploying this file to. If you already have a "[CommandSettings]" section (see above), just add the "DBSYSTEM" entry. If you are deploying the DBSYSTEM file to the same as your application you can set this to "." (i.e., DBSYSTEM=.) — the "." stands for "current directory". As with the errorlog setting mentioned earlier, you should be concerned with the UAC requirements of Windows. The path to where the DBSYSTEM.DB file is stored needs to be one that the user has the ability to read and write to. On a standalone computer it might be something similar to:

```
DBSYSTEM=C:\Users\username\AppData\Local\MyCompany\MyApp
```

On a network you would want to point to a folder on the file server, perhaps the one containing the tables, or in a folder in the same path structure.

Items You Can Add

You can add some settings to the .INI file that may not be there to start with, but will be recognized by dBASE and acted upon as needed. These include things like a "Default Fonts" group:

```
[Default Fonts]
Application=FontName,Size Controls=FontName,Size
```

Note that you need to do this with the name of a font and with the fontsize, so you could do something like:

```
[Default Fonts]
Application=Arial,10 Controls=Times New Roman,12
```

No Data Engine

It is possible, if your program does not do any work with tables, to tell the executable to start without using the BDE. This can be done with a couple of lines added to your application's .INI file:

```
[DataEngine]
DefaultEngine=NONE
```

If you use the Project Explorer to build your application, there is a way to set this there, rather than manually modifying the .INI file yourself. On the "Inno" tab, there is a set of tabs, and on the ".INI" tab you will see an option "BDE Not Required" – if you check that box, the entry as above will be included in your application's .INI file.

It is not recommended that you do this with the PLUS.INI file, unless you are sure you won't be working with tables.

This will cut some overhead and startup time when your program runs, but if you need to use tables at all, or any of the data objects, this will cause them to not work as dBASE (and the runtime) needs the BDE to handle them.

You can also add your own entries to a .INI file – custom entries that are used specifically by your own application.

A Recommended "Base" .INI File For a Deployed Application

For your own application you should consider the following as a "base" .INI file – one that could be used as a starting point for your application. See online help in dBASE for details for SET EPOCH, SET CENTURY, SET LDCHECK, etc.:

```
[CommandSettings]
EPOCH=1950
LDRIVER=WINDOWS

[OnOffCommandSettings]
CENTURY=ON
LDCHECK=OFF
BELL=OFF
TALK=OFF

[CommandWindow]
Open=1
Maximized=0
Minimized=1

[ComponentTypes]
ComponentTypeNumeric=1
ComponentTypeDate=1
ComponentTypeLogical=0
ComponentTypeMemo=0
ComponentTypeBinary=0
ComponentTypeOLE=0
ComponentTypeNumericForTables=1
ComponentTypeDateForTables=1
ComponentTypeLogicalForTables=0
ComponentTypeMemoForTables=0
ComponentTypeBinaryForTables=0
ComponentTypeOLEForTables=0

[Grid]
DefaultMemoEditor=0

[Toolbars]
Format=0

[ObjectPath]
```

```
objPath0=c:\path
...
objPath9=c:\anotherpath
```

The "LDRIVER=WINDOWS" setting ensures that no matter what your application's BDE Driver your source code will be saved as ANSI. *(There is a problem with this setting and the SoundEx() function – otherwise this setting will enhance the speed of text processing immensely).*

The "TALK" setting is very important – if Talk is not set OFF (either here or in your code), there will be a serious performance degradation, as dBASE will go through the motions of echoing commands to the Command Window. In dBASE PLUS this isn't as important, as the Runtime Engine automatically assumes talk is off.

The "CommandWindow" settings are there just to be sure there are no other problems – having the runtime try to open the Command Window is probably not a good idea. If you set the "Open" value to "0" this will tell the dBASE runtime to not even consider opening it when your application runs.

The "ComponentTypes" section may cause some datatype mismatch errors if not included, particularly if you are using the grid component on your forms. You should copy the section shown above from your own PLUS.INI, as you may have different settings than those shown above.

The "Grid" section is used to set the default *columnEditor* type for memo fields in a grid. If DefaultMemoEditor is set to zero, the default (*columnEditor*) is used, if set to one (1), the *columnEntryfield* is used (the original way the grid handled memos).

The "Toolbars" section – there's one entry that should be checked out, that's the "format" option. If it is set to "1", the format palette appears when a form opens that has an editor control; if it is set to "0", the format palette does not appear.

The "ObjectPath" section – this is your DEO paths section. You can have from 0 to 9 object path entries, each of them pointing to different folders.

Using Project Explorer Options

Using the Project Explorer for your application is discussed in Chapter 26, but briefly there is an option on the "Inno" tab to modify the .INI for your application, and one of the options on the ".INI" tab is "Include default INI entries". If you check this, the following will be automatically included in the .INI file:

```
[Toolbars]
Standard=0
StandardFloat=0
StandardStyle =0
[Desktop]
Maximized=0
StatusBar=0
[CommandWindow]
Open=0
[ObjectPath]
objPath0=C:\YourObjectPath
```

This may be a good start, although I have found the settings in the "Base" .INI file noted above may be a bit more useful.

Reading/Modifying a .INI File in an Application

If you do not create a .INI file for your application, the first time you start a .exe, it will create a .INI file with the following information (note, the .INI will have the same name as the .EXE, so if your executable's name was MYAPP.EXE, the .INI would be named MYAPP.INI):

```
[Toolbars]
Standard=1
StandardFloat=0
StandardStyle=0
StandardPosition=-2 38 37 69

[CommandWindow]
Open=1
Maximized=0
Minimized=1

[Directories]
0=C:\GPFBugHunt
Current=0

[Database]
Name=
```

If you wish to, you can use the .INI file for your own purposes. For example you can use code calling the Windows API as explained in earlier chapters of this book, you can use the File class in dBASE, or you can use an existing custom class that is in the freeware library of code called the dUFLP (dBASE Users' Function Library Project) called INI.CC. This class allows you to read, modify or delete entries and a lot more. It's worth checking out, rather than writing your own code to do what is already written.

What kinds of things would you want to code into a .INI file?
- Form position – the top and left positions of a form, which means that the next time a form was opened it would open in the same position it was last in when closed. This of course would mean reading the information from the .INI file before opening the form, then writing it when the form is closed.
- Preferences for an application – if you allow the user to modify how an application looks (color scheme, for example), or functions – in one of my applications, the code imports data in three different ways, and the user can specify through a small form if it should do all three at once, if it should delete the original data it was imported from, that kind of thing.
- If you can think of it, it is probably doable.

Setting Paths In the .INI File

One of the more interesting aspects of setting up an application for use is when deploying them – getting the paths set correctly. Using Inno Setup you can specify the paths (using the Windows path structures among other things) for things such as User BDE Aliases, the APPDATA folder paths and more. These can be stored properly in the .INI file before it is deployed, making it easier to get the settings correct in the first place. This will be discussed in the next chapter.

Deploying the .INI File

One of the big concerns with a UAC style application is how to properly deploy the .INI file for the application. This is covered in detail in Chapter 2 of this book, but to summarize:

In a UAC application, the .INI file should not be in the folder the executable is in. This is because the folder is expected to be a read/execute folder, but not a writable folder.

It is recommended that you store the .INI file in the folder path defined by the Windows variable CSIDL_LOCAL_APPDATA. On a Windows 7 or later operating system, and current versions of dBASE, this will point to a path similar to:

```
C:\Users\username\AppData\Local
```

where "username" is the login for Windows for the current user. Taking this further, you should have a folder for your application in this path, similar to:

```
C:\Users\username\AppData\Local\MyCompany\MyApp
```

This assumes that the executable is stored in a folder structure similar to (using the Windows variable CSIDL_PROGRAM_FILES):

```
C:\Program Files (x86)\MyCompany\MyApp
```

Using this folder structure, the dBASE Plus Runtime engine will create the folder structure if it does not exist:

```
C:\Users\username\AppData\Local\MyCompany\MyApp
```

It will also create a default .INI as specified earlier in this chapter for your application if it does not exist.

However, if when the application is installed you create the folder structure and a copy of the .INI file you WANT to be there, when your executable is run, dBASE will read that .INI file instead. This is preferable behavior. For more details on this, see Chapter 2 for the folder structures as well as the next chapter of the book on how to deploy your application.

One difficulty is if your user changes the installation paths during the install process. In many installations this may not be an issue, but there could be one where the user changes something and your executable cannot find the .INI file. You would most likely have to either have the user uninstall and re-install without changing the paths, or work with them to find the .INI file and put it in the correct location.

Summary

The INI file is not all that hard to understand once you get a feel for the basics. For the most part, you may never need to understand all of the entries in the PLUS.INI file, but it does help to know what is happening in the .INI file of your own applications.

NOTES:

Chapter 28: Preparing an Application for Deployment

Once you have done everything, put all the files together and built the executable, tested everything, possibly with the help of some other folk including the users, you now have to actually deploy the application.

After much searching and testing of what was available on the internet, it was decided to give developers a free (and constantly evolving) software package called Inno Setup, created by Jordan Russel. This software should be on your dBASE PLUS CD with updates available from the Inno Setup website.

This chapter will discuss using the Project Explorer to deploy "My Fish", as well as using Inno Setup to manually deploy an application. At the end of the chapter we will discuss what files are required for a deployment so you can either use a different installer, or deploy the files yourself in some fashion.

Code Signing Your Executable

What is Code Signing and why is it so important that I would put this at the start of the chapter?

Windows Vista and later versions of Windows came with the UAC (User Access Control – discussed in multiple places in this book). The UAC, among other things, checks to see if an executable has been Code Signed, verifying that in theory the executable comes from a trusted source.

When your user runs an executable on a Windows computer with the UAC enabled, if the program has not been Code Signed, they will see a dialog similar to this *(this is from my Windows 8 computer with the UAC enabled)*:

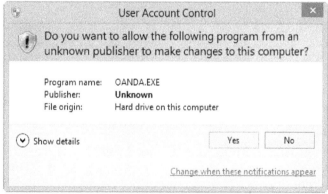

Figure 28-1

Your user then has to confirm that they wish to actually run the program. If the executable has been Code Signed, then the dialog will change appearance – it will not be a warning, but just a question, with the name of the publisher (your business name).

Citing an article on Wikipedia (http://en.wikipedia.org/wiki/Code_signing):

"**Code signing** is the process of digitally signing executables and scripts to confirm the software author and guarantee that the code has not been altered or corrupted since it was signed by use of a cryptographic hash."

In addition to the article above, the Knowledgebase for dBASE has an article written by Marty Kay about Code Signing that you should read (it is in the FAQ section):

    http://www.dbase.com/Knowledgebase/faq/CodeSigningHowTo.asp

Is Code Signing Necessary?
In the grand scheme of things, no, Code Signing is not 100% necessary – your executable should work fine without it, but your users will see the dialog each time they run your application.

How Do I Code Sign My Executable(s)?
How does one go about signing their code so that it is acceptable to Windows? This is a fairly complex process and the documentation keeps moving around on the Microsoft website (they change the addresses). It is also not exactly inexpensive.

Obtain a Digital Certificate and Private Key
Basically you have to sign up with a "Trusted Certificate Authority" (CA), create the digital certificate and public key necessary, then "Sign" your executable.

The FAQ at the dBASE website lists the following Certificate Authorities and if you search the web you will most likely find more:

Comodo:
    http://www.tech-pro.net/code-signing-certificate.html

Thawte:
    https://www.thawte.com/code-signing/index.html?click=buyssl-buttonsleft

VeriSign:
    https://www.symantec.com/products-solutions/families/?fid=code-signing

I note that the VeriSign link goes to the Symantec website and these can get a little pricey, ranging from $179 a year and up – meaning you have to pay again every year. I did find a site that offers a Comodo license for $95 a year (KSoftware) – this is at the time I am publishing the book – note that it could change at any time:

    http://codesigning.ksoftware.net/

Obtain a Code Signing Utility
Once you have purchased your Certificate and your Private Key from the authority you have selected *(be sure to write down your Private Key password, as you will need it in several parts of the process)*, save the files (something like "MyCert.spc" and "MyKey.pvk") to a safe location on your computer.

dBASE and executables created using dBASE have been tested by dBASE, LLC using Microsoft's Authenticode signing utilities. There are other utilities but they have not been tested by dBASE, LLC according to their own documentation on this topic.

The Authenticode signing utilities are, at this time, FREE from Microsoft. You will need to download the appropriate version for the operating system you are developing on.

Details on the process can be found on the MSDN (Microsoft Developer's Network) site at:

```
http://msdn.microsoft.com/en-us/library/ms537364%28v=vs.85%29.aspx
```

and

```
http://msdn.microsoft.com/en-us/library/aa379872%28v=vs.85%29.aspx
```

Keep in mind that Microsoft, like most businesses, often modifies their web site and by the time you read this, the information may have moved to a different web address. I searched for keywords "Code Signing" on the MS website to find the pages noted above.

I have not chosen to digitally sign any of my applications at this time, as the process is fairly involved and a bit pricey. If you are interested in Code Signing beyond what I have mentioned here, you will need to spend time working out the complete process.

Working with Windows' User Account Control (UAC)

Before we delve into this chapter, it is vital that you understand how to make your application work with the UAC, so it is important to have a grasp of the UAC options. Various other chapters of this book have been updated to include details you may need to know to make an application fully UAC compliant and Chapter 2 attempts to clarify the topics in general. This chapter is aimed at the actual deployment.

First, why is this so important? Windows provides, via the UAC, a lot of security for your application and the data used by your application. I am basing the following off of a description in the build notes for dBASE Plus 2.70 released in March, 2011, as well as referencing some other resources.

UAC Rules as a Software Developer
The first question is "What are the UAC rules?"

First, Windows' UAC rules are intended to:
- Protect installed program files from being modified or damaged by users or programs that should not have access to them.
- Keep each user's files, configuration settings, etc. separate from other users, except where shared files or settings are needed.
- Restrict access to any machine wide settings to the maximum extent possible.

By default, only users with Administrator privileges have access to machine wide settings.

Windows Vista and Windows 7 implement these rules by carefully limited default permissions on folders under the "Program Files" folder tree, the "Program Data" folder tree, the Windows folder tree and the Users folder tree. Permissions to registry keys are also carefully limited so that standard users will not be allowed to modify any settings that can affect other users.

UAC Rules and Your Application
In order for an application to be UAC compliant:

- Executable code (your program) must be placed under the Program Files folder tree and must not attempt to modify or create new files under this tree while running the program *(this is a very different approach for most dBASE developers).* Standard users – the default rights for a dBASE application –have read and execute permissions to files under this folder tree. Programs may be configured to require administrator privileges which would prevent Standard users from running them.
- Configuration and Data files should be under the ProgramData folder tree – but your application should *not* attempt to modify or create new files under this folder tree while running the program. By default, Standard users have read-only access to this folder tree.
- Master copies of files needed by each user should be placed under the ProgramData folder tree – to be copied to each user's private folder tree.
- Set up a private folder tree under the Users folder tree for each user when a user first runs the program so that each user can modify their private files however they wish without interfering with other users.

This sounds complicated, in some ways it is. Following the information given above, on a standard Windows 7 computer, US/English, the folder structures mentioned above are typically (to help keep it clear in your mind, I have included the CSIDL references from Chapter 2):

Program Files folder tree (CSIDL_PROGRAM_FILES):
```
C:\Program Files (x86)\company name\application name
```

Program Data folder tree (CSIDL_COMMON_APPDATA):
```
C:\ProgramData\company name\application name
```

Users folder tree (CSIDL_LOCAL_APPDATA):
```
C:\Users\username\AppData\Local\company name\application name
```

On a network, you will most likely want to store the data on the network file server, in a location that makes sense based on the network configuration, the network administrator's requirements, and so on.

Using Inno Setup

For most of the discussions for deployment of dBASE applications to your user/customer's computers, I am assuming the use of Inno Setup. For this to work, when you install Inno Setup, be sure to enable the installation of ISPP (Inno Setup Preprocessor) – see Figure 28-2.

Figure 28-2

Using the Project Explorer to Deploy Your Application

The Project Explorer is a useful front-end for many purposes, one of which is setting up the deployment of your application. You may have used Inno Script Generator with versions of Project Explorer prior to dBASE 2.8. Starting with 2.8 the script is being generated internally by Project Explorer and its supporting files. *(Note that there is a separate section of this chapter that discusses using Inno Setup to manually create your install.)*

Whether or not you have chosen to Code Sign your application, you will want to go over this process as shown below if you choose to use the Project Explorer.

For the examples in this chapter I have copied the sample files from Chapter 26, using the same file names. If you have the sample code files you will see that the same files are in the folder for this chapter. These have some minor changes in the source code for the purposes of this chapter. There are, in addition to the files copied from Chapter 26, some other files that are used in this chapter.

Make sure that the Project you are working with includes files that you need to deploy with your application. If you do not, then the process will not allow you to select the files to deploy, you will not be presented with options for where to deploy individual files, and so on.

Before starting this process, you should be sure to have built your executable in the current folder, so you have the current MyFish.exe file.

You should note that using the Project Explorer to set up your installation/deployment for your application you will still be using Inno Setup. As such, once you have gone through the process, you could modify the script as needed. Once you have built the executable *(and as noted elsewhere in this chapter, possibly "Code Signed" or not ...)* – open your project in the Project Explorer, and click the "Inno" tab:

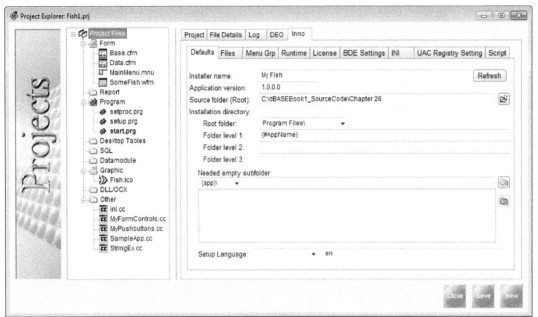

Figure 28-3

Note that while on the "Inno" tab you will see multiple sub-tabs – we will discuss each, starting at the first and working across.

This application is set as a UAC enabled application from the main "Project" tab and was compiled with that setting. As you may recall, this sets the property of the _app object *useUACPaths*.

The *Defaults* Tab

This tab allows you to define various aspects of your application, including the folders needed. See Figure 28-3 for an example of what this screen looks like when you first bring it up.

For the folders, you may want to determine first which of the "Root" folders to use. If you wish to deploy to the "Program Files" folder on the users' computer, then this is automatically selected. If you click the down arrow on the combobox, you will see:

```
Program Files\
Common Files\
Windows\
System\
Root Drive\
```

On a standard Windows Vista (or later) installation, these would be the following paths:

Path Name	Path
Program Files\	C:\Program Files (x86)\
Common Files\	C:\Program Files (x86)\Common Files
Windows\	C:\Windows\
System\	C:\Windows\System32\
Root Drive\	C:\

Once you have selected the installation path, you need to determine if you want to have your business/company name as part of the path. You may have multiple applications used by your customers and might wish to keep everything grouped by "company". For example, if I modify the entry as shown above, I could have the following as "Folder level 1":

```
dBASEBook
```

And then add:

```
{#AppName}
```

for "Folder level 2:".

You should note the Inno Setup constant "{#AppName}" above – this will use the name of your executable as the folder name. If you wish, you could change this.

The levels as shown above would then give you a path such as:

```
C:\Program Files (x86)\dBASEBook\{#AppName}
```

where the constant would be replaced with the name of the executable.

If you wish to store the data in a specific folder (which is recommended for UAC deployments), you would then use the "Needed empty subfolder:" option. To place the tables into the "Program Data" folder structure, you would use the Inno Setup constant: "{commonappdata}\" where the Project Explorer shows "{app}\".

Then in the entryfield to the right of that put the path that would be in the Program Data folder *(if you wanted you might also add the "{#AppName}" constant)*. For this one we will assume the company name, the application name, and then a "Tables" folder. So entering something along the lines of *(the example is also using the business name)*:

```
dBASEBook\{#AppName}\Tables
```

Then click the "Add Folder" button to the right. You should see something like (Figure 28-4):

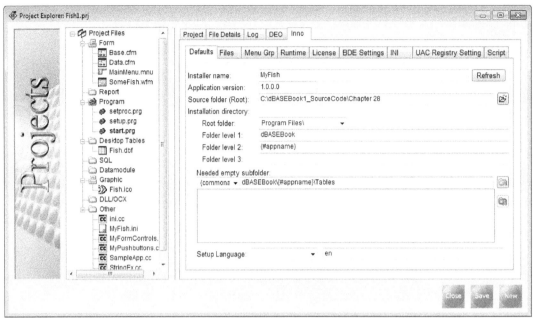

Figure 28-4

You can add as many folders as needed, removing ones you don't need, etc.

> **📝 NOTE:**
> The list under the "Needed empty subfolder" does not update as it should. I have been told this will be addressed in a future release of the Project Explorer.

You would want to set up each "empty" path you needed. Later you can define which folders individual files can be deployed to.

Note, for example, I am including an empty path pointing to the {localappdata} tree structure (CSIDL_LOCAL_APPDATA) – this is the users' folder structure and according to the Windows UAC rules is the correct place to store the tables that will be modified by your application (see Figure 28-5).

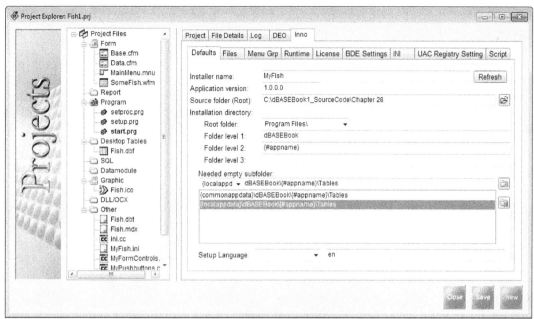

Figure 28-5

The "Setup Language" option deals with the install routine – it defines which language to use in the installer. This will not allow for multiple languages, but will at least let you set the specific one. You could create different installers for multiple languages if you wanted. The default is English *(as shown in Figure 28-5)*.

The *Files* Tab

The files tab is where you specify which files your application needs to deploy, and to where.

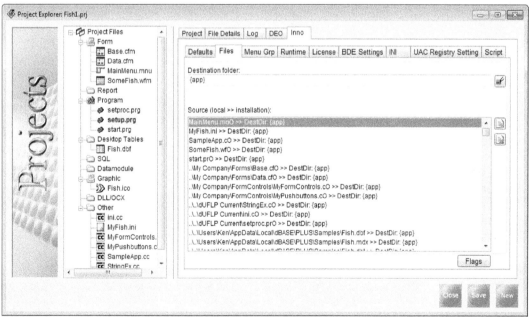

Figure 28-6

For some reason, even though this application is set as "non-DEO", meaning that the checkbox on the "Project" tab for "DEO Application?" is *not* checked, all the files for the application (including the tables) are included. You should double-check this – for example, the file "start.pro" is not shown in this list, because it is being built into the executable by definition.

This particular example is not a DEO application, but for any form of DEO application (as mentioned in other chapters of this book), when you deploy the files, all files not included IN the executable need to be deployed. However, if the file is included in the executable (your startup program, or whatever it happens to be, for example), it does not need to be in this list.

If you do not wish to deploy these files, you can select them and click the "Remove a file entry" button on the right.

You can also add files to the list. For example "MyFish.exe" is not included. Assuming you have built this file, you should add it here, as you cannot deploy it with the Project Explorer otherwise. In addition if you are using a Manifest file, you should include it. Any other files you wish to deploy that may not be in the file list should be added.

> **NOTE:**
> A Manifest file is used by Windows Vista and later versions of Windows to work with the Windows Themes, among other things. It also deals with application rights. The Manifest file needs to have the same name of the executable as part of the filename:
>
> ```
> MyFish.exe.manifest
> ```
>
> I copied the one for dBASE Plus from the folder the Plus.exe file is stored in, then renamed it. When you open it in WordPad or some other editor, you will want to be sure that you change references for "Plus.exe" to "MyFish.exe" (or the name of your own executable). You will then want to add this to the list of files to be deployed. It should be in the folder with the executable.

The executable should be stored in the folder represented by the "{app}" constant.

To add a file, or files (such as your tables), you would need to do the following (this example shows deploying the table for this application):

- Change the "Destination folder" to what you need. For the tables, use the folder created on the "General" tab:
  ```
  {commonappdata}\dBASEBook\{#AppName}\Tables
  ```
- Click on the file in the list, then click the "Change selected items to destinationfolder" button to the right.
- Click the next file, and note that it changes back to {app}, so you will have to enter the path again, then repeat the process for each file. For a table, be sure to include all files (.DBF, .DBT, .MDX) as needed for specific tables.

If you wish to deploy your own .INI file with the application, rather than have the Project Explorer create one, then you should be sure it is in the files listed in the Project Explorer, and it should be included on the screen here. Make sure to deploy it using the {app} constant.

Other notes, if you wish to deploy the tables to the user folder structure, you would need to add them to the list of files to be deployed *again* and assign the second location (for this example {localappdata}\dBASEBook\MyFish\Tables). However, the Project Explorer currently does not allow you to add files to the list twice, so after we generate the Inno Setup script at the end of this process we will need to add the tables a second time to allow us to deploy to the second location.

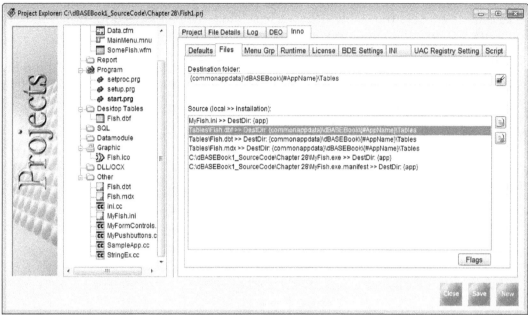

Figure 28-7

Setting Flags on Files

You can select individual files and set specific flags. To do this, click on the file in the list, then click the "Flags" button in the lower right corner of the Project Explorer. You should see something like:

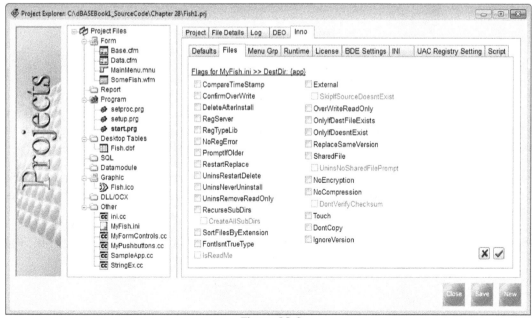

Figure 28-8

These flags can be found in the Inno Setup help, if you need to know what they mean. For this application I am not checking any of them.

One of my editors notes that he uses a few flags for some of his files:

- For an icon file (.ICO) he sets the "IgnoreVersion" flag.
- For a .DLL file that he distributes he also sets the "IgnoreVersion" flag.
- For a table he sets the "OnlyIfDoesntExist" flag – this makes a lot of sense because if you are deploying an update you would not want to overwrite the data.

You should check to make sure. For example, if you are deploying a "ReadMe" type file that is displayed for the user at the end, note there is a checkbox in the first column of flags.

The *Menu Grp* Tab

The "Menu Grp" tab deals with what appears on the Start Menu of Windows.

This defaults to the following when you first click on the tab:

Figure 28-9

If you wish to add other items into the menu group (for example, if you wish your users to access the Borland Database Engine Administrator, not always a good idea, but …) you could add these items.

If you wish to have an icon placed on the users' desktop to run the application, click the checkbox "Support Desktop icon". If you wish to include a "Quick Launch" icon (on the status bar of Windows), you can check that.

Other options for Uninstall and so on are defaults and is a good idea to leave them. For this simple application I am not going to add anything else to the group menu.

The *Runtime* Tab

Clicking the Runtime Tab will show you this screen:

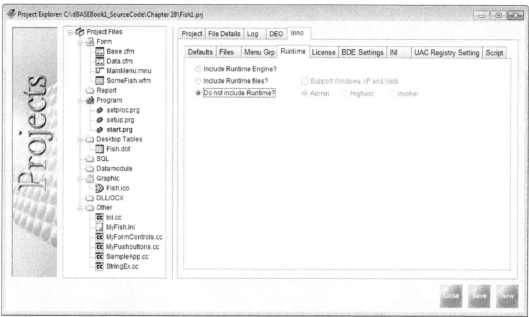

Figure 28-10

Note that by default the option is "Do not include Runtime?". I am not quite sure why the developers at dBASE decided this should be the default setting.

If you are deploying an update for your application and the Runtime engine has not been updated since the last time you sent files to your customer, you could set up the install to not use the runtime engine for dBASE, but most of the time you will want to.

What is the difference between the first two options?

The first one ("Include Runtime Engine?") assumes you need to deploy both the Borland Database Engine (BDE) and the complete Runtime engine for dBASE. (For a first-time installation of an application this would be required. However, it should also be noted that deploying an application using the Project Explorer, the developers at dBASE have added the ability to check to see if the BDE and Runtime has been installed and if so, not install them again.)

The second option ("Include Runtime files?") will assume that the Borland Database Engine(BDE) and the full runtime have been installed previously and that perhaps there has been an update to the runtime. This will only install the updated runtime files.

For the first time out, we need the first option, so click that radiobutton. The screen will change rather dramatically to:

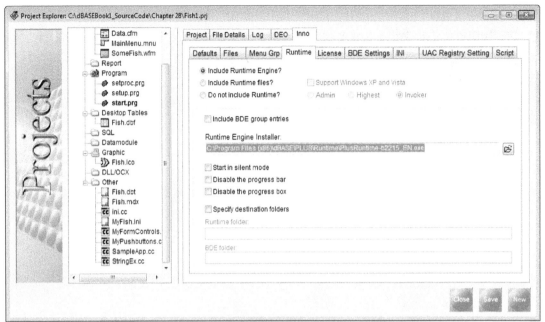

Figure 28-11

You have a lot of choices here. Very importantly you have to specify the runtime engine installer you wish to use. Before we get to that, let us move down one item at a time:

Include BDE group entries: This assumes you might want to add in the program group that is installed in Windows for your application the icon for the BDE Administrator. It is up to you if you wish to allow your user to have access to this. I am going to leave this at the default.

Runtime Engine Installer: This assumes you have downloaded a runtime installer from the dBASE website. I always store these in the Runtime folder. Click the folder button to find it, then select the appropriate file.

The path for the installer (which includes the BDE) will most likely be (for Windows Vista or later) under the "C:\Program Files (x86)" folder structure. See *Figure 28-11* …

Start in silent mode: When your installer runs, you can run the BDE/Runtime installer in "silent" mode, so the user does not see that it is being installed. I am going to leave this at the default setting.

Disable the progress bar: The runtime installer has its own progress bar that can be displayed during installation. Checking this option would turn the display of the progress bar off during the install. If you are running in silent mode, it seems like you would probably not want to display this either.

Disable the progress box: This is similar to the progress bar, it displays what is being installed for the BDE/Runtime installation. Again, if you are running in silent mode, you probably would want to disable this as well.

Specify destination folders: This option will, if checked, enable the two entryfields below for the specific paths for the BDE and the Runtime – you can specify specific paths. If you use Inno Setup constants you pass those to the installer. Checking this checkbox will show some defaults and you can modify them from there. For this example I am going to leave this unchecked.

> **⚙ BUG**
>
> There is a bug when using the BDE/Runtime installer here but it only occurs when you run the installer created at the end of this section. The bug will be discussed again when you are walked through the actual deployment screens. When the BDE/Runtime installation gets near the end an error dialog occurs, the user must cancel the installation, then re-start it. Since the BDE and Runtime were actually installed correctly, no error occurs the second time and the installation completes.
>
> The R&D team at dBASE, LLC plan on fixing it, but at the time I am completing this chapter of the book it has not been addressed.
>
> One developer has provided a workaround by using the Pre-Text option (see The License Tab section below) to explain to the person installing the application that they will need to cancel the installation at the point of the error and re-run it, that it is a known issue.

The *License* Tab

If your application requires a License Agreement (End-User License Agreement or EULA), this tab of the Project Explorer is where you can set this up.

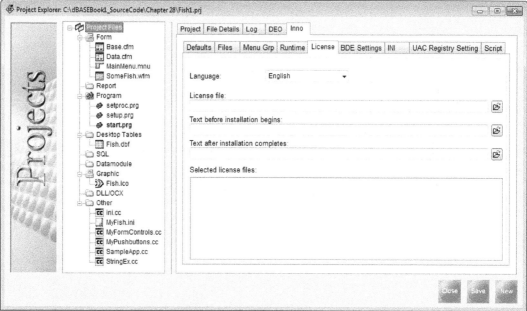

Figure 28-12

Basically the EULA is a set of text files – in this case some text that will display before the user can complete installation, typically asking the user if they have read and agreed to the License Agreement. The "License file:" is the actual licensing agreement and if you wish you can add text to display after the installation completes.

You can of course get more information on License Agreements online with a quick search. You can even find suggested wording that may be useful for your specific application.

The following is from an email by one of my editors, who has used the licensing options for at least one application:

● The License file runs at the beginning of the install and requires the user performing the install to select a radioButton that says, "I accept the agreement" or "I do not accept the agreement" which is the default. The user cannot proceed with the install without first accepting the agreement. You could put any kind of text you want in the TEXT FILE but all the surrounding verbiage that Inno supplies references a "License Agreement". *(The samples here are using a standard License agreement from the GNU website.)*

● If you have anything else that you specifically want to communicate to the person performing the install BEFORE the install actually starts such as my text regarding working around the illegal BDE path you can use the second entryField on the page titled "Text before installation begins". This text appears immediately following the user accepting the agreement and then clicking the next pushButton in "a" above. On this page the user then has the choices "Back". "Next" and "Cancel".

● At the end of the installation if you want to provide a "What Now" synopsis you can put it in a Text File in the third entryField titled "Text after installation completes".

It should be noted that you can set different language files. So for your installation, if you wanted to have a version in English, German and French, you could specify the appropriate files by selecting the language in the combobox, and so on ...

For this example, I downloaded a license agreement from the GNU website, and put together a couple of simple files to be used for the other two settings.

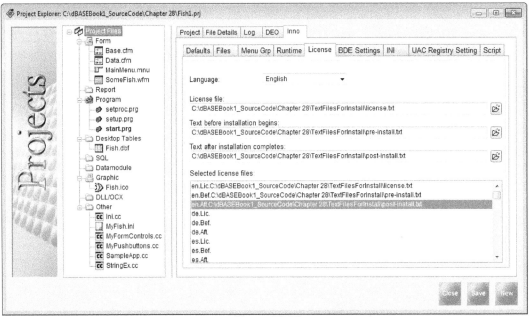

Figure 28-13

The *BDE Settings* Tab

This tab is where you can set up your BDE Aliases. It should be noted that this will set up "permanent" BDE Aliases, not "User BDE Aliases". The differences between these are mentioned in *many* places throughout this book, starting in Chapter 2 and working forward.

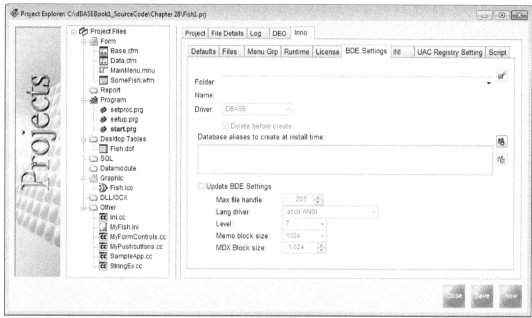

Figure 28-14

To do this you need to select the folder you wish to create a BDE Alias for from the dropdown at the top. This will be one of the folders you created on the "Defaults" and "Files" tabs.

Then you assign a BDE Alias name and select the driver. The checkbox "Delete before create" defaults to being checked *(meaning that if the installer finds the BDE Alias already created, it will delete it, then re-create it)*. Once you have your BDE Alias settings, click the button "Add BDE entries".

If you are using *User BDE Aliases*, rather than "hard-coded" BDE Aliases, then do NOT select anything here. This sample application is using *User BDE Aliases*.

Under the checkbox "Update BDE Settings" you can change default BDE settings. This will allow you to specify optimal settings for the BDE, and/or for the BDE and your application. See the appendices for discussions of "optimal" settings.

I set the "Max file handle" setting to 2048 and "Lang driver" setting to "WEurope ANSI" *(see Figure 28-15)*. The "Max file handle" is one of the optimized settings for the BDE from the appendices and the language driver I am setting is the one I always use for all of my applications. If the program you are deploying needs to create temporary files, it is a good idea for the language driver to be set to the one you need ...

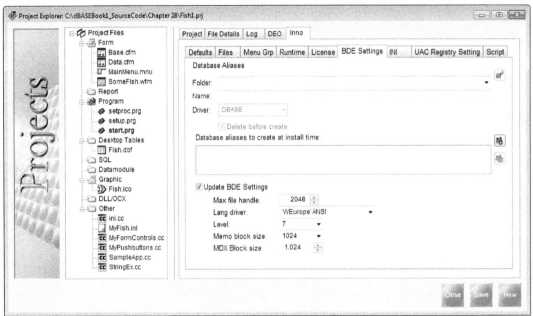

Figure 28-15

The *INI* Tab

This tab will create a .INI file for your application. If you have your own .INI file, then you will want to deploy it separately. For this example/walk-through we will have the Project Explorer not create its own .INI file. To that end, you will need to go back and add the .INI file to the file list (it will appear under "Other"). Make sure it shows up in the "File" tab, the default location of "{app}" should be fine.

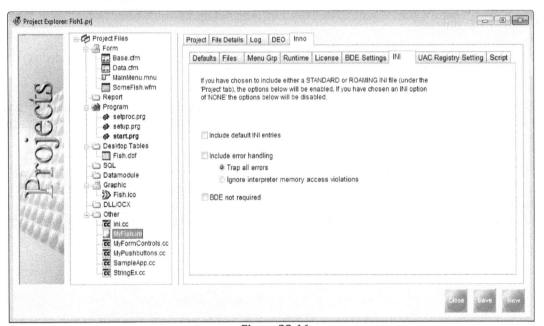

Figure 28-16

If you did click the "Include default INI entries", the Project Explorer would add the following entries:

```
[Toolbars]
Standard=0
StandardFloat=0
```

```
StandardStyle =0
[Desktop]
Maximized=0
StatusBar=0
[CommandWindow]
Open=0
[ObjectPath]
objPath0=C:\YourObjectPath
```

The last entry shouldn't be added if the DEO settings are "off", as it is only necessary for a DEO application.

Sometimes the Error Trapping can be useful. You can turn this on/off ... see Chapter 27 for details on these settings.

And finally if your application does not use tables, you could check the "BDE not required" checkbox, which would place the appropriate entry into the .INI file, so the BDE is not loaded with your application. However, keep in mind that if you use tables of any sort you need to use the BDE.

For this application/example, as we are deploying our own .INI file (among other things it includes a User BDE Alias), we are leaving the screen "as is".

The *UAC Registry Setting* Tab

This tab gives three specific options, with quite a bit of description:

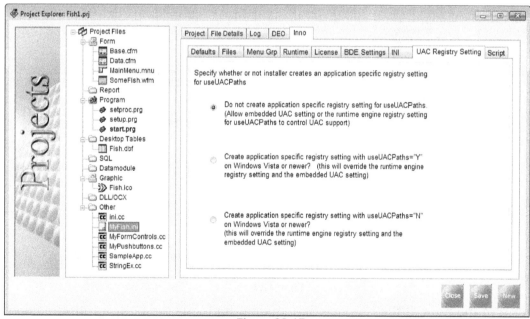

Figure 28-17

As the "Build as UAC App" checkbox was set for this application on the "Project" tab, we can leave this at the default. However, if you did not set it there, you could choose the second option, or if you want this application to specifically *not* be a UAC application, you would use the third option.

The *Script* Tab

This tab allows you to define and view the Inno Setup script generated by the Project Explorer.

At the time of this writing, the first time you click this tab for a project, it defaults to a folder that does not exist and you will receive an error (see Figure 28-18):

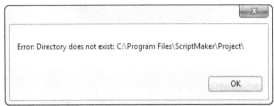

Error: Directory does not exist: C:\Program Files\ScriptMaker\Project\

OK

Figure 28-18

Click "OK", then you can change the path to where you want the Inno Setup script to be created and assign a filename to it. *(I have been assured that in a future release of the Project Explorer this error will not occur, as the entryfield will default to a blank value ...)*

Click the "Folder" button on the right which gives a screen tip of "Change Scriptname", select the folder (I recommend the same folder that the Project file is in) and assign a name. For this example I am using "Fish1" – the same name as the Project File.

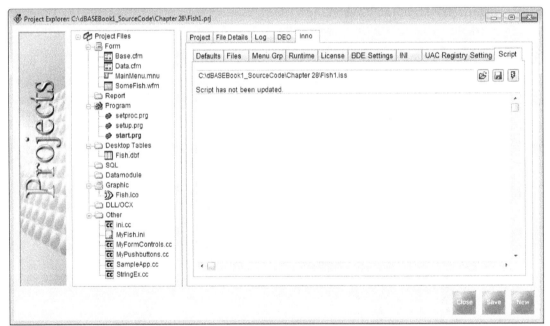

Figure 28-19

The button to the right of the "Change Scriptname" button is the button with the floppy disc image which if you hold the mouse over it gives a screen tip that says "Generate script with settings". Click that button and you should see the script in the large editor control on the dialog:

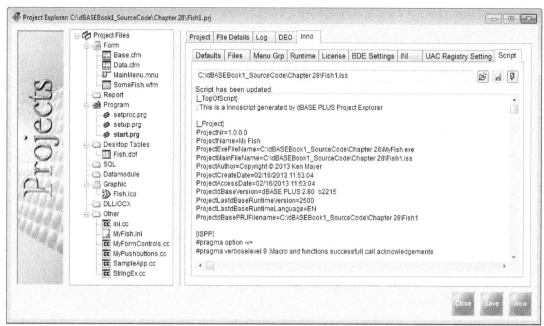

Figure 28-20

This screen is "read-only" – meaning that if there is an option you wish to change, you cannot do it in the editor control. You can change options in the Project Explorer if needed, then if you click the same button the script will be re-generated with those changes reflected.

The last button (the lightning bolt) will generate the Install program using Inno Setup to do so.

One thing that is quite important, which I forgot to do it while writing this chapter, is that somewhere along the line you need to build your executable (discussed in depth in Chapter 26). If you click the "Log" tab, if needed click the "Empty Log" button, then on the toolbar click the "Rebuild All" button, your .EXE should be created (or re-created).

Once you have your executable what actually happens when you click the "Generate Install Program" button is that your new script is opened in Inno Setup. You should see a screen very much like:

Figure 28-21

If you feel comfortable with Inno Setup, you could modify the script here. We will make a couple of change to the script generated here and in a good portion of the rest of this chapter we will examine what can be done with an Inno Setup script.

Before continuing you may want to close the Project Explorer (save any changes) and also close dBASE itself.

A Few Changes to the Script

In order to make this deployment Windows UAC compliant, we must deploy the tables to a specific location. We are going to add a little more to this script. However, keep in mind if you change anything in the Project Explorer and then re-create the script, these changes will need to be added back into the script.

Tables

Scroll down in the script to find the [Files] section, and note the table is listed with three files. We are going to copy those three lines, and paste this directly underneath. The file section looks like the following (note that these lines wrap inside the margins, each line begins with the word "Source:"):

```
[Files]
Source: MyFish.ini; DestDir: {app}; Flags: IgnoreVersion
Source: Tables\Fish.dbf; DestDir:
{commonappdata}\dBASEBook\{#AppName}\Tables; Flags: OnlyIfDoesntExist
Source: Tables\Fish.dbt; DestDir:
{commonappdata}\dBASEBook\{#AppName}\Tables; Flags: OnlyIfDoesntExist
Source: Tables\Fish.mdx; DestDir:
{commonappdata}\dBASEBook\{#AppName}\Tables; Flags: OnlyIfDoesntExist
Source: MyFish.exe; DestDir: {app}; Flags: IgnoreVersion
```

```
Source: MyFish.exe.manifest; DestDir: {app}; Flags: IgnoreVersion
```

We are going to copy the lines with the fish table and two auxiliary files (.MDX and .DBT) and paste them back in, then change the DestDir part of the lines just a little:

```
Source: Tables\Fish.dbf; DestDir:
{localappdata}\dBASEBook\{#AppName}\Tables; Flags: OnlyIfDoesntExist
Source: Tables\Fish.dbt; DestDir:
{localappdata}\dBASEBook\{#AppName}\Tables; Flags: OnlyIfDoesntExist
Source: Tables\Fish.mdx; DestDir:
{localappdata}\dBASEBook\{#AppName}\Tables; Flags: OnlyIfDoesntExist
```

This will ensure that the table is placed in the correct location.

User BDE Aliases

Next we need to have the Inno Setup script add the User BDE Alias to the MyFish.ini file. For this scroll down a little further in the script, and add the following several lines at the end of the [INI] section (again these will wrap between the margins, so each line begins with the word "Filename:"):

```
Filename: {app}\MyFish.ini; Section: "UserBDEAliases";
Filename: {app}\MyFish.ini; Section: "UserBDEAliases"; Key: "0"; String:
"dBASEFish";
Filename: {app}\MyFish.ini; Section: "dBASEFish";
Filename: {app}\MyFish.ini; Section: "dBASEFish"; Key: "Driver"; String:
"DBASE";
Filename: {app}\MyFish.ini; Section: "dBASEFish"; Key: "Options"; String:
"PATH: ""{localappdata}\dBASEBook\MyFish\Tables""";
```

Save your changes by clicking on the standard "Save" icon in the toolbar for the Inno Setup window.

Testing Your Installation

If you want to test the install routine then there are a couple of buttons for this – one will simply build the installation program, the other will be to build it and then run it.

The "Compile" button will just compile the program. This is useful to find errors (hopefully the Project Explorer did not create any, but ...).

The "Run" button will compile the setup program if it has not been and will then run it.

Either way, this builds the install program into a folder called "Output" in the same folder as your .ISS file.

So assuming the path being used for this chapter of:

```
C:\dBASEBook1_SourceCode\Chapter 28
```

The folder "Output" would be under that, with a program called "Setup.exe".

```
C:\dBASEBook1_SourceCode\Chapter 28\Output
```

Test the Installation

The following series of screen shots are from running the setup program based on what we did to this point in the chapter. I went to my Notebook computer which has Windows 8 on it, made sure dBASE and the Runtime were not on the computer, copied the file "setup.exe" to the drive and ran it. This is what the installation looks like:

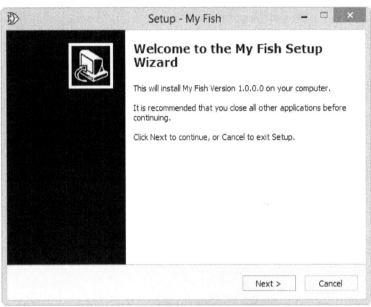

Figure 28-22

Clicking the "Next" button:

Figure 28-23

This screen shot shows the License Agreement. Note that to continue the user must click the "I accept the agreement" radiobutton.

Figure 28-24

Figure 28-24 shows the "Pre-Install text". The sample file I created was really simplistic for this example, but it shows where it appears in the process of the install (after the License Agreement). See the note above about the BDE/Runtime installation bug, for example. You could put explicit directions here, if that is what was needed, in case your installation was more complicated than this simple one, or you could just ask the user to not change the settings, and click through the installation process using the "Next" button.

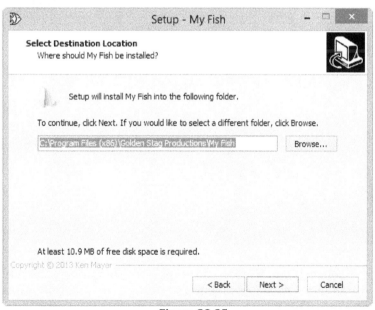

Figure 28-25

This screen allows the user to change the path to install the application to. Note that it shows the path that was created in the Project Explorer on the Defaults tab.

Figure 28-26

Here (Figure 28-26) we can change the name of the folder that will appear in the Start Menu. Note that the default settings assume you want to allow your user to change this.

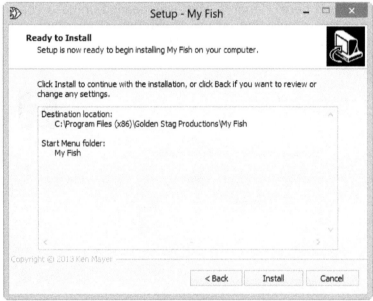

Figure 28-27

The user is shown the settings and if needed the user could click the "Back" button and change something. Keep in mind that this is a very simple installation, so there aren't a lot of options available.

At this point the option is to click "Install", rather than "Next". Doing so we will see the dBASE PLUS Runtime install screen:

Figure 28-28

Clicking "Next" we continue to:

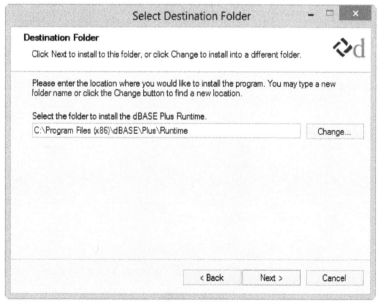

Figure 28-29

Leaving the default settings, we can then move on to:

Figure 28-30

This is the standard dBASE Plus Runtime and BDE (Borland Database Engine) setup wizard. It has been passed options to it by the settings selected in the Project Explorer, which are then streamed out to the Inno Setup script. Clicking "Next" ...

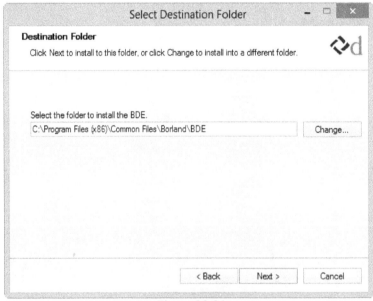

Figure 28-31

Again using the default setting, if we click the "Next" button again:

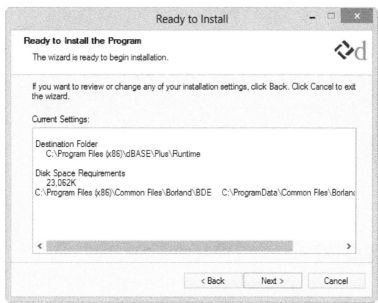

Figure 28-32

If you needed to change a path, you could use "Back" and do so, but we are again using the default settings, so clicking "Next":

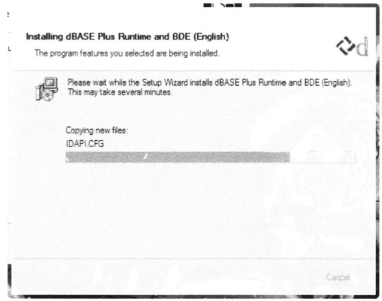

Figure 28-33

The progress bar as shown here will vary as to what you see. The screen was quite busy when I grabbed this screen shot ... It is possible when I pressed the PrtScn button that it was in the middle of a refresh, which is why it doesn't look so clean. That's okay.

> 🐞 **BUG**
> It is at this point that the bug will be encountered as mentioned earlier in this chapter. I am showing the two screens that will come up, so that if you choose to follow the lead of one of my editors you know what to expect.

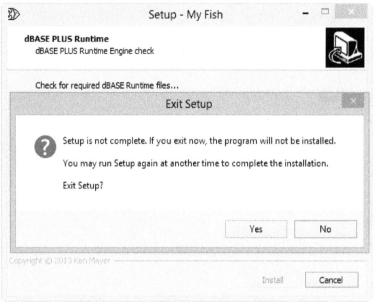

Figure 28-34

The error shown above is the first of two that are currently showing up when installing from a script created by the Project Explorer. See boxes explaining in more detail. Your user will need to click "OK" here, and on the next screen cancel the installation (click "Yes" on the dialog). When they re-start the installer, the BDE and Runtime have been successfully installed so the install will not try again, and the error will not re-occur, the installation should complete successfully.

Figure 28-35

If you click "Yes" here, restart the installer and complete it, you should see:

Figure 28-36

When you click "Finish" you are taken back to the main setup routine from Inno Setup – your application, which will look like:

Figure 28-37

In this case if you selected a "Post-Install Text" file, this is what you would get here. This could be again some specific instructions. This is not the "ReadMe.txt" file, which is not an option that the Project Explorer lets you set up, but Inno Setup does have as a setting for *(we will look at that later in the section on using Inno Setup manually)*.

Figure 28-38

Clicking the "Finish" button automatically opens Windows Explorer to the folder in the Start Menu for your application.

Your user can either run the application from there, from a Desktop Icon if you chose to allow for this (it is an option in the Project Explorer explained earlier in this chapter). The user can also go to the Start Menu and open the folder "My Fish" and run the application from there.

If you go to the folder structure under "C:\Program Files (x86)" where the application was installed, you will see an "Uninstall Information" folder. This contains the uninstall program (named "unins000.exe"). Your user can uninstall the application from there.

The folder with the executable in it should also have a copy of the .INI file. However, when you run the program, if anything in your code modifies the .INI file, under a standard UAC installation (which is how this was set up), you will see those changes were made in a completely different folder structure – a copy of the .INI file was made in the path:

```
C:\Users\Ken\AppData\Local\dBASEBook\My Fish
```

Where "Ken" is the "username" of the person logged in to Windows and everything after "Local" is the path to the folder that contains the .INI file.

Again, using the information we discussed earlier and looking at the computer with Windows Explorer, if you look for the table (or tables for a more complex application) you will find it is stored in the path:

```
C:\ProgramData\dBASEBook\My Fish\Tables
```

Keeping in mind that this is a read-only location, the tables were also copied to:

```
C:\Users\Ken\AppData\Local\dBASEBook\My Fish\Tables
```

And if you examine the User BDE Alias definition in My Fish.ini stored in the path mentioned above, you will see it points to this location as well.

What have we learned through this part of the chapter? That the Project Explorer *can* be used to create the installation script and that it works as advertised.

The one thing that is missing is the ability to truly customize your installation. The next part of the chapter will get into working with Inno Setup directly and not using the Project Explorer to install your application. This gives you more flexibility, but it can also make the initial setup a bit more complex. There are advantages to using a tool like the Project Explorer, much depends on your needs as a developer.

What Next?

Once you have your .ISS file created, you can leave it as is and use it to create your setup routine, or you can work with the script in Inno Setup and customize the installation. The next section of this chapter deals with working with Inno Setup by hand. There may be parts of the samples shown you would want to copy into a script created by the Project Explorer, for example.

Using Inno Setup Manually

Inno Setup is a program that was written in Delphi[tm] and has constantly evolved from well before it was discovered by the folks at dBASE *(to be truthful I discovered it when trying to find a different installer when I worked for them, as the license that Borland had with InstallShield was no longer valid)* to the present. The author of Inno Setup has created a very useful tool, and many folk who use it have created third-party add-ins and a lot more. My preference is to simply get my hands in and work directly with the script as shown in this part of the chapter.

Inno Setup works great with dBASE applications. The example in this chapter is a "manual" version of the same installation from earlier in the chapter constructed using the Project Explorer.

Although Inno doesn't look like much – it doesn't offer the kind of drag and drop functionality that you might be used to from other install programs – it's actually quite powerful and very functional. It also produces very fast install programs. If you work with it a bit you will see that it provides a wizard, as well as other features, including syntax highlighting (colors for specific parts of the script, etc.).

The sample script (MyFishInstall.iss) will be included with the source code for the book in the Chapter 28 folder.

Some Basic Information

This screen is simply an editor that can be used to create a setup script. The script created will have an extension of .ISS (Inno Setup Script). The program is also a "compiler" – it will attempt to create your setup program based on the contents of the script – if there are errors during the "compile process", they will be described and the setup program will not be created.

Figure 28-39

The script itself is an ASCII file, so you could create it elsewhere rather than using this program, although using the program to create/edit the script makes as much sense as anything else, as it performs some error checking and color coding to show different elements.

Most of the script contains name/value pairs – a name which references a value. These values will be things like filenames, or destinations for where to deploy to. These can also have parameters – modifiers for what you want the deployer to do with them.

Note that Inno Setup performs a top-down execution of your script. However, Inno includes quite a bit of functionality including IF preprocessor directives and more. These are defined in the help for Inno Setup.

Inno Setup also allows for some coding of your own in a version of Pascal. The script we will examine in this chapter has some code to deal with BDE Registry issues.

ⓘ **SUGGESTION**

Inno Setup has different "Sections", which will be discussed below. To test everything when I was figuring out how to install to the folders used by a "proper" UAC complaint application, I created a temporary folder and created setup routines for each section, keeping in mind that the [Setup] section is required to let Inno Setup know what to call the install program, and where to put it, if nothing else. This allowed me to try installing parts of the application and verify that I was using the correct constants and options. It took some time, but it provided for a pretty solid and nice looking installation.

Inno Constants

Inno supports the use of special constants which represent certain directories on either your computer or the person using your install's computer. Some of these are defined by you in the setup section.

Also note that the constants defined below cannot be used in the SOURCE parameter of the Files section.

{app}
The application directory, which the user selects on the Select Directory page of the wizard. For example: If you used {app}\MYPROG.EXE on an entry and the user selected C:\MYPROG as the application directory, Setup will translate it to use C:\MYPROG\MYPROG.EXE.

{sd}
The Windows System Drive. On a local computer this is typically C:\.

{sys}
The system's Windows System directory (System32 in a 32-bit installation on Windows NT). For example: If you used {sys}\CTL3DV2.DLL on an entry and the system's Windows System directory is C:\WINDOWS\SYSTEM, Setup will translate it to use C:\WINDOWS\SYSTEM\CTL3DV2.DLL.

{src}
The directory in which the Source files are located. For example: If you used {src}\MYPROG.EXE on an entry and the user is installing from "S:\", Setup will translate it to use "S:\MYPROG.EXE".

{pf} or {pf32}
Program Files. The path of the system's Program Files directory, typically "C:\Program Files" for Windows XP and earlier, or "C:\Program Files (x86)" for later versions of Windows. *(Use of {PF} means that Inno Setup will place the files in the correct location for 32-bit vs. 64-bit applications, which may be useful if dBASE is converted to full 64-bit in the future …).*

{cf}
Common Files. The path of the system's Common Files directory, typically C:\Program Files (x86)\Common Files.

Other constants that are important match up with the CSIDLs:

CSIDL	Inno Setup Constant
CSIDL_PROGRAM_FILES	{pf}
CSIDL_COMMON_APPDATA	{commonappdata}
CSIDL_LOCAL_APPDATA	{localappdata}

There are others, which you can look up in help.

Using Other Languages

The author of Inno Setup has written the code in such a way that the message strings used during an actual install are pulled from a file (*.ISL) – this file contains the strings used, which can be changed for different languages.

You can download a new file for a specific language from a third-party website:

```
http://www.jrsoftware.org/files/istrans/
```

When you find the language file you need, it is suggested that you either store this file in the folder that Inno Setup was installed to, or that you put it in your application directory – my inclination would be to store it with Inno Setup.

Getting Started

When I first started preparing to rewrite this chapter I spent some time creating very simple scripts to test individual sections as described below, for setting up folders, copying files, etc. This allowed me to just focus on the individual parts of the installation to see what worked, where files were placed with specific constants, and so on. This may be a useful trick for you as well.

Creating an Install

The sample script is going to end up being very similar to the one created by the Project Explorer, but there will be some additional items and possibly some simplifications in places.

Most of the following came from the Inno help, except for the information on installing the dBASE Plus Runtime and the BDE, which comes from the development team at dBASE, LLC.

Most of what is discussed below is specifically related to the Inno Setup Script needed to deploy this application, but there are a few places that digress into general topics.

You can include comments by using the semicolon ";" at the beginning of the line. As you look through the script below you will see that there are a lot of comments to help understand the sections. It is a good idea to document what you are doing and why.

Important: There are many places throughout the script where the book's page width has caused the lines to wrap. When reading the script, or using it for an example, remember that these commands are actually complete on one line. Most commands begin with a keyword followed by an equal (=) sign, or a keyword followed by a colon (:). Also note that a semi colon (;) at the beginning of a line indicates a comment; in any other position it is a separator.

The Setup Section

As you might imagine, this is important in a few ways. Note there are a lot of comments in the code below to help understand what is happening:

```
[Setup]
; These two entries following are required:
AppName=MyFish
AppVersion=1.0.0.0

; This is used on the Welcome page of the setup
; dialog, and in the Add/Remove Program entry
; in Windows:
AppVerName=MyFish 1.0.0.0

; The directive AppID is used for your uninstall
; program. It is probably a good idea to use it.
; The suggestion is to use the name of the program,
; similar to AppName as shown above:
AppID=MyFish
```

```
; Copyright information (the copyright symbol is
; created by using the alt key and the numeric
; keypad on the right side of your keyboard: alt+0169:
AppCopyright=Copyright © 2013 Ken Mayer

; If you wish to allow your users to Select the path
; to install to (which is a default setting). You can
; find more on this directive in the Inno Setup help. The
; constant {pf} references "C:\Program Files (x86)", or
; "C:\Program Files" depending on the operating system.
; This path is what is referenced in the script by the
; Inno Setup constant {app}:
DefaultDirName={pf}\dBASEBook\MyFish

; If you expect your user may be installing updates,
; you can include this directive as well:
UsePreviousAppDir=yes

; This is the group in Windows, where a link to the
; executable and any other related files will be placed
DefaultGroupName=MyFish

; The following directive defaults to "Yes", the difficulty
; is that it can confuse your end-users as it shows all the
; components that will be installed. It is a good idea
; to not do that unless you have a fairly complex installation:
AlwaysShowComponentsList=no

; This tells Inno Setup where to find the source
; code for your application. Rather than having
; to continually reference it in this script,
; you can then refer to the files in the path
; without having to put the full path in. If
; a subfolder is used, you would just reference
; the subfolder followed by files (i.e.,
;     Main\*.wfm    )
SourceDir=C:\dBASEBook1_SourceCode\Chapter 28

; Output directory is where you want Inno Setup
; to place the generated install program (the
; Project Explorer uses a folder called "Output",
; I prefer having some control over my folder
; names ...):
OutputDir=InstallImage

; What is the name of the actual setup program?
OutputBaseFilename=MyFishSetup

; The two following directives are used in
; the install screen and the uninstall screen:
AppPublisher=Golden Stag Productions
AppPublisherURL=http://www.goldenstag.net/Golden Stag Productions

; Appearance of the installer -- this section is not
; required, but is handy to personalize your install:
SetupIconFile=C:\Users\Ken\AppData\Local\dBASE\PLUS\Samples\Fish.ico
WizardImageBackColor=clGreen
WizardImageFile=Images\SmallStag.bmp
```

```
WizardImageStretch=no

; -- Text Files --
; License file - the license here was copied from
; http://www.gnu.org/licenses/#GPL - it is a generic
; General Public License ... for your own software
; you would obviously want to determine the license
; you would need with any specifics ...
LicenseFile=TextFilesForInstall\license.txt
; Information to be displayed after license is
; accepted, but before installation starts.
InfoBeforeFile=TextFilesForInstall\pre-install.txt
; Information displayed after installation,
; but before any "readme.txt" type file.
InfoAfterFile=TextFilesForInstall\post-install.txt


; ------------------------------------------------------------
; ----------------- End of SETUP section -----------------
; ------------------------------------------------------------
```

There are a lot of other options that can be set there, read the online help if you are interested. When the installer is started, a screen like this is shown:

Figure 28-39

The Dirs Section

The directory section is used to define directories to be created, besides the application directory. It uses the constants that are defined elsewhere in the script. While you aren't required to create directories first before copying files to them in the [Files] section, directories will not be deleted by the uninstaller if they are not specified here.

```
[Dirs]
; If your application needs to store files in multiple
; folders, this is where you would define them.
; For example, you might want to store the data
; in the C:\ProgramData folder, then any sub-folders
; you might need. The first location is:
```

304

```
;        C:\ProgramData\dBASEBook\MyFish\Tables   and should be read &
execute only:
Name: "{commonappdata}\dBASEBook\MyFish\Tables"; Permissions: users-
readexec;
; The second location is the real location of the data -- where
; the data can be modified:
;        C:\Users\username\AppData\Local\dBASEBook\MyFish\Tables
Name: "{localappdata}\dBASEBook\MyFish\Tables"; Permissions: everyone-
full;


; ----------------------------------------------------
; Where the dBASE Plus Runtime Engine will go: "C:\Program Files (x86)" if
on
; 64-bit versions of Windows, or on 32-bit versions, "C:\Program Files"):
Name: "{pf}\dBASE\Plus\Runtime"; Permissions: everyone-readexec; Flags:
uninsneveruninstall;


; ----------------------------------------------------
; Where the BDE will go:
Name: "{cf}\Borland\BDE"; Permissions: everyone-full; Flags:
uninsneveruninstall;


; If you were going to do a DEO installation, you
; might want to have a folder stored either locally
; or on the network (if this is a network application).
; See information in The dBASE Book, Chapter 28, on
; setting up folders for a network application,
; and dealing with "type" of installation.


; --------------------------------------------------------
; ----------------- End of DIRS section ------------------
; --------------------------------------------------------
```

If you wanted to perform a DEO installation, you would need a folder (or multiple folders) to store your DEO objects in. If you are working with a network-based application, you will want to see information below, but some of what you would need would be placed in the DIRS section as well. There is a discussion of this later in the chapter, as well as a sample Inno Setup script in the sample code.

The Files *Section*

The documentation for Inno Setup states this "is optional, but necessary for most installations." Since this section defines all of the files that are copied to the user's system, it is required unless you don't wish to actually deploy any files.

Each file has a "Source" and a "DestDir" and there are some parameters that you should examine.

```
[Files]
; The executable itself, to the application folder:
Source: "MyFish.exe"; DestDir: "{app}"; Flags: ignoreversion

; INI File --
; if you have an existing .INI file with specific settings in it
; then you will want to copy this to the application folder.
Source: "MyFish.ini"; DestDir: "{app}"; Flags: ignoreversion

; Tables, indexes and .dbts to the application\data folder --
```

```
; note that you can use wildcards in some cases (i.e., *.dbf):
Source: "Tables\Fish.dbf"; DestDir: "{commonappdata}\dBASEBook\MyFish\Tables";
Flags: onlyifdoesntexist;
Source: "Tables\Fish.mdx"; DestDir: "{commonappdata}\dBASEBook\MyFish\Tables";
Flags: onlyifdoesntexist;
Source: "Tables\Fish.dbt"; DestDir: "{commonappdata}\dBASEBook\MyFish\Tables";
Flags: onlyifdoesntexist;
Source: "Tables\Fish.dbf"; DestDir: "{localappdata}\dBASEBook\MyFish\Tables";
Flags: onlyifdoesntexist;
Source: "Tables\Fish.mdx"; DestDir: "{localappdata}\dBASEBook\MyFish\Tables";
Flags: onlyifdoesntexist;
Source: "Tables\Fish.dbt"; DestDir: "{localappdata}\dBASEBook\MyFish\Tables";
Flags: onlyifdoesntexist;


; Add any other files that would need to be deployed, which might
; include such things as a Readme file, image files, DLL files
; that may be required, etc. This would include putting files
; on the network for DEO applications, or other (see note
; above for details in Ch. 28 of the book).

; BDE/Runtime Installer for dBASE Plus (install to Temporary folder):
Source: "C:\Program Files (x86)\dBASE\Plus\Runtime\PlusRuntime-
b2215_EN.exe"; DestDir: "{tmp}"; Flags: ignoreversion deleteafterinstall


; --------------------------------------------------------
; Manifest file for runtime:
Source: "C:\Program Files (x86)\dBASE\PLUS\Runtime\plusrun.exe.manifest";
DestDir: "{pf}\dBASE\Plus\Runtime"
; Manifest file for BDE:
Source: "C:\Program Files (x86)\dBASE\PLUS\Runtime\bdeadmin.exe.manifest";
DestDir: "{cf}\Borland\BDE"
; Manifest file for application, must be in same folder as .EXE file:
Source: "MyFish.exe.manifest"; DestDir: "{app}";


; --------------------------------------------------------
; ----------------- End of FILES section ------------------
; --------------------------------------------------------
```

As with the DIRS section, if you were deploying a DEO or Network-based application, there is more that might need to be done here. For a DEO application that is *not* on a network, it is simpler – you would deploy the files to local folders as needed. For a network-based DEO application, see below.

Using the "Standard" dBASE PLUS Runtime Installer

NOTE: The folk at dBASE provide a runtime/BDE installer. This is stored on your dBASE CD, in a special RUNTIME folder. I recommend that you copy the file or files that you wish to use for your application(s) to the dBASE directories, perhaps in the folder called Runtime. The sample below assumes that this is where the runtime file is stored. You may want to be sure that the runtime installer you are using matches the version of dBASE you are using. You can download updates from the dBASE website.

There is a discussion here of using the "normal" runtime installer in your Inno Setup script, but there are difficulties such as modifying the Windows Registry with your setup. However, after some research, discussions with support for Inno Setup and some dBASE developers, there are also solutions.

Also note that there are six different install programs for the BDE/Runtime, one contains all languages currently supported and there are five for specific languages. If you wish to deploy the full multi-language runtime/BDE installer, use the file named: dBASEPlusRuntimeEngineNNNN.exe.

The "NNNN" is the build number of dBASE PLUS.

If you wish to use a language specific installer (which has the advantage of being smaller), you would use one of the files named

dBASEPlusRuntimeEngineNNNN_xx.exe, where the "xx" letters correspond to one of the following:

```
EN = English
DE = German
ES = Spanish
IT = Italian
JA = Japanese
```

Back to the Inno Setup script ... Note that this script uses standard DOS wildcards (*.* means all files of all file extensions in the folder) to make the script easier to work with. You can specify filenames if you wish, but it makes the script a lot longer. If you want all the files in a specific folder, this is the simplest way to go.

```
[Files]
; ... other files listed above ...

; dBASE Runtime Installer
Source: "C:\Program Files (x86)\dBASE\PLUS\Runtime\PlusRuntime-
b2215_EN.exe"; DestDir: "{tmp}"; Flags: ignoreversion deleteafterinstall
```

The biggest issue here is that this does not run in the sequence you might expect – there is an option discussed below for updating the Windows Registry – that section will be executed *before* the Runtime installer is executed. Then, when your script runs the Runtime installer, changes made to the registry are not executed. In addition, updating the Windows Registry is an issue with Windows Vista and later versions of Windows. There are some other issues with the Runtime installer that may or may not be resolved by the time you read this.

The INI Section

This section of the script allows you to modify or add keys to the .INI file for your application. For example, with the MyFish program, I can put the User BDE Alias references in, using the locations installed to via the Inno Setup constants.

```
[INI]
; -----------------------------------------------------
; Update the .ini file for the User BDE Alias:
Filename: {app}\MyFish.ini; Section: "UserBDEAliases";
Filename: {app}\MyFish.ini; Section: "UserBDEAliases"; Key: "0"; String:
"MyFish";
Filename: {app}\MyFish.ini; Section: "MyFish";
Filename: {app}\MyFish.ini; Section: "MyFish"; Key: "Driver"; String:
"DBASE";
Filename: {app}\MyFish.ini; Section: "MyFish"; Key: "Options"; String:
"PATH: ""{localappdata}\dBASEBook\MyFish\Tables""";

; -----------------------------------------------------
; ------------------ End of INI section ------------------
; -----------------------------------------------------
```

For a DEO application, or a network application where some files are on a file server (or both), you would need to add to the .INI file the paths where files are stored. See the sample script MBIInstall.ini in the sample code for this chapter.

The Run Section

This section is used to define programs that are to be executed during the installation process. You can execute more than one program and Inno Setup will, by default, wait for the next to complete. Any programs defined here will be run in the sequence given after the Files section is executed.

For our purposes, this section deals with running the dBASE Plus Runtime and BDE Install. Note that if you are using the second method shown above for the Runtime, you do NOT need to run the installer for the Runtime.

This script sets up the installer program to install the dBASE Plus Runtime and BDE in "silent" mode, but to show the user what is happening some text is displayed on the installer screen.

Back to the example:

```
[Run]
; Silent install of runtime suppresses the runtime install display, and
the installshield stuff ...
; PlusRuntime-bNNNN_en.exe -s -a Runtime=d:\dBASEPLUS\Runtime
BDE=d:\dBASEPLUS\bde Silent -sr
; In order to get this to work properly, the double-quotes are doubled up
in a few places
; if you look at the statement ... that embeds a single double-quote (as
it were) in the
; parameters needed for the runtime and bde installs.
;
; It should be noted that this version with the silent flag does not
appear to
; be very "silent" ... however, this runs without the error created by the
Project
; Explorer version:
Filename: {tmp}\PlusRuntime-b2215_EN.exe; Parameters: "-s -a
Runtime=""{pf}\dBASE\Plus\Runtime"" BDE=""{cf}\Borland\BDE"" Silent -sr";
StatusMsg: "Installing dBASE Runtime and BDE..."; Flags: runascurrentuser;
WorkingDir: {tmp};

; ----------------------------------------------------------
; ------------------ End of RUN section ------------------
; ----------------------------------------------------------
```

It should be noted that the "Silent" option for the BDE/Runtime installer does not appear to be working as silently as one might expect. However, this version of the BDE/Runtime install does not have the error discussed in the first part of the chapter when you set up your deployment using the Project Explorer.

You could add other programs you might wish to execute at this point.

Displaying the Group After Installation

Someone in Jordan Russel's newsgroups for Inno Setup asked about displaying the newly created group for the user after the install is complete. This is a nifty idea, especially since the install can be very fast. You can do this by adding the following lines:

```
; Display the group when done:
Filename: "{group}\"; Flags: shellexec
```

The Icons Section

As with the files section above, this may not be 100% required, but it is really pretty much a necessity. This section determines what files you want to be in the application group window.

```
[Icons]
; Application icon
Name: "{group}\MyFish"; Filename: "{app}\MyFish.exe"; WorkingDir: "{app}"

; Desktop icons:
Name: "{userdesktop}\MyFish"; Filename: "{app}\MyFish.exe"; WorkingDir:
"{app}";

; ---------------------------------------------------------
; ----------------- End of ICONS section ------------------
; ---------------------------------------------------------
```

If you wanted to, you could put an icon in the Group for the BDE Administrator. I would do this only if you needed your users to have access to the program, however.

The Registry Section

This is where you can place any registry keys your application may require. If you are not using any, you can leave this section out of your Inno Setup script, or if you would rather set registry keys in your application directly, see the chapter on working with the Windows API. However, this has some issues in a UAC compliant application, however (discussed in that chapter).

BDE Registry Settings

There are issues with Registry settings, in that this section of the script is actually run *before* the "Run" section. This means that if you wanted to create special settings for the BDE in the Windows Registry you would run into problem – you would set them, then the Runtime installer for dBASE would execute and overwrite those settings in the registry.

However, there is a way around this. The Inno Setup script has the ability to run code in a "Post-Install" function. If you examine the sample script "MyFishInstall.iss", the code at the end of the script includes the recommended settings for the BDE that are described in the appendices of this book. You should be able to copy the whole section into your own Inno Setup script and have it run without making changes (you might wish to change specific settings, but it will run just fine). This code does two things:

1. It checks to see if the BDE registry keys exist – if not, it displays an error message letting the user know that the application installed will not run properly;
2. If the BDE registry keys *do* exist, it then updates them to the specified settings.

You will want to examine this code, copy and modify as needed for your application.

Other Registry Settings

It is possible to set some registry settings. I have one application where I need to store the path of the data used by the application in the Windows registry. I then read that in another script that deploys updates to the data. This looks like the following:

```
[Registry]
; Also from the dBASE OLH:
; Install any user specific registry keys for the
; application under HKEY_CURRENT_USER\Software node
;
; For this application, where is the main tables folder?
; HKEY_CURRENT_USER\Software\GSP\Oanda\DataFolder
Root: HKCU; Subkey: "Software\GSP\OandA\"; ValueType: string; ValueName:
"DataFolder"; ValueData: "{commonappdata}\GSP\OandA\Data"
```

The second script (the one that updates the data) uses some code to determine where to place the data. In the SETUP section of the script:

```
; Default directory name, get from the Windows
; Registry:
DefaultDirName={code:OandADir}
```

This calls a function at the end of the script:

```
; ------------------------------------------------------------
; Code to get the folder I need from the Registry:
; New version is using HKEY_CURRENT_USER (HKCU)
;      Looking for: HKEY_CURRENT_USER\Software\GSP\Oanda\DataFolder
[Code]
function OandADir( Default: String): String;
var ResultStr: String;
   begin
      if RegQueryStringValue( HKCU, 'Software\GSP\OandA', 'DataFolder',
ResultStr)
      then
         Result := ResultStr
      else
         Result := ExpandConstant( '{pf}\Data' )
   end;
```

Uninstall Option

The uninstall program created by Inno Setup is stored in the same directory as your application, and will be named: UNINS000.EXE, as well as a couple of other files (UNINS000.DAT and UNINS000.MSG). The uninstall is quick. Note that this does not uninstall the BDE or the Runtime files, which are installed from a separate program.

Compiling and Testing

Click on the "File" menu and first save your script (always a good idea). Then click on the "File" menu again and select the "Compile" option.

This script will create a file called MyFishSetup.exe. By default it will appear in the source code folder. However, this script uses the "OutputDir" directive in the Setup section and instead it will be placed in a folder called "InstallImage" which will be under the source code folder.

It is a good idea to run and test your install, preferably on a clean computer if you can.

The example script (MyFishInstall.iss) creates a relatively simple installation. Below we will discuss other ideas, but I will not be putting all the code samples here.

Borland Database Engine Issues

When you install the BDE there are often specific settings that need to be made, after the application is installed.

If your application is UAC compliant, which is what I have been aiming at in this book, there may be some difficulties with the BDE. The Borland Database Engine, in order to modify any of the settings, must be run "elevated", meaning when you run the BDE Administrator, you have to do so with Administrator rights (which as noted throughout this book is not the same as the user having Administrator rights) – you have to right-click the BDE Administrator icon and select "Run as Administrator".

This means that modifying the BDE through dBASE code has become trickier as well. In the appendices is a listing of suggested settings for the BDE, some of which are the default settings, some of which are not.

To accomplish this in a different fashion, you can add some code to the your Inno Setup script that modifies the registry at the end of the installation. That is what is being done in the example Inno Setup script here. This code is fairly complex and is not shown in the book. You can view it by looking at the "MyFishInstall.iss" script in the sample code for this book. See also the information earlier in this chapter on the "Registry" section of an Inno Setup script.

In addition, there are two files that you need to be aware of that may be an issue for your application that are specifically related to the BDE:

PDOXUSRS.NET

The PDOXUSRS.NET file is used by the BDE to handle record and file locks. For a standalone application this is not generally a problem, but for a networked application it can be.

There is a lot of discussion in the dBASE newsgroups by users about this. What it all seems to boil down to is that for a multi-user application you need to know where the BDE thinks this file should be.

Under current installations of the BDE this file defaults to:

```
CSIDL_COMMON_APPDATA\Borland\BDE
```

On my computer this is:

```
C:\ProgramData\Common Files\Borland\BDE
```

On a networked application you don't want this file being used on the local workstation or there will be record (and file) locking issues.

This file should most logically be placed somewhere such as the folder that contains the data for the application on the network server. This is not easy to accomplish inside a dBASE application and I have not seen a way to do this in an install routine.

Andrew Shimmin is working on a dBL code solution (ccs_BDE.cc and ccs_InstanceManager.cc) to help with issues with this file and others.

In the meantime, you may have to work with your users to go to the individual work stations and open the BDE Administrator (Run as administrator), change the setting under the "Configuration" tab, then open the "Configuration" tree item, "Drivers", "Native", "Paradox", and manually set the path for "NET DIR". At this time I cannot see another solution.

DBSYSTEM.DB

This file is used by the BDE to handle encrypted tables. While personally I don't recommend doing this with local tables (.DBF and .DB), it is something developers use, as a way to deal with security issues. The whole process of encrypting tables is covered in Chapter 11 "Security".

If you are using encryption, this file should be deployed to a location that is read and writable, so that your database administrator for the application can work with it. The simplest location to put this in would be the path that the data is stored in, as this folder is already read and writable.

If you encrypt the files before deploying your application, the default location of the DBSYSTEM.DB file is:

```
C:\ProgramData\dBASE\Plus\BIN
```

assuming you are working with current versions of Windows (Vista, Windows 7, Windows 8), as well as current versions of dBASE. This is discussed in Chapter 11 in more detail.

When you deploy your application make sure you deploy this file. As noted, it should most likely be placed in the same folder as your data, but whatever you do should be in a read/write enabled folder.

In order for the BDE to be able to find this file, you need to have an entry in the .INI file for your application, along these lines:

```
[CommandSettings]
DBSYSTEM=C:\ProgramData\dBASE\Plus\BIN
```

The path should match your application's data path. See information earlier in this chapter about adding information to the .INI file in your Inno Setup script.

Database Aliases

Database Aliases are suggested and used with many dBASE applications. However, the difficulty lies in the ability to create them from your own application, so that it will find and recognize the tables. This has been discussed extensively throughout this book. The examples here are using User BDE Aliases, and storing the required information in the .INI file for the application. This is the recommended method at this time.

SQL Links Drivers

When your user installs the dBASE PLUS Runtime and BDE using the programs provided, all of the current SQL Links files necessary will be installed on your users' computer. This means that the Oracle, InterBase, Sybase, and other SQL Links drivers will be installed – you do not have to do anything special to install them.

In addition, just because SQL Links drivers are installed does not mean you can just assume that your user has whatever Client software that may be needed for the specific SQL Server (i.e., Oracle, etc.). SQL Links are the native drivers for these servers, but they will not allow your application to work without the proper software for the SQL Server/SQL Client being installed. See the documentation for the SQL software you are using for more details.

ActiveX Controls

ActiveX controls can make things difficult sometimes, because they need to be registered with Windows. However, Inno Setup has the ability to call the Windows setup routines necessary to register the control allowing it to work. The following code was provided by Rich Muller, and goes in the Run section. It assumes that the ActiveX control has been deployed to the correct location already (in the "Files" section of the script):

```
Filename: "{sys}\regsvr32"; Parameters: " ""{app}\Common
Files\Others\dunzips32.dll"" /s "
```

As usual the above is one statement. The path shown includes the name of an ActiveX control ("dunzips32.dll").

Network and/or DEO Applications

If you are creating your own installer using Inno Setup and need to deploy to a network there are a variety of issues to be concerned with.

1) Is the application a DEO application, if so are you storing the files on the network server?
2) Are you storing the data on the file server?
3) Are you installing the executable locally (generally considered to be a good idea)?

In the sample code that comes with this book, in the Chapter 28 folder, is a script that I haven't modified in a long time, but worked last time I checked for a former client of mine. The script is titled "MBIInstall.iss". I owe a lot of thanks to Lane Coddington and Jonny Kwekkeboom for helping get this script to work. It does not include the UAC compliant things we've been discussing in this chapter, and does not use User BDE Aliases, as it is an older script, but there are sections of code you may wish to examine – these still work.

The script includes code to ask the user if they are installing the Network files (data, etc.) or to a workstation. The script then deploys the appropriate files accordingly. Note that as you have NONE of the files needed for this, trying to actually test it will cause a lot of frustration as you will not be able to create a viable installer. It is here as a sample so you can copy the sections you might need and read the code and comments to help understand what it is doing.

Creating a CD Image

When you run your CD Burner software, whatever it is, you should be allowed to set up your CD image in whatever fashion works for you, including adding other software, if you feel that you need to. (And have space on the CD, which you probably will.)

One thing I found was not documented in my own CD software was how to tell the operating system what program to run, if Windows had AUTORUN set to on (which is the default).

After digging around, it is actually very simple. There is a file on any CD that is used when autorun is enabled, called AUTORUN.INF. It should contain the following three lines – modify these as necessary for your own application/CD layout – NOTE that this file must be created/saved as a DOS TEXT file:

```
[autorun]
OPEN=setup.exe
ICON=MyApp.ico
```

If your CD layout is with all your files in folders, you would want to be sure that you point to the folders, using the root as "\", for example, if you examine the AUTORUN.INF file on the dBASE PLUS CD, you will see that the OPEN option points to the SETUP program in the root of the CD, but the ICON option points to a different folder. Anyway, this is much easier than it sounds like it ought to be.

Contacting the Author of Inno Setup

For assistance with Inno Setup, please contact the author via information at his website:

```
http://www.jordanr.dhs.org/isinfo.php
```

In addition, Jordan has newsgroups for additional support for Inno Setup at:

```
http://www.jordanr.dhs.org/newsgroups.php
```

Manual Deployment – What Files Are Needed?

Some developers would rather deploy an application themselves, either with their own deployer (a software package either that they have written or someone else has and they have purchased or downloaded), or they want to manually copy files to the users' computers. This part of the chapter will discuss what files are needed. Personally I don't recommend doing it this way, it can be difficult to get everything "just right".

Application Files (DEO vs. non-DEO)

If your application is not a DEO application – meaning that all of the objects are compiled *into* the executable, there is not much you have to deploy. The following are the items that should be considered:

- The application executable and manifest file
- The application .INI file
- Any icons or other images used
- Any tables and auxiliary files (for a .DBF that includes .MDX and .DBT files; for Paradox files there are sometimes many).
- Any .DLL files that you may be using (such as a DLL that contains strings or images, etc.).

If your application is a DEO application, in addition to the files noted above, you will need to be sure that you include the object files that you need and if you are using DEO folders, you will want to be sure you place them in the appropriate places. The object files are the following:

Source File Extension	Object File Extension	File Type
.wfm	.wfo	Form
.cfm	.cfo	Custom Form
.mnu	.mno	Menu
.pop	.poo	Popup Menu
.rep	.reo	Report
.crp	.cro	Custom Report
.lab	.lao	Label
.prg	.pro	Program File
.sql	(none)	SQL File
.dmd	.dmo	Data Module
.cdm	.cdo	Custom Data Module
.cc	.co	Custom Class

If you change a file for a user/client and need to update just that file, re-compile the source file and send the user (or client) the object file (telling them which DEO folder to place it in). You might make sure the user (or client) does this when no one is running the application to be sure the files are updated properly.

Installing the dBASE PLUS Runtime with Your Application

Your best bet to install the Runtime for dBASE PLUS is to use the installer that comes with the product. This installer includes the BDE and can make life a lot easier.

However, for whatever reason, you may wish to deploy only the runtime files (an update to your application or some other reason). You may decide that you don't want to use the default runtime installer, or you may even be installing an application that does not need the BDE, so you only want to install the runtime files.

If that is the case, you need to install the following:

File	Description
PlusRun.exe	The Runtime Library
PlusR_en.dll	Language String File (Note: you need the specific language version, see table below)
Resource.dll	Image Resource File (If deploying a web application, probably not necessary)
PlusRun.exe.manifest	If you wish to deploy an application that uses the default Windows Theme and all that, then you should deploy this file as well. If this is left out, your application will not use the theme, and its appearance may not match what you expected. There may be other issues with Windows as well.

Note: the runtime DLL file (PlusR_xx.dll) needs to have the correct language reference — the default is "en" for English — use the following for the two-letter language code:

Language	Code	File
English	en	PlusR_en.dll
German	de	PlusR_de.dll
Spanish	es	PlusR_es.dll
Italian	it	PlusR_it.dll
Japanese	ja	PlusR_ja.dll

In addition, you should make sure that the appropriate language entry is in the application's .INI file, such as:

```
[CommandSettings]
Language=DE
```

(Note: the default setting is English, so if this is left out of the .INI file and you are using English you should be fine.)

If you wish to place the runtime in a folder other than the one your executable is in, then you will need to create a registry key for the dBASE Runtime, so that when your executable runs it can find it.

For example, if you copied these files on a user's computer to:

```
C:\Program Files\dBASE\Runtime
```

You would need to open the Registry Editor ("Start" button, "Run", enter "REGEDIT" and click "OK"), and add a key:

```
HKEY_LOCAL_MACHINE\SOFTWARE\dBASE\Plus\series1
```

Please note, that on a 64 bit system, this path is a bit more complex:

```
HKEY_LOCAL_MACHINE\SOFTWARE\WOW6432Node\dBASE\Plus\series1
```

(If you do this in an install script, or via code, Windows will handle putting the key in the appropriate location.)

The key needs to be under the "series1" folder in the path above, it needs to be called "RuntimePath", the value needs to be the path which in this example would be: "C:\Program Files\dBASE\Runtime". You will not be able to do this programmatically in your application because it will need to be able to find the runtime path to execute in the first place.

BDE Files

The following list is from the BDE online help, and should give you everything you need to deploy with your application to install the BDE on a client's computer.

File	Description
IDAPI32.DLL	Primary BDE DLL
BLW32.DLL	International Language Driver support functions
IDBAT32.DLL	Contains the batch operations
IDQBE32.DLL	QBE Query Engine
IDSQL32.DLL	SQL Query Engine
IDASCI32.DLL	ASCII Text Driver
IPDX32.DLL	Paradox Driver
IDDBAS32.DLL	dBASE Driver
IDODBC32.DLL	ODBC Socket Driver (allows the use of any ODBC 3.0 driver)
IDR2009.DLL	Resource file for error messages
IDDA032.DLL	Access Driver for Access 95 and Jet Engine 3.0
IDDA3532.DLL	Access Driver for Access 97 and Jet Engine 3.5
IDDR32.DLL	Data Repository
BDEADMIN.EXE	BDE Administrator utility for managing configuration information stored in the Windows Registry and aliases in the IDAPI.CFG file
BDEADMIN.HLP	Help file for the BDE Administrator
BDEADMIN.CNT	Table of Contents file for BDEADMIN.HLP. This must remain in the same directory with BDEADMIN.HLP.
BDE32.HLP	The online reference for the 32-bit BDE.
IDAPI.CFG	File containing application specific BDE configuration.
*.BTL	Ctype information (casing, soundex, etc.)
*.BLL	Related to the above
CHARSET.CVB	Character set conversion

If these are placed in the same folder as your application, they should work fine. By default the BDE is installed to:

```
C:\Program Files\Common Files\Borland\BDE
```

If you are using a SQL Server database and need the native drivers, you should consider copying the sql*.* files (all files that begin with "sql") – they aren't that big and don't take a huge amount of space on the users' computer.

Summary

By the time you get to here, your brain may be all alive with possibilities and perhaps even a bit of confusion. Deploying an application is the last step to completing a project, except perhaps documenting it (if you didn't do so while you were creating it). It can get fairly complex, although once you get some of the ideas worked out, it isn't really all that bad.

A lot of work went into revising this chapter in order to include details on getting your application to work with the UAC. I know that some developers still want to avoid it, but as noted elsewhere in this book, I feel it is a good idea for our (dBASE developers as a whole) applications to be more compliant with Windows than they have been in the past.

I also have to thank Gerald Lightsey again for his being very critical of how I explained some of what is here. While it sometimes got a bit frustrating, I think the chapter came out much better for it.

The Appendices

Like any book of this nature there is material that doesn't really fit into the main text that really ought to be included somewhere ... that's where we're at now. These appendices include an interesting mix of information that you may find useful.

Appendix 1: Resources Available

dBASE developers have available to them a large quantity of resources, including newsgroups, libraries of source code, freeware applications where you can download and "borrow" code, tutorials and a lot more. This appendix is literally a list of places to go to find assistance with building your applications.

dBase, LLC

These are the people who own and are developing and selling dBASE PLUS, dQuery (there is a standalone version of it), dbEverywhere (a web-database/application solution) and dBDOS (a Windows application able to run your dBASE/DOS applications in the current versions of Windows). You can find an overview of the company at:

```
http://www.dbasellc.com/
```

And specifically you can find information about dBASE and other products at:

```
http://www.dbase.com
```

If you need to purchase dBASE, need to talk to Customer Support, etc., this is where you would go. There are links on the website for email addresses of who to talk to for specific situations.

Newsgroups

One of the most useful ways of gaining help when trying to develop an application is through the free newsgroups out there. There are two that are specifically dBASE oriented.

- dBase, LLC. provides free newsgroups for support. These include a place to report bugs and post wishlist requests, which get read by the R&D team, but also a lot of different newsgroups *(including some that are language specific – German, etc. so that users who don't speak English have somewhere to go)*. Details on these newsgroups are available from the dBASE website:

    ```
    http://www.dbase.com/dBase_NewsGrpForums.asp
    ```

    The dBase newsgroups are monitored by members of the dBVIPS *(volunteer technical support – users and developers like you)* as well as members of the R&D team. Answers are given by anyone ranging from dBVIPS, dBase personnel and the dBASE community (other users). One can learn a lot from these newsgroups.

- Rich Muller has a special site aimed at archiving messages from all of the newsgroups out there. Details can be found at:

    ```
    http://www.alldbase.com
    ```

dBASE PLUS Tutorials

In the time before Borland sold dBASE to dBASE, Inc. *(now dBase, LLC)* and after Visual dBASE 7.01 was released, there was a period when there was little support for dBASE. I worked with various developers to create a tutorial. Professor Michael Nuwer took that tutorial, ran with it and improved and enhanced it. Over the years he has added modules to the tutorial to assist in learning more about how to create dBASE applications.

The main tutorial can be found in the dBASE Knowledgebase (see below) and was put there with Michael's permission, but you can also get to other tutorials and modules for the main tutorial at Michael's website:

```
http://www.mnuwer.dbasedeveloper.co.uk/dlearn/
```

dBASE Knowledgebase

In earlier versions of dBASE (everything after Visual dBASE 7.5 and before dBASE PLUS 2.5) the CD included a copy of the dBASE Knowledgebase, which was installed on your hard drive when you installed the dBASE application.

The Knowledgebase is still available on the dBASE website and you can view it either by going to the "Help" menu in dBASE and selecting "Knowledgebase", or going straight to it:

```
http://www.dbase.com/dBase_Knowledgebase.asp
```

dBASE Users' Function Library Project (dUFLP)

The dUFLP, which is referenced throughout this book, is a vast library of freeware dBL code created by many authors over a span of nearly 20 years. The code is redistributable with your applications with the only caveat being that the comment headers for the programs or functions you use are left intact, specifically the name of the authors of the code (we believe strongly in credit where credit is due).

The dUFLP was created by myself years ago when I was a developer working with dBASE IV, release 1.1. I got code from a variety of sources and put it in a single procedure file. Over time it got too large and unwieldy, so it was split up to smaller files. Over the years many developers have contributed code, helped fix bugs or enhance existing code in the library, making it a huge open-source dBL project. Instructions for the use of the library are both on my website and in the readme.txt file included in the collection of code.

The name: dBASE Users' Function Library Project was created so that we could pronounce the acronym as "duh-flop". It's a silly thing, which was meant to be silly and I wouldn't want to change it now.

The current version can be downloaded from my own website:

```
http://www.goldenstag.net/dbase
```

If you decide to use this library of code you should follow the directions given for setup (see "Readme.txt"), then you can use the form "Library.wfm" to get an understanding of what is in the dUFLP – this is a vast library of code and this form can help you find a specific item you need.

dBulletin

Jean-Pierre Martel created an online newsletter that is a great resource to the dBASE developer community called dBulletin. At the time of the current edition of this book, the dBulletin was discontinued some years earlier. The authors were people from all parts of the international dBASE community and there are often translations of some of the English articles to other languages and it is worth checking out. The main page for the dBulletin newsletter is:

```
http://www.jpmartel.com/bulletin.htm
```

There are other sites around the globe that also host the newsletter, but this is the primary source (links can be found at my website noted above under the "dUFLP" heading).

MarshallSoft Computing

MarshallSoft Computing provides libraries that give dBASE the ability to do email (POP3) serial communications, FTP and more. For more information you should visit their website at:

```
http://www.marshallsoft.com
```

dBASE Related Websites

Various other people have websites of interest and are quickly noted below:

- **Ken's dBASE Page** – my own dBASE related website:

  ```
  http://www.goldenstag.net/dbase
  ```

- **Golden Stag Productions** - Ken's Business website *(the business is closed, but I left the site up)*:

  ```
  http://www.goldenstag.net/GSP
  ```

- **The dBASE Webring**: Sponsored/hosted by Francois Ghoche (in France), this is a webring that allows you to view related websites – in this case, all about dBASE:

  ```
  http://www.fghoche.com/dbasering.htm
  ```

- **VdB-Logic** – Marc van den Berghen also has some useful dBASE tools available at his website:

  ```
  http://www.vdblogic.de/dbl/
  ```

These are just a few of the various websites out there. You may want to spend some time exploring to see what else is available *(the web-ring will be useful for that)*!

Other dBASE Books

Since the first Edition of this book was published, a German author, Ulf Neubert, has stepped forward with at least two books on dBASE and may be working on more. If you can read German, you might go to Ulf's website and check out his books:

```
http://www.ulfneubert.de/autor/dbasebuecher/index.html
```

I have published one other book, The dBASE Reports Book, which takes the information in the Reports chapters of this one and expands them in much more detail. The dBASE Reports Book is available from the same publisher as this book, AuthorHouse.

NOTES:

Appendix 2: A Brief History of dBASE

dBASE has a fairly long history, all things considered. It has been around since even before the PC "Revolution" in the computer industry in the early 1980s. The following history is based on information from various sources, which I will cite as I go.

This is extracted and simplified from the introduction of <u>dBASE Language Reference with Annotations</u>[1].

1975   C. Wayne Ratliff, working for the Martin Marietta Corporation at the Jet Propulsion Laboratory in Pasadena, CA, was responsible for a ground support database for the Viking lander project. Wayne's group used MFILE, a primitive data storage and retrieval system, using punch cards.

        The movie <u>2001: A Space Odyssey</u> was released and the HAL 9000 computer inspired Wayne to research artificial intelligence, natural language and database management.

1976   A friend of Wayne's bought and built an IMSAI 8080 hobby computer. Wayne followed suit and built his own. The first home software project Wayne took on was a small database manager modeled after the MFILE system.

1978   The first DBF file was developed around midnight, January 29 when Wayne finished implementing the CREATE command. He added DISPLAY STRUCTURE, DISPLAY, APPEND, and EDIT to round out the first commands in the next few months.

        After some hardware failures and such, Wayne continued to add more commands, some of which he borrowed from BASIC, such as ? and INPUT; from FORTRAN he used DO WHILE and from COBOL he got ACCEPT. Other commands, he says "came out of thin air." Wayne called the program Vulcan.

1979   Wayne invited Jeb Long, the lead developer from the Jet Propulsion Labs to look at Vulcan. After this JPL bought a license for Vulcan and requested several changes. He also moved it to the new CP/M operating system and got serious about making the program a commercial success.

        When MicroPro, the company that sold WordStar started to sell DataStar, Ratliff took the challenge to turn the program into a full-screen application and put B-tree indexing into the heart of Vulcan.

1980   Vulcan sold 61 copies in nine months and got the attention two marketing wizards, George Lashlee and Hal Pawluk. They met with Wayne in August and Wayne gave them a one-year exclusive right to market and sell Vulcan.

        A company in Florida named Harris Computers threatened to sue over the name "Vulcan" because that was the name of their operating system. Vulcan was renamed to dBASE II shortly thereafter. Wayne, Hal, and George Tate created an advertising campaign "dBASE II vs. the Bilge Pumps", which included the company named "Ashton-Tate".

Before selling the first copies of dBASE II, Ratliff made some architectural changes and George Tate started giving copies away. Wayne upgraded the indexes to B*-trees and added the @ command.

1981   Deliveries of dBASE II started in February 1981 and sales took off.

In late 1981, Jeb Long was hired to help with programming. Jeb modified the screen driver to handle Osborne computers and translated 8080 assembler code to the 8086 instruction set. This was critical because IBM had shipped the first PC and software vendors were adjusting their plans to take advantage of the new software market.

1982   Ratliff quit his job with Martin Marietta at JPL and began working full time on dBASE. Microrim started shipping R:Base amidst fanfare and an aggressive ad compaign.

1984   Ratliff and crew released dBASE III, shipped in June and became the de facto standard for customers and became an industry archetype.

The following is based on an article in dBulletin by J. P. Martel[2] with some additional notes by Ken Mayer (KJM):

1987   dBASE III Plus or dBASE III+ was on most PC computers sold, as well as many Macintosh computers. A variety of compilers and add-ins were available including Clipper, dBXL, Quicksilver, Arago *(Randy Solton's software – this name will become quite important later)* and Force.

1988   In October Ashton-Tate released dBASE IV, version 1.0. Unfortunately, it was released prematurely due to marketing pressure. The promised compiler was not there, there were many memory problems and a *huge* slate of bugs, making it almost impossible to use.

1990   About a year and a half after dBASE IV, version 1.0 was released, Ashton-Tate finally released version 1.1, which resolved many of the issues in the first release. In the meantime Windows 3.0 had appeared, giving a lot of promise to a new platform, however folk were hoping for a GUI interface which dBASE IV did not provide.

The release of dBASE IV 1.1 was through a series of Technical Sessions. I attended one at the cost of the company I was working for, and won the door prize – a free copy of dBASE IV release 1.1! That was fun because I didn't own a copy for my home computer and let me work with the software at home, learning it better. – KJM

1991   Borland bought out Ashton-Tate and took over dBASE *(and InterBase)*. Ken Mayer and several others over the next year or so (including in no particular order: Angus Scott-Fleming, Keith Chuvala, Jim Sare, Bowen Moursund, Marilyn Price, Rachel Holmen, Jay Parsons, Gary Thoenen, Romain Strieff, Paul Franks, and Ken Chan) were asked to join TeamB (Team Borland) – a group of developers who were to provide technical support on the Ashton-Tate BBS and later on the Compuserve forums for dBASE. Charles Miedzinski and Rick Fillman, among others, came to Borland from Ashton-Tate and worked on the dBASE team.

1993   Under the guidance of Tom Burt, Borland released dBASE IV, release 2.0, which was reliable, fast and had a compiler (finally!). At the same time dBASE for Windows was in the works, but was having problems. It was not very user-friendly and hard to use. Borland ended up buying WordTech, hence the development team of Arago *(Randy Solton and his team)* and they got to work on dBASE for Windows.

1994   In the one year Borland released dBASE 5.0 for DOS and dBASE 5.0 for Windows. The DOS product was developed by an independent team from the Windows team and was "Object-Based", but not fully object-oriented. On the other hand, the DOS product was fully 32-bit and ran like greased lightning on the computers of the day. It was incredibly fast – operations that had been taking 10-15 minutes were done in sometimes 1-2 minutes!

       Unfortunately, before dBASE for Windows was released, Microsoft had released Access and were giving it away as part of their Office Suite providing an easier to use *(not necessarily better, just easier)* and FREE GUI database. At some point after dBASE 5.0 for Windows as released, Alan Katz was asked to join TeamB for dBASE.

1994-1995

       A short-lived monthly magazine <u>dBASE Advisor</u> was created by the publishers of <u>Databased Advisor</u> and I (Ken Mayer) was invited to be an author, eventually I was a "Contributing Editor". The magazine lasted about a year and a half. Ken Chan, either in 1994 or 1995 started working at Borland.

1995?   Visual dBASE 5.5 was released, it was more stable and easier to use fixing many of the problems in dBASE 5.0 for Windows. Somewhere in here – within a year or so – a new build was released as Visual dBASE 5.6. These were the 16-bit versions of the Windows version of dBASE.

1996   I (Ken Mayer) was hired by Borland as a QA Engineer to work on the Visual dBASE project, specifically to work on Visual dBASE 6.0 (which never appeared). This happened because Ken Chan was working on the documentation team and knew they were looking for someone.

       Shortly after I started working there in April or May of 1996, Randy Solton and his team had convinced Borland that the internet was the way to focus efforts and an internet database tool would be a killer application.

       The QA team was told to learn JavaScript. Most of us really knew nothing about it. The product we worked on was IntraBuilder. The first release was in 1997 at the Borland Conference that year. Borland put a lot of marketing effort into it, but the approach wasn't quite right and except for a few users, most people didn't know what to do with it. A second release was done to fix some bugs and some interesting enhancements were worked on, but the product really never took off.

1997   The R&D team were told to go back and work on Visual dBASE again. Visual dBASE 7.0 was created and released in 1997. This was the first release of the 32-bit version of dBASE and there were a few things left in the software from the IntraBuilder days – it was the same code-base. The items specifically left in the product from IntraBuilder are the String, Date and Math classes.

       In the fall Borland released a fix for some of the more egregious bugs in Visual dBASE 7.0 and released it as Visual dBASE 7.01.

1998   Borland did a reorganization in the spring and I got laid off when they decided to dismantle the dBASE team. Many folk got the axe, some moved to other departments at Borland (such as Randy Solton and most of his R&D team, Ken Chan, etc.).

1999   Alan Katz worked with some private investors and got the capitol together to purchase the source code for Visual dBASE from Borland, along with the rights to use the Borland Database Engine (but not to modify it). The newly formed company was called dBASE, Inc.

In May of 1999 I was hired on as a QA Engineer to work under Charles Miedzinski (manager of the QA and Tech support departments). A small team was assembled to get the company going including Jim Sare as head of R&D, Marty Kay (a former employee of Alan's at Ksoft), Bowen Moursund, Rick Fillman, and others, some whom are familiar to the dBASE community.

1999-2004
During the time that I worked for dBASE, Inc. we released Visual dBASE 5.7 (a Y2K fix for Visual dBASE 5.6), Visual dBASE 7.5, dB2K (releases 01 through 04) and dBASE PLUS (releases 2.2 0 2.21). A lot of work was done on dQuery – a replacement for the data module designer that was built into dBASE, as well as a standalone version of dQuery to be sold as a separate tool.

Somewhere in here Jim Sare left the company and Alan Katz took over as the head of R&D.

2003   A group of users in Europe created the first user-run dBASE conference dBKON.

2004   In the late spring/early summer (May) dBASE, Inc. hired Larry Foster as CEO. On June 1 they reorganized and let several folk go including myself Charles Miedzinski, Bowen Moursund and Rick Fillman.

On the same day the layoffs occurred, the newsgroups went down and stayed offline for some time. In the meantime the user community came together. Rich Muller created a basic set of newsgroups, followed by George Burt with a more robust set of newsgroups (www.dbasetalk.com). These have less traffic these days than the newsgroups provided by dBase, LLC (see later in the timeline).

Since that time the company has built back up, hiring more developers. There were various internal changes of personnel (people shifting positions). Alan Katz became Chief Technology Officer rather than head of R&D as he was before. Shortly after, they changed their name to dataBased Intelligence, Inc. (using "dataBI" for a nickname).

J. P. Martel and Michael Nuwer held the first North American conference about dBASE in years, dBCon 2004, in Montreal based on the relative success of the European dBKon in 2003. While not heavily attended, they came close to breaking even and everyone felt it was a success. This proved hopeful for further conferences in the future *(sadly no one has since stepped up to create a new conference)*.

Late in the year dataBI released dBASE PLUS 2.5 with some new features for the grid and more. Some interesting things happened with the software, including promised updates to the Microsoft Foundation Classes, which enhanced the appearance and functionality of the visual controls in dBASE.

2005   I started writing the first edition of this book in the fall of 2004while trying to find a real job, finding some contract work, and the occasional contract work. dataBI was working on dBASE PLUS 2.6 *(in the first edition I had called this 2.51 as it hadn't been released at the time I was writing it)*, which fixed some bugs introduced in the software as well as quite a few enhancements to dBASE and dQuery *(including the ability to display Windows XP style controls as defined by styles and themes, using manifest files)*.

2006-2007

dataBased Intelligence continued to work on dBASE, dQuery and more. Version 2.6 was released (referred to above as 2.51) and several subsequent "patch" releases including 2.61, 2.61.2 & 2.61.3 as I was working on the 2nd edition of this book (February 2007).

Release 2.61 (July, 2006) included dBI branded ODBC drivers by DataDirect Technologies. These were intended to make it simpler to connect to Oracle, SQL Server, Sybase ASE, DB2, Informix, FoxPro, Visual FoxPro, Clipper and Pervasive SQL (formerly Btrieve) databases.

There were also several changes in personnel with Alan Katz no longer working for dataBased Intelligence in any capacity and Marty Kay promoted to Chief Technology Officer.

2008

Release 2.61.4 (March, 2008) – dBASE and all product executables introduced Code Signing, which is an issue with the User Access Control (UAC) in Windows Vista and Windows 7. In addition the ability to Code Sign your own executables with a digital signature was added. *(This is in addition to some enhancements and bug fixes.)*

Marty Kay and company put a lot of effort into the software and continued to improve it. The dBASE Community is still out there. Microsoft released Windows Vista and Windows 7, both of which have been making things more "interesting" for developers.

2011

dBASE 2.7 was released to the public in March. This was a big change, as it is the first attempt at dealing with the Vista and Windows 7 UAC rules for security and further updates (2.7.0.1, etc.) built upon this. Aspects of this book (3rd Edition) have been updated to include as much useful information as possible.

2012

In March the company went through a complete reorganization and restructure, with new owners and a new name, *dBase, LLC*. The new CEO, Michael Rozlog has stepped up to the plate, with some interesting ideas for the future direction of the company and the community is starting to get excited about it.

Marty and his development team have completed migration of the dBASE code to a more recent version of Microsoft's C compilers, giving better integration with Windows among other things.

Michael contacted me earlier in the year about making the 2nd Edition of this book available to dBase, LLC for distribution as they wished. The process of getting the PDF available for distribution with dBASE encouraged me to work on the 3rd Edition of the book.

April, 2012 – dBASE 2.8 was released with many fixes to the software and a new installer.

May, 2012 – dBDOS 1.0 was released by dBase, LLC – an application designed to run older dBASE/DOS applications in Windows without the need to rewrite the software in the Windows GUI style … time will tell how well this works out.

September, 2012 – As I continue to work on the 3rd Edition of this book, the developers are fixing some bugs in dBASE Plus 2.8, including deployment issues. This has slowed the release of this book a little (not much, the other big issue being my full-time job).

I have seen some information about a proposed dBASE Plus 8 *("Project Aloha")* as well, but as it is privileged information, I cannot divulge what may or may not be involved in this at this time. This version of dBASE will most likely require a 4th edition to this book! I am excited about what I saw and hope that it will be close to what they suggested it could be.

December, 2012 – Michael Rozlog announced a partnership with GlyFX – a graphics company that provides, among other things, icons for pushbuttons in Windows. This will most likely be a first-step in upgrading the appearance of future releases of dBASE.

[1] dBASE Language Reference with Annotations, Borland Press, 1993, Michael P. Masterson, with annotations by C. Wayne Ratliff and Jeb Long, ISBN: 0-679-79173-6 *(this may be out of print, sadly …)*

[2] dBulletin Issue 3, A Personal History of dBASE, J.P. Martel (http://www.jpmartel.com/bu03_b.htm)

Appendix 3: Colors, Images and Graphics in dBASE Applications

Any software as complex as dBASE has issues to deal with, one of them is the way graphics are handled. In some cases (such as the Image object) you can use almost any graphic format, in others things get more specific, such as working with icons or pushbutton images. This appendix is meant to help put as much of this information in one place as possible.

Colors

There are many ways to work with color properties for objects in dBASE when using the *colorNormal*, *colorHighlight*, and other color properties. This has not really been discussed elsewhere in this book and should be at least mentioned here.

16-Bit/DOS Color Names

dBASE still recognizes the old DOS color strings, which were often just the first letter of a color name, such as "W" for "White" (actually more of a grey color), and the use of the "+" sign showed a brighter color (so "W+" is brighter than "W" and is more of a true white). The online help, under *colorNormal* shows a table listing these colors, as well as other options listed in this appendix.

To show a text control with white text on a blue background, you could set the *colorNormal* property to "W+/B" and dBASE would recognize that and display it with those colors.

JavaScript "Safe Palette" Color Names

While the DOS color strings work, there are actually other ways of handling colors in dBASE. One is to use the standard JavaScript names for the "safe color palette" of colors, of which there are 256. The listing is in the online help – it seems nonsensical to list them all here. Suffice it to say that you can do some neat things with these, such as using colors named "aquamarine" or "salmon".

You can use these colors exactly as you would the DOS colors. In other words, to put white on a blue background:

```
colorNormal := "white/blue"
```

Hexadecimal BGR Colors

You can also use the hexadecimal equivalent of any color using the hexadecimal triplet in the sequence BGR (notice this is not the same sequence shown in the table in the online help), so to use "blue" as defined in JavaScript, and say, "Snow" for the text color (this would be snow/blue as shown below):

```
colorNormal := "0xFAFAFF/0xFF0000"
```

Windows Named Colors

Windows-named colors are taken from the settings in the Windows Display Properties dialog. If the colors are changed in the Display Properties while a form is open, the form and any controls that use these values will change automatically. You can use any of the

Windows-named color settings for either the foreground or background color. These are also in the online help (search for "colorNormal").

You can use these names for colors used by Windows in your application. For example, if you wanted your forms to use the same background color as the "Window" setting, you would set the form's *colorNormal* to "Window" (the default is *BtnColor*). The advantage to using these colors is that your application can take on the color scheme that your user may have defined for Windows itself.

User Defined Color Name

To use a user-defined color name, you have to use the dBASE command DEFINE COLOR. If I wanted to use a specific shade of green, I might name it "KensGreen":

```
DEFINE COLOR KensGreen 19,79,33
```

To get the actual colors (Red Green Blue), I used the built-in getColor() dialog:

```
? getColor()
```

And found the color I wanted to use. When I clicked "OK", dBASE output to the Command Window:

```
19,79,33
```

Which is what I used to define "KensGreen". This program statement would need to be set in a form's startup, or in an application startup for dBASE to recognize it in your application. The colors remain defined until your application closes. Once you have your colors defined you can use them in forms and reports instead of the names defined earlier in this chapter. It should be noted that you cannot redefine one of the colors specified earlier – in other words if I wanted to redefine "forestgreen" to this color, I could not.

Working with DLL Files

A DLL or Dynamic Link Library file has many uses, including what we have looked at so far – the ability to work with code that has been compiled and stored in the file. Indeed, dBASE itself uses DLL files to store character strings used in the software itself for different languages. If you examine the folder (by default when dBASE is installed):

```
C:\Program Files (x86)\dBASE\PLUS\Bin
```

You should see "PLUS_en.dll" if you are using English, "PLUS_es.dll" if you are using the Spanish translation for dBASE and so on. These files contain character strings that are translations of strings used in the menus, dialogs and other parts of dBASE.

Another use of .DLL files used by dBASE is a place to store images. You can place icon files, bitmap images and so on, in a .DLL file, then use it in your own application. This is particularly handy, because it allows you to deploy a single file, rather than a set of custom images and by storing them in the .DLL your customer won't *(normally, anyway)* be able to use them for their own purposes – important if you are using copyrighted materials.

By default, dBASE uses resource files such as bitmaps and icons from Resource.dll for forms and controls, as well as the toolbuttons used in the toolbars and so on.

If you want to use your own DLL file, or one that you have obtained from someone else, you would simply change the normal syntax when you use it. For example, if you had created a pushbutton that used "Resource #104" (the light blue arrowhead – see figure below) the source code in the form would look like:

```
upBitmap = "RESOURCE #104"
```

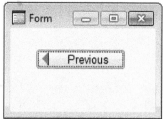

Figure A3-1

To use an image from a different .DLL file you would either use the appropriate number or name, if a name is used for the resource, followed by a space and the name of the .DLL file:

```
upBitmap = "RESOURCE ARROWLEFTBLUE GSPRES32.DLL"
```

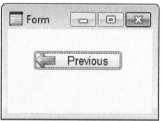

Figure A3-2

"ARROWLEFTBLUE" is the name given to resource in the .DLL in question and "GSPRES32.DLL" is the resource file (this is one that I put together and use for my own applications, GSP for "Golden Stag Productions", RES for Resource and 32 means 32-bit). I would distribute this with the examples for the book, but it contains copyrighted images that I have paid for the rights to use but may not be distributed to others for use in their own applications.

You can make these changes in the designer, rather than by hand-coding them. The Form Designer has a useful preview window that allows you to view images in .DLLs. To get there, click on the pushbutton in the Form Designer, then click on the bitmap property you wish to use (in this example the *upBitmap* property) and click on the tool button. You will firstly get a dialog that asks if you want to use a Filename or a Resource file. Select the Resource file, then then click the tool button on the right which will bring up the viewer, which looks like:

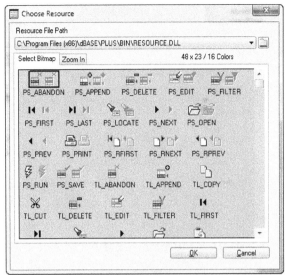

Figure A3-3

If you select a different .DLL in the combobox, such as GSPRES32.DLL, you will see the images change to show the ones in that DLL file:

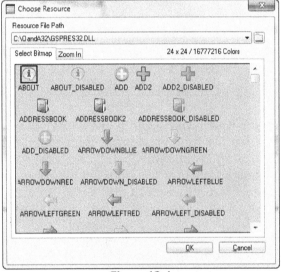

Figure 13-4

Choosing an image from here will allow you to use the image and the Form Designer will stream out the full information including the name of the resource file itself to the property as needed.

Of course, the question that is most important to a developer interested in creating their own DLL files, is HOW? dBASE does not ship with a way of creating or modifying DLL files. There are a variety of programs on the web that might be used and over time I have experimented with a few. With the assistance of some of the user community, I stumbled across "XN Resource Editor", which is free:

```
http://www.wilsonc.demon.co.uk/delphi_2006.htm
```

📝 NOTE

In case you are wondering about the images I used in the DLL example file called GSPRES32.DLL, these are copyrighted images that I paid for from a company named *incors*. Their website (when last I looked) is:

```
http://www.iconexperience.com/
```

They are quite good although a little pricey (you do get images in five sizes and .ICO files for each image set you purchase) and the creators are very helpful. If you decide to purchase a selection of images, however, you will need to set the background color to the default dBASE transparent background using some software package such as PaintShop Pro, or whatever is your favorite. The default dBASE transparent background is:

```
Red: 128
Blue: 128
Green: 0
```

In addition, the good folk at *incors* created a program that is available on their website, written in Java to do this work for you. Click on the "Technical" link and you will be able to download this utility from there. *(I have used it and it works quite well, including the batch processing of image files).*

Planning ahead, the folk at *incors* have created a set of icons and images for use with Windows 8 and the new theme that is the default. It is interesting, but may be worth getting hold of.

There are bound to be others on the web (if you use a web search engine you will find multiple websites that have this available). You can use this to modify .DLL files, adding and removing resources, strings, etc. to them. It is a very useful and invaluable tool, if you wish to work with dynamic link library files to manage your resources. You will need a blank or other 32-bit dll file to use. There is one in the dUFLP, in the .zip file named "EmptyRes.zip" – for dBASE PLUS you would want to use Empty32.dll, copy it, rename it to what you want, then you can start working with it from there.

There are of course other tools you can use, this is just one that falls into my personal budget (not very big) and is easy to work with and use.

Other Ways to Store Images

You may not be comfortable with working with a resource file as discussed above. There are always alternatives in dBASE for handling almost any issue. For example, you might want to store your images in a table (use a BINARY field). You would then need to use a *datalink* for the images, or some other means of making the images available.

Graphics Issues for Icons and Buttons (Pushbuttons and Toolbuttons)

dBASE has some very specific issues when working with images and the following is an attempt to de-mystify them and put the information in one place.

The online help is rather vague about image formats, the only place that says much appears to be in the help about the Image Class which is not really useful, because not all of the image types listed as being acceptable for use with the Image Class are useful with Icons, Toolbuttons and Pushbuttons.

Icons

Icons must have the .ICO extension or be stored in a .DLL file as an icon image. An icon is a 16x16, 24x24 or 32x32 or 48x48 pixel bitmap file that has a .ICO extension if used as a file and can have either a color depth of up 4 bit, 8 bit, 24 bit and 32 bit.

dBASE only supports some of these combinations. J.P. Martel did some testing and these are the results he came up with:

A .ICO file can contain more than one icon image. When such a file contains more than one image, each of these are called "frames". dBASE does not support .ICO files containing 24x24 pixel frames. The following is a breakdown of the way dBASE deals with icon frames:

- 16x16 pixel (4 bit): dBASE does not use this.
- 16x16 pixel (8 bit): Preferred frame of the Form Designer when the developer selects the icon property for the form. Also the preferred frame of Windows Explorer under all of its view modes except the "Large Icons" mode to represent the dBASE executable.
- 16x16 pixel (24 bit): When the 8-bit frame is not available, used by the Form Designer when the developer selects the icon property for the form, etc. as above.
- 24x24 pixel - any - dBASE does not use this.
- 32x32 pixel (4 bit): dBASE does not use this.
- 32x32 pixel (8 bit): Preferred frame of dBASE for the upper left icon when the form is running. Also the preferred frame of Windows Explorer for "Large Icons".
- 32x32 pixel (24 bit): When no 8-bit frame is available, used as above.
- 48x48 pixel – any – dBASE does not use this.

In a nutshell dBASE only uses 16x16 pixel and 32x32 pixel icons. When it needs a small image, it prefers 16x16 pixel 8-bit icons, when it wants a larger icon, it prefers 32x32 pixel 8-bit icons. When an 8-bit icon is not available, it will use a 24-bit icon.

Icons can be used for:

- The _app.framewin icon (this would be set when building an application using the Project Explorer)
- For a form's *icon* property
- For a TreeView or TreeItem's various image properties:
    - treeItem.*image*
    - treeView.*checkedImage*
    - treeView.*image*
    - treeView.*selectedImage*
    - treeView.*uncheckedImage*

Images for Pushbuttons

This gets more interesting, because an image used for a pushbutton in dBASE can be handled in multiple ways, including a "split image" – one that has two different images offset from each other; transparent background; different sizes.

And as with icons, these images can be stored in a .DLL file, as well as used directly as image files.

A "split image" is one that literally has two pushbutton images stored side-by-side in the same image. When used on a pushbutton, you *must* include ":2" after the word

"RESOURCE" or "FILE" when assigning the image. If you use the dialog that is part of dBASE that is used to assign images, there is a checkbox for "Split Image" that you can use that will do this for you.

To see what a split image looks like you can look at the first set of images in the standard Resource.dll that ships with dBASE. (Create a form, place a pushbutton on it, go to the *upBitMap* property in the Inspector, click the "tool button", select "Resource" rather than "Filename" and unless you previously used a different resource file, the default for dBASE will appear – you will see a series of images named "PS_ABANDON" and so on – these are split images.) The advantage to Split Images is that the first image will be used for the *upBitmap* and the second will be used for the *disabledBitmap* properties and you don't need to set them.

Transparency Under dBASE

dBASE recognizes transparent backgrounds in a limited fashion. An image is a rectangle by definition. A transparent background for an image is one that changes part of the image to the color of the object it is placed on. This is useful if you have a logo *(for example)*, which you only want the image to display, but not the rectangle. If your form is blue and you have an image object that uses an image with a transparent background defined, the image should show the background as same color as your form. This is very useful for pushbuttons or toolbuttons – where you may only want to show an arrow (again as an example), but not a background color behind it, using the color of the button for the background of the image.

dBASE recognizes the transparency in different ways depending on what object is using an image. There is a specific color *(mauve)* that dBASE recognizes for pushbuttons, but this same color is not recognized as transparent for images:

```
Red:   128
Blue:  128
Green: 0
```

Some testing shows the following ("Button" refers to Pushbutton and Toolbutton objects):

	Image Object	PushButton
Mauve GIF	No	Yes
Mauve BMP	No	Yes
Transparent GIF	Yes	No
Transparent PNG	No	No
Transparent WMF	Yes	Yes
Transparent EMF	Yes	Yes

A Pushbutton can use an image for one of these four properties:

- *upBitmap* – the standard image for a pushbutton – when the pushbutton is up. If you only want to use one image, this is the property you use.
- *downBitmap* – the image that displays when a pushbutton is down.
- *disabledBitmap* – the image that displays when a pushbutton is disabled. This is typically a greyed out version of the image, but can be whatever you wish.
- *focusBitmap* – the image that displays when the pushbutton has focus (tab to it, click it once). Note that if you use a pushbutton with text on it as well as an image, this is not required, as the text will be given a border when the pushbutton has focus. If you are working with image-only pushbuttons, it may be a good idea to have a special image to show that it has focus.

Images for Toolbuttons

Toolbutton images may have an image size limitation, but I am not so sure about that.

You can also create a single image file that contains a set of images side-by-side, then tell dBASE to use the images by passing specific coordinates. This is done by using the *bitmapOffset* and *bitmapWidth* properties. In addition, toolbuttons can use split images as discussed above for Pushbuttons.

In all other ways Toolbutton images have the same requirements as Pushbuttons.
A Toolbutton can use an image for one of these properties:

• *bitmap* – the image that is displayed

Toolbuttons do not have as many options as those used for pushbuttons, but if a Toolbutton is disabled, an attempt is made by dBASE to grey it out. If you use a split bitmap (as described above) and the Toolbutton is disabled, the second image is automatically used instead of greying out the image.

There is one issue reported by J.P. Martel when changing a toolbutton's *bitmap* property on the fly *(in your code)*, the line of code has to be stated twice and *all* the *speedtip* properties have to be restated. For example:

```
form.T1.Toolbutton4.bitmap = ;
   "Resource AnImage MyImages.dll"
// same line of code twice is required:
form.T1.Toolbutton4.bitmap = ;
   "Resource AnImage MyImages.dll"
// restate the speedTips:
form.T1.Toolbutton1.speedTip := "Previous"
form.T1.Toolbutton2.speedTip := "Next"
form.T1.Toolbutton3.speedTip := "Refresh"
form.T1.Toolbutton4.speedTip := "Search"
form.T1.Toolbutton5.speedTip := "Quit"
```

An Undocumented Feature

An interesting and undocumented feature of dBASE that you may find useful is the ability open an image from the Navigator window (by double-clicking on it) and view it. This viewer has capabilities most developers are not aware of! You can actually convert an image type to another. For example, if you open a .JPG file in the image viewer, you can convert it to a .BMP *(or other file type in the list)*! To do this, simply right click on the window and select "Export Image ...". This will allow you to select a different file type, export that image to that file type - converting it in the process – the list is not large, but it is still useful.

Appendix 4: Borland Database Engine and Table Specifications

The Borland Database Engine, or BDE, is currently vital to dBASE developers, although there are hopes that someday a new data engine will be created by the R&D engineers at dBASE. In the meantime, the following limitations and specifications will be of interest to developers using the BDE with their dBASE applications. The Borland Database Engine that ships with dBASE PLUS 2.5 and later is 5.2.0.2.

General Limits

48	Clients in system
32	Sessions per client (3.5 and earlier, 16 Bit, 32 Bit)
256	Sessions per client (4.0, 32 Bit)
32	Open databases per session (3.5 and earlier, 16 Bit, 32 Bit)
2048	Open databases per session (4.0, 32 Bit)
32	Loaded Drivers
64	Sessions in system (3.5 and earlier, 16 Bit, 32 Bit)
12288	Sessions in system (4.0, 32 Bit)
4000	Cursors per session
16	Errors in error stack
8	Table types per driver
16	Field types per driver
8	Index types per driver
48K	Size of Configuration (IDAPI.CFG) file
64K	Size of SQL statement (RequestLive=False)
4K	Size of SQL statement (RequestLive=True)
6K	Size of SQL statement (RequestLive=True, 4.01, 32-Bit)
16K	Record buffer size (SQL or ODBC)
31	Table and field name size in characters
64	Stored procedure name size in characters
16	Fields in a key
3	File extension size in characters
260	Table name length in characters (some servers might have other limits)
260	Path and file name length in characters

dBASE/DBF Table Limits

256	Open dBASE tables per system (16 Bit)
350	Open dBASE tables per system (BDE 3.0-4.0, 32 Bit)
512	Open dBASE tables per system (BDE .01, 32 Bit)
100	Record locks on one dBASE table (16 and 32 Bit)
100	Records in transactions on a dBASE table (32 Bit)
1	Billion records in a table
1	Billion bytes in .DBF (Table) file
4000	Size in bytes per record (dBASE 4)
32767	Size in bytes per record (dBASE for Windows)
255	Number of fields per table (dBASE 4)
1024	Number of fields per table (dBASE for Windows)
7	Number of index tags per .MDX file
254	Size of character fields

Paradox Table Limits

127	Tables open per system (4.0 and earlier, 16 Bit, 32 Bit)
254	Tables open per system (4.01, 32 Bit)
64	Record locks on one table (16 Bit) per session
255	Record locks on one table (32 Bit) per session
512	Open physical files (4.0 and earlier, 16 Bit, 32 Bit) (DB, PX, MB, X??, Y??, VAL, TV)
1024	Open physical files (4.01, 32 Bit) (DB, PX, MB, X??, Y??, VAL, TV)
300	Users in one PDOXUSRS.NET file
255	Number of fields per table
255	Size of character fields
2	Billion records in a table
2	Billion bytes in .DB (table) file
10800	Bytes per record for index tables
32750	Bytes per record for non-indexed tables
127	Number of secondary indexes per table
16	Number of fields in an index
255	Concurrent users per table
256	Megabytes of data per BLOB field
100	Passwords per session
15	Password length
63	Passwords per table
159	Fields with validity checks (32 Bit)
63	Fields with validity checks (16 Bit)

Suggested BDE Settings

Obviously no two situations are going to be identical, but the following is a listing of the default settings for the BDE and some suggested changes. You can modify these settings in the BDE Administrator. If you need to modify them for an end-users' computer, there is code available in the dUFLP (mentioned in Appendix 1, with details on where to find it) that will allow you to create a program you can have your application run on startup that will create the appropriate settings. More help for what each of these options are will be found in the BDE help which you can get to from the BDE Administrator.

There are some difficulties as mentioned in Chapter 2 (and elsewhere) with modifying the BDE's IDAPI.CFG file, as by default it is placed in a "read-only" folder. Changes can only be done by running the BDE Administrator with elevated privileges (right click the icon for it and select "Run as administrator"). You shouldn't ask your users to do this kind of thing and code can also be tricky. The chapter on deploying an application should address some of this.

To see/modify these settings, start the BDE Administrator and:

- Click on the "Configuration" tab on the notebook
- Click the "+" by the word "Configuration" which will expand a treeview
- Click on "System"
- Click on "Init"

You should see a screen like (the settings may not be exactly identical):

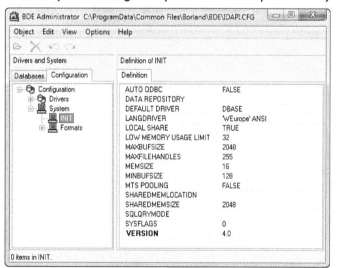

Figure A4-1

Suggested changes:

Key	Metric	Minimum	Maximum	Multiples of	Default	Recommended
LOCALSHARE	N/A	N/A	N/A	N/A	FALSE	TRUE
MAXBUFSIZE	KB	128	65535	128	2048	8192
MINBUFSIZE	KB	32	65535	32	128	2048
MAXFILEHANDLES	# of file handles	5	4096	48	48	2048
MEMSIZE	MB	16	205	16	16	64
LOW MEMORY USAGE LIMIT	KB				32	32
SHAREDMEMSIZE	KB	2048	2048			4096

If your application uses dBASE tables, you might change the "DEFAULT DRIVER:" to: DBASE *(to date I am not sure I see this making any difference).*

Note that in dBASE Plus 2.6, the LocalShare default is now TRUE; MaxFileHandles default is now 255 and SharedMemSize is now 2048.

The *Recommended* column in the table above could be expanded to the following. Both of these tables are the results of work done by Robin Reed, who posted this in the newsgroups having watched various discussions over time. The following is based on the amount of available RAM in a computer:

Key	256 MB	512 MB	>512 MB
MAXBUFSIZE	4096	8192	8192
MINBUFSIZE	2048	128	4096
MAXFILEHANDLES	96	200	4096
MEMSIZE	128	64	205
LOW MEMORY USAGE LIMIT	32	32	32
SHAREDMEMSIZE	2048	8192	8192

The important thing here is that you may have to tweak your settings.
You may want to make some changes for the default dBASE driver. To do that click the "+" by the word "Drivers" and:

- Click the "+" by "Native"
- Click on "DBASE"

Set the LANGDRIVER to: 'WEurope' ANSI

> *(Or whatever language driver is appropriate for your application – as a Windows application it **should** be an ANSI driver ...)*

Make sure you use ⌨Ctrl+Ⓐ (Apply) to save your changes.

The following webpages provided by someone who has made the information available at his own expense, that may be able to help you make decisions about some of the settings used, as well:

Performance: http://www.bdesupport.com/perform.htm
Stability: http://www.bdesupport.com/stability.htm
Common Errors and Solutions: http://www.bdesupport.com/errors.htm

dBASE (.DBF) Table Information

The following information ranges from basic to extremely technical, some of which may be more information than you could want.

dBASE (DBF) Files

When you create a .DBF, other files may be created that you do not realize.

File Extension	Description
DBF	The Table
MDX	Master/Multiple Index File
DBT	Memo/Binary/OLE data
NDX	dBASE/DOS (level 2-4 single index file. These are not used in dBASE Plus's OODML, and are allowed only for compatibility with older tables.

dBASE (DBF) Field Types

Field Type	Default Size	Maximum Size	Index Allowed?	Allowable Values
Character	10 characters	254	Yes	All keyboard characters
Numeric	10 digits, 0 decimals	20 digits	Yes	Positive or negative numbers. *The maximum size must include the digits to the right of the decimal, the decimal point itself, and if necessary, a minus sign (-) to show the number is negative./A*
Float	10 digits, 0 decimals	20 digits	Yes	Positive or negative numbers. Identical to Numeric; maintained for compatibility.
Long	4 Bytes	N/A	Yes	Signed 32 bit integer, range approximately +/- 2 billion. Optimized for speed.
Double	8 Bytes	N/A	Yes	Positive or negative number. Optimized for speed.
Autoincrement	4 Bytes	N/A	Yes	Contains long integer values in a read-only (non-editable) field, beginning with the number 1 and automatically incrementing up to 2 billion. Deleting a row does not change the field values of other rows. Be aware that adding an autoincrement field will pack the table.
Date	8 Bytes	N/A	Yes	Any date from AD 1 to AD 9999
Timestamp	1 Double	N/A	Yes	Date/Time stamp, including the Date format plus hours, minutes, and seconds, such as HH:MM:SS.
Logical	1 Byte	N/A	No	True (T, t), false (F, f), Yes (Y, y), and No (N, n)
Memo	10 Bytes	N/A	No	Usually just text, but all keyboard characters; can contain binary data (but using binary field is preferred).

Field Type	Default Size	Maximum Size	Index Allowed?	Allowable Values
Binary	10 Bytes	N/A	No	Binary files (sound and image data, for example)
OLE	10 Bytes	N/A	No	OLE objects from other Windows Applications

Differences Between dBASE (DBF) Table Levels

There have been changes to the DBF table structure over the years. The following table shows the difference in what field types are allowable in which table levels:

Field Type	Level 3	Level 4	Level 5	Level 7
Character	✓	✓	✓	✓
Numeric	✓	✓	✓	✓
Memo	✓	✓	✓	✓
Logical	✓	✓	✓	✓
Date	✓	✓	✓	✓
Float		✓	✓	✓
OLE			✓	✓
Binary			✓	✓
Long				✓
Timestamp				✓
Double				✓
Autoincrement				✓

Other differences: In level 4, MDX style indexes were introduced. In level 7, the field name can be mixed case, and up to 31 characters in length, where earlier field names were restricted to upper case and 10 characters. In addition, level 7 tables can have custom properties (some built-in) for fields.

dBASE (DBF) Table Header and File Structure

The following specifications break down the dBASE table header and go into incredible detail. Most of the time you will never need to get into this level of the dBASE table's information.

Table File Header

n above is the last byte in the field descriptor array. The size of the array depends on the number of fields in the table file.

Byte	Contents	Description
0	1 Byte	Valid dBASE for Windows table file, bits 0-2 indicate version number; 3 for dBASE Level 5; 4 for dBASE Level 7. Bit 3 and bit 7 indicate presence of a dBASE IV or dBASE for Windows memo file; bits 4-6 indicate the presence of a dBASE IV SQL table; bit 7 indicates the presence of any .DBT memo file (either a dBASE III Plus type or a dBASE IV or dBASE for Windows memo file).
1-3	3 bytes	Date of last update: in YYMMDD format. Each byte contains the number as a binary. YY is added to a base of 1900 decimal to determine the actual year. Therefore, YY

Byte	Contents	Description
		has possible values from 0xFF, which allows for a range from 1900-2155.
4-7	32-bit number	Number of records in the table. (Lease significant byte first.)
8-9	16-bit number	Number of bytes in the header. (Least significant byte first.)
10-11	16-bit number	Number of bytes in the record. (Least significant byte first.)
12-13	2 bytes	Reserved; filled with zeroes.
14	1 byte	Flag indicating incomplete dBASE IV transaction.
15	1 byte	dBASE IV encryption flag.
16-27	12 bytes	Reserved for multi-user processing.
28	1 byte	Production MDX flag; 0x01 if a production .MDX file exists for this table; 0x00 if no .MDX file exists.
29	1 byte	Language driver ID.
30-31	2 bytes	Reserved; filled with zeroes.
32-63	32 bytes	Language driver name.
64-67	4 bytes	Reserved.
68-n	48 bytes each	Field Descriptor Array (see below).
n+1	1 byte	0x0D stored as the Field Descriptor terminator.
n+2	See below for calculations of size	Field Properties Structure

Field Descriptor Array
(One for each field in the table)

Byte	Contents	Description
0-31	32 bytes	Field name in ASCII (zero-filled).
32	1 byte	Field type in ASCII (B, C, D, N, L, M, @, 1, +, F, 0 or G).
33	1 byte	Field length in binary.
34	1 byte	Field decimal count in binary.
35-36	2 bytes	Reserved.
37	1 byte	Production .MDX field flag; 0x01 if field has an index tag in the production .MDX file; 0x00 if the field is not indexed.
38-39	2 bytes	Reserved.
40-43	4 bytes	Next Autoincrement value, if the Field type is Autoincrement, 0x00 otherwise.
44-47	4 bytes	Reserved

Field Properties Structure
This contains a header describing the Field Properties array, followed by the actual array, followed by property data. It is contained in the .DBF header and comes immediately after the Field Descriptor terminator *(See Field Descriptor Array Table)*.

Byte	Contents	Description
0-1	16-bit number	Number of Standard Properties
2-3	16-bit number	Start of Standard Descriptor Array. (See below)
4-5	16-bit number	Number of Custom Properties.
6-7	16-bit number	Start of Custom Property Descriptor Array. (See below)
8-9	16-bit number	Number of Referential Integrity (RI) properties.
10-11	16-bit number	Start of RI Property Descriptor Array. (See below)
12-13	16-bit number	Start of data – this points past the Descriptor arrays to data used by the arrays – for example, Custom property names are stored here.
14-15	16-bit number	Actual size of structure, including data (Note: in the .DBF this will be padded with zeroes to the nearest 0x200, and may have 0x1A at the end). If the structure contains RI data, it will not be padded.
16-n	15 bytes each	Standard Property Descriptor Array (n = (15 * number of standard properties) + 16) (See below)
(n+1)-m	14 bytes each	Custom Property Descriptor Array (m = n+14*number of custom properties). (See below)
(m+1)-o	22 bytes each	RI Property Descriptor Array (o = m+22*number of RI properties). (See below)

Standard Property and Constraint Descriptor Array

Byte	Contents	Description
0-1	16-bit number	Generational number. More than one value may exist for a property. The current value is the value with the highest generational number.
2-3	16-bit number	Table field offset - base one. 01 for the first field in the table, 02 for the second field, etc. Note: this will be 0 in the case of a constraint.
4	8-bit number	Which property is described in this record: 01 Required 02 Min 03 Max 04 Default 06 Database constraint
5	1 byte	Field Type: 00 No type - constraint 01 Char 02 Numeric 03 Memo 04 Logical 05 Date 06 Float 08 OLE

Byte	Contents	Description
		09 Binary 11 Long 12 Timestamp 13 Double 14 AutoIncrement (not settable from the Inspector)
6	1 byte	0x00 if the array element is a constraint, 0x02 otherwise.
7-10	4 bytes	Reserved
11-12	16-bit number	Offset from the start of this structure to the data for the property. The Required property has no data associated with it, so it is always 0.
13-14	16-bit number	Width of database field associated with the property, and hence size of the data (includes 0 terminator in the case of a constraint).

Custom Property Descriptor Array

Bytes	Contents	Description
0-1	16-bit number	Generational number. More than one value may exist for a property. The current value is the value with the highest generational number.
2-3	16-bit number	Table field offset - base one. 01 for the first field in the table, 02 for the second field, etc.
4	1 byte	Field Type: 01 Char 02 Numeric 03 Memo 04 Logical 05 Date 06 Float 08 OLE 09 Binary 11 Long 12 Timestamp 13 Double 14 AutoIncrement (not settable from the Inspector)
5	1 byte	Reserved
6-7	16-bit number	Offset from the start of this structure to the Custom property name.
8-9	16-bit number	Length of the Custom property name.
10-11	16-bit number	Offset from the start of this structure to the Custom property data.
12-13	16-bit number	Length of the Custom property data (does not include null terminator).

Referential Integrity Property Descriptor Array

Byte	Contents	Description
0	8-bit number	0x07 if Master (parent), 0x08 if Dependent (child).
1-2	16-bit number	Sequential number, 1 based counting. If this number is 0, this RI rule has been dropped.
3-4	16-bit number	Offset of the RI rule name - 0 terminated.
5-6	16-bit number	Size of previous value.
7-8	16-bit number	Offset of the name of the Foreign Table - 0 terminated.
9-10	16-bit number	Size of previous value.
11	1 byte	Update & delete behavior: Update Cascade 0x10 Delete Cascade 0x01
12-13	16-bit number	Number of fields in the linking key.
14-15	16-bit number	Offset of the Local Table tag name - 0 terminated.
16-17	16-bit number	Size of previous value.
18-19	16-bit number	Offset of the Foreign Table tag name - 0 terminated.
20-21	16-bit number	Size of previous value.

(Foreign = in the other table, Local = in this table)

Property Data

For standard properties, everything is stored exactly as it is in the Table records. Custom property data is stored as the Name string, followed immediately by the Value string and a null terminator. The Constraint text is stored as a null-terminated string.

Table Records

The records follow the header in the table file. Data records are preceded by one byte, that is, a space (0x20) if the record is not deleted an asterisk (0x2A) if the record is deleted. Fields are packed into records without field separators or record terminators. The end of the file is marked by a single byte, with the end-of-file marker, an OEM code page character value of 26 (0x1A).

Storage of dBASE Data Types

Except for autoincrement fields, all types are initialized to binary zeroes. In addition, any fields which have been assigned a default property will contain the default value.

Symbol	Data Type	Description
B	Binary, a string	10 digits representing a .DBT block number. The number is stored as a string, right justified and padded with blanks.
C	Character	All OEM code page characters - padded with blanks to the width of the field.
D	Date	8 bytes - date stored as a string in the format YYYYMMDD.
N	Numeric	Number stored as a string, right justified, and padded with blanks to the width of the field.
L	Logical	1 byte - initialized to 0x20 (space) otherwise T or F.
M	Memo, a string	10 digits (bytes) representing a .DBT block number. The number is stored as a string, right justified and padded with blanks.
@	Timestamp	1 double floating point number, indicating the number of milliseconds since 01/01/01 00:00:00 (January 1, 1901, midnight).[1]
I	Long	4 bytes. Leftmost bit used to indicate sign, 0 negative.
+	Autoincrement	Same as a Long
F	Float	Number stored as a string, right justified, and padded with blanks to the width of the field.
O	Double	8 bytes - no conversions, stored as a double.
G	OLE	10 digits (bytes) representing a .DBT block number. The number is stored as a string, right justified and padded with blanks.

Binary, Memo, OLE Fields and .DBT Files

Binary, memo, and OLE fields store data in .DBT files consisting of blocks numbered sequentially (0, 1, 2, etc.). SET BLOCKSIZE determines the size of each block. The first block in the .DBT file, block 0, is the .DBT file header.

Each binary, memo or OLE field of each record in the .DBF file contains the number of the block (in OEM code page values) where the field's data actually begins. If a field contains no data, the .DBF file contains blanks (0x20) rather than a number.

When data is changed in a field, the block numbers may also change and the number in the .DBF may be changed to reflect the new location.

Paradox (.DB) Table Information

In addition to the dBASE (.DBF) table type, the Paradox (.DB) table is native to dBASE via the BDE. The following information will hopefully help understand these tables a bit better.

Files Associated with a Paradox Table

The Paradox table format has quite a few field types, which to someone used to working with .DBFs may find a bit overwhelming, here they are:

---

[1] The original Borland BDE documentation states that this is "8 bytes - two longs, first for date, second for time. The date is the number of days since 01/01/4713 BC. Time is hours * 3600000L + minutes * 60000L + Seconds * 1000L." This is apparently incorrect, as John Hazzard discovered when attempting to convert dBASE Timestamp fields to a MySQL database. This information was posted in the dBASE newsgroups (July 9, 2012).

File Extension	Description
DB	The table
PX	Primary index
MB	Memo
VAL	Validation and integrity rules
Xnn, Ynn	Secondary single-field index
XGn, YGn	Composite secondary index

Paradox Table Field Types

Some field types are not fully supported in dBASE, the last column in the table below will give that information.

Field Type	Description	Supported?
Alpha	Contains letters, numbers and any printable character. Comparable to a DBF character field.	Yes
Number	Contains numbers up to 15 significant digits. Similar to DBF Float.	Yes
Money	Exactly like Number, formatted to display decimal places and currency symbol automatically.	Yes
Date	Same as DBF date field.	Yes
Short	Contains integers from -32,767 to 32,768. If you attempt to replace a field with a value out of this range, an incorrect value is stored.	Yes
Memo	Similar to DBF memo field. Size of memo is limited by amount of disk space. Memo data is stored in an MB file.	Yes
FmtMemo	Rich-text memo. Cannot be viewed in dBASE.	No
Binary	ObjectPAL binary field. Cannot be viewed in dBASE.	No
Graphic	Contains pictures. Similar to placing an image in a DBF binary field.	Yes
OLE	Similar to the DBF OLE field. Contains objects placed in your table from other applications taht support OLE.	Yes
Time	Contains time data; the length is four digits.	Yes
Timestamp	Same as DBF Timestamp field or DateTime() value.	Yes
Long	Contains large numeric values, used to perform scientific calculations. (PDX Level 5 only)	Yes
Logical	Similar to DBF logical, stores boolean (true/false) values. (PDX Level 5 only)	Yes
Bytes	Used in ObjectPAL applications, this sort of works in dBASE, but this author is not certain why it does or why. (PDX Level 5 only)	Yes?
BCD	Binary Coded Decimal. Similar to DBF numeric. (PDX Level 5 only)	Yes
Autoincrement	Identical to DBF Autoincrement field. (PDX Level 5 only)	Yes

Appendix 5: Undocumented Features

While the R&D team and the documentation team at dBase, LLC have documented many features of dBASE, there are always a few features that have not made it into the help.

It is not a good idea to assume that these features will always be available, as any functions or commands that are undocumented may be removed from the software. There may be a reason they are undocumented (buggy, duplicates some other aspect of the product, unnecessary).

This appendix will show the ones this author is aware of, the information has come from several sources.

Easter Egg

Many programs have what are called "Easter Eggs" – little hidden things that appear if you use the correct combination of things.

In dBASE a list of credits for the software can be found by going to the Help menu, selecting the "About dBASE PLUS" dialog. When this dialog appears, press ⎇Alt+⎵ and a listing of contributors to dBASE will appear. It will continue until done, or you close the dialog.

Figure A5-1

Functions

The following are XBASE DML functions that are undocumented:

- FCOUNT() – this is the same as FLDCOUNT(), it returns the number of fields in a table.
- PDXRECNO() – Returns a logical record number for a Paradox DB table, similar to the record number in a .DBF table that is returned by RECNO(). *(You should use the BOOKMARK() function instead, and with OODML this is not an issue as logical record numbers are ignored ...)*
- UPDATED() – Actually a totally useless function in dBASE PLUS, because it was used with the old @/SAY/GET commands which have been removed from the software, this function returned a logical value if the contents of any @/GET fields or variables were updated.

Date Functions

There are two (that this author is aware of) undocumented date functions which may be used to output the date in a different format, although the two appear to be identical. The *DtoH()* and *DtoJ()* functions will output the date in a different format than you normally get:

```
? date()
? dtoh( date() )
```

Will result in:

```
04/17/2005
Sunday, April 17, 2005
```

System Variables

There is only one undocumented system memory variable, _UPDATED. This works exactly like the UPDATED() function, but you can query it directly:

```
? _updated
```

This memory variable returns a logical (*true* or *false*) value just as the UPDATED() function does and is just as useless in dBASE PLUS.

Hiding a Variable

When you list all of the memory variables available using LIST MEMORY or DISPLAY MEMORY, dBASE lists everything. However, if you create a variable with a tilde (~) as the first character of the variable name, these commands will not display it.

```
a = "Test"
b = 5
c = date()
~Hidden = "Hidden Variable"
```

The following is the first part of the output in the output pane of the Command Window:

```
          User Memory Variables

A               Pub   C   "Test"
B               Pub   N          5.00 (5.00000000000000)
C               Pub   D   04/17/2005
      3 variables defined,       5 bytes used
    497 variables available,  4091 bytes available
```

Custom Controls and the Component Palette

A developer who works with custom controls a lot might like to place those controls on the Component Palette for use in the designer. Currently this happens, but all custom controls are placed on the "Custom" tab of the Component Palette and by default they use an icon that represents the base class. For example, if you create a custom pushbutton class used to navigate in a table, you might not want a pushbutton icon to appear on the Component Palette, but something more representative of what the control is for.

As it turns out, this can be done. The Component Palette uses a table to store information about custom controls. You can add your own information (you could modify the default information, but that is generally a bad idea – it's best to leave the system defaults alone), including the name of the tab to display your controls and the image used on the Component Palette.

It should be noted that if you modify the icons used in the Component Palette, then uninstall dBASE or update to a newer release, you may need to do it again. There is some code in the dUFLP *(see Appendix 1)* that you might want to copy and modify called "ComponentPaletteUpdate.prg". The following is based on that code, but is much more simple.

If we assume that you did the exercises in the chapters on working with the Form Controls in dBASE and specifically custom controls, you have a set of custom pushbuttons referenced by the Source Code alias :MyFormControls: and stored in the file MyPushbuttons.cc. If you wish to follow along, the following will add some entries to the table used by the Component Palette and add information to show your pushbuttons on their own tab and assign images specific to the purpose of the pushbuttons.

- Using the Navigator, click on the Tables tab.
- Use the "Look in:" part of the Navigator, click on the Folder button.
- Navigate to the folder under the location dBASE is installed:

```
C:\Users\username\AppData\Local\dBASE\PLUS\Designer\form
```

Click the "OK" button. You should see two tables, CREG0009.dbf and SCHS0009.dbf – the first is the one we want, the other is used by the Form Wizard for schemes (something we didn't really discuss in the chapters on the Form Designer). Note that the last four digits may be different, depending on the language you have installed for dBASE, but the important thing is the table starts with "CREG".

- If you double-click this table, you will see something like:

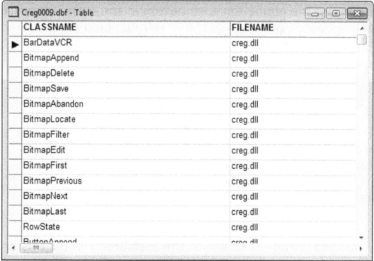

Figure A5-2

- We are going to add some rows to this table, but we need specific information first. The information that is absolutely required here is used in these fields:
  - CLASSNAME – as it says, the name of the class
  - FILENAME – the name of the DLL file that contains the image to be used – note that this is either no path, which tells dBASE to use its own internal path mechanism (which starts at the folder this file is in), or a fully qualified path up to 254 characters in length (such as C:\MyFiles\somefile.dll).

353

- BITMAPID – Number of the image as stored in a .dll file
- XOFFSET and YOFFSET – used to handle SPLIT Bitmaps *(discussed in Appendix 3)* and the exact offset. If you are not using split bitmaps, set this to zero (0).
- WIDTH – in pixels *(20x20 pixel images appear to be the largest the Component Palette can handle)*
- HEIGHT – also in pixels *(20x20 pixel images appear to be the largest the Component Palette can handle)*
- CATEGORY – the name you wish to use for the tab on the Component Palette.
- ORDER – The order you wish the control to appear in on the Component Palette – the first one would be 1, the second would be 2, etc.
- DESIGNER – Which design surface (Form or Report) you wish this to appear for – a letter of either F or R should be used. "N" sometimes appears in some entries, which appears to be "None".

There is more information about these fields in the file CREG0009.TXT in the dUFLP, written originally by Jim Sare with some annotations by myself.

- To get started, you will want to add a new row, and this is the place you will "repeat" to/from for each item you wish to add to the Component Palette:
  - Click the "Add Row" tool button
  - Enter "FirstButton" for the CLASSNAME field, press Tab
  - Enter "creg.dll" for the FILENAME field, press Tab
  - Enter 2 for the BITMAPID field, press Tab 3 times (skip the XOFFSET and YOFFSET fields)
  - Enter 16 for the WIDTH field, press Tab
  - Enter 15 for the HEIGHT field, press Tab
  - Enter "My Buttons" for the CATEGORY field, press Tab
  - Enter 1 for the ORDER field, press Tab
  - Enter "F" for the DESIGNER field
  - Click the "Save Row" button
- You will want to repeat the above for each button in the class, changing the CLASSNAME for the name of the classes (as below), the BITMAPID field (as shown below) and the ORDER (as below). All other entries should be exactly the same.

CLASSNAME	BITMAPID	ORDER
LastButton	5	2
NextButton	4	3
PreviousButton	3	4
AddRowButton	12	5
EditRowButton	14	6
DeleteRowButton	13	7
SaveRowButton	15	8
AbandonRowButton	16	9
CloseButton	1005	10

NOTE: you will want to change the path to the Resource File for this one in the FILENAME field:

```
C:\Program Files\dBASE\PLUS\BIN\resource.dll
```

RowState	28	11
MySpeedBar	6	12

- Once you have done all of that, you can close the table. You may want to set your working directory back to some other location. To see that this worked, in the Command Window type:

```
set procedure to :MyFormControls:MyPushbuttons.cc additive
```

- Start a new form in the Form Designer and go to the Component Palette. Click on the tab on the notebook that says "My Buttons". You should see something like:

Figure A5-3

- If you hold the mouse over a button you will see an appropriate speedtip with the name of your control, and if you drag it to the design surface you should get the correct button *(make sure, if you want to do this, that you set the form's metric property to "6-Pixels", or you may get odd results for the speedbar).*

This is a handy thing to do if you use a lot of custom controls – it allows you to group controls on different tabs, assign your own icons to the controls rather than using the defaults created by dBASE. The code in the dUFLP's "ComponentPaletteUpdate.prg" program adds all of the visual controls in the dUFLP, assigning appropriate tabs and images for the various controls in the library. As noted, you might want to examine that code to create your own version for your custom controls.

You can examine the images in the CREG.DLL file using some code in the dUFLP (CREG2.WFM) and you can even use a form in the dUFLP (CREG0009.WFM) to add your own entries, edit entries and see the images assigned to controls in the table.

Multi-Language Application Using DLL Files

Strictly speaking, this is not an undocumented feature, as it uses a function called *resource()* that is part of the dBL, but the online help does not really delve into the topic in much detail. The following is based on some experimentation and some work I did for a project *(which is under NDA, so I cannot discuss the project directly)*, and a bit of help from an article in dBulletin (Issue 5, "A Language Independent Application") by Robert Bravery. The following is a very simple example, but hopefully it will get you through the basics and you can expand it as needed (Robert's article has a more detailed example).

There are many ways to do multi-language applications, but one that is particularly useful is to store character strings in a string table of a DLL file. By doing this you could have a different DLL for each language your application was used for, such as English, German, French, etc. This is a technique used by dBASE itself for the menus, speedtips and many other aspects of the software.

The string table stored in a.DLL is in a particular format. While I recommend elsewhere using a free software package called XN Resource Editor, I have not found it easy to create a brand new string table. However, if you go to the article mentioned above you can copy one of the DLLs that Robert uses, and then XN Resource Editor will allow you to modify the string table. *(Of course, you can also use other software to do the same things as shown here.)* You can add or remove strings as needed. You need to make sure that each number you use is unique, but the string itself does not need to be. The limit to the length of the string is 32K characters – that is a large string – any string longer than this will be truncated by dBASE as it will not read a string longer than that from the dll.

Note that you can modify the string table by adding, removing, and changing values. For example, to change the string associated with the number "1" to something like "A Test Form", click on the text and change it. Once you have made any changes you might want, click the "Compile Script" button to ensure that this DLL has been re-built. Then save it.

To use the strings in this dll file, you can do a simple test from the Command Window:

```
? resource( 1, "english.dll" )
```

And if you changed the string as noted above, will display:

```
A Test Form
```

in the output pane of the Command Window.

To use this in your application, you would create a form, then assign the value as needed. The one difficulty you will note if you try this is that the design surfaces always evaluate calls to functions and for example, if you were to modify the source for a form so that it used this string in the form's *text* property, you would find that it was actually streamed out. So code that looked like:

```
class TestResourceForm of FORM
   with (this)
      height = 16.0
      left = 50.0
      top = 0.0
      width = 40.0
      text = resource( 1, "english.dll" )
   endwith
```

Would be evaluated in the Form Designer and streamed out the next time you modified the form to:

```
class TestResourceForm of FORM
   with (this)
      height = 16.0
      left = 50.0
      top = 0.0
      width = 40.0
      text = "A Test Form"
   endwith
```

The solution would be to use an overrridden *open()* or *readModal()* method as has been discussed in earlier chapters of this book many times. Then you could assign the strings you needed to easily for each control, something like the following for this *simple* example:

```
function form_open
   class::Init()
return TESTRESOURCEFORM::open()
```

```
function form_readModal
    class::Init()
return TESTRESOURCEFORM::readModal()

function Init
    // assign text values properly to form ...:
    form.text := resource( 1, "english.dll" )
    // etc.
return
```

Of course, there is still the difficulty of the need to be able to change the name of the dll file. This can be done by storing a value as a custom property of the _app object, such as:

```
_app.AppLanguageDLL = "english.dll"
```

or

```
_app.AppLanguageDLL = "german.dll"
```

Your form would then be able to do something with this value, such as:

```
function Init
    // assign text values properly to form ...:
    form.text := resource( 1, _app.LanguageDLL )
    // etc.
return
```

You could do this for as many strings as you wanted or needed to use in your application. While a bit of extra work, it is a good way to make this transparent to your users. The only changes needed to switch languages would be to the custom property noted above and to have the appropriate language dll file available.

For other languages once you have your first .DLL set up, you could simply copy the .DLL file to a new file, then open that DLL in XN Resource Editor (or your favorite program for this purpose) and modify the string table.

For more suggestions and ideas, it is recommended that you read Robert's excellent article, but as noted, this should get you going.

NOTES:

Appendix 6: ANSI Chart

The ANSI (American National Standards Institute) Character set (used for Windows) is particularly useful to any dBASE developer. The chart here maps the decimal number to the associated character – this is the 1252 Windows Latin 1 ANSI character set.

ANSI Chart

0	null	32		64	@	96	`	128	€	160		192	À	224	à
1	□	33	!	65	A	97	a	129	$	161	¡	193	Á	225	á
2	□	34	"	66	B	98	b	130	,	162	¢	194	Â	226	â
3	□	35	#	67	C	99	c	131	ƒ	163	£	195	Ã	227	ã
4	□	36	$	68	D	100	d	132	„	164	¤	196	Ä	228	ä
5	□	37	%	69	E	101	e	133	…	165	¥	197	Å	229	å
6	□	38	&	70	F	102	f	134	†	166	¦	198	Æ	230	æ
7	BEL	39	'	71	G	103	g	135	‡	167	§	199	Ç	231	ç
8	BS	40	(	72	H	104	h	136	^	168	¨	200	È	232	è
9	TAB	41	)	73	I	105	i	137	‰	169	©	201	É	233	é
10	LF	42	*	74	J	106	j	138	Š	170	ª	202	Ê	234	ê
11	□	43	+	75	K	107	k	139	‹	171	«	203	Ë	235	ë
12	□	44	,	76	L	108	l	140	Œ	172	¬	204	Ì	236	ì
13	CR	45	-	77	M	109	m	141	$	173	-	205	Í	237	í
14	□	46	.	78	N	110	n	142	Ž	174	®	206	Î	238	î
15	□	47	/	79	O	111	o	143	$	175	¯	207	Ï	239	ï
16	□	48	0	80	P	112	p	144	$	176	°	208	Ð	240	ð
17	□	49	1	81	Q	113	q	145	`	177	✂	209	Ñ	241	ñ
18	□	50	2	82	R	114	r	146	'	178	²	210	Ò	242	ò
19	□	51	3	83	S	115	s	147	"	179	³	211	Ó	243	ó
20	□	52	4	84	T	116	t	148	"	180	´	212	Ô	244	ô
21	□	53	5	85	U	117	u	149	•	181	🖳	213	Õ	245	õ
22	□	54	6	86	V	118	v	150	–	182	¶	214	Ö	246	ö
23	□	55	7	87	W	119	w	151	—	183	✄	215	℗	247	①
24	□	56	8	88	X	120	x	152	~	184	¸	216	Ø	248	ø
25	□	57	9	89	Y	121	y	153	™	185	¹	217	Ù	249	ù
26	□	58	:	90	Z	122	z	154	š	186	º	218	Ú	250	ú
27	ESC	59	;	91	[	123	{	155	›	187	»	219	Û	251	û
28	□	60	<	92	\	124			156	œ	188	¼	220	Ü	252	ü
29	□	61	=	93	]	125	}	157	$	189	½	221	Ý	253	ý
30	□	62	>	94	^	126	~	158	ž	190	¾	222	Þ	254	þ
31	□	63	?	95	_	127	DEL	159	Ÿ	191	¿	223	ß	255	ÿ

Microsoft indicates that character 0 to 31 are not supported in Windows – 0 to 31 are also non-printing, but have special meanings, most of them to DOS, the ones that may be of interest to dBL programmers are described below.

Special Meanings for Non-Printable Characters
According to Microsoft, the characters 0-31 are not recognized by Windows. However, dBL developers have found this is not necessarily the case.

0	= Null	Null character
7	= Bel	Bell: ? Chr(7) will play the "bell" in a dBASE application
8	= BS	Backspace
9	= Tab	Tab Character
10	= LF	Line Feed
13	= CR	Carriage Return
		Characters 10 and 13 are the standard end of line in DOS and Windows applications.
27	= ESC	Escape
32	= Space	*(Not really a "non-printable" character by the standard definition, as a space is a valid character ...)*

127 = DEL Delete
128 = EURO this character looks like: € *(see comment about specific fonts displaying characters below)*

Characters in the range from 128 to 159/160 may be font dependent – in other words, in some fonts you may see characters that do not display in other fonts.

ANSI Charts on the Web
Some of the charts on the web that you can find give a huge amount of detail beyond what is covered here. Rather than duplicating effort, you might want to check the following sites:

```
http://www.microsoft.com/globaldev/reference/sbcs/1252.htm
http://en.wikipedia.org/wiki/ISO_8859-1
http://www.unicode.org/charts/
```

Using ANSI Characters
To use ANSI characters in dBL – in code you may use the CHR() function:

```
? chr( 223 ) // ß
```

In order to use ANSI characters properly you may want to be sure that you have the BDE set to use a Windows (ANSI) driver, and the LDRIVER entry in PLUS.INI is set either to WINDOWS or perhaps a specific language driver from the BDE, again using ANSI.

You may also create a string using characters by carefully doing the following:

- Hold the ALT key
- Using the NUMERIC KEYPAD (not the numbers at the top of the keyboard, but the ones on the right), type the number, but add a leading zero. To get the character "ß", you would type: 0233
- Let go of the ALT key

The character should now appear.

If ANSI Characters Do Not Appear in a Table
The primary reason that ANSI characters may not appear properly in a table is if the table was created with a DOS (ASCII) driver. This can cause problems when migrating from DOS applications, if you need characters from the ANSI character set. You may want to make sure the BDE is set properly, then create a new version of the table and copy the data from the old table. Then you will want to check characters to make sure they translated properly. You can get more information about these issues by going to the help in dBASE and using "Character" as a topic to look at.

Font Sets and ANSI Characters
Not all fonts (True Type or other) used in Windows have mapped all characters of the character set exactly the same. Some font designers wish to use their own meanings for each character. This can be a little confusing if you try to use some special character and get unexpected results.

If you use the dUFLP (mentioned in Appendix 1), you may wish to take a look at ANSIChart.wfm which calls a report called ANSIChart.rep. This allows you to display all the characters in any font set from 0 to 255. This might be useful if you wanted a specific character to display on a form or report.

NOTES:

Appendix 7: Windows Application Interface Design and Standards

Microsoft has a book that is a guideline for Windows Application design, standards, and such. It discusses the concepts of good design. It is worth a read – the URL is:

```
http://social.msdn.microsoft.com/Search/en-
    US?query=windows%20application%20design%20guidelines&ac=2
```

In addition to the Microsoft book, there are of course many other books on user interface design available. Another one on the internet is at:

```
http://www.joelonsoftware.com/uibook/chapters/fog0000000057.html
```

(The author, Joel Splosky, notes that if you purchase the book there are seven chapters in the printed version not available on the web.)

What Is A Good User Interface?

What is a good user interface? One could discuss industry standards for design, things that don't work, things that do and make a lot of comparisons. The key thing to note is that a good user interface is one that does what the user expects and needs it to do. In the long run, that sums it all up.

When designing the user interface you need to work with the user(s). Your user is going to have some ideas for what they want it to look like and what they need it to do. They may have some odd ideas that either will not work, or could be done better – this is where your own design sense and understanding of the software comes in.

When working with your user and designing the interface you probably do not need to tell them (in most cases) all of the details that occur behind the scene. They don't need to know that you had to write a huge one thousand line routine in code that is executed when a specific pushbutton is clicked to perform this task or all of the twists and turns in the logic necessary to do it – as long as it gets there, the user will be happy. Yes, there are the few rare people who really want to know, or at least think they do – but most of them do not. You will find this out when you start explaining and their eyes glaze over but that's okay, it is why they paid you to do the job, right?

Points to consider:
- *When you give the user a choice, they have to make a decision.* Many users just want it to work – "stop asking me questions!" Giving a user too many choices will frustrate them. Make sure that when a choice occurs in the use of the application that it is an important one. Obviously the user will need to make choices to do the tasks the application is designed for, but make sure they are meaningful.
- *Be consistent throughout your application.* If you use custom forms, custom controls, and custom reports, you enforce this. Make sure the pushbuttons are always in the same places from form to form and don't change the text or images used to do the same thing from form to form. When your application uses dialog boxes, be consistent and use the same styles, pushbuttons, and images, etc. Consistency means that the user won't

move from one screen to another and suddenly have no clue how to do the task at hand.

- *Don't show off just to show off ...* don't do flashy things in your application just because you can. The user may be wowed by it at first, but if they can't use those features and they don't make sense to the task at hand, is it really worth it? This includes beautiful designs that are hard to use and confuse the user.
- *Sometimes you have to break the rules.* There are reasons to follow industry standards, but if you have a situation where "breaking the rules" is really going to make the application better, by all means, do so. There are very few real hard-and-fast rules when designing an interface.
- *Users don't read the manual.* One point made by Joel Splosky (the second website cited above) is: "Users don't read the manual!" He also notes that if they have the manual, they still won't read it. How many times have you sat down and installed a software package and jumped in without reading the manual? Your users will do the same thing. Beginners assume that it will work as is; advanced users assume they know enough and don't bother with the manual. In either case if the user has it, they most likely won't read it. Of course, there are exceptions to the rule, but in most cases the manual won't be read.
- Keeping in mind the bit above, long explanations on the screen are not all that useful, either.
- *Keep it simple.* Many people are intimidated by computers and get scared that anything they do will screw up the computer, the data, their lives – keep it all simple – the more complex it appears the more concerned they will be. (The "KISS Principal" comes into play here: "Keep It Simple, Stupid!") Of course, the concept of keeping it simple for some applications may seem silly, because by the very nature of what your application needs to do, the process may not be simple. In those cases, avoid cluttering the screen with unnecessary options or descriptions, use multiple forms or multiple pages of a form or a notebook to break things down into smaller parts.

In earlier versions of the book I provided examples of good design from a few developers who gave me permission to display screen-shots of their applications. Those designs were excellent at the time, but are out of date. At this time, your best bet is to work with the tools, work with your customer or employer, and come up with what works best for you, keeping the "rules" above in mind.

Appendix 8: Glossary

The following is a short glossary of terms used in this book - it does not cover all possible terms, because in some cases the definitions are well defined in the chapters of the book.

ActiveX – objects written to a Microsoft standard, often in Visual Basic (but not always). These can be used in dBASE through the use of the ActiveX component.

Alias – An alias is an alternate means of referring to something. In dBASE an alias is generally one of these:

- A database (or BDE) alias, used to point to either a SQL Server database file, or to a folder containing local tables.
- A source code alias, used to point to a folder containing source code libraries.

API – Application Programming Interface. A means for a developer to interact with a piece of software from outside of that software. For example, this book has a chapter (23) dedicated to the Windows API, which discusses the ability to use functions of Windows in your dBASE application by calling them directly from your code.

Autoincrement Field – A field that, upon saving a row, automatically increments to a new number. This is useful for primary keys, and linking for Parent/Child tables, because the value by definition is unique. Paradox (.DB) and dBASE level 7 (.DBF) tables have an autoincrement field built-in, so no code is required to use this field. To use something similar for other table types, some extra code is required.

BDE –Borland Database Engine. This is the data engine that ships with dBASE, and is required for any dBASE application that works with tables.

BDE Alias – *see Alias*

Calculated Field – A field in a table whose value is calculated. This value may be calculated as the table is retrieved or perhaps as navigation occurs in the table. The field can be datalinked to a control on a form (or report), but a user cannot change the value – it is a readonly field by definition. You can create these with a SQL statement using the SQL SELECT command, and in the OODML you use a Field Object.

Class – A definition of an object. A class is used to define the properties, events and methods of an object. An object is created *(instantiated)* from the class definition.

Codeblock – A codeblock is a method of storing a small amount of dBL code within curly braces ({}) which can be executed as needed. A codeblock is sometimes used to create an *event handler* for a simple bit of code. *(Details in various chapters of this book.)*

Column – Another name for a field in a table, or a column (vertical listing) in a grid, report, etc.

Constant – A memory variable whose value does not change. If created using the preprocessor directive #DEFINE, the variable *cannot* be changed, accidentally or otherwise, unless it is undefined and redefined in the code.

Container – An object that can contain other objects. This is part of the *object hierarchy*, *dot notation* is used to show the relationship of the objects.

Custom Class – A *class* defined by a developer and stored in a custom class file (by default ending with a .cc file extension, but a developer can create custom forms, custom reports, etc. as well). This class is always *subclassed* from a stock class in dBASE (even if it is the stock "OBJECT" class which has no *properties*, *events* or *methods*), and the developer adds his own *properties* and/or *methods* to the subclass.

Database – A collection of tables stored in one place. With *local tables* this is normally a folder that contains the tables. If using a *SQL server* database, the tables are generally stored in a single file. This term is also the name of the OODML *object* used to reference a *database* or database *alias*.

Database Alias – *see Alias*

DataLink – To link the data to a visual control.

DataSource – The source of the data used in a combobox, listbox, notebook, tabbox, or image control. This should not be confused with a *dataLink* – the dataSource cannot normally be modified (directly) by the user of the control.

DBF7 – A way of referencing a dBASE Level 7 table, in order to difference it from any other levels (3, 4, 5, or even a FoxPro table which uses the same file extension).

DBL – The dBASE Language. This consists of a combination of forms of language, including the XDML (XBASE Database Manipulation Language), OODML (Object-Oriented Database Manipulation Language), Local SQL, and other commands and functions built in to the software.

Designer – A designer is used to design a dBASE object in a visual and interactive fashion. dBASE has built into it a Form Designer, a Report (and Label) Designer, a data module designer (dQuery), a Menu Designer, a Table Designer, and a SQL Designer.

Dot Notation – The syntax used to show the parentage of objects in *containers*, and to reference *properties*, *events* and *methods* of an *object*.

dQuery – The data module designer built in to dBASE. This designer is actually much more robust than just a data module designer, although that was its original purpose when it was created. It can be used to design tables, create "One-Click" applications – both Windows and Web, import and export data from or to other formats (including Excel spreadsheets and more), and it can read and write Borland C++ and Delphi data modules.

Event – An action that a program may act upon, if an *event handler* is written to perform a set of program statements when the event occurs.

Event Handler – Code that is written to be executed when a specific *event* occurs.

Field – A single element of data in a *row* or *record*. A field will have a name, a type, a width and optionally may have if numeric a setting for the number of decimals. In a row that contains customer information a single field might be the customer's First Name.

Field Object – The elements of a *Fields Array*. A new field object can be used to create a *calculated field* in the dBASE OODML model.

Fields Array – An *object* that is contained by a *rowset* object, specifically to contain *object reference variables* for the *fields* (see also *Field Object*) in a *rowset*.

Filter – A means of limiting the data to a specific subset based on an expression that must evaluate to either *true* or *false*.
- A filter can be defined in a SQL SELECT statement using the WHERE clause.
- When using the OODML, a filter is created by using the *filter* property of the *rowset* object, or by using a combination of the *beginLocate()* and *applyLocate()* methods.

Foreign Key – In a parent/child relationship, a foreign key is the key field in the child table used to link to the *primary key* in the parent table.

Index – A means to order the data in a specific sequence using the values in the *fields* of the table. An index may be a single field index, or it may, in the depending on the table type, be able to use a combination of fields and dBASE expressions (these can only be used with dBASE tables).

Instantiate – To create an instance of an *object* as defined in a *class*. The usual syntax to instantiate an object is:

```
oMyObj = new ClassName()
```

Key Field – The field used in the *primary index* of a table, this is normally a field that must have a unique value for each row in a table.

Local Tables – Local tables are literally tables that are "local" to dBASE. dBASE defines local tables as DBF (dBASE File), Paradox (.DB) and FoxPro (also .DBF, but with some differences). The definition is through the Borland Database Engine (*BDE*). Any other tables that can be used by dBASE are SQL Tables, and require a SQL Server Engine be running to use them.

Method – A method is code that is built in to a *class* definition that is called as needed to execute specific tasks. In some cases with the *stock classes* of dBASE there are related *events*. An example of this might be the rowset's *save()* method has two events associated with it – *canSave()* which fires before the *save()* method and *onSave()* which fires after the *save()* method. A developer can add their own methods to an instance of a class, or in their own *custom classes*.

Modal – A Modal form is one opened with the form's *readModal()* method. It must be closed for any code outside of the form to be executed, or it must call another form.

Null – Literally, nothing. This is the default for many fields in a DBF table when a new row is added and is used to blank out memory variables and such.

Object – An instance of a *class* as described in the class definition. See also *instantiate*.

Object Hierarchy – When working with classes, this is the hierarchy of containership, or in the case of custom classes, it is the hierarchy of the classes. For example, if a custom pushbutton class is defined, then another custom pushbutton class is derived from the first, a class or object hierarchy exists and code in the first pushbutton is inherited by the second pushbutton.

Overwrite – To change the way a method predefined in a class definition works. This is usually done when creating a subclass of a class definition.

Parent – The parent of an object is the object that it is contained by. For example, if a form contains objects that are displayed for the user to interact with, the parent of these controls is the form.

Popup – A menu that appears when you use the right-click mouse button.

Primary Key – A field that must, by definition, contain a unique value. When working with a parent/child table relationship the primary key of the parent table is linked to by a field of the child table. The field used to link to the parent table from the child table is called the *foreign key*.

Primary Index – An index on the *primary key* field.

Project – A collection of the programs, forms, reports, etc., needed for an application. These are managed in dBASE PLUS by the Project Explorer. The Project Explorer creates a .PRJ file that is used to store the information for each file in the project.

Property – The characteristics of an *object*, created in a *class* definition.

Query – A dBASE *object* used to extract data from a table. The result of the query is the *rowset*.

Record – A collection of data about a specific entity in a *table*. A *table* may contain information about, say, a customer. Each record would contain information about an individual customer, the information would be broken down into *fields*.

Row – Another name for a *record*.

Rowset – An object in the OODML used to reference the rows in a table and to navigate and access the row in a completely object-oriented fashion.

SQL Server Database – A database software package that has its own table definitions and uses its own variation of the SQL database manipulation language. dBASE may use databases and tables created by a SQL Server Database through the *BDE*. A SQL Server data engine must be running to access the databases and tables. These include InterBase, Oracle, MSSQL, and many others.

SQL – Originally "Structured Query Language", although the authors of the language claim that this means no such thing, and was just a series of letters put together. This is a standardized language used to work with databases and tables, used by most database software in the world. The standard used by dBASE, built in to the *BDE*, is ANSI 92.

Stock Class – One of the many classes that are built in to dBASE and available for use by developers. All *custom classes* are subclassed from the stock classes in dBASE. If no class type is used in the class definition, the *custom class* is derived from the stock OBJECT class in dBASE.

Subclass – To create a *class* that is based on another *class*. When subclassing, all properties, events and methods of the original class are inherited in the subclass, and may be used by it, modified, etc.

Tab Order – In a form the sequence in which a user tabs (or back-tabs) through controls. This is controlled by the *z-order*, or sequence in which controls are defined in a form class definition (or by the use of properties of the controls ...).

Table – A collection of rows, which is a collection of fields. Tables are the means of storing data in a database. You may create relationships between tables (see *Primary Key, Foreign Key*, etc.).

User Access Control (UAC) – Windows Vista and later versions of Windows include enhanced user security. Unfortunately, as a developer, this complicates development and deployment of applications. This is referenced in many places throughout this edition of the book.

User Interface (UI) – The interface a user works with to perform their tasks. The UI can be a form, toolbar, menu, popup, etc.

Z-Order – The sequence in which controls are streamed out in a class definition. This controls the *tab order* in a form, and the sequence in which controls are rendered in a report.

NOTES:

Index

F

T